# CAMBRIDGE TEXTBOOKS IN LINGUISTICS

*General Editors*: B. COMRIE, C. J. FILLMORE, R. LASS, R. B. LE PAGE, J. LYONS
P. H. MATTHEWS, F. R. PALMER, R. POSNER, S. ROMAINE, N. V. SMITH,
J. L. M. TRIM, A. ZWICKY

# PHONOLOGY

*In this series:*

P. H. MATTHEWS *Morphology*

B. COMRIE *Aspect*

R. M. KEMPSON *Semantic Theory*

T. BYNON *Historical Linguistics*

J. ALLWOOD, L.-G. ANDERSON, Ö. DAHL *Logic in Linguistics*

D. B. FRY *The Physics of Speech*

R. A. HUDSON *Sociolinguistics*

J. K. CHAMBERS and P. TRUDGILL *Dialectology*

A. J. ELLIOT *Child Language*

P. H. MATTHEWS *Syntax*

A. RADFORD *Transformational Syntax*

L. BAUER *English Word-formation*

S. C. LEVINSON *Pragmatics*

G. BROWN and G. YULE *Discourse Analysis*

R. HUDDLESTON *Introduction to the Grammar of English*

R. LASS *Phonology*

B. COMRIE *Tense*

W. KLEIN *Second Language Acquisition*

A. CRUTTENDEN *Intonation*

A. J. WOODS, P. FLETCHER and A. HUGHES *Statistics in Language Studies*

D. A. CRUSE *Lexical Semantics*

F. R. PALMER *Mood and Modality*

# PHONOLOGY

## AN INTRODUCTION TO BASIC CONCEPTS

### ROGER LASS

DEPARTMENT OF LINGUISTICS
UNIVERSITY OF CAPE TOWN

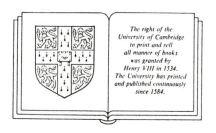

The right of the
University of Cambridge
to print and sell
all manner of books
was granted by
Henry VIII in 1534.
The University has printed
and published continuously
since 1584.

CAMBRIDGE UNIVERSITY PRESS

CAMBRIDGE

NEW YORK    NEW ROCHELLE

MELBOURNE    SYDNEY

Published by the Press Syndicate of the University of Cambridge
The Pitt Building, Trumpington Street, Cambridge CB2 1RP
32 East 57th Street, New York, NY 10022, USA
10 Stamford Road, Oakleigh, Melbourne 3166, Australia

First published 1984

Reprinted 1985, 1988

Printed in Great Britain by The Bath Press, Avon

Library of Congress catalogue card number: 83–23915

*British Library Cataloguing in Publication Data*
Lass, Roger
Phonology. – (Cambridge textbooks in Linguistics)
1. Grammar, Comparative and general – Phonology
I. Title
414    P217

ISBN 0 521 23728 9 hard covers
ISBN 0 521 28183 0 paperback

NP

# CONTENTS

*Preface*                                                    *page*      xiii
*To the student*                                                        xvii

  1  **Preliminaries: what is phonology? and some
     related matters**                                                1
1.1  The domain                                                          1
1.2  Areas of agreement                                                  3
1.3  On facts, theories, and 'truth'                                     6
     Notes and references                                             9

  2  **Foundations: the phoneme concept**                               11
2.1  Segmentation and classification                                    11
2.2  Units, realizations, distributions                                 14
2.3  'Excess' of data: the phoneme as a solution                        15
2.4  Criteria for phonemic status                                       18
2.5  Phonemic analysis and restricting conditions                       21
2.6  Simplicity, symmetry, pattern: the 'as-if' argument                25
2.7  Problems, I: biuniqueness and overlapping                          27
2.8  Problems, II: linearity violations                                 30
2.9  Problems, III: separation of levels                                31
2.10 Problems, IV: 'failure' of allophonic rules                        34
2.11 A salvage operation for separation of levels: 'juncture'
     phonemes                                                        36
     Notes and references                                            38

  3  **Opposition, neutralization, features**                           39
3.1  Neutralization and the archiphoneme                                39
3.2  The structure of phonological oppositions                          41
3.3  Multiple neutralization                                            46
3.4  Neutralization types and archiphoneme 'representatives'            49
3.5  Neutralization vs. defective distribution: reprise                 51
     Notes and references                                            53

*Contents*

4   **Interfaces: morphophonemic alternations and
      sandhi**                                                        55
4.1   Morphophonemic alternations                                    55
4.2   Morphophonemics as an 'interlevel'                             57
4.3   Process morphophonemics: Bloomfield                            59
4.4   The Unique Underlier Condition                                 63
4.5   The UUC and the Latin consonant-stems                         64
4.6   Summary: implications of underlying forms and processes       68
4.7   Sandhi                                                         69
      Notes and references                                          73

5   **'Ultimate constituents', 1: binary features**                 75
5.1     Feature theory                                               75
5.1.1   Jakobsonian distinctive features                             75
5.1.2   Distinctiveness and redundancy                               78
5.2     Features and 'natural classes'                              80
5.3     A tentative set of segmental phonological features          82
5.3.1   Major class features                                        83
5.3.2   Cavity features                                             84
5.3.2.1 Primary strictures                                          84
5.3.2.2 Tongue-body features                                        85
5.3.2.3 Some problems in vowel specification                        86
5.3.3   Multiple articulations                                      87
5.3.4   Lip attitude                                                88
5.3.5   Length of stricture                                         89
5.3.6   Secondary apertures                                         89
5.3.7   Manner features                                             89
5.3.8   Source features                                             90
5.3.9   Aspiration                                                  91
5.3.10  Long vowels, diphthongs, and long consonants                91
5.3.11  Airstreams                                                  92
5.4     Features in phonological description: first steps           93
5.4.1   Segment inventories                                         94
                                                                    95
5.4.2   Phonological rules                                          97
5.5     Capturing natural classes: the role of acoustic features    97
        Notes and references                                       100

6   **'Ultimate constituents', 2: non-binary features and
      internal segment structure**                                 102
6.1     The homogeneity assumption                                 102
6.2     Dissolving binarity: arguments from vowel height           104
6.3     Non-binary consonantal features                            107

vi

6.4 Internal segment structure, 1: sequential values 111
6.5 Internal segment structure, 2: the concept of 'gesture' 113
6.6 A problem: auditory/articulatory asymmetry in vowels 118
Notes and references 122

7 **Phonological systems** 125
7.1 The status of systems 125
7.2 The English Vowel Shift: the argument from non-participation 126
7.3 The argument from cyclical shifts 129
7.4 Phonological universals and markedness 131
7.5 System typology, 1: vowel systems 134
7.5.1 Introduction: what phonemes does a language 'have'? 134
7.5.2 Long vowels and diphthongs 135
7.5.3 Basic vowel system types 139
7.6 System typology, 11: consonant systems 147
7.6.1 Obstruents, 1: stops 147
7.6.2 Obstruents, 2: fricatives 151
7.6.3 Some generalizations about obstruents 153
7.6.4 Sonorants, 1: nasals 155
7.6.5 Sonorants, 2: 'liquids' 157
7.6.6 Sonorants, 3: 'semivowels' ('glides', vocoid approximants) 159
7.7 What phonemes does a language 'have'? revisited 160
7.8 Polysystematicity and neutralization 163
Notes and references 166

8 **Phonological processes** 169
8.1 The concept of process: terminology, theory, problems 169
8.2 Assimilation and dissimilation 171
8.2.1 Direction and contiguity 171
8.2.2 Basic assimilation and dissimilation types 173
8.2.3 Acoustic assimilation 175
8.3 Phonological strength 177
8.3.1 Lenition and fortition 177
8.3.2 Preferential environments and 'protection' 181
8.3.3 More on strength hierarchies 183
8.4 Whole segment processes: insertion, deletion, reordering 183
8.4.1 Insertion 184
8.4.2 Deletion 186
8.4.3 Reordering 188
8.5 Complex processes and abbreviatory notations 190
8.6 Natural processes, evaluation measures, and explanation 195
Notes and references 201

*Contents*

9 **The limits of abstraction: generative phonology** 203
9.1 The conceptual core: 'relation by mediation' 203
9.2 Abstract analysis: the German velar nasal 205
9.3 'Abstract segments' and absolute neutralization: Hungarian vowel harmony 208
9.4 Some arguments against abstract solutions 211
9.5 Testing abstract analyses: the role of external evidence 214
9.6 Constraining the theory 222
9.7 Abstractness: some conclusions 232
Notes and references 233

10 **Beyond the segment: prosodies, syllables, and quantity** 236
10.1 'Reduction': how primitive are primitives? 236
10.2 Prosodic phonology 238
10.2.1 A first approach to prosodies 238
10.2.2 Types of prosodies 242
10.2.3 The prosodic treatment of vowel harmony 244
10.3 Syllables 248
10.3.1 Preliminaries 248
10.3.2 The reality of the syllable: quantity 250
10.3.3 Canonical quantity and 'compensation' 257
10.3.4 More arguments for the syllable 260
10.3.5 Delimiting syllables 262
10.3.6 Interludes 267
Notes and references 268

11 **Dependency relations** 271
11.1 The concept of dependency 271
11.2 Intrasegmental dependencies: the structure of vowels 274
11.3 Vocalic processes in a dependency framework 279
11.4 The structure of consonants: the categorial gesture 282
11.5 The articulatory gesture 285
11.6 The initiatory gesture 289
11.7 Lenition revisited 291
Notes and references 293

12 **Non-static phonology: connected speech and variation** 294
12.1 Preliminaries 294
12.2 Connected and casual speech 295
12.3 Systemic effects, tempo hierarchies, and rule interactions 298

12.4 Variation and variables: the social dimension 304
12.5 Individual variation: the lexical dimension 310
Notes and references 313

13 **Phonological change** 315
13.1 What changes? Phonetic change and phonologization 315
13.2 Split and merger 318
13.3 Morphophonemic rules, morphologization, and analogy 320
13.4 The mechanism of sound change 322
13.4.1 'Regularity' and reconstructability 322
13.4.2 Lexical diffusion and the origin of regularity 324
13.4.3 Phonetic gradualness: variation and change 329
13.4.4 Phonetic gradualness and 'missing links' 332
Notes and references 338

Appendix: phonetic and other symbols 339
References 343
General index 353
Index of names 361

We shall have to evolve
   problem solvers galore –
since each problem we solve
   creates ten problems more.

The road to wisdom? – Well, it's plain
   and simple to express:
Err and err and err again
   but less and less and less.

Our choicest plans have fallen through,
   our airiest castles tumbled over,
because of lines we neatly drew
   and later neatly stumbled over.

   Piet Hein, *Runaway Runes*:
   *Short Grooks, I* (1968)

# PREFACE

It is probably impossible to write a satisfactory textbook on a contentious and evolving subject like phonology. Certainly one that's comprehensive, up-to-date, and accessible, and hits the right level without being patronizing. But I thought I'd try, even if I am bound to fail on some if not all of these desirable qualities. At this stage there seems to be a need for a book that is neither a history of phonology (like the indispensable Fischer-Jørgensen 1975, or the collection of papers in Makkai 1972a), nor an attempt to sell a particular school or orthodoxy. Rather one that offers a broad and eclectic coverage of the field, takes seriously a wide range of competing theories, analytical strategies, and notational systems, and depicts phonology as a discipline with historical continuity, not a series of 'revolutions'. (There are plenty of the former on the market, from the fairly self-controlled to the blatantly evangelizing.)

I see phonology as a developing, essentially problem-centred discipline, growing through the interaction of complementary approaches with a complex mass of data. Much of yesterday's theory and practice is silently incorporated into today's, and this will continue as long as the subject does. There do not exist anything like full alternative phonological theories; we have a host of partial approaches, each of which does some things well, others badly, and still others not at all. I am suspicious of attempts to push any framework as THE theory; so almost everything, Prague phonology, American structuralism, prosodic analysis, generative phonology, gets a hearing, because all have something to offer, and all have their part to play in the continuing endeavour to understand how phonology works. My aim is to indicate where each approach works best, and the contribution each has made – and in many cases still can make.

This breaks down into two sub-aims: (a) to explore some important aspects of the phenomenology of sound structure, by singling out what is most salient for particular theories; and (b) to introduce some characteristic modes of argument in phonology, and some major controversies. I have tried to be reasonably fair; but my selection is naturally personal, guided by my own interests and assumptions. I have undoubtedly judged some potentially rich approaches to be dead ends, and worried issues that have rolled over and died without my knowing. But my guiding principle has been theoretical pluralism: whenever I'm tempted to think I have the answer to something, I recall Popper's dictum (1973): 'Whenever a theory appears to you as the only possible one, take this as a sign that you have neither understood the theory nor the problem it was intended to solve.'

This will explain a curious feature of this book; a number of digressions into rather arcane matters in philosophy of science, like realism vs. instrumentalism, the status of theoretical constructs, etc. I think it's good for students to be aware of such issues from the beginning, so that they see how difficult a discipline linguistics is, become a bit sceptical and suspicious of 'strong' claims, and so on. This kind of thing rarely appears (even superficially, as here) in linguistics texts; but it is an integral part of the way I teach, and therefore ought to be reflected here. The book can of course be read perfectly well without the digressions, and my generally 'uncommitted' stance might serve as a good take-off point for a theoretically committed teacher. But I have made no effort to hide my opinions, or to be uncontroversial.

A few general points on presentation and coverage. I have started off rather slowly, often labouring the (apparently) obvious, since in my experience if certain fundamental points aren't hammered home in the beginning, nothing else ever gets clear. Hence the length of chapter 2, on phonemes, distinctiveness, redundancy, and the like. The density and complexity increase thereafter, but I have tried to lay the groundwork for each new development in what came before. The text as a whole is 'introductory', in that it presupposes very little linguistics – except for a good command of phonetic taxonomy. Maybe this is asking a lot, but lack of space precludes building in a phonetics text, and attempts I have seen to do this in phonology texts come off badly. Besides, this information can be obtained elsewhere. To help, I have included a complete list of phonetic symbols used, and keyed discussion of complex or exotic matters to standard sources.

Since my overall conception of the subject is not particularly 'abstract' or 'cognitive', but quite phonetic, this seemed the best way to proceed.

The range of languages treated in detail is perhaps smaller than usual. This can be defended on the ground that if phonology is a 'universal' subject, it shouldn't matter too much what the languages of exemplification are, as long as the typological range is fairly wide. And students seem to prefer getting into new areas through relatively familiar examples. Hence the emphasis on various forms of English. Also, I prefer where possible to talk about languages I know at first hand, which accounts for the preponderance of Germanic and Dravidian. In some areas (e.g. system typology) I've had to depend on others' descriptions of languages I've never heard, and can only hope (fondly) that I have avoided any major howlers.

A word on bibliography and coverage. I have been selective and wide-ranging, but in no way comprehensive; everyone will find some favourites missing. As a matter of principle, I have normally excluded reference to 'informal' publications (working papers and the like); though I have mentioned a few unpublished PhD theses. I think that in general nothing in theoretical linguistics is of such pressing immediate importance that it has to be read fresh from the author's pen or word-processor; at least not for the audience for this book, who can wait until work has undergone the kind of assessment and peer review that (ideally) precedes publication in books or established journals. Anything that goes out of date so fast that it must be read in pre-published form is either ephemeral, or so technical and near the frontiers of the discipline that it has no place in an undergraduate or beginning postgraduate course. We can always afford to wait till the dust has settled a bit.

For this reason, I have had virtually nothing to say about metrical phonology (except indirectly, in discussing syllable structure), or about autosegmental phonology; this is not to be taken as a negative comment on these approaches, but a matter of not wanting to be so up-to-date that I have to get into controversial material still in the midst of extensive re-working. For this reason also I have omitted any systematic consideration of accent and tone; these topics are now so embroiled in the two approaches mentioned above that they ought to be postponed until a more advanced stage in the student's career. They certainly require (or ought to) a solid background in more traditional kinds of phonology.

The only exception I have made with respect to 'novel' approaches is in devoting a chapter to dependency relations; the notions involved here are conceptually so different (and I think so important) as to be a necessary corrective to the paradigmatic or syntagmatic bias of other theory types.

Most importantly, however, students today lack, to put it crudely, a sense of the 'classical': I think that pre-generative (and certainly pre-metrical, autosegmental, natural) phonology is the 'indispensable foundation' for considering newer developments. Linguistics in my view is not a 'science' in the strict sense anyway, but at least as much a scholarly discipline, and nothing ever gets genuinely 'superseded'. This book is an introduction, and presumably the interested student will read beyond it.

I am grateful to all those people who have read all or part of this text in draft and commented, often harshly: particularly Eugénie Henderson, John Laver, Nigel Love, Gill Brown, Heinz Giegerich, and Betsy Uldall. I am also grateful to Penny Carter and Cambridge University Press in general, for waiting patiently while I took an unconscionable time to finish. And perhaps most of all I owe a debt to my students at Edinburgh over the last few years, who were captive audiences for a lot of this material, and read drafts of some of the chapters. They taught me the valuable lesson that teaching is nearly impossible, and their questions and puzzlements often helped me to formulate things more clearly; whether clearly enough is for the reader to judge.

# TO THE STUDENT

Students often find phonology difficult. One reason, perhaps, is that compared with other branches of linguistics, like syntax or to some extent semantics, it's rather 'technical': seemingly remote from our everyday experience of language, and requiring from the beginning command of another technical discipline – phonetics. Facts about syntax and meaning – and even some about phonetics – are more 'available' than the rather abstract but no less important matters that much of phonology is about. You can get a preliminary grasp of syntax, for instance, with little more equipment than an idea of sentence structure and some traditional grammatical terminology, elements of which are probably part of your general educational background. Everybody comes into linguistics knowing pretty much what nouns and verbs are; just nobody comes in knowing what stops and fricatives are. And even in phonetics, some of the facts are available at the beginning through rather simple observation (what is your tongue doing when you make a [t]?). However, you normally approach phonology pretty much cold, while at the same time needing a technical vocabulary and a set of concepts (place of articulation, state of the glottis, vowel height, etc.) that you've probably just learned, or are in the process of learning. It seems as if you have to superimpose one relatively new subject on another, almost from the start.

I'm afraid there's no way out of this: phonology is about things that are basically phonetic (see §1.1 for details of the distinction between the two); it requires the concepts, terminology and notations of phonetics, in addition to erecting on top of this a whole new set of its own. In an ideal world, you'd not begin to do phonology until you had a solid background in all aspects of phonetics; but university courses aren't long enough for that, and things are usually studied in parallel that ought to go in sequence.

Nonetheless, I find it impossible to talk intelligently about phonology without presupposing a certain amount of phonetic knowledge; more as one gets deeper into things. As a teacher, I can get around this by providing verbal footnotes at the appropriate times, explanations or definitions of things I assume my own students, whose backgrounds I know, are unfamiliar with. And I have the advantage of feedback from a class as well. But in a book, written for a various and invisible audience, following all kinds of different courses, I don't have this resource.

To cope with this inevitable problem I have tried to distinguish carefully between new material, which you're not expected to know, and the background, 'old' material which you might be expected to know. Terminology and concepts that are specifically phonological or related to the contents of this book will be handled this way: the first occurrence of a new term will be in **bold type**, along with a definition or illustration. All major discussions involving this term will be listed in the index. So if in the course of reading you forget something, you should be able to recover the introductory treatment. If on the other hand you come across general phonetic concepts that are not explained and unfamiliar, the best thing to do is look them up in some reliable text. The phonetics text in this series (Laver: forthcoming) should be especially valuable, as the author and I have tried to key our books to each other. Other useful sources are Heffner (1950), Malmberg (1963), Abercrombie (1967), Brosnahan & Malmberg (1970), O'Connor (1973), and Ladefoged (1975). For unfamiliar phonetic and other symbols, see the appendix.

In order to make the text clearer and easier to follow, I have avoided footnotes, and kept the references to a minimum. But each chapter is followed by a section of notes and references, which gives the major bibliography and notes on issues of interest which are subsidiary to the main text. As a rough guide through the large amounts of literature cited, I use the following conventions: * marks works of importance that are either good introductory accounts of certain matters, or technical but relatively accessible; ** marks works that are important and rewarding, but difficult. I have tried not to star too many items, but this does not mean that the others aren't worth reading.

The notes also give sources for the more exotic linguistic examples; data not credited is either so familiar as not to need reference (English, French, German, Latin); or is based on my own work with the languages in question or data given to me by colleagues.

The notes and references are conceived so that the best way of using them is to read each section of the text first, and then the notes to that section, first for comment on the text, then further reading. I have tried to make the book as self-contained as possible, but it's always worth following up some of the professional literature, and looking at other textbook accounts of given material. No two writers, even of introductory texts, will present things in the same way, and differing approaches can be useful: successful grasp of material often seems to be a matter of getting on a writer's wavelength, and we all have different ones.

# I
# Preliminaries: what is phonology? And some related matters

## 1.1 The domain

Phonology, broadly speaking, is that subdiscipline within linguistics concerned with 'the sounds of language'. More narrowly, phonology proper is concerned with the function, behaviour, and organization of sounds as LINGUISTIC items; as opposed to phonetics, which is a rather more 'neutral' study of the sounds themselves as phenomena in the physical world, and the physiological, anatomical, neurological, and psychological properties of the human beings that make them. Phonology, that is, is 'linguistic', in the sense that syntax, morphology, and to a large extent semantics are; while phonetics shades off at various points into neurophysiology, perceptual psychology, acoustics, and so on.

Really clearcut distinctions between related branches of the same subject are of course excessive; the lines aren't really that sharp, as we will see. But we do need some initial partitioning of our subject-matter into manageable chunks. We must however be aware of potential points of contact, and even of areas where one sub-field shades off into another; so one might talk about 'linguistic phonetics', 'experimental phonology', and the like. (Chapters 5–6 are really about linguistic phonetics, and experimental phonology of a sort comes up in ch. 9.) We cannot, for instance, study the function of sounds in language without reference to their articulatory and/or acoustic properties (cf. terms like 'dental stop', 'dark *l*') – if only to use them as labels to tell us what we're talking about. And similarly, we cannot study 'sounds' in a vacuum, with no reference to their linguistic function. Or rather, we CAN do these things for the sake of attacking individual, highly specialized problems; but not in terms of linguistics as a general and unified field of inquiry. For that we need cross-reference and connection.

1

In the long run, neither a totally 'abstract' (i.e. non-phonetic) phonology nor a totally 'concrete' (i.e. non-linguistic) phonetics is likely to be of very much interest. So, although the emphasis in this book will be on the 'grammatical' (in the widest sense) behaviour of sounds, I will always try to maintain – as indeed most serious theories of phonology have done – connection with the phonic properties of the material. Indeed, I will try to stress throughout that phonology is a very phonetic field: one might define it as the combination of universal phonetics (see especially chapters 5 and 6) and language-specific phonetics, with an emphasis on the interaction of these two areas with linguistic structure in general.

How does phonology relate to the whole of linguistics? Or, to narrow it a bit, how does the phonological side of language relate to the rest of it (semantics, syntax, morphology)? And how if at all ought linguistic description to capture this connection?

We might introduce the relation rather sketchily in terms of an important distinction made by Saussure (1916 [1959]: 122) between **form** and **substance**. A language in one sense is an abstract, formal set of relations (somehow, perhaps, represented in the brains of its speakers). But it is manifested in use as 'substance', as sounds, marks on paper, etc. To put it another way, still using Saussurean terms, every linguistic symbol (*signe*, 'sign') is a conjunction of two elements: a signified 'concept' (*signifié*) like 'dog' or 'third person singular', and a 'vehicle' embodying or carrying it, a 'signifier' (*signifiant*). The union of these is a 'word' or other formative. Thus (crudely) the concept 'dog' in a language is carried by a string of phonetic segments: [dɒg] in English, [hʊnt] in German, [ʃjɛ̃] in French.

Further, language is characterized by what some scholars have called a **double articulation**: at one level, we have essentially 'meaningless' elements (e.g. phonetic segments), with their particular rules of combination and other non-semantic properties. And at another, we have 'meaningful' combinations of these meaningless elements. But the relation between the meaningful and the meaningless is essentially ARBITRARY (Saussure's doctrine of *l'arbitraire du signe*): there is no particular reason why 'dog' should be [dɒg], as [hʊnt] etc. indicate. It is this essentially arbitrary relation that guarantees to phonology, as a 'structural' study, a considerable if not total autonomy: though, as we will see, the extent of this autonomy – the independence of phonology from semantics, and especially from

2

morphology and syntax – is one of the central debating points in theoretical discussion (see especially chs. 4, 9).

To go a step further, a language may be defined from one point of view as a set of sound–meaning correspondences; and a description or 'grammar' of a language is a formal object that states these correspondences. The particular range of items that go into the description, and the total set of phenomena that it can be held accountable for, are, again, matters of debate. Different theoretical frameworks suggest different versions of what an 'adequate' description is. In essence, though, we can say that phonology has a twofold task: (a) to explore the nature of the substantial (phonic) realization or representation of the formal core of language, both in general and for specific languages; and (b) to relate this substantial representation to the form itself, i.e. determine its place in and relation to other aspects of a total description. I would see (b) as a subsidiary goal, though others would not (see ch. 9 in particular).

## 1.2 Areas of agreement

For as long as the structure of language has been seriously studied, there seems to have been general agreement about certain properties of the phonic medium it is realized in. Notably:

(i) Sounds in themselves are meaningless (see 'double articulation' above). There is no point to the question (independent of some particular language) 'what does [v] mean?'

(ii) But within the structure of a language, either alone or in combination with others, sounds can carry meaning. Thus [v] means nothing in English, but is one form of the Polish preposition *w* 'in' ( [ɣvarʃavɛ] 'in Warsaw').

(iii) Each language has an 'inventory' of sounds, selected from the whole range of possible human noises, which is (or may be) different from the inventories of other languages. Thus English doesn't have voiceless lateral fricatives, but Welsh does, French has the vowels [y ø] but Swahili doesn't, and so on.

(iv) There are patterns in the organization of phonic substance which vary from language to language: constraints on the distribution of sounds, predictability of certain sounds in certain positions, etc. Thus all final stops and fricatives are voiceless in German, Dutch, Russian, Polish; [ŋ] does not occur syllable-initially in English, but only after a vowel and before either pause, another vowel, or [k g];

3

a voiceless uvular fricative [χ] occurs in French only after another voiceless segment ([kaʈχ] 'four'); no syllable in Maori may end in a consonant.

(v) Two languages may have the same sound types, but use them differently with respect to semantic distinctiveness: both English and Hindi have voiceless aspirated and voiceless unaspirated stops, but this difference is not information-bearing in English, while it is in Hindi. So distinctions like those between Hindi [pʰəl̪] 'fruit' and [pəl̪] 'moment' are impossible in English, where aspiration is position–dependent, i.e. for most dialects with aspiration, stops are aspirated before stressed vowels (unless [s] precedes) (*pit* vs. *spit*), and often finally (*pip, pit, pick*), but unaspirated before unstressed vowels (*upper*): see §2.3.

(vi) There are also cases where sound distribution seems to be implicated in morphosyntactic structure. Thus in English the segments [aɪ]/[ɪ], [iː]/[ɛ], [ɛɪ]/[æ] act as 'sets' or units in certain **alternations**: e.g. *divine/divinity*, *sign/signify*, *crime/criminal*; *serene/serenity*, *clean/cleanliness*; *humane/humanity*, *grain/granary*, etc. These alternations show certain similarities with those between (say) English aspirated and unaspirated stops, but differences as well; a linguistic description obviously has to cope with them, but precisely how, as we will see, is a problem.

Observations like (i–vi) above partly define the subject-matter of phonology; though careful examination leads to much more subtle and complex observations. And we can add some other points of general agreement:

(vii) There are limits to the number of sound types that can be used in human languages. For example, no language has consonants made with the tip of the tongue against the vocal folds, or vowels made with simultaneous spreading and rounding of the lips (for obvious reasons); but no language appears to have segments made with the tongue-tip against the left premolars, and the reasons for this are not obvious.

(viii) There exists a reasonable phonetic **taxonomy** (classification), including such items as places of articulation, airstreams, positions of the velum, states of the glottis, etc., which can be used to classify, nearly if not fully exhaustively, the sounds that occur in languages. And phonological descriptions ought to be responsive to this prior classification.

(ix) Of the sounds that humans do make, only certain ones are 'linguistic': laughs, belches, grunts, shrieks are not linguistic items (even if their use can carry meaning of a sort). There is no direct mapping between a laugh and the proposition 'I am amused' of the kind that exists between the string of sounds [aɪæməmjuːzd] and that proposition.

Given this preliminary sketch of our data-base and agreed matters to be accounted for, we can look at what aspects pose the most interesting descriptive problems, and how these problems have suggested theories about both the details and the overall organization of phonology. In particular, we will be concerned throughout this book with a number of basic questions:

(i) What are the UNITS of phonology? Just 'sounds', or something else (larger or smaller)? Is there only one basic type of unit, or more? (chs. 2, 5–6, 10, 11.)

(ii) What are the PRINCIPLES OF ORGANIZATION controlling the units in (i)? (chs. 6, 7, 8–10, 11.)

(iii) How much abstraction, idealization, etc. will be needed for adequate description? Are we to be content with simple listing of things we perceive, or are there 'deeper' principles involved, which may require fairly or highly abstract theoretical models? (chs. 2, 3, 4, 9.)

(iv) Given answers of some sort to (i–iii), where is the dividing line between what is 'truly' phonological and what is morphological, syntactic, or semantic? In particular, where do things like the *divine/divinity* alternation mentioned above fit in? (chs. 4, 9.)

(v) Given possible answers to any or all of (i–iv), what are the argument strategies for justifying them?

(vi) To what extent (if any) should phonological theory be tied in with psychological theory? Are the constructs of phonology intended to reflect 'properties of mind', or to be part of a larger-scale theory of human 'mental structure', cognition, etc.? Or is phonology 'autonomous', not necessarily or relevantly connected with anything outside itself, i.e. a study of 'pure' structure in a quasi-mathematical sense?

(vii) From (vi) arises the question of 'external' justification: to what extent (if any) is data from language change, language acquisition, language pathology relevant to phonological theory? Can internal issues (e.g. decisions as to which of two or more competing descriptions

5

is 'correct' or at least 'better') be decided on the basis of external evidence of this kind? (ch. 9.)

(viii) What do we want from a phonological theory/description anyway?

I will not necessarily allude to all of these questions directly as the discussion unfolds, but they will always be there in the background, along with others that will arise from time to time. But they do represent the key questions that animate current debate.

### 1.3 On facts, theories, and 'truth'

This section may appear out of place in an introductory textbook, as it deals with rather abstract matters of philosophy and method. But I think it's an error to expect students to be simple-mindedly unaware of such things, even if they cause a bit of mental indigestion. You can probably read this book quite successfully without this section, but the material interests ME, and the attitudes expressed here show up in the way I look at the subject.

It's a commonly held view that 'facts' are just lying about in the world, and the way we make theories is by collecting these facts and then seeing what theories they lead to. Nothing could be further from the truth: in a way, there are no facts without theories. One might even define a theory as – in part – a framework that tells you what a fact is.

Let me clarify a bit. Even though the 'theory-dependence of facts' is a sound general principle (we will see it in operation as we go along), certain facts are 'privileged': those determined by such low-level and indispensable theories that we can take them as **pre-theoretical**, i.e. 'given' by observation or perception. For instance: it's a fact (observational) that the further away an object is from the eye, the smaller the image it casts on the retina. Hold your two hands about six inches from your eyes, and then move your right hand a foot further away. Are your two hands still the same size? If you answer 'yes', as you probably will, you are making a theoretical judgement. That is, the brain has a 'theory' that physical objects retain constant size, and it disregards the actual evidence of the size of the projected image. Size-constancy thus becomes a pretheoretical fact for the user of a particular brain – even though some kind of theoretical operation went into establishing it.

6

Consider three types of relatively pretheoretical facts about one variety of English:

(i) In pronouncing [f], the tongue is at rest on the floor of the mouth; for [v], it is somewhat raised towards the alveolar ridge.

(ii) The segment [pʰ] occurs before stressed vowels except after [s]; [p] occurs before unstressed vowels and before stressed vowels after [s].

(iii) The segments [k]/[s]/[ʃ] have a 'special relationship', in that they alternate in morphological paradigms: *electric/electricity/electrician*, *critical/criticize*, etc. *Example/model*

Virtually no phonological theory would take (i) as a genuine (phonological) fact, because there is no theory in which tongue position is 'relevant' for labiodental fricatives; but (ii) and (iii) involve variant distributions, under some apparent systematic control, of perceptually different items: the controls in (ii) are phonological, those in (iii) partly morphological. All phonologists would agree, I think, that (ii) and (iii) somehow ought to be accounted for in a description of English; and probably that there ought to be general principles to tell us how things like this should be treated in ALL languages; i.e. these phenomena are clearly of theoretical interest, and part of a theory of universal phonology – under the assumption that there are at least SOME properties that are invariant across languages (otherwise there would be no such discipline as phonology, but only 'English phonology', etc.).

But the question of HOW they ought to be treated is more complex, and here is where we get into debate: there is no general agreement as to whether things like (iii) are part of 'phonology proper', or belong to morphology, or come somewhere between (see chs. 4, 9). (Terms like 'stressed', 'vowels', 'aspirated' are of course also theoretical, but they belong to **background knowledge**, i.e. they come from a theory – phonetics – that is pretheoretical for phonology, not having to be justified within phonology itself. Phonology takes the classifications of phonetics as 'factual' input, part of what philosophers call its **observation language**.)

Throughout this book I will be looking at many different theories of phonological organization; most are in one way or another manifestly inadequate, and some may represent positions that nobody nowadays holds in their pure form. This may sound like a perfectly

7

good reason for not considering them at all, but it isn't, for two reasons: (a) no science is capable of giving final or ultimate answers to its questions, so that at any time it is not necessarily the case that all earlier answers and methods of getting them are superseded; and (b), because it is not possible to understand any body of evolving theory in isolation from its history.

So just because a particular theoretical stance seems at the moment to have been abandoned doesn't mean that all its insights have been discarded. Even revolutionary developments in science don't usually mean beginning again from the beginning; the history of any discipline involves a lot of old wine in new bottles (as well as new wine in old bottles, new wine in new bottles, and some old wine left in the old bottles). Even ideas that seem at the moment self-evidently true don't arise out of nowhere, but are products of a long series of trial-and-error interim solutions to perennial problems, illuminated by occasional flashes of creative insight and inspired invention. Improvement or even radical restructuring of a theory doesn't (or shouldn't) imply the rejection of everything that went before.

As the philosopher of science Sir Karl Popper reminds us (1972), 'progress' in science or any other intellectual field is the result of 'conjectures and refutations'. The story of phonology, like that of any other subject, is one of hypotheses proposed, subjected to criticism, defended, revised, rejected if need be, and so on. There are never any 'decisive' solutions, none that can with certainty be known to be right. The best we can ever know about a theory, and even this isn't often attainable, is that it's wrong: a theory that hasn't yet been falsified or otherwise rejected has a certain claim on our confidence – until a better one comes along. As it will, given the boundlessness of human invention. I will therefore treat competing phonological theories in this light: the main difference between phonology (or any other branch of linguistics) and the 'hard' (natural) sciences is that a discipline concerned with human symbolic behaviour is so much more complicated than one dealing with inanimate nature, or non-human animate nature, that the opportunity for decisive refutation is much rarer. There are no episodes in the history of linguistics like the triumph of heliocentric over geocentric cosmology, and there aren't likely to be.

This view affects the structure of this book as follows: since phonology is fluid and developing, it is not so much a set of facts and 'correct' theories accounting for them as a set of PROBLEMS and attempted solutions. In the present state of our knowledge, we are rather in the position of the blind men and the elephant in the old story: to the one who had hold of its tail, the elephant was 'very like a rope'; to the one who had its leg, it was 'very like a tree', and so on.

Since our elephant is very complex and elusive, it's often necessary to approach a description of its overall organization by putting the reports of the blind men together – through detailed and intricate arguments about the structure of its individual parts. And since these structures are often not very obvious, we may have to approach them indirectly, and it will be impossible to give hard-and-fast precepts about how to analyse them, or even to give once-and-for-all definitions of what they are. Thus my approach will be based on particular problems, and the advantages and disadvantages of particular solutions that have been offered: above all, on ARGUMENTS.

That is, since many of the things we will be talking about are **unobservables**, i.e. structural principles, hypothesized units, etc. that 'lie behind' the observable reality we are trying to fathom, we will have to talk in terms of whether particular systems of hypotheses do better or worse jobs of making sense of the data. If anything, that's what the whole enterprise is about: making sense of things. This book will succeed if you come away with some idea of how difficult this is, and how interesting it can be.

## NOTES AND REFERENCES

1.1 Arbitrariness: there are some marginal (relatively) non-arbitrary relations between sound and sense, e.g. **onomatopoeia** (imitation: *moo, cluck, cuckoo*), and various kinds of 'sound symbolism'; but these are in no way central or basic.

Description: some theories claim that description isn't enough, but that an adequate theory should 'explain' its observations. This is a contentious and difficult problem, which I will take up briefly in chs. 8–9. For discussion see Lass (1980) and the papers in Cohen (1974).

Phonic realization: I don't imply that the form/substance relation means that phonic substance is the only direct realization of linguistic form. It's a common error to assume that writing is merely an indirect manifestation of language, 'secondary' or 'parasitic', exclusively mediated through phonology. See McIntosh (1956), Householder (1971: ch. 13).

1.2 Phonology and psychology: for some schools of linguists the 'representation of language in the brain' is the central issue in linguistic theory. This is usually treated in the literature under the heading of 'psychological reality'. For Chomsky and his followers this is what linguistics is about; for some of Chomsky's opponents as well. For a committed Chomskyan view see Smith & Wilson (1979); for a critique of Chomsky see Derwing (1973), Linell (1979). For an elegant argument to the effect that psychology is no concern of linguistics proper, Matthews (1979). These are difficult issues, and you should probably not worry about them at this stage (especially as much of the literature requires a good deal of technical knowledge). I will return to these matters in §§6.1, 9.3ff.

1.3 'Science': whether linguistics is a 'science' is much debated. My guess is that it isn't, but I will occasionally use the term rather loosely. For literature on this difficult issue see Itkonen (1978), Lass (1976a: Epilogue), Ringen (1975). On progress in knowledge as a matter of conjectural solutions to problems, see Popper (1972, 1973); for an excellent introduction to such general problems of the philosophy of science see Chalmers (1978).

# 2

# Foundations: the phoneme concept

## 2.1 **Segmentation and classification**

This chapter spells out some terms and analytical concepts which are basic to virtually all forms of phonological theory. Emphasis and definition have changed, but the concepts and terms remain (if sometimes in thickish disguises), and we will be using them throughout.

Let us approach this conceptual/terminological background a bit *study of* *wd. formation* obliquely, through a 'higher' level of analysis: morphology. This will indicate parallelisms between different levels of description, and characterize the analytical level with which phonology interacts most intimately.

Utterances can be segmented into recurring elements, which appear in various combinations (*cats eat mice, mice dislike cats, John eats mice, Mary dislikes John*, etc.). Some of these are what we would call 'words' (*John, mice*); others, like the suffixes in *eat-s, cat-s*, while 'meaningful', are of a different (dependent) status. The former might broadly be called 'lexical formatives', the latter 'grammatical formatives'. Somewhere between 'full' lexical items and inflexional affixes like *-s*, we find derivational affixes (*un-* in *un-pleasant, -ness* in *good-ness*).

All three types, however, can be taken as belonging to a higher-order unit type or category: they are **morphemes**. We can define a morpheme (roughly and a bit controversially) as a minimal (indivisible) 'meaning-bearing' element. Or a minimal syntactic 'building-block'. Thus *cats* can be segmented into *cat* and *-s*; but neither of these can be segmented without loss of sense: *ca-* doesn't mean anything (or better, does not belong to the set of English formatives); but while *-at* does mean something, it's not the same as *cat*. It **represents** or **realizes** a different morpheme (see §2.2). The

11

**lexicon** of a language is the inventory of all its morphemes, lexical and grammatical.

The criterion of minimalness is important: in a number of types of linguistic theory, broadly classifiable as **taxonomic** or classificatory, the most important analytical operation is the segmentation of linguistic material into decreasingly complex series of units. (All theories rely on this to some extent: the primary difference is whether these operations are 'background' or 'foreground'.)

Consider the sentence *the cat hates dogs*; its structure might be represented as:

(2.1)

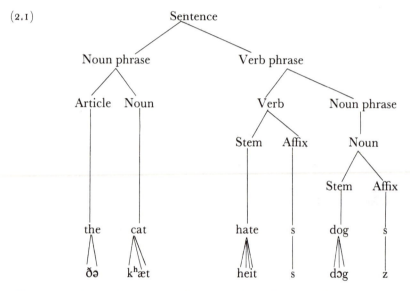

(The form of the diagram and the labels and transcriptions are just for convenience; the details are not to be taken seriously.)

Diagram (2.1) displays a series of 'is-made-of' or **constituency** relations. The sentence is made up of a noun phrase and a verb phrase (in that order), the verb phrase of a verb plus a noun phrase, and so on down to the phonetic level where *the* is a string of segments [ð] plus [ə]. This segmentation is a progressive application of the notion 'minimal unit in any domain'. Morphemically, we reach the level of basic units with *cat*, *hate*, *-s*; phonetically, with the 'sounds' which are themselves (apparently, but cf. chs. 3, 5, 6) indivisible. We will see shortly that this is oversimple.

We observe further that certain morphemes can occur in various contexts: *cat* in *cat, cats, cat's, catty, cat-like*; and *-s* 'plural' in *cats, dogs*. But while *cat* has the same phonetic shape everywhere, this isn't true of *-s*. There are instances of what seems – with respect to minimalness and sameness of sense – 'the same morpheme' in different phonetic shapes: [s] after *cat*, [z] after *dog*. And we'd probably want to include [ɪz] in *fishes* as yet a third occurrence of '*-s*'.

We must now refine our use of 'morpheme'. It's not that *cat* (either orthographically or phonetically) 'is' a morpheme, but rather that all occurrences, phonetic and orthographic, **represent** or **realize** a morpheme {cat}. (We will include morphemic representations in braces here to indicate their status; for other uses of braces see below.) What we find actually occurring are **morphs**: pieces of substance representing the formal category 'morpheme'. Phonetically, we get strings of sounds; any such string, without specific reference to the structure of a language, is a **morph**: but in terms of its 'place' in a linguistic system, it is a morph representing a specific morpheme – an **allomorph** of that morpheme (Greek *allos* 'other', *morphē* 'form'). Thus [kʰæt] is an allomorph (the only one, as it happens) of {cat}, and [s z ɪz] are allomorphs of {-s} or {plural} or whatever you want to call it. (This is actually inaccurate; the proper formulation will be presented in §2.3.)

So it seems that we can interpret a morpheme not strictly as an 'entity' but as a **class**: and the allomorphs of a morpheme are objects of a particular structure that are the members of that class. (There are other definitions; but for phonological purposes this is the most useful.)

Now observe the particular relations among allomorphs that let us assign them to a given morpheme. With {cat} there's no problem, since the representation in 'sound' is invariant. But even for {plural} it still seems reasonable to assign the three diverse objects to one class, because of two properties: (a) **invariance of meaning**, and (b) **predictability of occurrence**. Consider these English noun plurals:

(2.2)  
$\left\{\begin{array}{l}\text{(a) cap[s], cat[s], back[s], muff[s], heath[s] ...} \\ \text{(b) cab[z], cad[z], bag[z], love[z], ham[z], hill[z], bee[z] ...} \\ \text{(c) dish[ɪz], patch[ɪz], kiss[ɪz], buzz[ɪz] ...}\end{array}\right\}$

The phonetic shape of {plural} is predictable from the segment preceding it. We can express this generalization in the following rule:

(2.3)

$$\{\text{plural}\} \rightarrow \begin{cases} [\text{ɪz}] \text{ after sibilants} \\ [\text{z}] \text{ after non-sibilant voiced segments} \\ [\text{s}] \text{ after non-sibilant voiceless segments} \end{cases}$$

(The arrow '→' means 'is realized as'; the braces with items one above the other enclose mutually exclusive choices.)

The selection of an allomorph on the basis of its segmental environment is called **phonological conditioning**. There is however another kind of conditioning: consider {knife}, which ends in [v] before {plural}, but otherwise in [f] (*knives, knives'*, but *knife, knife's*). Here the stem allomorph is conditioned by the MORPHEME that follows it: this is **grammatical** or **morphological conditioning**. An extreme subcase of this is **lexical conditioning**, where allomorphy is determined by the presence of specific lexical morphemes. Thus in addition to the vast bulk of English nouns that follow the 'regular' plural rule (2.3), there are those with other suffixes (*kibbutz, ox*), internal vowel change (*man, foot*), vowel change plus a different suffix (*child*), and zero plural (*sheep, deer*). But there is still a case to be made for including them under {plural}, on semantic grounds.

These different types of conditioning can interact; take {knife} again. Here a rule gives us the [v]-allomorph before {plural}, but not before {genitive} (*knives* vs. *knife's*). But note that the rule for the allomorphy of {genitive} is the same as that for {plural}: *cat'*[s], *dog'*[z], *fish'*[ɪz]. Thus the stem allomorph is grammatically conditioned, but the suffix is phonologically conditioned. Note also that the 'choice' of stem allomorph has to be made 'before' that of the suffix, since the former conditions the latter. I will return to the problem of **process** or **rule order** later (chs. 4, 9).

## 2.2 **Units, realizations, distributions**

Perhaps we ought to clarify the notions 'unit' and 'realization'. A simple approach is through units of another kind. Consider these shapes:

(2.4)    A  a  *A*  *a*
         B  b  *B*  *b*
         C  c  *C*  *c*

It's reasonable to say that each row of characters is a set of 'different versions' of one basic character or unit in the writing systems of Roman-based scripts. In the first line they are all 'different forms of the letter *a*', and so on.

But 'the letter *a*' itself has no shape independent of one of its realizations: it is an ABSTRACT UNIT IN A CODE, realizable only as one of a determinate number of shapes, but without 'a shape of its own'. (We will see later that this condition may be argued not to be the case in phonology.) That is: if you were asked to specify 'what an *a* is', you would have to answer in terms of one of these shapes, even though you know perfectly well that there is something abstract 'underlying' and common to all of them – their '*a*-hood', as it were. Each shape is in fact a member of the abstract class 'a', a realization or **exponent**. Using ⟨ ⟩ to enclose a symbol for a class of realizations, or a graphic unit, we can say:

(2.5)

$$\langle a \rangle \rightarrow A, a, \ldots$$

The unit is a **grapheme**, and the realizations **allographs**.

But each basic symbol type (here reduced to two) has a distinctive **distribution** or **privilege of occurrence**: we don't normally get *\*ideA*, *\*americA*, *\*banAna* (an asterisk signifies an 'ungrammatical' or 'illegal' form). Though we can get *Apple*, and we must get *America*. For this restricted sample, then, the distribution of forms is:

(2.6)
$$\langle a \rangle \rightarrow \left\{ \begin{array}{ll} A & \left\{ \begin{array}{l} \text{sentence-initially} \\ \text{at the beginning of proper names} \end{array} \right\} \\ a & \text{elsewhere} \end{array} \right\}$$

And of course there are rules that govern the distribution of the class ⟨a⟩ as a whole (*China*, but *\*history*). So: (a) every unit has a specific **macro-distribution** as a unit; and (b) every realization of a unit has its own **micro-distribution** within the macro-distribution of the unit as a whole.

The crucial notions are **unit**, **distribution**, **realization**; they form the conceptual core of the bulk of pre-1960s 'structural' linguistics, regardless of level of analysis. And indeed, they are the implicit basis of every other kind of phonological model.

## 2.3 **'Excess' of data: the phoneme as a solution**

The discussion in §2.1 suggests a straightforward mapping between morphological form and phonetic substance: morphemes are realized as strings of sounds. But this is too simple; there is evidence for some intervening level or levels, more 'abstract' than the phonetic, more 'concrete' than the morphemic. Could phonology too be organized in levels of abstraction, with classes and realizations of its own?

Probably no phonologist would deny this; though the precise nature of this organization is still debated. We will be concerned here with what is often called the **classical phonemic** answer to this question – an answer that in one form or another dominated phonological thinking in the first half of this century, and is still with us.

Let us begin with some relatively 'raw' data. Here is some from a dialect of British English, transcribed in considerable detail ([k̟ g̟] are 'advanced' velar stops, [ʔpº ʔtº ʔkº] are pre-glottalized and unreleased, [Ṽ] is a nasalized vowel, [ɫ] is velarized or 'dark'):

(2.7)

| | | | |
|---|---|---|---|
| 1 kʰiːɫ 'keel' | 1 kʰuːɫ 'cool' | 1 skiː 'ski' | |
| 2 k̟ʰeɪɫ 'kale' | 2 kʰʌɫ 'cull' | 2 sk̟eɪʔtº 'skate' | |
| 3 k̟ʰɪʔkº 'kick' | 3 kʰʊd 'could' | 3 sk̟ɪf 'skiff' | |
| 4 k̟ʰɛ̃nʔtº 'Kent' | 3 kʰɔːʔtº 'caught' | 4 sk̟æ̃mʔpº 'scamp' | |
| (a) | (b) | (c) | |

| | | |
|---|---|---|
| 1 skuːʔpº 'scoop' | 1 giːs 'geese' | 1 guːɫ 'ghoul' |
| 2 skʌɫ 'skull' | 2 g̟eɪʔtº 'gate' | 2 gʌɫ 'gull' |
| 3 skɔːn 'scorn' | 3 g̟ɛ̃nʔtº 'Ghent' | 3 gɔːʔkº 'gawk' |
| 4 skɒʔtº 'Scot' | 4 g̟æʔpº 'gap' | 4 gʊd 'good' |
| (d) | (e) | (f) |

1 liːʔkº 'leek'
2 læʔkº 'lack'
3 lʊʔkº 'look'
(g)

What is the point of this untidy display? Consider the initial velar stops in (2.7). In (a) we find an advanced voiceless one, articulated toward the front of the velum or even the back of the palate: in (b) we find a relatively back velar. Both the advanced and retracted ones are aspirated. A little consideration shows us, however, that there is a relation between the frontness of the stop and that of the following vowel: front before front(ish), back before back(ish).

Further: if we look at (c–d), we find the same front/back variation, only without aspiration. And we note that the voiceless unaspirated ones occur only if an [s] precedes. So English has four voiceless velar stops, [kʰ k̟ kʰ k]. And if we look at the voiced velars in (e–f), we find two kinds again: so we add [g̟ g] to our inventory. And if we add velars in final position, we find another one: glottalized unreleased [ʔkº]. But do we really want to say that English 'has' seven velar stops?

As a matter of simple observational fact we do 'have' all these velars. But leaving it at this misses an interesting generalization. Given the two sets [k$^h$ k k$^h$ k ʔk°] and [g g], the members of each are distributed so that the occurrence of one or another is totally PREDICTABLE. Thus all velars are advanced before front vowels and retracted before back; voiceless velars are aspirated before stressed vowels unless [s] precedes; and glottalized and unreleased only finally.

But this doesn't hold for one group AS A WHOLE vs. the other. Substituting the [k$^h$] of *keel* for the [k$^h$] of *cool* may give us a rather odd version of *cool*: but one that's still *cool* and no other word. But if we substitute [g] for [k$^h$] we get *ghoul*. So: the difference between front and back velars in English is not lexically **information-bearing** (though it may give **indexical** information, i.e. not about word-meaning but about speaker-characteristics, like sex, effeminacy, foreignness, etc.). Whereas that between voiceless and voiced velars is: the presence or absence of voice tells us that one word rather than another has been said, but frontness and aspiration are **redundant**. They are conditioned automatically by properties of the speech chain. Such variants are not normally under the speaker's control: he 'chooses' either voice or voicelessness, but not frontness or aspiration: one might say that the system does the choosing for him.

So we have two kinds of entities: **systemic**, belonging to the language as a signalling system or code, and **non-systemic**, predictable exponents of the systemic units. We could say that in English there is some 'abstract structural element' corresponding to the range of [k]-types, and another to the [g]-types. In these ranges, the '[k]-ness' or '[g]-ness' is an idiosyncratic or 'free' property, while the others are constrained. The same is true in (2.7) of non-velarized [l] and velarized [ł]: the former only occurs syllable-initially, the latter only syllable-finally (see a. 1–2, b. 1–2 vs. g. 1–2). Or of nasalized vs. non-nasalized vowels (see a. 4, e. 3 vs. any other forms), etc.

In other words, there are two types of 'sound' inventory: the very large set of actually occurring noises, and the smaller set of fundamental units they realize. We have now reached the kind of decision we reached in §2.1 about 'meanings': morphemes are not directly represented in sounds, but sounds themselves are part of (at least – see ch. 4) a two-level structure, of classes and their realizations or members. And morphemes are represented as strings of these structural units of the phonology.

17

These units, parallel on their level to morphemes on theirs, are **phonemes**, and the realizations of a phoneme are its **allophones**. (An actual sound, with no reference to its class membership, is a **phone**.) If we now represent (allo)phones in square brackets, phonemes in solidi, and morphemes in braces, we can illustrate the levels of representation as follows:

(2.8)

| Class-level unit | e.g. | next-level realization |
|---|---|---|
| Morpheme | {plural} | /s/, /z/, /ɪz/ ... |
| Phoneme | /k/ | [k̟ʰ], [k̟], [kʰ], ... |

And so, for *cats*:

(2.9)

| Morphemic representation | {cat} + {plural} |
|---|---|
| Phonemic representation | /kæts/ |
| Phonetic representation | [k̟ʰæʔts] |

Morphemes are mapped onto phonemically-realized allomorphs, and phonemes onto phonetically-realized allophones. (We will have to revise some of these simple notions, but the principles will remain.)

## 2.4  Criteria for phonemic status

How do we determine which sounds in a language represent which of its phonemes? How do we go about setting up phoneme systems, and organizing the phonetic material we encounter? To begin with, any pair of phonemes, like /k/ and /g/, are **contrastive**: their function is to separate entities. Two words that are phonemically different (with certain exceptions – see below) are different words. We must now examine the relation between distribution and contrastiveness, to see how the distribution of phones can, in a fairly precise way, be used to establish contrast, and thus determine the phoneme inventory of a language.

Let us return to English velar stops. In the dialect exemplified in (2.7), voiceless stops (not only /k/) are aspirated before stressed vowels unless /s/ precedes (we will take the phonemic status of /s/ for granted; we'll see below how it can be established). Thus [k] does not occur before a stressed vowel unless /s/ precedes, and contrariwise, [kʰ] doesn't occur if /s/ does precede. The two phones occur in mutually exclusive environments: they are in **complementary distribution**. In general – with provisos to be discussed below – two phones in complementary distribution are allophones of the same phoneme, i.e., if they can never appear in the same environment, they obviously can't contrast; the prime situation for contrast is **parallel distribution**, e.g. the initials of *cat, tat, pat*. By the above criterion, [kʰ] and [k] must represent one phoneme: therefore *cot* [kʰɒʔtᵒ] and *Scot* [skɒʔtᵒ] can be phonemically represented as respectively /kɒt/ and /skɒt/ (the rule for [ʔtᵒ] is obviously the same as that for [ʔkᵒ]).

But consider the case of [h] and [ŋ] in English. These are in complementary distributions: [h] only before a vowel, [ŋ] only after, as in *hang* [hæŋ]. A form *[ŋæh] is impossible in English, though there are languages with initial [ŋ] (Maori) and final [h] (Mohawk). Do we say then that [h] and [ŋ] are allophones of one phoneme, either /h/ or /ŋ/? By our previous definition we do. And there's no problem in deriving a phonetic representation from a phonemic one, and vice versa: all we need is a simple realization rule telling us which allophone appears where, and we could represent *hang* as /hæh/ or /ŋæŋ/.

But should we? To a speaker of English, this seems outrageous; one would like these two phones to belong to two separate structural units, regardless of their complementarity. So we introduce a further condition: to qualify as allophones of one phoneme, two phones must not only be in complementary distribution, they must be **phonetically similar**. This is a tricky criterion; but we can accept it as intuitively plausible, and in practice workable, even if not formally definable. There is a clear sense in which [k] and [k̟] are phonetically similar, and an equally clear one in which [h] and [ŋ] are not.

We take contrast as a fundamental notion: two phones are contrastive (represent different phonemes) if substitution of one for the other produces a 'different word/morpheme' in the language, or, to stretch it a bit, if substitution produces a word that ISN'T in the language for either accidental or structural reasons. Thus substitution of [kʰ] for [pʰ] in *pang* produces the non-word [k̟ʰæŋ], which is certainly a possible English word – though it happens not to exist ('Try delicious orange-flavoured *Kang* for breakfast tomorrow'); whereas substitution of [f] for [s] in *snoop* produces *[fnuːʔpᵒ], which violates English rules of phoneme combination (but cf. §12.3).

Substitution (or **commutation**) gives us a useful tool for establishing contrastiveness: two phones are in contrast if they are commutable in the same 'frame'. Thus we can establish the phonemes /p b t d k g/ for English by commutation in the frame 'before [ɒt]': *pot ≠ bot ≠ tot ≠ dot ≠ cot ≠ got*, etc. This is **minimal contrast** (the forms contrast in one segment only), and a pair like *cot*:*got* is a **minimal pair**. In classical phonemics, the isolation of minimal pairs is the basic method of establishing a phoneme inventory (and in practice, especially in field-work with an unknown language, this is a prerequisite for almost anything else). We will see, however, that minimal pairs may be misleading: they can point to structural properties better described as something other than phonemic contrast proper (§§2.7ff).

Of course these techniques aren't always available: not all potential phonemes contrast in every context. There are extreme cases of **defective distribution** (as with [h] and [ŋ] in English), which are not commutable in any frame. Nonetheless they can be shown to be phonemic in their own macro-distributions by contrast with other (independently established) phonemes: one could use *cat*:*pat*:*hat*, *ham*:*had*:*hang*, etc. Further, ONE minimal contrast with another independent phoneme may be enough. Thus [ʒ] in English has an extremely limited distribution, and minimal pairs are difficult to find. But if we establish /ʃ/ as phonemic *vis-à-vis* /s/ (*ship*:*sip*), then *azure*: *Asher* (for dialects that don't have /zj/ in *azure*) establishes /ʒ/. And even if there are no minimal pairs, 'near-minimal' ones can make the case for contrast: /ʒ/ could be established on the basis of *vicious*:*vision, delicious*:*derision*.

So a phoneme may be defined – roughly – as 'a class of phonetically similar phones in complementary distribution'. This is a **procedural** or **operational** definition: phonemes 'arise' as the product of operations on data. It has nothing to say about the embedding of phonology in the rest of grammar, about 'psychological representation' (what kinds of 'mental entities' phonemes might be), etc.

We have been dealing so far with **categorical** ('either'/'or') properties, e.g. contrast vs. non-contrast, general rules for allophony in particular environments. It would be nice if these were all we had to consider, but there are cases of a rather different sort as well. Consider for instance dialects of English in which final voiceless stops can appear as follows ('~' = 'varies with', [C'] = **ejective**, i.e. with glottalic – not pulmonic – egressive airstream):

(2.10)     *cap*: khæp$^h$ ~ khæʔp° ~ khæp'
           *cat*: khæt$^h$ ~ khæʔt° ~ khæt'
           *back*: bæk$^h$ ~ bæʔk° ~ bæk'

We can predict initial aspiration, etc., but the final allophones seem to be unpredictable. So there is another relation that can hold among allophones: so-called **free variation**. This is (apparently) unpredictable vacillation or 'optionality' (within prescribed limits) in certain positions. (This is actually too unsophisticated a statement, though it holds within the limits of the framework we're considering. For extensions of predictability, and some refinements, see ch. 12.)

Not only phones, but – apparently – phonemes can occur in free variation. Thus for some English speakers /iː/ ~ /ɛ/ in *evolution* (but never in *revolution*), /iː/ ~ /ai/ in *either, neither*. Here the distinctive function of a phonemic contrast (cf. /iː/ vs. /ɛ/ in *beet:bet*, /iː/ vs. /ai/ in *beet:bite*) is suspended in certain lexical items; but this is a marginal, nonsystematic effect. (For suspension of contrast as a systematic property see §2.8 and chs. 3, 4, 9.)

2.5 **Phonemic analysis and restricting conditions**
What then is a 'phonemic analysis' or 'taxonomic phonology' of a language? Essentially it is an inventory, together with realization rules for its members, and statements of distribution, that characterizes exhaustively the substantial structure of its morphemes.

It will be a set of lists, of three major types:

(i) **Phoneme inventory**. What phonemes does language L have?
(ii) **Allophonic rules** (exponence or realization statements). A set of rules, or a list of allophones for each member of the inventory.
(iii) **Phonotactics**. Statements of permissible strings of phonemes (e.g. clusters, sequences, distributional restrictions, admissible syllable types).

Some comments on these are in order.

(i) *Inventories*. These are characteristically displays or lists of phonemes, with some particular symbol chosen – normally on phonetic grounds – for each. Thus one might give 'the phonemes of Grodno Yiddish' as:

(2.11)

| | | | p | t | | k | | m | n | | ŋ |
|---|---|---|---|---|---|---|---|---|---|---|---|
| ɪ | ʊ | | b | d | | g | | | l | ʎ | ʁ |
| ɛ | ɔ | | f | s | ʃ | x | h | | | j | |
| | a | | v | z | ʒ | | | | | | |
| ɛɪ | aɪ | ɔɪ | ts | tʃ | | | | | | | |
| | | | dʒ | | | | | | | | |

21

This displays says: this language has 32 phonemes, of which 8 are vowels and 24 are consonants; of the latter, 17 are **obstruents** (stops, fricatives, affricates), and 7 are **sonorants** (nasals, laterals, etc.: see §5.3.1). And these phonemes may be 'naturally' represented by the symbols chosen: i.e. the relation between symbol and phonetic exponent(s) is non-arbitrary. Therefore we would not expect a form which is phonemically /harts/ to be phonetically [kɪʃkɛ]. (On phonemic systems in general, see ch. 7.)

But symbol choice also depends partly on the USE to which a description is put. For instance: in my variety of English, the lateral phoneme is a velarized dental [ɫ] in nearly all positions (non-velarized only before /j/ as in *million*), voiceless after voiceless stops and fricatives (*clay, flay*). But one could perfectly well represent it as 'unmodified' /l/, with the details supplied by rule, if the only concern is the contrast between some kind of lateral and a non-lateral **liquid** (non-nasal sonorant) /r/. A representation like /ɫ/, on the other hand, would be chosen for a language with a velarized/non-velarized contrast (like Irish or some forms of Polish), and one like /l̪/ for a language with a dental/alveolar contrast. Though even for English one might – if the purpose of a description were contrastive or typological – use /l̪/ to distinguish a dialect type like mine from another with a velarized alveolar /ɫ/, and from still others (like Hiberno-English or some Northumbrian varieties) with only non-velarized /l/, or dialects where the 'norm' is unmodified, but [ɫ] appears in some positions (like RP). In other words, the amount of detail given in the symbols themselves depends on what you're trying to show, and the extent to which you're interested in PHONETIC TYPES as well as PHONEMIC CONTRASTS.

(ii) *Allophonic rules.* These can often be given as simple prose statements (as was often the case in the earlier literature), or in some kind of formal notation: this matters little in the framework we're discussing here. What counts is exhaustiveness of statement and the avoidance of 'mixing of levels' (see below), i.e. statements involving non-phonological conditioning. (But cf. §§2.9–10 for some cases where one might not want to do this.)

The format we will use for allophonic rules is based on the formalism current in most forms of phonology nowadays; the following conventions will be used throughout:

(2.12)

$$X \rightarrow \left\{ \begin{array}{l} y/ \underline{\hspace{1cm}} A \\ z \ /B \underline{\hspace{1cm}} \\ x \end{array} \right\}$$

To interpret: 'Some unit X is realized as (its member) y before A, as z after B; and as x elsewhere'. Braces, as in (2.6), indicate either/or choices. The **environment bar** '\_\_\_\_' indicates the position in which the statement 'X → ...' holds: thus X → y/\_\_\_\_ A is another way of saying that a sequence XA on one level becomes yA on another. We will see later that the arrow can have other meanings than 'is realized as', depending on theory; and that the formalism shown here can handle many things besides allophonic rules.

(iii) *Phonotactics.* Two or more languages with similar, even identical phoneme inventories may have very different rules governing the distribution of phonemes in morphemes, words, syllables. Thus both standard North German and English have stop systems that can be represented /p b t d k g/ and both have the sibilants /s z ʃ/. But whereas these are all distributed quite freely in English, in German none of the voiced ones may appear word-finally (but cf. §§3.1, 4.3 for a different interpretation of this). Further, while German allows both /s/ and /z/ medially, only /z/ occurs initially in native words before vowels: G /zoːn/ 'son' vs. E /sʌn/; and only /ʃ/ occurs initially before consonants: G /ʃtʊrm/ vs. E /stɔːm/.

Another aspect of phonotactics is higher-order generalizations about syllable structure (see ch. 10). Here we can often operate with general 'cover' categories like C(onsonant), V(owel), etc. Thus the **canonical** (permitted) form of a Maori syllable is CV (all syllables are **open**: no *VC, *CVC); whereas syllable formulas for a freely clustering language like English or Russian would be much more complex.

A few remarks on the purpose and nature of phonemic representation are in order. One main purpose, obviously, is to give us tractable systems of transcription, techniques for representing linguistic forms so that they can be studied further (note the subtitle of Pike's *Phonemics* (1947): 'a technique for reducing languages to writing'). But there is more to it than this: in effect, by removing allophonic minutiae from the transcription, we produce simplified representations, useful for any kind of additional analysis (except of course detailed phonetics, which is what the phoneme concept is designed to get us away from). And the description as a whole, of course, is an account of 'the structure of L' for any language L.

On the simplest level a phonemic transcription is a string of segmental representations, each standing for an occurrence of a structural category or systemic unit; and it can, given the relevant conventions (allophonic rules) be mapped onto a phonetic transcription. Ideally, it is a redundancy-free transcription, including only 'structurally relevant' information. (Or better, the conjunction of phonetic and phonemic representations is the sum of the structural information available about the phonology.) The point can be made by simply juxtaposing a phonemic and phonetic representation of a word in my variety of English, *can't*:

(2.13)  Phonetic

Phonemic

(The broken line between /n/ and [æ̃ː] suggests a possible indeterminacy: should nasalization be regarded as 'part of' /n/ or solely of /æ/ before /n/?) But given properly formulated rules, it should be possible (except in the limiting case of free variation) to 'read off' – unambiguously – one transcription from the other, in either direction. Whether this is a sufficiently exhaustive and interesting goal for phonology, and whether it's even possible, are other questions: we will be returning to them throughout this book.

To ensure this exhaustive analysability of phones into phonemes, and interchangeability of transcriptions, it's necessary – or so classical phonemics in its 'purest' form would claim – to impose certain conditions on phonemic analyses. These can be incorporated into something like a theoretical *credo*, which I give below in a rather condensed form: I will draw out some of its implications later on.

I  **Primacy of phonemes.** The 'atomic' units of phonology are segment-sized contrastive elements, i.e. phonemes as defined above.

II  **Biuniqueness.** Any phone in a given environment must be an allophone of one and only one phoneme – to prevent ambiguity and secure unique read-off.

III  **Linearity.** The location of a contrast in a phonetic representation is the same as in the corresponding phonemic one: if two phonemic representations contrast only in their third segments, the associated phonetic representations may not contrast only in their second, etc.

IV  **Separation of levels.** Phonology is fully independent of morphology and/or syntax; there is no information available for analysing the phonological structure of an utterance except the phonetic segments in it.

I will save (1) for later chapters (3, 5, 6); we will concentrate here on (II–IV). But first there is one important point about the 'imposition' of conditions on analyses that remains to be dealt with.

### 2.6  **Simplicity, symmetry, pattern: the 'as-if' argument**

Phonology, like other sciences or semi-sciences, imposes certain overall, quasi-'aesthetic' constraints on the shape of descriptions. Thus good descriptions are as simple as is consistent with the facts, as coherent, orderly, highly patterned and structured as possible. These **metaconditions** (overarching conditions on descriptions) often lead to problems in handling given data; and their interaction with the data brings important problems, and even unsuspected properties of the data itself, into focus. Phonologists in general seem, whatever their theoretical allegiances, to operate on three rather general principles:

(i)  Make systems as simple as possible: minimize phoneme numbers, types, etc., i.e. take the greatest advantage possible of predictability of realization, and use rules to minimize units.

(ii)  Make systems as symmetrical as possible.

(iii)  In trying to achieve (i) and (ii), get maximum mileage out of systematic regularities of all kinds.

It is uncertain whether constraints like these derive from the nature of the data or that of linguists; but the fact that they can often be utilized without excessive violence to the data suggests that in some way our desire for symmetry, simplicity, etc. reflects – if indirectly – properties of 'the real world'.

This furnishes a preface to a very important and highly characteristic phonological (and general linguistic) argument type: the **'as-if' argument**. One often comes across the following sort of argumentation in the literature:

Here is a phenomenon X; if we simply analyse X as what it – superficially – appears to be, our analysis will contain the **primitive** (basic) elements X and Y. But in fact X behaves in some ways rather as if it were 'really' a Y (and Y is already an independently motivated category that we can't get rid of). So if we treat X 'as-if' it were Y, we get rid of X as a basic element, capture an interesting generalization, and simplify our description.

We will see this type again and again; I will illustrate it here with a rather simple distributional example, a case of what might by called the 'phonotactic as-if'.

English has two phonetic items that are described as 'palato-alveolar affricates', voiceless and voiced (*church, judge*). The question is: should these clearly phonemic items be treated as units ('affricates'), or as clusters of (phonemic) stop + fricative? The phonetics don't give us an answer one way or the other: we write [tʃ], [dʒ]; but phonemically we could treat them either as units (traditionally /č ǰ/) or as 'complex' or bi-segmental (/tʃ dʒ/). If we treat them as bi-segmental, should they have any particular status? That is: should (for now) /tʃ dʒ/ be analysed as parallel to say /t d/, or as parallel to clusters in general? This has inventory implications: one would not normally want to say that English 'has the phonemes' /ts dz/, etc.

If we look at the general pattern of distribution of the affricates as compared to other stop + fricative clusters, we find the following ('#___' = word-initial, 'V___V' = between vowels, '___#' = word-final):

(2.14)

| #___ | V___V | ___# |
|---|---|---|
| tʃ (choose) | tʃ (pitcher) | tʃ (rich) |
| dʒ (Jew) | dʒ (budgie) | dʒ (budge) |
| — | ps (absent) | ps (apse) |
| — | bz (observe) | bz (cubs) |
| — | ts (ritzy) | ts (ritz) |
| — | — | dz (adze) |
| — | ks (exit) | ks (Max) |
| — | gz (exam) | gz (eggs) |
| — | pθ (naphtha) | pθ (depth) |
| — | — | tθ (eighth) |
| — | — | kθ (length) |
| — | kʃ (action) | — |

(This applies only for established 'native' vocabulary, not loans like *Dvořák, tsetse*, etc., which may be considered phonologically 'foreign'.)

That is: it's a general fact about English that stop + fricative clusters (except for the two in question) can't occur initially. This suggests, on the grounds of distributional patterning (**pattern congruity**), that the affricates ought to be taken as units, not clusters: in fact as stops that just happen to have a sibilant release. Their distribution is then parallel to that of /p b t d k g/; and in many dialects the voiceless one is also aspirated before stressed vowels, and glottalized finally, making the parallel even closer. This simplifies the phonotactics, and avoids positing two 'clusters' with unique distributions. Both distribution and system are now more coherent, and one phonotactic statement (for stops, regardless of release) suffices. Here 'phonological' criteria take precedence – for reasons of systemic neatness – over simple phonetic ones.

A further spin-off from this analysis is that the system of stops and fricatives in English is now more symmetrical, with a palato-alveolar series /č ǰ ʃ ʒ/ paralleling the labial, alveolar, and velar series. (But not fully symmetrical, since there are no phonemic dental stops to match /θ ð/.)

Unfortunately (and characteristically) there is a hitch: the distributional argument can be turned round to make the affricates unique again. Unlike the other voiceless stops, /č/ doesn't cluster with /s/ in any position: /sp st sk/, final and medial /ps ts ks/ but no * /sč čs/. This brings up the problem of **non-uniqueness** or **indeterminacy**: formal arguments (among others) don't necessarily lead to unique answers. In a case like this it may be a matter – ultimately – of personal preference and subjective judgement which argument is stronger. (For more on affricates see §§ 5.3.7–8, 6.3.)

### 2.7 **Problems, 1: biuniqueness and overlapping**

The biuniqueness requirement (often paraphrased as 'once a phoneme, always a phoneme') is designed to prevent phonetic/ phonological 'ambiguity'. The idea is that the listener's 'decoding' of the speech signal is a segmentation-and-classification routine: and this is not feasible unless a given phone in a given (phonological) environment is always an allophone of one particular phoneme. On the face of it, this seems sensible.

But as often happens, real-language data throws up problems that make desirable theoretical principles hard to maintain. Consider the following: many varieties of English have an optional (actually variable: see §12.4) rule which creates the following variants:

(2.15)

| Morpheme | → Form 1 | ~ Form 2 |
|---|---|---|
| {bat} | bæt | bæʔ |
| {butter} | bʌtə | bʌʔə |
| {cap} | kʰæp | kʰæʔ |
| {back} | bæk | bæʔ |

The natural interpretation is that /p t k/ are optionally realized as [ʔ] word-finally, and /t/ as [ʔ] also intervocalically. (But not /p k/: we don't get *[bæʔə] for *backer*, etc..) But under biuniqueness, this analysis is impossible: if [ʔ] is an allophone of /t/, as its wider distribution for /t/ suggests, then in one position (finally) it can't also be an allophone of /p k/. This would mean that any string [bæʔ] was ambiguous between /bæt/ and /bæk/, etc.

The classic way out is to shift the problem into the morphology, this way:

(i) {cat} has the allomorph /kæt/ (optionally → [kʰæʔ])
(ii) {back} has the allomorphs /bæk/ and /bæt/ ( → [bæʔ])
(iii) {cap} has the allomorphs (kæp/ and /kæt/ ( → [kʰæʔ])

So: {back} has one allomorph homophonous to {bat}, and {cap} has one homophonous to {cat}. And further, if the /-t/ allomorph is chosen in either of these cases, the /t/ → [ʔ] rule is **obligatory** ({cap} never appears as *[kʰæt]) – whereas it is **optional** if the /-t/ allomorph is the only one that exists (as in {cat}).

The biunique solution is thus counter-intuitive and messy. The obvious solution is to permit extensive **overlapping**, giving a realization pattern like:

(2.16)

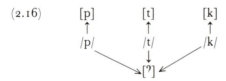

But this means that phonetic strings can be ambiguous. We seem to need a loosening up of the condition – to allow ambiguity of phonetic representations, with contextual or some other sort of disambiguation.

In order to avoid counter-intuitive or otherwise undesirable solutions, we seem to be forced to relax the very criterion that makes phonemic analysis possible (i.e. strict one-to-one correspondences between code-units and realizations). So what do we do? Fight our intuitions (we THOUGHT it impossible for {back} to have an allomorph homophonous to {bat}, but the theory tells us we were wrong)? Or give up biuniqueness, and get along as best we can without it?

Such situations display theoretical 'weak points': here speaker intuition vs. theoretical constraints leads to conflict. Theories have hidden consequences, which emerge only through confrontation with data; and these consequences may force us into revision or rethinking.

What's really the problem here? Is something wrong with the phoneme concept itself, or with one condition on analyses, or something else? Perhaps the real difficulty is the idea that leads to biuniqueness in the first place: strict separation of phonology and morphology, and the desire to preserve a simple and direct inter-level relation. Maybe we need to assume some basic idea like 'morpheme-identity': people may be assumed to know what they're saying and hearing, and many (most?) cases of phonological ambiguity are only apparent.

In any case, we must allow for simple homophony, like /rait/ representing *rite, right, write, wright*: here the question of different phonemic representations doesn't normally arise, but the problem is shunted to the lexical level, where it belongs. In principle, then, there's not all that much difference between this and the *bat/back* problem. And homophony is a pseudo-problem anyhow, since most instances are automatically disambiguated IN SPEECH: it is surely unrealistic to expect a speaker, given some realization of /rait/ in isolation, to know which of the four homophones it represents. By the same token, it might be just as perverse to expect an instance of [bæʔ] in isolation to be unambiguous.

Here is the nub: classical phonemics is predicated on forms IN ISOLATION: the properties of connected speech are irrelevant to phonological 'structure' in this restricted sense. There is a distinction (usually implicit) between the STRUCTURE of a language (a general, theoretically describable system of relations) and the USE of a language, i.e. the deployment of this structure in an indefinitely large number of real-speech situations.

Another problem is that classical phonemics (like many other kinds) is **categorical**: based on presumed either/or relations. But the case under consideration here involves **variation**, which is outside the ambit of any phoneme theory in the strict sense (as one can judge by the *ad hoc* strategies – like multiplication of allomorphs – used to handle it). In fact, a good many apparent violations of biuniqueness involve variation: either 'free' within one speech style, or conditioned by different styles, registers or tempi. And even when variation is not involved, there are other factors which help to disambiguate. As a preliminary example, consider these inter-tempo relations in my dialect:

(2.17)    Morphemic:    it        can't      be
          Phonemic:     /ɪt       kænt       biː/
          Slow:         [ʔɪt      kʰæːnʔt    biː]
          Fast:         [ʔɪk      k̟ʰæːp      b̥iː]

It looks as if this dialect has the following overlap:

(2.18)

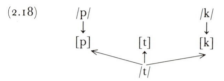

But not really: because (a) the phones [p k] as 'allophones of /t/' are predictable from the SYNTACTIC context (we now have to go beyond word level in talking about class membership: see 4.7); and, in fact, (b) rapid speech would be uninterpretable except by reference to the 'normal' slow or **citation form**. That is, one knows, on the basis of prior knowledge of the language, particular discourse context, etc., what is being presented: the sequence [...ɪt k...] can be from /...ɪt k.../ if the material involved is *it can't be*, but is from /...ɪk k.../ if the material is *pick carrots*. The phonetic/phonemic relationship is primarily available, perhaps, only to someone who knows the language already, not mechanically to any outsider.

The moral might be that phonemic representations are style-specific, and really appropriate, in their 'classical' form, only for slow speech. It may be misleading to try and assign phonemic representations in the strict sense to rapid, connected speech, but proper to derive it solely as a PHONETIC phenomenon, from the phonetic representations of slow speech, which are in turn based on the phonemic representations of basic word-phonology. (For detailed consideration of connected speech and variation, see ch. 12.)

## 2.8  **Problems, ɪɪ: linearity violations**

Classical phonemics imposes what has been called a **linearity** condition: phonemic and phonetic differences must match up one-to-one in linear strings. This seems to follow from the definitions. But consider this U.S. English data (in a transcription omitting a lot of non-significant detail):

(2.19)     (a) [raɪt] 'write' [rɑˑɪd] 'ride'
           (b) [raɪɾər] 'writer' [rɑˑɪɾər] 'rider'

(Here [r], by convention, stands for whatever the usual realization of this phoneme is, in this example an alveolar approximant [ɹ]). The (a) forms illustrate the normal distribution of the allophones of /aɪ/: [ɑˑɪ] being predictable before voiced segments, so that [aɪ] and [ɑˑɪ] are in complementary distribution. But: neither [t] nor [d] can appear between vowels, both being replaced by the alveolar tap [ɾ] (thus [mæɾər] 'matter/madder', etc.). Yet it's clear that the 'base' of *writer* is /raɪt/, and that of *rider* /raɪd/, as the simple forms show. So here we have (a) an apparent violation of biuniqueness, and (b) a linearity problem: because the only way that *writer* and *rider* can be distinguished is by their VOWELS – yet elsewhere the distinction between these two vowel types is not information-bearing, and if the two forms contrast anywhere it should be in their medial consonants. If we allow for total overlap of /t, d/, then the phonetic vs. phonemic picture is like this:

(2.20)

| | (a) | | (b) | |
|---|---|---|---|---|
| Phonemic: | r aɪ t | r aɪ d | r aɪ t ə r | r aɪ d ə r |
| | 1 2 3 | 1 2 3 | 1 2 3 4 5 | 1 2 3 4 5 |
| Phonetic: | r aɪ t | r ɑˑɪ d | r aɪ ɾ ə r | r ɑˑɪ ɾ ə r |
| | 1 2 3 | 1 2 3 | 1 2 3 4 5 | 1 2 3 4 5 |

In (a), there is both phonemic and phonetic contrast in position 3; in (b) the phonemic contrast is in position 3, but the phonetic contrast is in 2. That is, two normally non-contrastive phones carry meaning difference, while two (supposedly) contrastive phones fail to contrast. There are, as it happens, perfectly respectable ways of dealing with this – but not in the framework of classical phonemics. They necessitate a fairly extensive revision of the conceptual framework, and lead to a more complex picture of what natural-language phonologies are probably like.

## 2.9 Problems, III: separation of levels

The strictest form of phoneme theory aims at keeping phonology separate from morphology and syntax, to the point that there is no 'communication' between different levels of description:

a phonological analysis may not refer to non-phonological information. Again, a major source of this notion is a simple model of the
speaker as 'decoder'. If the only operations available to him are the
segmentation of phonetic strings and assignment of the results of that
segmentation to structural units; and if the only information available
to him is directly contained in the phonetic string, then by definition
morphosyntax is inaccessible.

Once again, an apparently sensible condition runs afoul of data –
and also of other principles of phonemic analysis. Consider the case
of vowel-length distinctions in Scottish English. In most varieties
there is a simple allophonic rule of (roughly) this form:

(2.21)
$$V \rightarrow V:/- \left\{ \begin{array}{c} r \\ v, \eth, z \\ \# \end{array} \right\}$$

(Where '#' = 'word-final position': see below.) That is, vowels are
long only in these environments, and short elsewhere; Scots lacks the
phonemic vowel-length characteristic of many other types of English.
The resultant distribution can be illustrated for some selected vowel
phonemes:

(2.22)

/i/ → $\left\{ \begin{array}{l} \text{[iː]: grieve breathe sneeze fear free ...} \\ \text{[i]: heap heat heed bean niece feel ...} \end{array} \right.$

/o/ → $\left\{ \begin{array}{l} \text{[oː]: grove nose loathe more no ...} \\ \text{[o]: grope note load loan mole ...} \end{array} \right.$

/ʉ/ → $\left\{ \begin{array}{l} \text{[ʉː]: move smoothe lose moor flew ...} \\ \text{[ʉ]: stoop foot food mousse moon cool ...} \end{array} \right.$

/ʌi/ → $\left\{ \begin{array}{l} \text{[aˑe]: five tithe prize fire die ...} \\ \text{[ʌi]: gripe bite bide mice nine file ...} \end{array} \right.$

(And so on; the quality-difference for /ʌi/ is an automatic accompani-
ment of its length, and will not concern us further.)

So long and short vowels are in complementary distribution, and
therefore length cannot be contrastive. But there are some exceptions:

(2.23)

| heed | [hid] | he'd | [hiːd] |
| road | [rod] | rowed | [roːd] |
| brood | [brʉd] | brewed | [brʉːd] |
| tide | [tʌid] | tied | [taˑed] |

These are clearly 'minimal pairs' in the usual sense. Comparing (2.22)
and (2.23), then, what do we say: that length ıs phonemic but only
before /d/? Surely this is a messy-looking solution, and one that we

32

would like to avoid. Closer examination in fact shows that length is PREDICTABLE before /d/ – if we take into account the 'kind of /d/' involved. All the 'long' /d/ are past tense or past participle markers. But this generalization simply isn't statable if we insist on separation of levels and the autonomy of phonology.

At first sight this looks like a genuine counter-example to the claim that phonology is independent of morphology; but it isn't. At least not under a marginally looser definition of 'phonology', as we will see. But this data raises the important point that what counts is not how 'right' a theoretical claim is, but how **testable** it is, and what we can learn from trying to push it as hard as possible. Strong claims, even if untenable, can be **heuristics**: methodological guidelines or strategies for analysis.

One's first impulse is to alter (2.21) by adding '/____ d/]$_{past}$' or something of the sort; i.e. allow morphological information in allophonic rules. But we have already allowed a certain morphological element – without saying so – into the most basic phonological concepts. We have defined phonemes as units that signal meaning-differences between morphemes. So 'phoneme' is already defined in terms of 'morpheme'; and this means that we must be able to delimit – in advance – the morphemes (so we can decide what pieces are having their semantic differences signalled). And, as we'll see later (chs. 4, 10), we need not only morphemes, but larger units ('words') as well, as domains for phonological generalizations.

And in our delimitation of the environments for length in Scots we already invoked the 'word' anyhow – when we said that vowels were long 'in final position': final, obviously, in the word. If we now add 'final in the morpheme' as well, we can state the length rule without mentioning specific morphemes like {past}, but invoking only two kinds of **boundaries** or **termini**: word and morpheme boundaries (symbolized as '#' and '+' respectively). Thus we restate (2.21) as:

(2.24)
$$ V \rightarrow V{:}/ \underline{\hspace{1cm}} \left\{ \begin{array}{l} r \\ v, \eth, z \\ \#, + \end{array} \right\} $$

There are a few cases, however, where this analysis seems at first not to work: for some speakers, long vowels occur in forms like *beetle*, *nylon*, *spider*, where there is no internal boundary: we don't want analyses like /bi + tl/, surely, just to save a neat generalization. Or do we? One possibility is that these cases can be accounted for as **false segmentation** by speakers – the insertion of a 'pseudo-morpheme-boundary'. Thus there is a 'pseudo-morpheme' {-tl} in English (*ra-ttle, ke-ttle, me-tal*), and another {-lon} (*py-lon, Fab-lon, Dra-lon*), etc. Speakers treat the forms in question – judging from their phonetic output – AS-IF they were bi-morphemic. If we allow this, then rule (2.24) is still valid. And the fact that speakers differ in the way they treat these words, and that even the same speaker may vacillate (whereas this never happens with *he'd*, etc.) is another indication of the marginal status – but not the unreality – of the false segmentation: it is unstable and variable because it is not deeply integrated into the linguistic structure.

## 2.10 **Problems, IV: 'failure' of allophonic rules**

Should one minimal pair be allowed to establish two phones as representing two phonemes? According to our definition of contrast, it should: though §§2.8–9 suggest that problems can arise when something disturbs the 'normal' biunique phoneme/phone relation. The case I want to look at here doesn't involve linearity violation or (except marginally) morphology, but something with a similar effect: apparent non-categorical application of an allophonic rule.

Many English dialects (including mine, from which the data below is taken) have a rule for the realizations of /æ/ of this type:

(2.25)

$$/æ/ \rightarrow \left\{ \begin{array}{l} [æ:]/\_\_\_\_ \left\{ \begin{array}{l} \text{Fricatives} \\ \text{Voiced stops} \\ \text{Non-velar nasals} \end{array} \right\} \quad \text{(a)} \\ [æ] \end{array} \right\} \quad \text{(b)}$$

Thus by (a) we get [æ:] in *half, halve, pass, jazz, cab, cad, man, ham*; by (b) we get [æ] in *cat, cap, back, hang, pal*.

Rule (2.25) holds for most forms: but there are a number of cases where it appears to 'fail', and we get minimal pairs:

(2.26)
| Expected [æ:] | Unexpected [æ] |
|---|---|
| hæ:v 'halve' | hæv 'have' |
| kʰæ:n '(tin) can' | kʰæn 'can' (aux) |
| æ:dz 'adds' | ædz 'adze' |

And there are a handful of others. Does this mean that there is a phonemic contrast /æ/ : /æː/, and that we must scrap the generalization (2.25) as 'accidental'? Must we do it even though (2.25) covers a vastly larger number of cases than there are contrasts? There are two basic solutions to this, involving different views of how rigid a phoneme theory ought to be:

(i) Stick to biuniqueness. (2.25) is not a 'generalization' about allophonics, but a statement of defective distribution. There are two phonemes /æ/ and /æː/, and there's no significance to the fact that /æː/ never occurs before voiceless stops. But it's precisely the ASYMMETRY of the exceptions that is the interesting and significant point, and this is lost under a two-phoneme analysis. Whenever we get an 'unexpected' vowel, it's always short where we expect long, never the other way round: there are no exceptions of the type *[bæːt]. And in addition, the environments where we normally get length are those where on phonetic grounds we might expect it (e.g. lengthening before voiced segments is very common).

(ii) Allow allophonic rules to have exceptions (but not to be variable: note that the exceptions here are not like the [ʔ]-forms of *bat*, etc., but are **invariant** for any lexical item). Within classical phonemic theory this is not a valid option: though other theories have accepted the essentially plausible notion 'exception to a rule', and incorporated it into their formalism. This is better than (i), because it manages to capture BOTH the generalization in (2.25) and the anomalies in (2.26): even if (2.25) is now not 'true', but 'largely true'. Further, the anomalies now take on a 'position' in the universe of the description by virtue of being referrable to (2.25): it's because of (2.25) that (2.26) can be seen to be 'exceptional', and (2.25) defines the precise nature of its exceptionality.

Note that abandoning separation of levels would take care of some of the exceptions, so that they could be 'predicted' by a revised (2.25): e.g. failure in auxiliary verbs could be written into the rule, and *adds* vs. *adze* might be described in terms of boundaries. But this won't work for further pairs, such as *cadge, Baddeley, Hadley* with [æ] vs. 'normal' *badge, badly*.

It turns out that situations like this are generally explicable in a rather simple way, but not in a framework that takes **synchronic** (non-historical) descriptions as fully self-contained. Categorical failures of allophonic rules (unlike variability, which is – or may be

– something else: §§12.4–5) are normally the debris left behind by historical change. But to admit this requires yet another conceptual revision of what phonology is, and we're not ready for that yet.

### 2.11 A salvage operation for separation of levels: 'juncture' phonemes

A number of U.S. structuralists, confronted with the problem of (apparent) morphological conditioning of allophonic rules, attempted to retain the principle of separation of levels by shifting the problem onto the phonological plane. This was typically done by incorporating (what I have been referring to as) 'boundaries' into phoneme inventories, as so-called **'juncture phonemes'**. I will illustrate this with a simple example.

In some dialects of German, there is virtual complementary distribution between the phones [x] and [ç]: [x] occurs after back and low front vowels ([buːx] 'book', [lɔx] 'hole', [bax] 'brook'; [ç] occurs after non-low front vowels ([byːçər] 'books', [lœçər] 'holes', [bɛçə] 'brooks'), after consonants, regardless of the preceding vowel ([manç] 'many', [mɪlç] 'milk', [dʊrç] 'through'); and word-initially ([çiːna] 'China', [çɛmiː] 'chemistry'). But there are also – in these dialects – minimal pairs involving these two segments: [kuːxən] 'cake' vs. [kuːçən] 'little cow', [tʰaoxən] 'to dive' vs. [tʰaoçən] 'little rope'.

The minimal pairs suggest that in spite of the applicability of the distributional generalization to most cases, there is in fact a phonemic contrast /x/ : /ç/. But there is a 'phonological' way of this, proposed by W. G. Moulton (1947), as follows. Let us introduce a 'phoneme of **open juncture**', / + /, which, since it is a phoneme, must have allophones: its allophones are 'potential pause' (at the beginning or end of an utterance), and 'brief pause' ∼ zero (utterance–internal). This is to be taken as a 'segmental phoneme' on a par with any other. If it is, then we do not need a phoneme /ç/, since the minimal pairs are now phonemically distinct: / + kuːxən + / vs. / + kuː + xən + /, etc. In addition, two other phenomena can be naturally accounted for by / + /: (a) word-initial aspiration of /p t k/; and (b) the presence of word- (or morpheme-) initial [ʔ] ([ʔɪç] 'I', [fɛrʔáen] 'union', represented as / + ɪx + /, / + fɛr + aen + /.

Unfortunately, as Moulton himself notes, the supposed occurrence of / + / normally coincides 'with syntactic and morphological boundaries' (p. 25); the only exception seems to be a group of forms where the 'brief pause' can come morpheme-internally: e.g. [pap$^h$íːr] 'paper', which he gives as / + pa + ˈpiːr + /. These are – interestingly – all French loanwords.

Why not, then, derive the occurrences that coincide with boundaries anyhow from boundaries, and take the others as having 'pseudo-boundaries' (see §2.9)? Moulton's answer is in three parts (p. 26n): (a) a methodological reason: 'I believe that the phonemes of a language should be analysed without reference to syntax or morphology'; (b) that since juncture sometimes doesn't coincide with morphosyntactic boundaries, the two can't always be equated; and (c) that the phenomena in question 'are more clearly described by / + /'.

Argument (a) is obviously a matter of 'religious' commitment (note that Moulton agrees that the morphosyntactic boundaries are necessary SOMEWHERE in the description); (b) can be taken care of by not insisting on strict one-to-one correspondence, and allowing for 'false segmentation'; and (c) seems to me merely an arguable matter of preference – and methodologically weak; if you need boundaries anyhow, why introduce extra phonemes, and ones with 'zero allophones' at that?

Another argument against juncture for separation-of-levels problems falls out naturally from the Scots length distinctions. If we don't want to introduce a phoneme whose ONLY 'allophones' are effects on other phonemes, but insist (I think rightly) that any phoneme must have independently perceptible allophones, then we're in trouble with e.g. [brʉd] vs. [brʉːd]. We could define our word boundary /#/ in terms of 'potential pause' (e.g. there is one before and after [brʉː], so we could represent it as / + brʉ + /). But what about [brʉːd]? There is surely no potential pause between the verb stem and the ending – the only way of doing this in fact is to create a disyllable *[brʉː ... d], which is neither 'normal' nor even acceptable. (Note that all of Moulton's potential pauses occur either between words or morphemes, or between the syllables of polysyllabic words.)

I think we can conclude that junctures are a methodological ploy for keeping levels separate, and have no claim to real independence as non-morphosyntactic (i.e. purely phonological) entities. We should probably take boundaries as objects in the morphosyntax, which happen to have effects on the phonological plane as well. They often behave as if they were segments, and for these cases they can be treated – in the phonology – as segment-like, though without losing their nature as boundaries, and without the need to posit separate 'junctures' in addition.

## NOTES AND REFERENCES

2.1 The definition of 'morpheme' skirts a number of issues: e.g. what does *cran-* in *cranberry* mean? But it will serve for this book. For a comprehensive recent discussion, *Matthews (1974: ch. v).

2.3–2.5 On the concept of the phoneme presented here (which is a distillation of the common core of a complex tradition), see the historical account in *Fischer-Jørgensen (1975: ch. 6). For recent textbook treatments, Hyman (1975: ch. 3), Sommerstein (1977: ch. 2). For textbook accounts representing aspects of the tradition by practitioners brought up in it, Hockett (1958: chs. 2–13), Gleason (1961: chs. 16–21). In the professional literature, many of the most important papers are collected in Joos (1957) and Makkai (1972a). To get a chronological idea of the development of phoneme theory, a good sequence of readings would be *Swadesh (1934), Hockett (1942), **Bloch (1948). Two complex but important papers, which still bear reading, are **Twaddell (1935) and **Chao (1934).

On contrast and methods of analysis see **Harris (1960: chs. 3–11).

There are other versions of phonemic theory as well, and an immense literature; for one other important view see Jones (1950) and Fischer-Jørgensen (1975: ch. 4).

2.6 The 'simplicity' principle is often called 'Occam's Razor', after the 12th-century English philosopher William of Occam, who said: *Entia non sunt multiplicanda praeter necessitatem* ('Entities are not to be multiplied beyond necessity'). This was intended as an overall constraint on theory-construction. For discussion of simplicity in general see Hyman (1975: ch. 4).

The particular as-if argument here is loosely based on one in Hockett (1958: 109f). On indeterminacy see Chao (1934), and more recently Schane (1968), dealing with the problem in a different theoretical framework.

2.9 On the Scots length rule see Lass (1974). The idea of a 'pseudo-morpheme boundary' is due to A. J. Aitken. The length rule itself is often referred to as 'Aitken's Law' in the literature.

2.10 The data is a simplified version of material from Lass (1976b, 1981).

2.11 On boundaries having 'segment-like' properties, see the arguments in Lass & Anderson (1975: ch. v).

# 3
# Opposition, neutralization, features

## 3.1 Neutralization and the archiphoneme

We saw earlier (§2.3) that phonological contrasts are not always relevant for all environments; this has some interesting theoretical implications. Recall that under the biuniqueness requirement we disallowed multiple class-membership; a phonetic transcription was to be read off a phonemic one, and vice versa. If we take the phoneme as a primitive category, something of the sort seems necessary, to avoid losing track of the identity of distinctive units. But in fact there are arguments for at least two other types of primitives in addition to phonemes – arguments developed in large part in the 1920s and 30s by linguists of the Prague School.

A relatively simple case will introduce the concepts. Modern Standard (North) German has the following phonemic stop/fricative system:

(3.1)

|         | Labial | Alveolar | Palato-alveolar | Velar | Glottal |
|---------|--------|----------|-----------------|-------|---------|
| Stop    | p  b   | t  d     |                 | k  g  |         |
| Fric    | f  v   | s  z     | ʃ ʒ            | x     | h       |

There are some curious asymmetries of distribution, particularly involving certain PAIRS of phonemes. Following is a table of distributions for the items in (3.1), in initial, preconsonantal, intervocalic, and final positions: $+$ = occurs, $-$ = does not occur, C = /p t/:

(3.2)

|   | #___V | #___CV | V___V | ___# |
|---|-------|--------|-------|------|
| p | $+$   | $-$    | $+$   | $+$  |
| b | $+$   | $-$    | $+$   | $-$  |
| t | $+$   | $-$    | $+$   | $+$  |
| d | $+$   | $-$    | $+$   | $-$  |
| k | $+$   | $-$    | $+$   | $+$  |
| g | $+$   | $-$    | $+$   | $-$  |

| (3.2) – *cont.* | # __ V | # __ CV | V __ V | __ # |
|---|---|---|---|---|
| f | + | − | + | + |
| v | + | − | + | − |
| s | − | − | + | + |
| z | + | − | + | − |
| ʃ | + | + | + | + |
| 3 | + | − | + | − |
| x | − | − | + | + |
| h | + | − | − | − |

Note the following patterns: first, for any voiced/ voiceless pair, like /p b/, /s z/, only the voiceless member can appear in final position. So /taobə/ 'dove' ≠ /daobə/ 'stave', /laetən/ 'to lead' ≠ /laedən/ 'to suffer'; but only /laot/ 'sound', no */laod/. Another pattern affects the sibilants: /s/ does not occur initially, whereas /z ʃ/ do: /zoːn/, 'son', /ʃoːn/ 'already', */soːn/; and before /p t/ initially, we get only /ʃ/:/ʃtʏk/ 'piece', */stʏk/. In fact NO consonant except /ʃ/ is legal in initial preconsonantal position. Further, /h/ appears only initially, and /x/ only finally.

These could all be treated as defective distributions; but there seems to be something more going on, since we can extract some generalizations. Particularly, no voiced obstruent can appear finally. The 'pairedness' of voiced and voiceless segments with respect to this distribution suggests a basic structural principle: the distribution of /p b/ seems 'controlled', in a manner replicated for other similar pairs; as opposed to that of /h/, say, which does not appear to be involved with any other distribution. And the sibilants fall between the two types.

Situations like the voiced/voiceless distribution can be given structural coherence if they are analysed, not as defective distributions, but as SUSPENSIONS OF CONTRAST, due to structural principles of the language. And this possibility, under the name of **neutralization**, forms one of the cornerstones of Prague phonology. The idea was most clearly developed in the work of N. S. Trubetzkoy, and we will follow his account to begin with.

Trubetzkoy starts with the simple fact that segments can appear in parallel distribution, in which case they are potentially distinctive, or in complementary distribution, in which case they are not (cf. English /p/:/b/ vs. [p]:[pʰ]). The latter case is simple allophony, the former a **constant phonological opposition**. But there is a third possibility: in Trubetzkoy's words (1936 [1964]: 187), 'oppositions which are relevant only in particular positions, because only in these positions can one or the other member appear, whereas in the other positions EITHER one OR the other appears' (my emphasis). So in German, initial and intervocalic, where /t d/ contrast, are **positions of relevance**, and final is a **position of neutralization**.

In a position of neutralization, according to Trubetzkoy, it is not in fact EITHER phoneme that actually occurs, but what he calls an **archiphoneme**: 'the totality of properties ... that are common to two phonemes' (*ibid.*: 189). In something like the German /t d/ opposition, what appears in final position is phonologically 'neither voiced nor voiceless'; it is 'the non-nasal dental stop in general' i.e. opposed to /n/ on the one hand, and /p b k g/ on the other. (We will return in §3.2 to the problem of 'common properties' and the details of what constitutes a phonological opposition.)

Trubetzkoy further distinguishes between genuine neutralization and defective distribution; his argument is intricate, and is better quoted than paraphrased (p. 189f):

> the fact that German *t* and *d* are not allowed word-initially before *l*, while *b* and *p* can appear ... does not produce a neutralization of the oppositions *d – b*, *t – p*: in a word like *Blatt* ['leaf'], *b* retains all its properties, i.e. it remains a labial voiced stop, and cannot be taken as the representative of an archiphoneme of the opposition *d – b*: because the phonological content of such an opposition can only be 'voiced stop in general' – and *b* in *Blatt* cannot be treated that way, because *g* in *glatt* ['smooth'] is also a voiced stop.

An archiphoneme then is the sum of the properties in common to two (or, under a different definition, more: see §§3.3ff) phonemes, and it appears in the position(s) of neutralization. The precise guise in which it appears, and its systemic status will be taken up in §§3.3ff. Under Trubetzkoy's original definition, only certain types of pairwise oppositions can be neutralized: as we will see, this restriction may pose some problems.

## 3.2 **The structure of phonological oppositions**

In Praguian terms, the phonemic system of a language is not just an inventory of contrasting segment classes, but a system of oppositions. These of course have phonetic (or phonemic) content; but most importantly, from the standpoint of linguistic analysis, they form a network of formal structures. In Trubetzkoy's view, the inter-locking system of oppositions takes priority over the phoneme inventory: the major role in phonology is played not by the phonemes themselves, but by the **oppositions** they enter into. 'Each phoneme has a definable phonemic content only because the system ... shows a definite order or structure' (Trubetzkoy 1939 [1969]: 67f).

To see what this means, we must return to the idea underlying the archiphoneme: 'common properties'. How are these defined? The key is already implicit in traditional phonetic classification: what do we mean when we say e.g. that [t] is a 'voiceless alveolar stop'? We mean that it is characterized by certain CONCURRENT articulatory properties, i.e. alveolar occlusion, a stricture of complete closure, no vibration of the vocal folds, etc. So [t], rather than being 'of a piece', is a **structure**, or at least a **set** (on this distinction see §6.5) of SIMULTANEOUS PROPERTIES: alveolarity, stopness, voicelessness. A segment, that is, may be taken as a set of **features**. Thus phonemes are not indivisible, 'atomic' entities, but 'molecules' (in the old-fashioned sense of these terms, not involving elementary particles; the image is mine, not Trubetzkoy's).

So we can represent the members of the German oppositions /p − b/, /t − d/, /k − g/ this way:

(3.3)

$$
\begin{bmatrix} \text{Labial} \\ \text{Stop} \\ \text{Voiceless} \\ /p/ \end{bmatrix}
\begin{bmatrix} \text{Labial} \\ \text{Stop} \\ \text{Voiced} \\ /b/ \end{bmatrix}
\begin{bmatrix} \text{Alveolar} \\ \text{Stop} \\ \text{Voiceless} \\ /t/ \end{bmatrix}
\begin{bmatrix} \text{Alveolar} \\ \text{Stop} \\ \text{Voiced} \\ /d/ \end{bmatrix}
$$

$$
\begin{bmatrix} \text{Velar} \\ \text{Stop} \\ \text{Voiceless} \\ /k/ \end{bmatrix}
\begin{bmatrix} \text{Velar} \\ \text{Stop} \\ \text{Voiced} \\ /g/ \end{bmatrix}
$$

Segments have the property of **componentiality**: they are 'made of' smaller, sub-segmental **components**. These components or features are independently combinable 'building blocks' out of which segments − and hence oppositions − are constructed. (We will return to features in detail in chs. 5–6, 11.) And the archiphoneme is derived by a kind of 'factoring out' process (e.g. the archiphoneme of /t − d/ is obtained by factoring out [voiced] and [voiceless], leaving the common [alveolar, stop]).

So an opposition in a phonemic system is not merely the fact that two phonemes exist which have distinctive function. Rather, since the phonemes themselves are structures, it is their components that determine the opposition. Any pair of phonemes has a **basis of comparison**, consisting not only in the properties they differ in, but also those they share.

Given the fundamental notion of opposition, there are two basic types to be found WITHIN ANY SYSTEM. The last phrase is emphasized, because the definitions below refer to the structures of particular systems; a pair of phonemes cannot be defined as opposed in any particular way in isolation from the system they occur in. Consider for instance the stop systems of English and a Brahmin dialect of Kannaḍa:

(3.4)

|            | Labial | Alveolar | Velar |
|------------|--------|----------|-------|
| Voiceless  | p      | t        | k     |
| Voiced     | b      | d        | g     |

English

|                  | Labial         | Dental         | Retroflex       | Velar          |
|------------------|----------------|----------------|-----------------|----------------|
| Voiceless        | p              | t              | ṭ               | k              |
| Voiced           | b              | d              | ḍ               | g̣             |
| Aspirated        | p$^h$          | t$^h$          | ṭ$^h$           | k$^h$          |
| Breathy-voiced   | ḅ              | ḍ              | ḍ               | g̣             |

Kannaḍa

The two major opposition types are:

(a) **Bilateral.** Here the basis for comparison is restricted to two phonemes only. Thus in English /k/:/g/ is bilateral, since [velar] and [stop] are common to no other members of the system: the disagreeing term is [voiced] vs. [voiceless]. But /k/:/g/ in Kannaḍa is not bilateral, since there are four velar stops; it is

(b) **Multilateral.** That is, the basis for comparison occurs in more than two segments. Since English only has two stop series, all the pairs are bilaterally opposed; since each place of articulation in Kannaḍa has more than two stops, the oppositions are multilateral. Whereas /k/:/p/ in both languages is multilateral, because [voiceless] and [stop] occur also in English /t/, Kannaḍa /t ṭ/.

This means that we typically get both kinds of oppositions in a phonological system: consider the English inventory:

(3.5)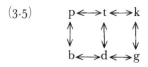

The 'vertical' oppositions are bilateral, and the 'horizontal' ones multilateral. There are three phonemes with the features [voiceless, stop], but only two with [labial, stop], etc. The importance of the distinction is that the bilateral oppositions are minimal, and play a crucial role in determining the overall shape of the system. Systems can be (largely) described as sets of minimal (pairwise) oppositions in the vertical dimension, organized into 'chains' of multilateral oppositions in the horizontal, with certain segments (see below) standing outside both types of classification.

Within this overall division, there are a number of subtypes in Trubetzkoy's scheme; I will sketch the most important ones here as a background to further discussion. These types depend not only on the structure of the system as a whole, but on the particular relations among pairs and n-tuples (sets of any number *n* of members) of phonemes within the system.

(a) **Proportional oppositions.** These are multilaterals of the structure a:b :: c:d, ... etc. That is, there is a sequence of at least two separate oppositions implemented in the same way. This is not the same thing as a multilateral opposition (in general), because it requires at least *four* members, and always an even number. Thus /p/:/b/::/t/:/d/ is proportional, but /b/:/d/:/g/ isn't. The presence of proportional oppositions is an index of the 'mileage' a language gets out of a particular feature: in Praguian terms, of the **functional yield** of that feature, i.e. how much 'work' it does. Oppositions like these are often implicated, as blocks, in both synchronic alternations and historical change.

(b) **Isolated oppositions.** Here only one pair in the whole system is distinguished in a particular way, i.e. the distinction has minimal functional yield. Thus in Swedish the vowels /ø/:/ʉ/ are distinguished as [outrounded] vs. [inrounded] (see §5.3.4), whereas all other pairs are distinguished as [outrounded] vs. [unrounded]. So, given the front vowel system

(3.6)    i    y
         e    ø    ʉ
         a

there is a proportional opposition /i/ : /y/ :: /e/ : /ø/, and an isolated one /ø/ : /ʉ/.

(c) **Privative oppositions.** One member is characterized by the presence, and the other by the absence, of some feature: usually a feature of a type that can reasonably be taken as 'added to' another articulation. Thus /m/ : /b/, /n/ : /d/, etc. are privative [nasal] vs. [non-nasal], and /b/ : /p/ etc. are [voiced] vs. [non-voiced]. The feature whose PRESENCE is critical is in Prague terminology called a **mark** (*Merkmal*), and the segment possessing this feature is said to be **marked** for it.

But how do we decide which segment of a privatively opposed pair is to be taken as marked? After all, [oral] vs. [non-oral] is logically equivalent to [nasal] vs. [non-nasal]. And if so, the opposition /n/ : /d/ could be privative in either direction. Decisions are usually made on two bases: general properties of phonological systems across languages, and neutralization behaviour. In the first case we might say that if there are no languages with only nasal phonemes, but there are languages (if rarely) with only oral ones, then there is a sense in which nasality is a 'marked' state: a nasal has 'something extra', beyond the (normal) minimal specification. Something of the same sort is often taken to hold for voiceless vs. voiced stops and fricatives: there are many languages with systems like /p t k/, but as far as I know ones like /b d g/ with no voiceless members are restricted to certain Australian languages (see §7.6.1). As for neutralization, we can say at least that – perhaps with greater than chance frequency – neutralizations of privative oppositions tend to be represented by the segment that by the first set of criteria would be considered 'unmarked'.

(d) **Gradual oppositions.** These depend not on presence vs. absence of a feature, but on degrees or gradations of some property. An example is vowel height: given a three-height system like

(3.7)      i     u
           e     o
           a     ɑ

the individual members are gradually opposed to each other in the vertical dimension along a continuum: thus here there are two sets of gradual oppositions, /i/ : /e/ : /a/, etc. It is also possible to take a three-way opposition like this as made up of two minimal oppositions:

i.e. instead of having one continuous parameter 'height', we have oppositions of the type [high] vs. [non-high], [low] vs. [non-low], or three independent features [high], [mid], [low]. But this will require some more background to state properly: see §§5.3. 2.2–3, 6.2, 11.2.

(e) **Equipollent oppositions.** Here the relation between the members of the opposition is one of logical equivalence, i.e. they cannot be considered as privative or gradual. Consider a system like this (Amsterdam Dutch):

(3.8)    p    t    k
         b    d
         f    s ∫    x

Here /p/:/b/ is privative, but is part of a proportional set /p/:/b/ :: /t/:/d/; but take /p/:/x/, or /f/:/k/. We can't define them in terms of any minimal criteria: they function in the system as non-minimally opposed (equipollent) pairs. It turns out that the larger number of (potential) oppositions in any system will probably be equipollent; but from the point of view of neutralization or participation in morphological alternations (see ch. 4), it is rare that equipollent oppositions are as important as the more constrained types.

So for instance we find alternations in Dutch involving neutralization of privative voiced/voiceless pairs: /ɪk hɛp/ 'I have' vs. /hɛb ək/ 'have I', /kiːs/ 'choose' vs. /xəkoːzən/ 'chosen'; this type is much more common than alternations involving equipollent series, like /k/ ∼ /s/ ∼ /ʃ/ in English (*electric* ∼ *electricity* ∼ *electrician*): and these latter usually belong to a rather different stratum of grammatical organization (see ch. 4).

### 3.3  Multiple neutralization

German voicing neutralization in final position is a simple suspension of bilateral privative pairs; using, as is conventional, a capital letter for an archiphoneme, a form like phonetic [laot] 'sound' (see §3.1) would be represented as /laoT/, and the opposition whose archiphoneme is /T/ would be represented in the neutralization position by its 'unmarked' member, /t/.

In order to guarantee determinate answers to the question of what contrast is being neutralized, Trubetzkoy restricted 'true' neutralization to bilateral oppositions. But there are other cases where we might want to talk of neutralization. Consider the nasals in Kannaḍa. A phonemic analysis will give the following system of paired stops and affricates: /p b/, /t d/, /ṭ ḍ /, /k g/ and the palatal affricates /č ǰ/. But the nasals are difficult: phonetically we have [m n ṇ ɲ ŋ], i.e. one nasal for each place with a pair of stops. Now the stops contrast relatively freely initially and medially; but the distribution of the nasals is peculiar. We can sum it up as follows:

(3.9)

| | #___ | V___V | V___C |
|---|---|---|---|
| [m] | magu 'child' | namage 'to us' | { kempu 'red'<br>{ kombu 'horn' |
| [n] | ni:ru 'water' | ka:nu 'touch' | { entʰa 'what kind?'<br>{ ondu 'one' |
| [ṇ] | — | ka:ṇu 'see' | { eṇṭu 'eight'<br>{ čeṇḍu 'ball' |
| [ɲ] | — | — | { aɲču 'skillet'<br>{ aɲǰu 'fear' |
| [ŋ] | — | — | { beŋki 'fire'<br>{ aŋgaḍi 'shop' |

[m] and [n] contrast in all positions; [ṇ] seems to have a defective distribution, not appearing initially, but clearly contrasting with [n]. But [ɲ ŋ] are difficult: they occur nowhere except before some stop or affricate, and this always has the same place of articulation as they do. If we look at the other nasal + stop clusters, we find that NO nasals contrast here: there is always place agreement. If we follow Trubetzkoy in allowing neutralization only for bilateral oppositions, we have a serious problem in phoneme assignment; or rather it gives rise to a number of competing solutions, none very good. If we adhere to biuniqueness, for instance, we must take [m] in [kempu], [n] in [entʰa] and [ṇ] in [eṇṭu] as respectively phonemic /m n ṇ/. But what about [ɲ ŋ]? Since they are in complementary distribution, they must be allophones of one phoneme: but which? Because they are in complementary distribution with ALL the other nasals.

Thus we could analyse [aɲču] as /amču/, /anču/, or /aṇču/, and [beŋki] as /bemki/, /benki/, etc., since [ɲ ŋ] are in complementation with the allophones of /m n ṇ/. But the choice is arbitrary. We could perhaps invoke phonetic similarity: [ɲ ŋ] are 'closer' (in articulatory distance) to /ṇ/ than /m n/, being further back in the oral cavity than /ṇ/, and thus proportionately further from /m n/. So we could say:

47

(3.10)

$$/\eta/ \rightarrow \left\{ \begin{array}{l} [\textrm{ɲ}]/\underline{\qquad} \quad \left\{ \begin{array}{l} /\check{c}/ \\ /\check{\jmath}/ \end{array} \right\} \\ [\eta]/\underline{\qquad} \quad \left\{ \begin{array}{l} /k/ \\ /g/ \end{array} \right\} \\ [\eta] \end{array} \right\}$$

Or we could take /n/ – on account of its greater freedom of distribution – as basic, and revise accordingly. But whatever we do, the pre-consonantal nasals in [kempu], [entʰa], [eɳʈu] must be phonemically distinct, and those in [aɲču], [beŋki] must fall in with one of the others.

This misses a generalization: is it an accident that there are no *[mt], *[np], etc.? On a strictly phonemic analysis, we have no choice but a messy indeterminacy, and no way of stating the obvious generalization: all /NC/ clusters are **homorganic** (agree in articulation); or all contrasts among nasals are suspended before stops and affricates. The only distinction is /VC/ vs. /VNC/: there is no choice about the nasal.

This problem provides an argument against restricting neutralization to bilateral oppositions; the Kannaḍa nasals couldn't even be handled neatly with defective distribution, since the question of WHAT is defectively distributed is still open. The solution is to allow less tightly specified archisegments (i.e. archiphonemes). Given the original definitions (§§3.2–3), we can extract from ALL the nasals the component [nasal]; the relevance of the rest of the articulatory features disappears under neutralization.

Thus we neutralize, not pairwise oppositions, but features or feature-sets, and have archiphonemes with much less phonemic content. Here we set up an archinasal /N/, nasality alone; our forms are now /keNpu/, /eNtʰa/, /aNču/, /beNki/. And /N/ is realized as [nasal] plus the features of the following stop. We thus have a unique solution, and are not forced to represent systematic lack of contrast by contrasting entities. Schematically:

(3.11)

$$\left[ \textrm{Nasal} \right] \left[ \begin{array}{l} \textrm{p} \\ \textrm{Labial} \\ \textrm{Oral} \\ \textrm{Stop} \end{array} \right] \longrightarrow \left[ \begin{array}{l} \textrm{m} \\ \textrm{Nasal} \\ \textrm{Labial} \end{array} \right] \left[ \begin{array}{l} \textrm{p} \\ \textrm{Labial} \\ \textrm{Oral} \\ \textrm{Stop} \end{array} \right]$$

(We can assume the rest of the features of /N/, e.g. [voiced], to be filled in by some general convention.)

So some realizations of /N/ will be [m], i.e. the same as those of /m/, some will be [n], etc. But two realizations, [ɲ] and [ŋ], will not coincide with the allophones of any nasal phoneme proper, but will belong only to /N/ in the neutralization environments, here before palatals and velars respectively:

(3.12)    Archiphonemic

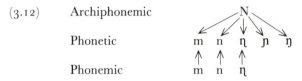

While this analysis is cumbersome (multiplying the number of segments and/or levels, obscuring unique read-off of phoneme membership, and introducing a new primitive), it has its advantages. It permits us to state a regularity explicitly, and does not force *ad hoc* and unrevealing assignments of phones to phonemes. The overall description derives from larger structural principles of the language. Instead of having only statements of distribution and membership, the concepts of neutralization (in this extended sense) and the archiphoneme allow us to draw together facts which on some other interpretation would remain unconnected. In effect we claim that what counts, linguistically, is nasality plus (some particular) stop, not (some particular) nasal plus (some particular) stop. (See further §§6.5, 10.2.1, where we look at the Kannaḍa nasals again.)

### 3.4  Neutralization types and archiphoneme 'representatives'

Neutralization types can be classified according to what segments appear in the neutralization environments as representatives of the archiphoneme. Schematically there are five basic types, definable by the implementation of the archiphoneme. The commonest, perhaps, is the one where one member of the neutralized opposition appears to the complete exclusion of the other. Thus in German, Dutch, Afrikaans, Polish, and Russian the opposition [voiced] : [voiceless] for stops and fricatives is neutralized in final position: given the stops /p b t d k g/, only /p t k/ (the 'unmarked' members) appear. So any form ending in phonetic [p t k] in this type of language will be represented with a final archiphoneme: German [tʰoːt] 'death', Dutch [doːt] would be /toːT/, /doːT/, since [d] – hence /d/ – never appears here, and no contrast is possible.

A rather different type can be illustrated by the distribution of /e/ and /ɛ/ in French. This opposition is distinctive in final position (*les* /le/ vs. *lait* /lɛ/, *aller* /ale/ vs. *allait* /alɛ/); the phones [e ɛ] appear in other positions as well, but they are predictable: [ɛ] in closed syllables (*laide*, *maître*), [e] in open syllables if non-final (*été* [ete], *étais* [etɛ]). Here BOTH members of the opposition appear, but in different neutralization environments. So given the forms cited above, and an archiphoneme /E/ of the opposition /e/ : /ɛ/, we have:

(3.13)  les /le/        lait /lɛ/
        aller /ale/     allait /alɛ/
        laide /lEd/     maître /mEtr/
        été /Ete/       étais /Etɛ/

thus [e] is phonemically /e/ in final syllables, but not elsewhere; phonetic identification is overridden by phonological structure.

There is another type of neutralization in which NEITHER member of the opposition appears as archiphoneme representative, but some third (non-phonemic) segment sharing properties of the others, but with some of its own. So in the U.S. English neutralization of intervocalic /t/ : /d/ (see §2.8), what we get in the neutralization positions is an alveolar tap [ɾ]: it has the alveolar articulation and complete closure of /t d/, the voice of /d/, and a 'rate' feature (see §6.3) – very brief contact – all its own.

In yet another type, we get both members of the opposition in the same neutralization position, apparently indifferently – but still non-contrastively, which is what counts. In Danish, the oppositions /p/ : /b̥/, /t/ : /d̥/ are neutralized in final position, with either member appearing (Davidsen-Nielsen 1978: 18, 37). Thus *lap* 'patch' is [lapʰ] ∼ [lab̥], and *ladt* 'loaded' is [latʰ] ∼ [lad̥].

The four types so far mentioned may be schematized this way:

(3.14)

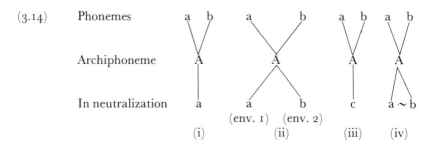

50

Case (i) is German or Dutch voice-neutralization; case (ii) is French /e/ : /ɛ/ (an extended version could handle the Kannaḍa nasals); case (iii) is U.S. English /t/ : /d/; and case (iv) Danish /p/ : /ḅ/.

The final type we will look at is more complex and harder to schematize. This is one we frequently find in the case of gradual oppositions, where only 'extreme' members appear. For example, early Old English probably had a phonemic short vowel system like this:

(3.15)      i        u

        e        o

        æ        ɑ

But in one environment – before nasal + consonant – the contrasts high vs. mid, low front vs. low back are neutralized, and only high vowels and the low back vowel appear (see Lass & Anderson 1975: 70ff). The six-vowel system (3.15) is reduced to

(3.16)      i        u

            ɑ

This could be seen as the product of three neutralizations:

(3.17)

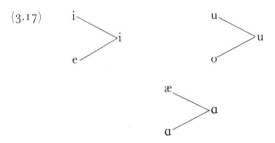

In cases like this it is difficult (if not impossible) to come up with a reasonable archiphonemic representation; this sort of pattern may be better handled in a very different way (§7.8).

### 3.5 Neutralization vs. defective distribution: reprise

It is not always clear whether a given instance of non-contrast should be taken as neutralization or defective distribution; indeed, this may be a matter not of 'fact' but of theoretical judgement. In cases like the OE short vowels, lack of German /tl dl/, and the Kannaḍa nasals, there are problems in deciding just which contrast is being neutralized, and hence what the archiphoneme – if there can be said to be one – represents. Trubetzkoy solved this – or bypassed it – by restricting neutralization to bilateral oppositions, but this turned out to be too constrained.

To see the difficulties more clearly, consider the (apparent) massive neutralization of consonantal contrasts in initial C + stop clusters in English. Phonetically we get only [sp st sk]: but how do we interpret these? We could say that the oppositions /p – b t – d k – g/ are neutralized after /s/, so we have /sP sT sK/. But in fact [s] is the only consonantal segment that appears here (except for a few Yiddish loans like *shtick* 'bit of actor's byplay' in some dialects). In effect, then, [s] might be said to represent the neutralization of ALL consonantal contrasts here, so that the clusters begin with a generalized archi-consonant /C/: thus [st] is /CT/, etc. And we note further that only /r/, not /l/ appears after [st]: so we have another neutralization, this time with the archiphoneme of /r/ : /l/ (or /r l/ and the nasals!). Thus a word like *string* begins with a triple neutralization /CTR/. This seems to be pushing things a bit far. A similar interpretation might hold for English vowels under low stress, where [ə] could be an archivowel representing the neutralization of all the short vowels.

Such difficulties have prompted some scholars to scrap the idea of neutralization, and reduce all apparent neutralizations to defective distributions. This can often lead to loss of generalization, but there is a theoretical point (de Groot 1939) of some interest. This hinges on what one regards phonemes as. In the Praguian view (e.g. to Trubetzkoy), phonemes are primarily **distinctive** entities: they have phonetic content (necessarily, since they have to be realized), but this is operative mainly as defining opposition (thus Jakobson & Halle 1956 define the phoneme as 'mere otherness'). For de Groot, however, the primary function is not distinctive but **identifying**: it is the phonetic content that tells us which phoneme is present, not the oppositional network: phonemes are independent and 'positive' entities.

That is, a /t/ is a /t/ by virtue of its '/t/-ness', not its 'not-/d/-ness', etc. In the English sibilant clusters there is no 'neutral' representative of an archiphoneme, but only a /p/ or a /t/ or a /k/. De Groot rejects Trubetzkoy's claim that (as in German) a phonetic [t] can be phonologically 'neither voiced nor voiceless'. In other words – though he doesn't say so – back to biuniqueness. De Groot seems to hold the rather commonsense position that speakers operate on a strictly 'local' level in segmenting utterances: all they know, as it were, is what unit is present, not its position in a larger system.

So the concept of neutralization is both useful and problematical, and the two aspects are more or less in balance. Perhaps the best strategy is to relegate the structure of oppositions to a secondary (though not trivial) position, and make feature-relevance primary (see §5.1). What counts is the role of particular features: an archiphoneme (as in Kannaḍa /N/) can simply be the 'lowest common denominator' of any number of oppositions. But it's still hard to rule out somewhat counterintuitive treatments of situations like English /s/-clusters.

We can get rid of simple indeterminacies like initial /tl dl/ by taking them as defective distributions (since there is typically a question of only one or two defective segments); but really massive ones are still open to either interpretation – and perhaps ought to remain so. The question is whether, when no unique solution is evident, we ought to solve the problem by a theoretical dictate (which may mean defining it away), or simply learn to live with a certain amount of 'fuzziness'. If there is no realistic alternative – as is often the case – then the two solution types are equally satisfactory, or unsatisfactory, depending on your point of view.

## NOTES AND REFERENCES

3.1 The Prague School is important and rather too little known in detail these days. On their linguistic theory in general, see the account in Vachek (1966), and the papers by Prague linguists in Vachek (1964a). For their phonological theory, Fischer-Jørgensen (1975: ch. 3). The best full-length study of neutralization is Davidsen-Nielsen (1978).

For Trubetzkoy's mature thinking, see the rich and important **Grundzüge der Phonologie* (1939), available in English (1969). The passages from Trubetzkoy (1936) are in my translation, with original notation retained. The theory of neutralization was developed in a series of earlier papers (e.g. *1936) and in *Grundzüge*. The term 'archiphoneme' was not Trubetzkoy's invention, but first appears in Jakobson (1929) in a different sense, not restricted to neutralization (see Davidsen-Nielsen 1978: pp. 22ff).

A few remarks on the treatment of German: (a) initial /x/, following §2.11, appears in [çiːna] /xiːna/ 'China'; /ʒ/ only in French loans like /ʒeniː/ 'genius' (though many speakers have /ʃ/ in these). (b) on lack of initial /s/: some speakers may have it in loans like /stiːl/ 'style', and younger speakers have it in English loans like /sɛks/ 'sex', /sɔŋ/ '(pop)song'. But these are marginal items.

3.2 On the structure of oppositions,** Trubetzkoy (1939, Part I, chs. I–V) is the most complete treatment.

The problem of arbitrariness in privative oppositions is resolved in some contemporary feature theories by using $+/-$ specifications like [+nasal] vs. [−nasal]; here there is no question of 'presence' vs. 'absence', but different values of one feature (see §5.1). Markedness is also a difficult notion: see the discussion in §§7.4, 8.6, and references.

3.3 On arguments for multiple neutralization, *Martinet (1936). Note that there is a partial archiphonemic analysis implicit in the treatment of homorganic nasals in English spelling: there is no symbol for [ŋ], but it is always written as $n + k$, $g$ (*sink, sing, finger*). Since in English, /NC/ clusters within the morpheme are normally homorganic, this is un-ambiguous (*nk* could never be *[nk] for most speakers). We COULD do this with /m/ as well (*limp* as *linp*), but we happen not to. Kannaḍa however has a special symbol for all pre-stop nasals: the forms discussed are spelled as if they had an archinasal, in transliteration *magu, keNpu, nīru, oNdu*, etc.

3.4 The characterization of final stop-neutralization in German and Dutch as archiphonemic is actually quite unrevealing, if we push the analysis further: see §§4.1, 4.3.

3.5 In contemporary generative phonology (ch. 9) the usual solution to the problem of the English /sC/ is to take /s/ as a kind of archiconsonant (no features except [consonant]), and [p t k] as /p t k/: but this is arbitrary.

# 4

# Interfaces: morphophonemic
# alternations and sandhi

## 4.1 Morphophonemic alternations

We have established phonemes as basic contrastive units,
and seen that their contrastiveness can be neutralized, suggesting a
need for archiphonemes; we have also seen that we need a primitive
smaller than the phoneme, the feature, to cope with neutralization.
But we have not yet exhausted the possibilities of contrast vs. non-
contrast. Let us look in more detail at the neutralization of voice in
final obstruents in German: we have barely scratched the surface.

Recall that voiced and voiceless obstruents contrast reasonably
freely in two positions (initially and medially), but not finally. From
an archiphonemic point of view, taking /t/ : /d/ as an example, we
could represent the facts this way:

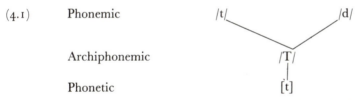

(4.1)      Phonemic                    /t/                    /d/

           Archiphonemic                    /T/

           Phonetic                         [t]

In the neutralization environment, only the principal allophone of /t/
appears; the contrastive categories are 'labial stop' vs. 'alveolar stop'
vs. 'velar stop', etc.: /liːP/ 'dear', /liːT/ 'song', /liːK/ 'lie!', predictably
ending in /p t k/ respectively.

But if we extend our examination to the morphological plane, things
begin to look different. German has a class of homophones, which can
be represented by the pair [raːt] 'counsel' and [raːt] 'wheel/bicycle':
let's call them {raːt}₁ and {raːt}₂. By the analysis in (4.1), these would
both be /raːT/. Now the homophony itself is not particularly interesting, but the two morphemes are not homophonous throughout their
inflexional paradigms:

| (4.2) | | $\{ra:t\}_1$ | $\{ra:t\}_2$ |
|---|---|---|---|
| | Nom sg | ra:t | ra:t |
| | Gen sg | ra:təs | ra:dəs |
| | Nom pl | re:tə | re:dər |

That is, when inflected, $\{ra:t\}_1$ has [t] before the suffix, and $\{ra:t\}_2$ has [d]. Since /t/ and /d/ contrast in non-final position, this would mean, in most forms of phoneme theory, that the two allomorph types of $\{ra:t\}_2$ must be phonemically different with respect to their final consonants: /ra:t/ vs. /ra:d-/. There are many other pairs like this: $\{bunt\}_1$ 'colourful' vs. $\{bunt\}_2$ 'league' (inflected [buntə] vs. [bundə] ), $\{bo:t\}$ 'boat' vs. $\{to:t\}$ 'death' (gen sg [bo:təs] vs. [tʰo:dəs] ), and so on; and the same holds for the other voiced/voiceless pairs (even if there are no actual homophones).

Is this a mere 'accident' or lexical idiosyncrasy, or a generalization about German? The facts can be summed up this way:

(i)      In final position (leaving aside the archiphoneme for the moment), only /t/ appears.

(ii)     Given forms with final /t/, there are two paradigm types: those with medial /-t-/ and final /-t/, and those with medial /-d-/ and final /-t/.

Or, German appears to have 'two kinds of /t/': a non-alternating or e and one that alternates with /d/: what we might call a 'morphologically inactive' and a 'morphologically active' one.

How is this to be represented in a description? One way is simply to give this information in allomorph rules for the morphemes in question:

(4.3)      $\{ra:t\}_1 \longrightarrow$ /ra:t/

$\{ra:t\}_2 \longrightarrow \begin{cases} \text{/ra:d/} & \text{/\_\_\_\_ + V} \\ \text{/ra:t/} & \end{cases}$

But note that this is not in fact a statement of a regularity: precisely the same formulation would do for the allomorphy of a totally irregular form like $\{good\}$:

(4.4)      $\{good\} \longrightarrow \begin{cases} \text{/bɛt/} & \text{/\_\_\_\_ + \{er\}} \\ \text{/bɛ/} & \text{/\_\_\_\_ + \{st\}} \\ \text{/gud/} & \end{cases}$

Since the voice-alternations in German are quite regular and extensive, it seems perverse to treat them the same way we would a **suppletion** or total irregularity like (4.4). But any solution that relies solely on listing allomorphs runs into this problem by virtue of its format.

This throws into relief the failure of the archiphoneme/neutral-ization analysis of alternations with morphological consequences. The archiphonemic treatment is defective precisely the way allomorph listing is: since an archiphoneme is by definition what appears where a systemic contrast is neutralized, there can never be contrastive /t/ : /d/ in the two {raːt} cases. Both the uninflected forms must be /raːT/; so we're right back with two homophonous morphemes, one of which has (arbitrarily) a pre-suffixal allomorph with /t/, and one with /d/. This loses generality the same way as (4.3).

For the moment we're left simply with the fact that German has forms in which certain phonemes alternate with others, and forms in which apparently 'the same' phonemes don't. Let's stabilize the concept by giving it a name: any instance where one or more phonemes in a language alternate(s) with some other(s) is a **morpho-phonemic alternation**. This covers the vowel alternations in *man* ~ *men, foot* ~ *feet*, the consonant alternations in *electri*[k] ~ *electri*[s]*ity* ~ *electri*[ʃ]*ian* or *knife* ~ *knives*, the /Ṽ/ ~ /V/ alternations in French *fin* /fɛ̃/ ~ *finir* /finir/, and so on. The problem is how to treat these in a unified phonological description; and there's a subsidiary problem, which we'll get to later (ch. 9) – whether we ought to. But for now we assume that we should.

## 4.2 **Morphophonemics as an 'interlevel'**

If simple statements of allomorphy are unrevealing, we can acccount for alternations by referring them to SEGMENTAL properties of the morphemes in question, i.e. creating a new level of representation, the **morphophonemic** – intermediate, as its name implies, between the morphemic and phonemic. And this gives rise to yet another unit, the **morphophoneme**. In analyses with a separate morphophonemic level (and there are many varieties), the non-alternating {raːt} would have a morphophonemic (henceforth MP) representation identical to its phonemic one, whereas the alternating {raːt} would have its final segment represented by some special symbol, say /T/ or /D/ (confusing because of the conventional use of capitals for archiphonemes), or /t∗/, or /t̃ᵈ/ or whatever: the precise form is unimportant, as long as the interpretive conventions are explicit (but see §§4.4f for treatments where the form of the MP symbol is important). In such an analysis, /t∗/ would mean '/t/ finally, but /d/ before +V', and /t/ would mean 'only /t/'. Some writers further distinguish the MP level by using verticals or double solidi (|t| or //t//); I will use the latter in this section.

So for our German forms:

(4.5)

| | | {raːt}$_1$ | | {raːt}$_2$ |
|---|---|---|---|---|
| MP | //raːt// | //raːt + əs// | //raːt∗// | //raːt∗ + əs// |
| Phonemic | /raːt/ | /raːt + əs/ | /raːt/ | /raːd + əs/ |

(leaving boundaries in at the phonemic level). The phonemic realizations would be produced by a **morphophonemic rule**:

$$(4.6) \qquad //t∗// \longrightarrow \begin{cases} /d/ & /\underline{\hspace{1cm}} + V \\ /t/ & \end{cases}$$

This has a particular advantage over simple allomorph listing. It indicates that there are in the language groups of phonemes with a 'special relation' (Harris 1960: 226 n7): not the kind that is necessarily deducible from oppositional structure (as this privative case might be). Examples from English would include the fricative pairs /f v/, /θ ð/, /s z/ (*knife: knives, mouth: mouthe, house* (n): *house* (v)), the triple /k s ʃ/ as in *electric: electricity: electrician, physics: physicist: physician*, and so on. So we could say that *knife* has the MP representation //naif∗//, where //f∗// → /v/ before {plural}, /f/ elsewhere, while a non-alternating form like *fife* is //faif//, /faif/. In terms of our notion of classes and members as primes (see §§2.1–2.3), we have another parallel: just as a morpheme is a class of allomorphs and a phoneme a class of allophones, so A MORPHOPHONEME IS A CLASS OF ALTERNATING PHONEMES.

By invoking this new level we can capture the fact that a language has certain fairly consistent or **productive** alternations; the MP symbol plus the attendant rule(s) allows us to state this once and for all. And most important: the MP level allows us to give to every (non-suppleting) morpheme a SINGLE REPRESENTATION at some level, even if not the phonemic. It seems desirable, as a working principle anyhow, to have some such device available, to allow larger-scale structural generalization, and in particular to create a linkage or interface between two separate but interinvolved levels of description. It is however quite a different question whether a separate MP level is the way to do this, as we will see.

## 4.3 **Process morphophonemics: Bloomfield**

We now turn to another type of MP description, pioneered in recent times by Leonard Bloomfield. This is a fairly radical departure from the theoretical framework we've been working in, and in some ways is more complex than the separate-levels analysis – though it may also be more revealing. This type of analysis actually predates the type set out in §4.2, associated with linguists like Zellig Harris, and was in use before the biuniqueness requirement became widely accepted. But I treat it out of chronological order here because it is much more in the historical mainstream, and is the foundation of the currently most widely practised types of analysis.

Recall that in the German and English alternations we've considered, a linguist like Harris would use a special MP symbol, and thus invoke an intermediate and distinct level, where alternating segments get different symbols from non-alternating ones, regardless of phonetic identity: in effect this is a **segmental coding** of an essentially morpho-syntactic property, since symbol-choice is determined by properties of morphological paradigms. In this way the MP symbol has a **bridging function** between two levels. And in each case there is a rule that tells us which phonemes expound a morphophoneme in which contexts.

Bloomfield's approach was rather different, though the 'bridge' principle still operated. He achieved the desired uniqueness of specification without introducing MP representations as a new level, but by doing away – in a sense – with purely phonemic representations. Or better, perhaps, redefining the phonemic level in a MORPHOLOGICALLY RELEVANT way, so that the bridging is achieved without the interposition of an independent level. To give a rough summary in advance, Bloomfield's procedure was this: wherever possible, take one allomorph (**alternant** in his terminology) as basic, and **derive** the others from it by rule. So in *knife*, he takes the phonemic shape /naif/ as the **basic alternant** or **underlying form**, and specifies a set of procedures for obtaining the correct alternants. Thus the 'peculiarity' of the plurals of *knife, mouth, house* can be described 'by saying that the final [f, θ, s] of the underlying singular is replaced by [v, z, ð] before the bound form [= plural suffix] is added' (1933: 213). A bound form is one that cannot occur in isolation. (The / / vs. [ ] convention was not in use in the 1930s.)

This means that the correct description here is a series of steps or procedures, two **processes** applied to /naif/: (1) CHANGE the voiceless finals to voiced; (2) ATTACH the appropriate alternant of the plural suffix (or – it's not clear from his description – its underlying form). The processes (1, 2) must be applied IN THIS ORDER; there is no way to get the correct alternant of the plural suffix unless the /v ð z/ are there 'already' to condition it. Bloomfield thus introduces two fundamentally important notions: (a) **mutation rules** (rules that change one thing into another, or replace one with another); and (b) **process** or **rule order**: processes (at least sometimes) must be applied in particular sequences to get the correct results. (The boldface terms are not Bloomfield's.)

He further remarks (*ibid.*) that these operations represent a purely **descriptive order**: 'the actual sequence of constituents', he says, is 'a part of the language, but the descriptive order of grammatical features is a fiction and results simply from one method of describing the forms'. That is, there is no sense in which the speaker performs these operations; nor are they intended to be analogues to anything he might do or that might go on in his brain. The speaker 'merely utters a form (*knives*) which in certain features resembles, and in certain features differs from, a certain other form (namely, *knife*)'.

This separation between what we attribute to the speaker and the linguist is now unfashionable, as there is a tendency to expect linguistic descriptions to be 'psychologically real'. Bloomfield was explicitly not a 'realist' in this sense, and the questions of (a) whether one ought to be, and (b) whether it's possible to tell if one is being, are still open. For Bloomfield, the 'data' is self-contained, and the linguist's aim is to produce the neatest and most structurally revealing description possible of it, not the speaker. (For Bloomfield the latter would in any case be outside the province of linguistics.) But descriptive theories in themselves are neutral with respect to the 'location' of what they describe: it might be that the best description would be best whether judged on psychological or aesthetic criteria. But there is a question about what linguists ought to be doing; it might be worth quoting Fred Householder's famous or notorious remark (1966: 100): 'A linguist who could not devise a better grammar than is present in any speaker's brain ought to try another trade.' (We return to the 'reality' problem in §9.5.)

Let us go a step further. In setting up an MP description, we first choose a basic or underlying form. On the face of it, the simplest choice would be some actually occurring **free** allomorph (i.e. one that can appear in isolation); but sometimes the most insightful description can be obtained only by constructing what Bloomfield calls an **artificial underlying form**, e.g. a **bound** allomorph, or in some cases even a form that doesn't occur in the data at all (see §9.3). For the German voice-alternations, Bloomfield chooses a bound form.

He justifies this on the basis of the following type of argument: he observes (p. 218) that voiced obstruents do not appear finally in German, and that further, if we took the voiceless forms as basic in all cases (alternating and non-alternating) 'we should have to give a long list to tell which ones appeared in derivatives' with voiced and with voiceless stem-finals (e.g. if both {raːt}$_1$ and {raːt}$_2$ had the base-form /raːt/). If however we construct an 'artificial' basic free form with a voiced final, the general 'law' or phonotactic constraint in German that voiced obstruents do not appear (phonetically) in final position will determine the correct output. He refers to this constraint as the 'rule of permitted finals'. We could schematize his description this way:

| (4.7) | | Nom sg | Gen sg | Nom sg | Gen sg |
|---|---|---|---|---|---|
| | Underlying form | raːt | raːt | raːd | raːd |
| | Add suffix | — | raːt-əs | — | raːd-əs |
| | Rule of permitted finals | — | — | raːt | — |
| | Output | raːt | raːtəs | raːt | raːdəs |

Bloomfield makes an extremely important point with this rule of permitted finals: it's not merely the case that the /t/ $\sim$ /d/ alternation represents a 'special relation' between (any) two phonemes, but rather that the relation itself is partly dependent on, or predictable from, a larger generalization about German phonology. This has the interesting effect of connecting what seems at first to be an idiosyncratic fact about certain classes of morphemes with other – independent – principles. It's not obvious on the face of it that a MEDIAL alternation should have any particular connection with a constraint on FINALS; but choosing a single base form virtually 'forces' the connection. Here a general theoretical or analytical principle has the effect of 'uncovering' structure. And in particular, the more 'abstract', inapparent relation falls out naturally from the more obvious one.

But there are difficulties here as well; or at least the need for a change in our idea of what 'phonemic contrast' is. And this casts a different light on the whole notion of what phonology might look like. Most important, the idea of contrast as a property of PHONETIC strings is bypassed; contrast is shifted now to an 'underlying' level (unobservable, but theoretically inferrable); and in essence we find ourselves back again with a two-level organization for phonology as a whole.

This time however it is best characterized, not as phonemic vs. phonetic, but as morphophonemic vs. phonetic. (Or in Bloomfield's and current terms, 'phonological' vs. phonetic.) This further means that we now require TWO sets of phonotactic rules: one for the phonetic (**'surface'**) level, and one for the underlying (**'deep'**) phonological, and there is no reason why they have to be the same. (The rule of permitted finals is 'surface-true', but not phonologically true.) The question now is whether the loss of classical distinctiveness is too high a price to pay for overall coherence and minimization of idiosyncrasy. (For the claim that it is, see §§9.4ff.)

It's important to note the effect of Bloomfield's treatment. By not separating levels, but having forms produced by a process of 'continuous derivation', we grant considerably more power to our descriptive techniques. We're allowed to do things that the old separate-levels approach didn't permit: to change segments into others (and as we'll see later, to delete, insert, and transpose them as well).

This new insight ($\{$raːt$\}_2$ can't have the phonetic form $*$[raːd] in isolation, but must end in [d] before a suffix, etc.) is achieved only by rejecting biuniqueness. It's not obvious, in this framework, whether any final [t] is 'in fact' underlying /t/ or /d/; this information is obtainable only from the description AS A WHOLE (i.e. by 'backtracking' the derivation). The typical argument against such a 'mixture' of morphophonemics and phonemics, of course, is precisely that unique recoverability of phonological structure from phonetic forms is lost, and that if we project our analysis to the speaker-hearer, it becomes difficult to see how he can segment and analyse his phonetic input.

If we want to get into this, the same counter-argument is available here as for the [ʔ]-for-/k/ problem (§2.7): the speaker must simply be assumed to 'know' in some sense the overall structure of his language. After all, language, to be used productively, must be structurally transparent to its speakers; in some way or other – if not in the way the linguist does – they must have access to forms and their relations.

4.4  **The Unique Underlier Condition**

Perhaps the principal characteristic of phonological structure (or the kinds of data phonologies are interested in) is ALTER-
NATION: many structural units show alternant realizations in different
(typically – but not always – **syntagmatic** or linear) contexts. Phones
alternate in phonemic contexts, morphs in partly phonological, partly
morphosyntactic ones. Since so much of our subject-matter, in both
'pure' phonology (allophonics) and (morpho)phonology is alternation, we are constantly faced with the problem of how to account
for it in a simple and structurally coherent way. And it is clear that
allophonics and morphophonemics, whatever their differences, can't
be kept strictly separate, since allomorphs are by definition phonological realizations of underlying morphemes.

In this and the following section I want to look at the general
conditions that most current schools of phonology tend to agree in
placing on (morpho)phonological descriptions (for the dissenting
voices see §§9.5ff), and the types of description and argumentation that
emerge from them.

The basic principle I will call the **Unique Underlier Condition**
(UUC):

(4.8)    **UUC**
         Every non-suppletive alternation is to be accounted for by
         assigning to each morpheme a SINGLE, PHONOLOGICALLY SPECI-
         FIED UNDERLYING REPRESENTATION, with the allomorphy derived
         by general (preferably phonologically specified) rules.

But just what do we mean by 'non-suppletive'? This is sometimes
tricky, but at least the extreme cases are clear. For example:

(4.9)    *go ~ went*                      *cat*/s/ ~ *dog*/z/ ~ *fish*/ɪz/
         Suppletive (one-off)             Non-suppletive (productive,
                                            regular, predictable)

         No general rule                  General rule
         No phonological motivation       Phonological motivation

We will see that 'phonological motivation' is not always obvious, and
that 'depth' of analysis plays a crucial role.

Let us now look at an analysis motivated by the UUC, and see what
kinds of rule systems and interactions we are led to postulate.

63

## 4.5 The UUC and the Latin consonant-stems

There is a subset of Latin nouns of the 'third declension' called **consonant-stems**: their inflections are added to the bare stem, rather than having a linking or **thematic** vowel between (e.g. nominative singular /luːk-s/ 'light' vs. /korp-u-s/ 'body'). Consider these paradigms:

(4.10)

|    |        | 'light'  | 'king'  | 'stone'   |
|----|--------|----------|---------|-----------|
|    | Nom    | luːks    | reːks   | lapis     |
|    | Gen    | luːkis   | reːgis  | lapidis   |
| Sg | Dat    | luːkiː   | reːgiː  | lapidiː   |
|    | Acc    | luːkem   | reːgem  | lapidem   |
|    | Abl    | luːke    | reːge   | lapide    |
|    |        |          |         |           |
|    | Nom/Acc| luːkeːs  | reːgeːs | lapideːs  |
| Pl | Gen    | luːkum   | reːgum  | lapidum   |
|    | Dat/Abl| luːkibus | reːgibus| lapidibus |

The paradigms (or at least their nom sg) are arranged in order of apparent increasing 'irregularity' from left to right. Our problem will be to see if these (and others to be introduced later) are as irregular as they look, or if there is a rational structure to this declension.

For 'light', there are no problems with underliers: both the stem and the suffixes are obvious (/luːk-/, nom sg /-s/, dat sg /-iː/, etc.). And the endings are constant throughout the paradigms.

Now 'king': what is the underlying form of the stem? The choice is between /reːk/ and /reːg/, since these are the only two allomorphs. We can use two principles for guidance:

(i) Where possible, select the most widely distributed allomorph. This is intuitively sensible, and minimizes 'interference' with the data. (Though as we will see, it's not always viable.)

(ii) Where possible, let the description fall out naturally from the phonotactic rules of the language.

We can begin with a fact about Latin relevant to (ii): all stop + fricative clusters agree in voicing. If the nom sg is /s/, we can use both principles: take /reːg/ as the underlier (the only place it DOESN'T appear is nom sg), and this will give /reːgs/, which by the condition on clusters will become [reːks]. (From now on I follow the practice of putting all non-underlying forms in [ ].) All other forms in the paradigm can be left untouched. This ploy – generating an illegal form in the course of a derivation, for good reasons – is sometimes known as 'taking a **false step**'; and the rule that destroys /reːgs/ and forms [reːks] is a '**rescue rule**'. We will see more of the motivation for these moves below.

But now 'stone': the nom sg is again 'irregular', but here by having a segment 'missing'. Should we take the base as /lapi/, with /d/ inserted in all the other forms? Given the cluster condition, */ds/ is illegal; and if we took /lapid/ as underlying, we would have /lapids/ → * [lapits]: not the attested [lapis]. But it would be nice if we could have /lapids/ → [lapits] → [lapis]; this would give us an underlying structure like that for 'king' and 'light', in that we would have a consistent stem-shape for the whole paradigm.

But wouldn't this be a needless complication? Why have this 'extra' form [lapits] when we could – if we insist on preserving constant stem-shape – simply go from /lapids/ → [lapis]? But if we look further, we will find some motivation for this false step.

First a fact, then a hypothetical argument. Fact: the cluster [ts] does not appear in Latin (non-compound) phonetic forms. Argument: assume that there exist forms where /ts/ → [s] is directly motivated, by arguments at least as strong as those for /gs/ → [ks] in 'king'. If this were so, we would need two rules: (a) /ts/ → [s] for our hypothetical forms, and (b) /ds/ → [s] for /lapids/ → [lapis]. Yet /ds/ → [ts] is already automatically provided for by our cluster condition. And there are forms that suggest the need for a /ts/ → [s] rule, here given only in sg for convenience:

(4.11)

|      | 'night' | 'race' | 'part' |
|------|---------|--------|--------|
| Nom  | noks    | geːns  | pars   |
| Gen  | noktis  | gentis | partis |
| Dat  | noktiː  | gentiː | partiː |
| Acc  | noktem  | gentem | partem |
| Abl  | nokte   | gente  | parte  |

(Disregard the vowel-length difference in 'race': we will return to this shortly.)

The paradigms suggest the underliers /nokt/, /gent/, /part/. Thus there is a motivation for a nom sg in /ts/ (/nokts/, etc), and a rule to reduce the cluster: /nokts/ → [noks]. To recapitulate: (a) [lapis] ~ [lapidis] suggests /ds/ → [s]; (b) [reːks] ~ [reːgis] suggests /gs/ → [ks]; (c) [noks] ~ [noktis] suggests /ts/ → [s]; (d) there is no phonetic [ts]. So: why not use the independently motivated voice-identity condition on clusters to create [ts] from /ds/ (/lapids/ → [lapits]), and then resolve this ill-formed sequence by the /ts/ → [s] rule we need anyhow? We thus give /lapids/ a **'free ride'** on the rules we need for another form. Our derivations then are:

(4.12)

|  | reːgs | lapids | nokts | parts |
|---|---|---|---|---|
| Cluster condition | reːks | lapits | — | — |
| ts → s | — | lapis | noks | pars |

We can state the rules in a simplified form as:

(4.13)   (a) Cluster condition

$$\left\{\begin{matrix} b \\ d \\ g \end{matrix}\right\} \rightarrow \left\{\begin{matrix} p \\ t \\ k \end{matrix}\right\} / \underline{\quad} s$$

(b) Cluster simplification

$$t \rightarrow \emptyset / \underline{\quad} s$$

(Where '→ ∅' means 'goes to zero', i.e. deletes: see §8.4. The labials are included in (a) because of [urps] ∼ [urbis] 'city', etc.)

   Now back to [geːns] ∼ [gentis]. There are a number of nouns in this declension with a long vowel in nom sg and a short one elsewhere. They all seem to have the basic structure [-Vːns] ∼ [-VntV-] (e.g. [meːns] ∼ [mentis] 'mind', [froːns] ∼ [frontis] 'forehead'). It is a general fact about Latin, however, that vowels are always long before [ns]; so any description will need a length rule for this environment, which is required independently of morphological considerations. That is, we can motivate [ns] in [geːns] as being from underlying /nts/, with /t/ removed by (4.13b); but not the [ns] in [eːnsis] 'sword' (gen sg. [eːnsis]). So we add the rule:

(4.14)   Lengthening

$$V \rightarrow Vː / \underline{\quad} ns$$

We can now add the derivation for [geːns] to the set in (4.12):

(4.15)

|  | reːgs | lapids | nokts | gents |
|---|---|---|---|---|
| Cluster condition | reːks | lapits | — | — |
| Cluster simplification | — | lapis | noks | gens |
| Lengthening | — | — | — | geːns |

   Let us look at some more forms, which display a new alternation, as well as one we've already looked at:

(4.16)

|       | 'soldier' | 'chief'    |
|-------|-----------|------------|
| Nom   | miːles    | priːnkeps  |
| Gen   | miːlitis  | priːnkipis |
| Dat   | miːlitiː  | priːnkipiː |
| Acc   | miːlitem  | priːnkipem |
| Abl   | miːlite   | priːnkipe  |

The consonant alteration in 'soldier' is obviously like that in 'night': /miːlets/ → [miːles]; but the [i] ~ [e] alternation raises a problem with respect to the choice of /miːlets/ as underlying. Shouldn't it be /miːlits/, on the 'majority rule' principle? But other facts suggest this might not be the best approach. Consider for instance the following pairs of simple and derived forms:

(4.17)

|          | Simple    |            | Derived      |
|----------|-----------|------------|--------------|
| teneoː   | 'I hold'  | attineoː   | 'I keep'     |
| sedeoː   | 'I sit'   | assideoː   | 'I sit by'   |
| premoː   | 'I press' | komprimoː  | 'I compress' |

That is, there is a widespread (though not exceptionless) tendency in Latin for [e] to alternate with [i], especially where the [e] comes in a non-initial penultimate syllable, and the preceding vowel is not [e]. Since this process is needed for [teneoː] ~ [attineoː], etc. (it's clear that the underlier is /ten-/), we can utilize it for nouns like those in (4.16) as well, under the general principle:

(iii) Get maximum mileage out of independently motivated rules; use 'free rides' when possible. So the underliers for (4.17) are /miːlets/, /miːletis/, etc.

The concept of **independent motivation** is especially important in this kind of description: a rule is independently motivated if its environment is transparent, and if it is required for the derivation of forms outside the set that a particular description is being constructed for. (This is in spirit rather like the legal notion of 'corroboration' or 'independent witness'.) I will not formulate the /e/ → [i] rule here, as it is immensely complex; but the point is clear.

The analysis so far raises a number of points of theoretical interest. First, observe that there are constraints on applying the three rules in (4.13–14). In order to get the correct results, they must apply in a particular order. For example, (4.13b) Cluster simplification must apply after (4.13a) Cluster condition, since it requires as input the [ts] created by the former rule; and similarly (4.14) Lengthening must apply after (4.13b), since the former produces the [ns] clusters, and these are necessary for lengthening to take place. Each of the rules was formulated independently of the others, but they turn out to interact when taken together as a system. So once again (see §2.7 on biuniqueness and overlapping) a theoretical model shows consequences that weren't envisaged when it was set up.

Note another important property of this analysis: even the 'irregular' forms we started with BECOME regular if the analysis takes a sufficiently **abstract** (distant-from-surface) point of departure, and we allow forms unacceptable on the surface to appear as underliers, or to be generated during derivations. And the regularity falls out as a natural consequence of syntagmatic restrictions on phoneme or phone sequences. It looks as if there's far less 'irregularity' in language than appears on the surface. If only you go deep enough, 'things are seldom what they seem'. There will always, of course, be an irreducible core of suppletion; the argument will centre around just how big it is, and what you're allowed to do to reduce it.

We might also observe another point that will become more significant later on: in a 'process' description with underliers and mutation rules, in the Latin case as well as the simpler German one, we come up against an entirely new phenomenon. Since the model we're using completely overrides biuniqueness, we now have – on the phonetic surface – 'two kinds of' [i], of [eː], of [oː], of [k], of [s], etc. What we might call **'original'** or **'underlying'** and **'derived'**. Thus the [i] in the third syllable of [priːnkipis] is original, from underlying /i/, but that in the second syllable is derived from /e/; similarly the [k] in [luːks] is original, but that in [reːks] is underlying /g/, while the [eː] in [reːks] is underlying, but that in [geːns] derived. It is no longer possible to tell from its phonetic form in isolation what the systemic status of any segment is; this information is obtainable only from the whole description, by retracing the derivation of a form to see what rules have operated on it.

### 4.6 Summary: implications of underlying forms and processes

The most obvious implication of §4.5 is that it's possible to do away with 'contrast' in the classical phonemic sense and still have a satisfactory – if radically different – form of description. A lot seems to depend on what you want in the first place: is class assignment or coherence of primary importance? And this in turn depends on preliminary theoretical commitments, e.g. the view of overall linguistic structure you hold, whether you are committed *a priori* to a unified or 'integrated' theory, where all levels interconnect in a seamless web, or to a more stratified or compartmentalized theory. To a large extent these are matters of preference, not empirical issues: given that the phenomena of contrast, non-contrast where you expect contrast, non-uniform distribution, morphophonemic alternation, etc. do exist, what's most important, what's basic, and what's peripheral? Perhaps in the end the most important element is PERSPECTIVE.

That is, the notion 'underlying form' derives from a shift of perspective. Take the German /t/ /d/ alternation again: there are essentially two ways of looking at it:

(i)    There are two kinds of morphemes, those with both /t/- and /d/-allomorphs, and those with only /t/-allomorphs; or
(ii)   There are two kinds of /t/, those that alternate with /d/, and those that don't.

Perspective (i) makes MP alternation a fact about morphology, which happens – because of the way morphemes are realized – to involve phonology; perspective (ii) makes MP alternations a fact about phonology, which happens – because phonological units occur in morphemes – to implicate morphology as well.

In chapter 9 we'll see how the extension of perspective (ii) in recent times leads to a radical increase in descriptive power and a strikingly different view of phonological structure. We will also see how this extension of descriptive power leads to a sharper focus on the issues raised here.

## 4.7   Sandhi

If MP alternations occur at the interface between phonology and morphology, there is another kind of process that occurs at the interface between phonology and syntax (though it is involved in morphology as well). Here we are concerned mainly with processes not within words themselves (whose structure, broadly speaking, is the province of morphology), but at the MARGINS of words in syntactic configurations (or the margins of morphemes in syntactically motivated contexts). That is, alternations not derivable from the inspection of inflectional or derivational paradigms (as in the Latin material in §4.5 or English *electric ~ electricity*, etc.). Though some of these phenomena may come into consideration as well.

It may seem odd at first to think of phonological phenomena that show up primarily in syntax (aside from intonation, which is not in question here), but the situation is quite common. As a fairly extreme example, consider the following Sanskrit data, involving word-forms in isolation and in syntactic combination:

(4.18)  (a) 1 na 'neg' + asti 'he-is' + iha 'here' → naːstiːha 'he is not here'

2 saːdhu 'well' + uktam 'spoken' → saːdhuːktam 'well spoken'

(b) 1 viːna 'without' + iːrṣjaja 'jealousy' → viːnerṣjaja 'without jealousy'

2 saː 'she' + uːvača 'spoke' → sovača 'she spoke'

(c) 1 aːsiːt 'there was' + raːjaː 'king' → aːsid raːjaː 'there was a king'

2 vaːk 'speech' + bhraːmjati 'is-excited' → vaːg bhraːmjati 'the speech is excited'

3 vaːk + me 'my' → vaːŋ me 'my speech'

4 tat 'this' + mama 'of mine' → tan mama 'this of mine'

(d) 1 tat + ča 'and' → tač ča 'and this'

2 tat + lebhe 'I-obtain' → tal lebhe 'I obtain this'

3 tat + jamma 'birth' → taj jamma 'this birth'

([č, j] are palatal affricates)

The processes here can be described as follows: at word boundary,

(4.18a)  Two like vowels coalesce to one long vowel, with loss of a syllable.

(4.18b)  Two unlike vowels coalesce to one 'intermediate' vowel, e.g. High + Low → Mid, with the backness of the resulting vowel determined by the right-hand vowel in the sequence.

(4.18c)  A stop becomes voiced before a voiced stop, and nasal before a nasal, retaining its original place of articulation.

(4.18d)  A dental stop becomes palatal before a palatal (1), and by (4.18c) voiced as well if the palatal is voiced (3); before a lateral a dental stop becomes lateral.

It is appropriate to illustrate this general type of process from Sanskrit, as the traditional name for it (after the usage of the ancient Indian grammarians) is **sandhi** (Sanskrit *sam* 'together' + *dhi* 'put' – yet another kind of sandhi!). What we have here is essentially syntactically conditioned allomorphy, with rules operating on the termini of the peripheral morphemes of words of any internal structure (or on the termini of morphemes in general in the limiting case of monomorphemic words).

One question that immediately arises is whether sandhi rules are really any different from, say, rules that constrain sequences within the word: from the data above it's not entirely apparent that they are. But further forms from Sanskrit show that here it is the boundary that counts: thus /aːtman/ 'spirit' violates (4.18c), and the existence of independent diphthongs (e.g. the dat sg ending /ai/, the nom/acc/voc dual /au/) shows that (4.18b) isn't an overriding constraint. Sandhi rules may be extensions of rules operating within the word or morpheme, but they do not have to be: e.g. Sanskrit has a homorganicity constraint on /NC/ sequences both within the morpheme and across boundaries. But the most important point probably remains – at least for this type of sandhi – the distinction between paradigmatic alternations and alternations belonging to syntactic configurations of virtually limitless scope (paradigms are closed sets, and syntactic combinations aren't).

A similar type of sandhi, though with some interesting complications, occurs in so-called **'non-rhotic'** dialects of English. These 'lack postvocalic /r/', i.e. have /r/-realizations only initially and intervocalically within the word, and not pre-consonantally, and show final /r/ only in syntactic configurations where the following word begins with a vowel (or in morphological ones where the following morpheme begins with a vowel). There are two types of dialects showing /r/-sandhi in English, one of them phonologically more complex than the other, and the two will serve to illustrate two different sandhi types, and their relation to larger phonological structures.

In both types, an /r/ appears at word boundary where the left-hand form in its isolative realization ends with a vowel, and the right-hand form begins with one. But in one type (4.19a below), the /r/ appears only after certain WORDS; in the other (4.19b) it appears after certain VOWELS, regardless of the forms involved. For example:

(4.19)   (a) 1 aɪdɪə 'idea'    5 ðɪ aɪdɪə ɪz 'the idea is'
             2 fɪə 'fear'      6 fɪər ɪz 'fear is'
             3 lɔː 'law'       7 lɔː ænd ɔːdə 'law and order'
             4 fɔː 'four'      8 fɔːr ænd faɪv 'four and five'
         (b) 1 aɪdɪə            5 ðɪ aɪdɪər ɪz
             2 fɪə              6 fɪər ɪz
             3 lɔː              7 lɔːr ænd ɔːdə
             4 fɔː              8 fɔːr ænd faɪv

Both dialects also show a similar phenomenon in cases where – apparently – word and morpheme boundaries coincide, as in [fɛə] 'fair', [fɛərə] 'fairer'.

In type (a), there are two classes of words, those that turn up with final /r/ before a vowel, and those that don't; in type (b), all forms ending with certain vowels turn up with /r/ (mainly non-high back vowels, and centre-gliding diphthongs: neither type would have *[friːr ænd iːzɪ] 'free and easy'). The first type of sandhi is generally called 'linking-*r*', the second 'intrusive-*r*'.

In analysing (4.19a), we would probably want to have 'fear', 'four' ending with an underlying /r/, deleted except before a form beginning with a vowel, and 'idea', 'law' without /r/; in (4.19b) we would have two choices: either to have all the forms end in /r/, with the same rule as for (a), or to have the /r/ inserted after certain vowels as a hiatus-breaker.

The sandhi rules we've been looking at so far seem to be strictly phonologically conditioned – even if their input is syntactic: i.e. phonological in the sense that no lexical or syntactic specifications (except boundaries) are required for their statement. But there are also sandhi rules that invoke specific morphological categories. Consider Swedish: here there is a general prohibition against two vowels in sequence across a boundary, under certain conditions, as in:

(4.20)  (i)    /flikːa/ 'girl' + /ɛn/ 'def art' non-neuter → /flikːan/
        (ii)   /flikːa/ + /ur/ 'pl' → /flikːur/
        (iii)  /øːga/ 'eye' + /ɛt/ 'def art, neuter' → /øːgat/
        (iv)   /øːga/ + /ɔn/ 'pl' → /øːgɔn/
        (v)    */flikːɛn/ 'the girl'
        (vi)   */flikːar/ 'girls'
        (vii)  */øːgɛt/ 'the eye'
        (viii) */øːgan/ 'eyes'

If our underliers are /flikːa + ɛn/, /flikːa + ur/, /øːga + ɛt/, /øːga + ɔn/, it's clear that given a sequence /V + V/, one vowel or the other deletes. But it is the left-hand vowel (that of the stem) if the suffixed item is the plural marker, and the right-hand vowel (that of the suffix if it is the definite article. (We will return to this example in §8.4.2.)

From this brief treatment we can see that any theory that attempts to make absolutely clear demarcations between phonology and morphology and even phonology and syntax will run into trouble:

it will fail to account for important phenomena involving phonological units. There is certainly a case to be made for the different
components of linguistic structure having access to each other; though
the extent and regularity of this access are debatable. This chapter
was designed mainly to show what the debate is about, and to
introduce morphophonology as a topic. We will return to it later on
(ch. 9).

## NOTES AND REFERENCES

4.1–4.2 Morphophonemics is an immensely complex matter, which has
absorbed an enormous amount of scholarly energy. For a historical
overview, *Fischer-Jørgensen (1975: §§6.33–40). Good structuralist
treatments can be found in *Hockett (1958: chs. 15, 32–35), and
**Harris (1960: chs. 13–14). See also *Matthews (1974: ch. xi),
**Matthews (1972: ch. 14). For a contemporary view, **Dressler
(1977). Many of the more problematical issues will be taken up again
in ch. 9.

4.3 The type of description considered here ('process-morphophonemics')
goes back in fact to the pre-Christian Sanskrit grammarians, but in the
modern context it's not doing too much violence to history to associate
it with Bloomfield. It's of some interest to note that the chapter in
Bloomfield (1933) dealt with in §4.3 is called 'morphology'; and in his
*Menomini morphophonemics* (1939) Bloomfield calls procedures like those
discussed here 'morphological analysis'. This will become relevant later
on (ch. 9). The general issues raised by the importation of processes
into non-historical description were much discussed in the 1940s and
50s: see particularly **Hockett (1954), and §10.2.1.

    Bloomfield's practice of conflating phonemic and morphophonemic
levels is difficult to interpret: did he mean this sort of analysis to be
applicable IN GENERAL, or was it to be proper only for morphophonemics,
while the usual phoneme/allophone type was to be used for 'pure'
phonology? Certainly he doesn't appear to make the distinction, and
his published descriptive work usually shows the combined approach.
We will see later (ch. 9) that Bloomfield's rejection of certain 'classical'
distinctions between levels of analysis finds a strong echo in much later
theory: it has been both fruitful and methodologically dangerous.

4.4 The term 'underlier' is non-standard, and comes from Coates (1977).
The term UUC is a pedagogical invention of my own, but it seems to
sum things up usefully.

4.5 The analysis in this section is not really 'Bloomfieldian', but is in the

spirit of, and includes some of the formalisms and concepts of, contemporary generative phonology (ch. 9). But since most of the modern
argumentation types are implicit in Bloomfield, the anachronism is
harmless: what counts is the conceptual framework of process-
morphophonemics, whatever it's called. On selection of underlying
forms, see *Hyman (1975: §3.4), **Zwicky (1975b); on the free ride
principle, **Zwicky (1970), and on false steps **Zwicky (1973). The
Latin data is 'selected', in the sense that a lot of types are omitted; the
third declension as a whole is a fascinating exercise in process-description,
since it includes so many other paradigms amenable to similar strategies
([homoː] ~ [hominis] 'man', [kor] ~ [kordis] 'heart', [floːs] ~ [floːris]
'flower', etc.): it would be a nice exercise to try to account for ALL the
'irregular' nom sg here. (For the data, see any good Latin grammar.)

4.7 On sandhi in general, see **Allen (1962), which is a classic. This is
concerned mainly with Sanskrit, but discusses the theoretical issues as
well. Sanskrit forms are cited in a rough phonetic transcription, unlike
the forms in the grammars, which are transliterations. For treatment
of sandhi in the context of morphology, slightly less restrictively defined,
*Matthews (1974). In some treatments, phenomena occurring at
boundaries within the word are called **internal sandhi**, and those
occurring across word boundaries **external sandhi**.

# 5
## 'Ultimate constituents', 1: binary features

### 5.1 Feature theory

#### 5.1.1 *Jakobsonian distinctive features*

Phonology requires primitives smaller than the segment; this much is clear. But what are these 'atomic' components, and what part do they play in theory and description?

The most generally held view is that a feature system is a kind of 'universal alphabet' for phonological description – an inventory of components available to languages for building their phonologies, and to us for describing them. But a proper feature theory must also include answers to some basic questions, like:

(i) What are the features for? Specifying all and only the PHONO-LOGICAL OPPOSITIONS available to languages? Or also specifying in some detail the PHONETIC PROPERTIES of the segments involved?

(ii) Given an answer to (i), what features are there? How many? How are they defined?

(iii) How are they deployed in segments? Are there co-occurrence restrictions? Are segments just 'bundles' of features, or do they have internal structure?

(iv) What are the formal properties of feature systems? What notational conventions do we need in order to use features in phonological description?

The first fully-fledged system of features was that developed by the Prague linguist Roman Jakobson and various co-workers, which came to fruition in *Preliminaries to speech analysis* (Jakobson *et al.* 1951: henceforth *PSA*). The general approach, which we can call 'Jakobsonian', is based essentially on the first view in (i): that the 'basis of phonology' is a relatively small set of **distinctive features**, utilized by all languages in the construction of oppositions.

For Jakobson and his collaborators, these atomic elements were primarily ACOUSTIC rather than ARTICULATORY, and defined on the basis of spectrographic and similar properties. There was a reason for this; the whole theoretical framework rested on two main tenets: (a) that a feature theory should model the way the HEARER processes utterances presented to him, and (b) that what really counts is pure DISTINCTIVENESS, not phonetic detail ('The sole information carried by the distinctive feature is its distinctiveness', *PSA* §1.3.)

If this is so, the way is opened to a radical reduction of the potential inventory: 'if certain phonemic distinctions possess a common denominator and are never observed to coexist within one language, then they may be interpreted as mere variants of a single opposition' (*PSA* §1.2). This bears some discussion, as it presents one serious problem that motivated a shift from acoustic to articulatory features in the late 1960s, and expanded the inventory.

The Jakobsonian 'reductionist' strategy can be exemplified by the feature [flat], which is defined (*PSA* §2.422) as 'a downward shift of formants in the spectrum'. Now this can be achieved by at least three articulatory gestures: labialization, retroflexion, and pharyngealization. Since, according to *PSA*, no more than one of these parameters is used distinctively in any language, the three can be grouped together as one, thus getting rid of two independent features.

Now this certainly reduces the universal inventory; but the problem is that once we get beyond specifying distinctive oppositions, and into allophonic and other generalizations (which ought, if the features are truly 'basic', to be treated in terms of them), we get into trouble. Take Arabic for instance, which has a phonemic opposition between pharyngealized and non-pharyngealized consonants, and a vowel system /i a u/, where /u/, though rounded, is not distinctively so (see §5.1.2). But vowels are pharyngealized adjacent to a pharyngealized consonant.

This creates the need for what McCawley (1967) calls a 'feature-interpretation component' as part of any description, which has to state things like: '[flat] = pharyngealized in consonants, and on /i a/ adjacent to pharyngealized consonants, but rounded and pharyngealized on /u/...' etc. And there would be a different component for any language that utilized the opposition of flatness.

This lack of phonetic specificity and attendant descriptive complication led to the abandonment of excessively constrained inventories and conflation of variant articulations under single acoustic **'cover**

**features'**. It also led for a time to the abandonment of acoustic features themselves; though this turned out to be too radical a move, and it seems that we need both types (see §§5.5, 6.6).

A more lasting, though still controversial Jakobsonian contribution is the concept of **binarity**: all phonological features are **two-valued**. For *PSA*, 'any minimal distinction carried by the message confronts the listener with a two-choice situation' (§1.1); i.e. the identity of a phoneme is defined as the sum of a set of answers to yes–no questions. Each successive answer eliminates one or more phonemes in the system, and the last question gives an identification. And there is, for the most part, a fairly natural hierarchical order in which the questions should be asked. Take a language with the inventory:

(5.1)
```
        p  t  k        i  u
        f  s            e  o
           r            a
        m  n
        (C)            (V)
```

We might construct an identification-procedure as a series of Question/Answer/Instruction routines:

(5.2)  (i)  Q. C?
            A. Yes.
            I. Eliminate /i e a u o/. Choice is now a member of (C).
       (ii)  Q. Obstruent?
            A. No.
            I. Eliminate /p t k f s/. Choice is now /r m n/.
       (iii) Q. Nasal?
            A. Yes.
            I. Eliminate /r/. Choice is now /m n/.
       (iv)  Q. Labial?
            A. No.
            I. Eliminate /m/. Answer is /n/.

Something like this lay behind the original notion that features ought to be thought of perceptually; but the same principle (if not with the same 'perceptual choice' interpretation) can be incorporated as a classifying device into a theory where for instance the componential structure of segments (phones as well as phonemes – see §5.1.2) is thought of in terms of 'instructions' from the brain to the vocal organs. It can also be incorporated into any theory attempting to specify, in Chomsky & Halle's phrase (1968: 295) 'the phonetic capabilities of man'. And it can be so incorporated as to be neutral with respect to the speaker/hearer distinction; as well as with or without anything approaching a neurological or other 'deep' interpretation. That is, simply as a device for enumerating the possible segment-types that occur, and framing structural generalizations. Leaving aside any conjectures about what features 'really are' at some level other than their simple physical definition, and leaving aside any guesses about whether either perception or production can be said to work in terms of such items, the point of feature-systems – and the ultimate test of their validity – is their utility in stating what we think to be true generalizations about linguistic structure.

### 5.1.2 *Distinctiveness and redundancy*

The informal procedure (5.2) suggests a formal analogue: we can characterize any phoneme system in terms of a set of **binary oppositions**, where each segment is specified 'plus' or 'minus' for a given feature, i.e. as possessing or not possessing that property. Two segments are **distinct** if for at least one feature one is marked '+' and the other '−'. So if [±voice] is a two-valued feature defining glottal state, /t/ and /d/ are distinct as [−voice] vs. [+voice].

A segment then can be represented as a **matrix**, a column of features, each with a **value** or **coefficient**. Say we want to distinguish the vowels /i y u/ in some language. Using for the moment only the binary articulatory features [±high], [±back], [±round], the matrices are:

$$(5.3) \qquad i \qquad\qquad y \qquad\qquad u$$

$$\begin{bmatrix} +\text{high} \\ -\text{back} \\ -\text{round} \end{bmatrix} \qquad \begin{bmatrix} +\text{high} \\ -\text{back} \\ +\text{round} \end{bmatrix} \qquad \begin{bmatrix} +\text{high} \\ +\text{back} \\ +\text{round} \end{bmatrix}$$

(These features are obviously insufficient to distinguish these vowels in a whole system: we'll add more later.) Note that /i y/ are **minimally distinct** (differing in only one feature-specification), but /i u/ are distinct in two. (You can begin to see how we might define a measure of 'phonetic similarity'.)

Now consider this system:

$$(5.4) \qquad\quad i \quad y \quad u$$
$$\qquad\qquad\quad e \quad \o \quad o$$
$$\qquad\qquad\qquad\qquad \alpha$$

Let us add the feature [±low] (defined intuitively, as the others above are, for now). The system is:

(5.5)

|        | i | e | y | ø | u | o | ɑ |
|--------|---|---|---|---|---|---|---|
| High   | + | − | + | − | + | − | − |
| Low    | − | − | − | − | − | − | + |
| Back   | − | − | − | − | + | + | + |
| Round  | − | − | + | + | + | + | − |

Two features, [±high, ±low] are sufficient to specify a three-height system. This reflects a mathematical property of binary systems: for n features, the number of specifiable distinctions is $2^n$. Thus one binary feature will provide $2^1 = 2$ contrasts, two will provide $2^2 = 4$, etc. This however can represent excessive power: we would not want to allow (under the usual definitions) a segment specified [+high, +low]: so we will need some kind of empirically based constraints.

Note also that the binary principle – for this case at least – dissolves a gradual opposition /u – o – ɑ/ into two binary oppositions /u – o/, /o – ɑ/. This property allows us to characterize virtually all multi-lateral or gradual oppositions as sets of bilaterals (but cf. §5.3.2.3 for some problems).

So far, though we have been using non-Jakobsonian articulatory features, we have been talking in Jakobsonian terms: features are specifiers of oppositions, i.e. they have a **classificatory function**. But they must also have a **phonetic function**, which can be illustrated as follows. Consider a language with the vowel system /i e u o ɑ/, which in terms of our features is:

(5.6)

|        | i | e | u | o | ɑ |
|--------|---|---|---|---|---|
| High   | + | − | + | − | − |
| Low    | − | − | − | − | + |
| Back   | − | − | + | + | + |
| Round  | − | − | + | + | − |

It is clear that [±round] is not distinctive in this system (as it is in (5.5)): the value [+round] can be predicted from the values [+back, −low], and [−round] from [−back] or [+low]. Thus at the phonemic level roundness is functionless or **redundant**. (These are **language-specific redundancies**; there are others that are **universal**, or **definitional**, such as that [+high] predicts [−low], [+low] predicts [−high].)

Now assume that language (5.6) has a phonetic (allophonic) rule that says that consonants are rounded before rounded vowels: surely this must be stated somewhere in our description. Even though the information about roundness is PHONOLOGICALLY redundant, it must still be available in order for the consonant to 'know' that it's supposed to be rounded (or for us to be able to state this). I put it both ways to suggest that there are two ways of looking at a linguistic fact: from the 'inside', as it were, on the assumption that one is modelling a speaker or a similar device, and from the 'outside', where no such assumption is made: the linguist is describing an object that for his descriptive purposes is completely external and independent.

At any rate, this hypothetical case, like the Arabic one in §5.1.1, suggests that both the phonetic and classificatory functions are equally necessary, and that pure distinctiveness in the Jakobsonian sense is not enough.

## 5.2 **Features and 'natural classes'**

Consider again the vowels in (5.6). We can see that a given specification, aside from its role in an oppositional system or in phonetic characterization, has two further meanings: (a) the possession of a property by a segment: (b) the membership of that segment in the class of all segments that share that property. Thus [−back] isn't just a property of /i/, it is also a label for the class /i e y ø/, which are all – whatever else they may be – [−back]. The set of feature specifications of a segment is thus on one interpretation a list of the set of classes it's simultaneously a member of.

So /u/, which is [+back, +high, −low, +round], is a member of the following set of partly independent and partly intersecting classes:

(5.7)    [+back]:    u   o
         [+high]:    u   i   y
         [−low]:     u   i   y   e   ø   o
         [+round]:   u   y   ø   o

Let us move from the members of a particular system to segments in general. Consider a voiceless velar stop [k]; according to the features to be given in §5.3, it would have, among others, the specifications:

(5.8)
$$
\begin{bmatrix}
k \\
+ \text{obstruent} \\
+ \text{back} \\
+ \text{high} \\
- \text{continuant} \\
- \text{voice}
\end{bmatrix}
$$

(where [ + high] indicates a raised tongue-body, and [ − continuant] a stop articulation). This means that [k]-types belong to the sets containing the following members:

(5.9)    [ + obstruent] :  all stops, fricatives, affricates
         [ + back]      :  all velars, uvulars, pharyngeals, back vowels
         [ + high]      :  all velars, palatals, palato-alveolars, and high vowels (front, central, back)
         [ − continuant]:  all stops and affricates
         [ − voice]     :  all voiceless segments, i.e. stops, fricatives, affricates, nasals, laterals, etc.

This suggests that we shouldn't be surprised to find a [k] behaving as if it belonged to any of these groups. In addition to the obvious ones like velars and stops, we can now see that raising of vowels before velars (since they are high, like high vowels) is quite reasonable: though without this sort of analysis we might not have found it plausible.

Now note that each of the one-feature classes in (5.9) is much larger than the five-feature (one-member) class (5.8); and that each addition of a feature reduces the class. The [ + obstruent, + back] excludes labials, dentals, palatals, palato-alveolars, all included in [ + obstruent], and the addition of [ + high] excludes uvulars and pharyngeals. So the number of feature specifications is INVERSELY related to the size of the class specified: the **simplest** specifications (in the numerical sense) are also the most **general**.

This has an interesting spin-off. Consider once again the vowel system in (5.6), and the specifications of the following subsets of vowels in it:

(5.10)    i, e:  [ − back]
          i, u:  [ + high]
          i, o:  [ + high, − back] OR [ − high, + back]

These are the specifications necessary to distinguish the given classes from any other vowels within the system. Now according to what we know of the way languages behave, it is much more likely that the classes /i e/ or /i u/ would be involved in some unitary phonological process than one like /i o/. Note that within this system the two 'likely' sets have the property of being distinguished AS SETS by fewer feature specifications than would be necessary to specify their MEMBERS distinctively: this is not true of /i o/. Classes like /i u/ which have this property are called **natural classes**; this term means essentially 'class that we would expect to find behaving as a unit'. There are natural classes that can't be defined in quite this way, as we'll see, and some formally natural classes that are 'unnatural'; but the concept is worth noting.

### 5.3 **A tentative set of segmental phonological features**

The inventory presented in this section is incomplete and idiosyncratic. These failings are unavoidable in the present state of our knowledge. But the set I propose seems pretty useful, and is generally not too far outside the most widely accepted tradition. And, more important, it gives an idea of what kind of enterprise the drafting of a proposed universal feature inventory is, and what the result might look like.

This set is based largely on the proposals in Chomsky & Halle's monumental *Sound pattern of English* (1968: henceforth *SPE*). This is as 'standard' as any; but in the years since 1968 a number of serious inadequacies have been found, and remedies proposed, from revision to scrapping and replacement. The modified framework here incorporates some proposals of my own, as well as of others. In fairness to the reader, who will have to cope with a bewildering array of partly different systems in the literature, I will indicate the sources of features not in *SPE*, either in the text or notes; those without sources are my own. All additions, revisions, or redefinitions are marked with a preceding *.

I just note before proceeding that the system here is not sufficient for describing all the contrasts (let alone phones!) in the world's languages (none yet proposed is). But it does provide for those that are necessary for all languages, or relevant to those most commonly met with. How well it performs its tasks is debatable; some problems will be dealt with in this chapter, and some fairly radical revisions suggested in chs. 6, 11.

### 5.3.1    *Major class features*

*SPE* specifies as basic phonemic types the following: **obstruents** (stops, fricatives, affricates), and four classes of **sonorants** or nonobstruents: **liquids** (laterals and '*r*'-types), **vowels**, **nasals**, and **glides** (essentially the 'semivowels' [j w] and the glottal segments [ˀ h]). This is dubious on both phonetic and phonological grounds; the classification I adopt here does not recognize glides as an independent category, but takes [j w] as either consonants (usually liquids) or vowels, depending on circumstances. Here too [ˀ] and [h] are grouped respectively with stops and fricatives, in the traditional way (see §5.3.2.1).

*SPE* uses the features [±sonorant], [±vocalic], [±consonantal]; I will use the two major class features [±obstruent] and [±consonantal], with some redefinition (see note at end of chapter).

*(i) [±obstruent]. *SPE* posits a difference in voicing type in obstruents and sonorants, but this has been shown to be untenable (Ladefoged 1971). I opt here for a 'relative' rather than an 'absolute' definition: obstruents show a minimal output of periodic acoustic energy, non-obstruents a large output. Or, the 'unmarked' state for an obstruent is voiceless, that for a sonorant voiced (though there are voiceless nasals and liquids and voiced obstruents). Stops, fricatives and affricates are [+obs], liquids, nasals and vowels [−obs].

*(ii) [±consonantal]. A feature of constriction: a stricture of full closure to close approximation is (in general) [+cons]; most degrees of open approximation are [−cons]. So obstruents, nasals and liquids are [+cons] and the opener approximants [−cons]. But this is not an absolute definition, and consonantality must often be defined phonologically, regardless of stricture (e.g. in terms of syllable position).

If semivowels are not a phonologically distinct class, then we have (so far) these major types:

(5.11) 

|      | Obstruents | Nasals | Liquids | Vowels |
|------|------------|--------|---------|--------|
| Obs  | +          | −      | −       | −      |
| Cons | +          | +      | +       | −      |

Nasals and liquids are distinct by [±nasal] (§5.3.6).

*(iii) [±syllabic]. If we should have to define segments like /j w/ as distinct in type from both /r l/ and vowels, we can use this. Certainly at some level (though not phonemically for most languages) we will have to specify certain segments for syllabicity: e.g. in a diphthong

[iu] one member would have to be so specified, and the [ɫ] in [bæʔtɫ̩] to take another case. If this feature is indeed classificatory, as argued in *SPE*, then all vowels would be [ + syll], as would phonemic syllabic sonorants (as in Czech /pr̩st/ 'finger'). Otherwise the feature would be introduced at the phonetic level by rule.

### 5.3.2 *Cavity features*

These locate strictures in the vocal tract. We assume that the same set of binary features can characterize both continuous scalar oppositions like vowel height and relatively 'discrete' locations along the front/back axis ('velar', 'dental'); and that the same features in general apply to vowels and consonants. This lets us specify classes of related segments in a way not possible in frameworks requiring different features for these types. For example, in Arabic [ɑ] occurs only in the vicinity of pharyngeal(ized) consonants; it's clear that there's a relation between the backness and lowness of both segments that is not captured by the labels 'low back vowel' and 'pharyngeal(ized) consonant'. But this in no way replaces traditional place-labels; it merely cross-categorizes them according to a different set of relations, and they can be redefined in terms of the features.

#### 5.3.2.1 Primary strictures

*(i) [±oral]. First proposed in Lass (1976a: ch. 6). This distinguishes articulations in the pharynx and oral cavity from 'laryngeals', i.e. [ʔ h ɦ]. Any segment made in the oral cavity or pharynx is [ + oral]; any articulation below the epiglottis is [ – oral]. Note that [ + oral] is not the converse of [ + nasal]; nasal consonants are (perhaps confusingly) also [ + oral]. Among other things, this allows us to specify naturally the relation between voiceless stops and [ʔ], between voiceless fricatives and [h] (§§6.5, 8.3.1).

(ii) [±coronal]. This and the tongue-body features in §5.3.2.2 are defined in *SPE* with reference to the so-called 'neutral position' of the tongue: the blade more or less at rest on the floor of the mouth, and the front slightly raised towards the palate, somewhere in the vicinity of [ɛ]. While this concept is phonetically dubious, it is widely accepted, and regardless of its status creates a workable reference point. In a coronal articulation, the BLADE of the tongue is raised above neutral position (the positions of the front and body are irrelevant). Dental, alveolar, retroflex and palato-alveolar consonants are [ + cor], and all other consonants and non-retroflex vowels [ − cor].

(iii) [ ± anterior]. This locates a consonantal stricture with reference to the palato-alveolar region. It's difficult to define accurately, but seems workable. Any stricture anterior to [ʃ] is [ + ant], and any one from [ʃ] back is [ − ant]. Labials, dentals, alveolars (henceforth 'dental' will be a cover-term for both, i.e. non-retroflex coronals) are [ + ant], and all other segments [ − ant]. Given the stricture features so far, we have:

(5.12)

|      | Labial | Dental | Palato-alveolar | Retro-flex | Palatal | Velar | Uvular | Glottal |
|------|--------|--------|-----------------|------------|---------|-------|--------|---------|
| Oral | +      | +      | +               | +          | +       | +     | +      | −       |
| Ant  | +      | +      | −               | −          | −       | −     | −      | −       |
| Cor  | −      | +      | +               | +          | −       | −     | −      | −       |

## 5.3.2.2 Tongue-body features

(i)[ ± high]. In this and the two following features, the criterion is displacement of the BODY of the tongue from neutral. [ + high] means raised above neutral; [ − high] not so raised. So high vowels and palatal, palato-alveolar and velar consonants are [ + high] and all other (non-multiply-articulated) consonants [ − high].

(ii) [ ± low]. For [ + low], the body is below neutral position. So low vowels and pharyngeal consonants are [ + low], all other segments [ − low].

(iii) [ ± back]. For [ + back], the body is retracted from neutral position. So back vowels, velar, uvular and pharyngeal consonants are [ + back], other segments [ − back]. We now have:

(5.13)

|              | Oral | Ant | Cor | High | Low | Back |
|--------------|------|-----|-----|------|-----|------|
| Labial       | +    | +   | −   | −    | −   | −    |
| Dental       | +    | +   | +   | −    | −   | −    |
| Retroflex    | +    | −   | +   | −    | −   | −    |
| Palato-alv.  | +    | −   | +   | +    | −   | −    |
| Palatal      | +    | −   | −   | +    | −   | −    |
| Velar        | +    | −   | −   | +    | −   | +    |
| Uvular       | +    | −   | −   | −    | −   | +    |
| Pharyngeal   | +    | −   | −   | −    | +   | +    |
| Glottal      | −    | −   | −   | −    | −   | −    |
| High front V | +    | −   | −   | +    | −   | −    |
| Mid front V  | +    | −   | −   | −    | −   | −    |
| Low front V  | +    | −   | −   | −    | +   | −    |
| High back V  | +    | −   | −   | +    | −   | +    |
| Mid back V   | +    | −   | −   | −    | −   | +    |
| Low back V   | +    | −   | −   | −    | +   | +    |

5.3.2.3   Some problems in vowel specification

We now have the features [± high, ± low, ± back] for the vertical and horizontal dimensions, but what about central vowels, or systems with more than three heights? How do we capture the traditional close/half-close/half-open/open scale in binary features?

The issue is complex, and involves areas of feature theory where there is no consensus. When the *SPE* features were proposed (and for a good time after), many linguists apparently believed that central vowels and the half-close/half-open distinction were not independently phonemic, but always reducible to other, 'primary', distinctions. Thus it was observed that many languages have what looks like a four-height front vowel system /i e ɛ a/, but where /e/ vs. /ɛ/ is phonetically [eː] vs. [ɛ]. In such a situation the fourth height could be accounted for by some non-height feature, with low-level rules producing the height distinction. Features like [± tense] or [± long] were the most common (see §5.3.10).

Similarly, languages were thought not to have back and central vowels of the same lip attitude and height. So if there are no systems /y ʉ u/, but /y u/ or /y ʉ/, for instance, /ʉ/ could be treated as a phonemic ('underlying') back vowel, with a 'late rule' to specify /u/ as phonetically [ʉ]. Procedures like this, it must be emphasized, are not *per se* objectionable; they represent a legitimate attempt to reduce the number of primitives.

They are also, fortunately, empirically falsifiable. In both these cases the problem was (as usual) the data-base. Rather surprisingly here, since the languages that refute both the above claims are reasonably familiar. Even though there are languages where four apparent heights can be reduced to three plus length, or where three front/back contrasts can be reduced to two, there are cases where this can't be done. Clear examples of four-height systems appear in Danish and dialects of German with /iː eː ɛː aː/ plus short /ɛ a/; and a system with irreducible central vowels appears in Norwegian, which has the high vowels /i y ʉ u/. Even if only one known language has a contrast, the universal inventory must be able to characterize it naturally.

Vowel systems of these types can be handled with the following features (there is no consensus, but these are possible options):

*(i) [± front]. With three front/back positions, we can take the poles of the horizontal vowel space as two-valued features, with the

intermediate position as 'minus' for both (like doing three heights with two features). So:

(5.14)

|        | Front V | Central V | Back V |
|--------|---------|-----------|--------|
| Front  | +       | −         | −      |
| Back   | −       | −         | +      |

*(ii) [±mid]. Four-height systems are commonly handled with the features [±mid, ±high]. Here [+mid] is a kind of **diacritic** or 'modifier', meaning 'one step lower than the other height specification'. Thus:

(5.15)

|       | i | e | ε | a |
|-------|---|---|---|---|
| High  | + | + | − | − |
| Mid   | − | + | + | − |

This is not a felicitous treatment, and may be little more than a notational trick; for a better approach to height, see §6.2, and alternatively §11.2.

### 5.3.3  *Multiple articulations*

Certain feature specifications may co-occur in the same segment, others may not. The basic rule is that no segment can be marked '+' and '−' for the same feature (but see §6.4). There are other specifications too that would give contradictory results, e.g. if they required the same organ to be in two different positions at once, like [+high, +low]. But there are no general restrictions on 'non-interfering' specifications.

Therefore so-called 'secondary strictures' like palatalization, velarization, etc. can be handled with double sets of features, defining both articulations. For instance: the /l/ in my dialect is a dental lateral with dorso-velar constriction: this means that two different articulators are involved, i.e. the blade articulation is [+ant, +cor] and the body is [+high, +back].

If we take secondary strictures like these as essentially vowel-like properties superimposed on consonants, we can define palatalization as [i]-ness, velarization as [ɯ]-ness, and pharyngealization as [ɑ]-ness. For example:

(5.16)

|  |  | Palatalized dental | Velarized dental | Pharyngealized dental |
|---|---|---|---|---|
| Primary | Ant | + | + | + |
| | Cor | + | + | + |
| Secondary | High | + | + | − |
| | Low | − | − | + |
| | Back | − | + | + |

Labialization may be handled with [+round] (§5.3.4).

### 5.3.4 *Lip attitude*

(i) [±round]. This defines roughly the narrowing or lack of narrowing of the lip orifice. This is phonetically highly variable; in most languages the degree of rounding of a vowel is directly related to its tongue height. But no language, as far as I know, uses degree of rounding contrastively; we can assume that [±round] will be sufficient for lip attitude in most languages.

*(ii) [±inrounded]. One exception is Swedish, which has not two degrees, but two TYPES of rounding, distinct for only one vowel. No reasonable feature has so far been proposed for this, but the available articulatory descriptions show retraction and vertical lip compression, as opposed to the neutral or spread attitude for unrounded vowels and the protruded lip-rounding for the other rounded vowels. This vowel, as in *hus* 'house', is half-close and front, i.e. at the same height and frontness as [e] and [ø], both of which Swedish has; only its rounding type is distinctive.

For want of anything better I propose a translation of the traditional Swedish term *inrundning* 'inrounding', as opposed to the *utrundning* 'outrounding' of the other vowels, which = [+round]. This makes the Swedish front-vowel system about the most complex known; using /ʉ/, traditionally and incorrectly, for the inrounded vowel, we get:

(5.17)

|  | i | y | e | ø | ʉ | ɛ | a |
|---|---|---|---|---|---|---|---|
| High | + | + | + | + | + | − | − |
| Mid | − | − | + | + | + | + | − |
| Round | − | + | − | + | + | − | − |
| Inrounded | − | − | − | − | + | − | − |

Note that [+inrounded] is dependent on [+round], but not vice versa: [−inrounded] is automatically predicted by [−round], but a [+round] vowel may have either value for inrounding.

5.3.5   *Length of stricture*

(i) [±distributed]. This refers to the relative length of a consonantal stricture. [+distrib] sounds have a relatively long constriction along the direction of airflow; [−distrib] ones relatively short constrictions. This is designed for pairs like laminal/apical, non-retroflex/retroflex, bilabial/labiodental, the first in each case being [+distrib]. This may have things backwards; it seems more plausible to take the articulatory types as primary, and derive stricture length from properties of the articulators (the apex is smaller than the blade, etc.). But this would require the redefinition of places as singulary, not as products of binary oppositions.

5.3.6   *Secondary apertures*

(i) [±nasal]. A [+nas] segment is produced with a lowered velum, allowing air to pass through the nasal pharynx; a [−nas] segment has velic closure. Thus nasal consonants and nasal(ized) vowels are [+nas].

*(ii) [± lateral]. *SPE* restricts [+ lat] to [+ cor] segments; but many dialects of English have velar laterals with no blade activity, and some Caucasian languages have velar lateral affricates and ejectives. In a [+lat] articulation, the airflow is not through the centre of the oral tract, but along one or both sides of the tongue.

5.3.7   *Manner features*

These characterize the way in which airflow through the vocal tract is impeded.

(i) [±continuant]. In a [+cont] articulation, airflow is not totally blocked at any point; [−cont] means a stricture of complete closure. Thus [+oral] stops and affricates and [−oral] [ʔ] are [−cont]; fricatives and vowels are [+cont]. Nasals should probably be interpreted generally as nasal stops, i.e. [+nas, −cont]. Laterals are a problem, because even though they often have complete closure, they are also rather 'vowel-like' in their behaviour; they should probably be handled on a language-specific basis. As for various types of /r/, the approximants and fricatives are [+cont], and so probably are trills; but taps are difficult: how short a closure qualifies as complete? (See §6.4.)

(ii) [±delayed release]. In an affricate the closure is that of a stop, and the release that of a fricative: i.e. full release of the stop is 'delayed'. This is a bit misleading: it does not imply that affricates are longer than plain stops. Perhaps 'gradual release' would be better. Affricates can be distinguished as [+del rel] from the [−del rel] stops. There are other ways of treating them as well: as clusters, with a special feature of [friction], or in terms of sequential features within the segment (§§6.3, 6.4).

### 5.3.8 Source features

These refer to the source of maximum distinctive acoustic output:

(i) [±voice]. This is an unsatisfactory if familiar feature; unfortunately there are a number of glottal states that don't fall naturally into this dichotomy, e.g. creaky voice, breathy voice. But the distinction is grossly workable for a large number of languages. The definition is obvious: if the glottis is vibrating, producing periodic output, the segment is [+voice]; otherwise it is [−voice]. But in order to distinguish at least two other major glottal states, I suggest:

*(ii) [±constricted]. If there is voice plus laryngeal constriction, e.g. in some forms of creak, the segment is [+voice, +const].

*(iii) [±murmur]. 'Murmur' is another name for breathy voice. In this state, the vocal folds ('ligamental glottis') vibrate, but the arytenoid cartilages ('cartilaginous glottis') are apart, allowing leakage of non-vibrating air along with the voicing. The 'voiced *h*' [ɦ] in *ahead* (vs. *head*) and the breathy-voiced stops /b̤/ etc. in Hindi or similar languages would be [+voice, +murmur].

(iv) [±strident]. This is not strictly congruent to the rest of the system, as it is essentially acoustic (a leftover from the Jakobsonian framework). But this isn't a real problem, as there is no reason to assume that all features should be either articulatory or acoustic (see §§5.5, 6.1). Strident sounds have high-frequency noise: hence sibilants like [s z ʃ ʒ] are [+strid]. The feature can also distinguish other fricative pairs, as follows:

(5.18)

| | Bilabial | Labio-dental | Dental | Alveolar | Palato-alveolar | Velar | Uvular |
|---|---|---|---|---|---|---|---|
| | − | + | − | + | + | − | + |

In some languages [+strid] can characterize affricates, without invoking a release feature: they are strident stops, i.e. [+obs, −cont, +strid]. This would work for English /tʃ dʒ/, German /pf ts tʃ/. But some languages will need both a release feature and specification for stridency, e.g. Chipewyan with contrasting /ts/ and /tθ/. Only fricatives and affricates can be [+strid].

### 5.3.9 *Aspiration*

*(i) [±aspirated]. It is often assumed that aspiration (whether allophonic or distinctive) is in some way related to 'tense-ness', 'force of articulation', or some possible correlate like 'heightened subglottal pressure' (the *SPE* solution). But the evidence is against this; aspiration is primarily a matter of timing, an aspirated consonant having its stricture released before the onset of voice on a following voiced segment, giving a period of voicelessness. One should probably take aspiration as an independent feature, or, if one wants to tie it in with timing, try

*(ii) [±premature release]. Under this definition, an aspirated segment has its closure released earlier than a corresponding un-aspirated one, without change in voicing value.

In neither case is '+' restricted to stops; affricates and fricatives may be aspirated as well (as indeed they are in some varieties of English).

### *5.3.10 *Long vowels, diphthongs, and long consonants*

The specification of length is unsettled and difficult, but I will make some preliminary comments (and see §§6.4, 10.3.2). In the tradition stemming from Jakobson (including *SPE*), length is treated not as a prime, but associated with 'tenseness', so that the feature [±tense] dichotomizes vowel systems, and length is a low-level exponent of tenseness. For *SPE*, 'tense' vowels are marked by relatively greater deviation from neutral position than non-tense ('lax') ones: so in German, for instance, /iː eː uː oː ɑː/ are [+tense] and /ɪ ɛ ʊ ɔ a/ [−tense]. In addition to the relative peripherality of tense vowels, it is usually assumed that in a tense/lax pair, the tense one (if non-low) will be closer than the lax one, giving characteristic pairings like [iː]/[ɪ], [oː]/[ɔ], etc. This is all right for some forms of German and English, but can't cope with Swedish [ɛː]/[ɛ] and the like. This suggests that length ought to be an independent parameter.

In addition, tenseness doesn't seem to have the empirical correlates assigned to it in the literature; it is rare indeed to find even a highly trained phonetician who claims to be able to recognize it as an independent segmental property. (This is bad news for a cognitively oriented theory like that of *SPE*, since one presumes that features identifiable by children acquiring language would be identifiable by phoneticians.) As far as I can tell there are no qualities attributable to [+tense] that can't be reduced to the traditional dimensions of height, backness and duration. The feature [±tense] can probably be discarded.

One easy way to treat length is with a durational feature [±long]. A [+long] segment (in a particular language) is simply longer in relative duration than a [−long] one – whatever other properties it may have. This can be used for both consonants and vowels.

In *SPE*, most diphthongs are treated as sequences of (tense) vowel plus 'glide', so that *bite, out* have something like (in their notation) [āy āw] ([y] = [j]; the macron over a vowel indicates tenseness). This however makes these closing diphthongs absolutely different in type from centring diphthongs like [ɪə] in *idea*, and the 'peripheral opening' type in some West Yorkshire dialects like [eä], [uä] (*spade, smoke*), or the front/back open type in Malmö Swedish ([æɑ]). *SPE* would treat the latter type as vowel sequences.

It seems better in general, especially since the second elements in diphthongs like those in *bite, out* are rarely if ever close enough to be responsibly written [j w], to take diphthongs as vowel clusters. It might then also be feasible to take long vowels as 'undifferentiated' diphthongs, i.e. clusters with identical members, or **geminates**. Thus German phonetic [ae] in *weiss* 'white', [ao] in *Haus* 'house', [iː] in *Wiese* 'meadow', [oː] in *Tod* 'death' are phonologically /ae ao ii oo/. This captures the natural relation between long vowels and diphthongs in a simple and revealing way. We can also then treat long consonants as clusters, parallel to others, and do away with a special length feature, except in rare cases. (See §§ 10.3.2–3, 11.3.)

### 5.3.11 *Airstreams*

In addition to pulmonic egressive segments, a feature theory must be able to handle at least three other main types: clicks, ejectives, and implosives. In *SPE* these are specified with features of glottalic suction, velaric suction, and glottalic pressure (implosives, clicks, ejectives), and in another (non-binary) framework (Ladefoged 1971) by a multivalued feature of 'glottalicness' plus a binary suction feature. *SPE* gives:

| (5.19) | Pulmonic stop | Click | Implosive | Ejective |
|---|---|---|---|---|
| Velaric suction | − | + | − | − |
| Glottalic suction | − | − | + | − |
| Glottalic pressure | − | − | − | + |

I suggest a different system, based on two primitives: (a) DIRECTION of airstream, and (b) INITIATOR (making 'suction' a primitive rather than distributing it over two unrelated features). Thus we specify any segment for airstream direction:

*(i) [±egressive]. In a [+egr] airstream the direction of flow is towards the lips; in [−egr], towards the lungs. So implosives and clicks are [−egr], and all other segments [+egr].

We then specify the initiators: i.e. the lungs, glottis, or a moving velaric closure. Thus ejectives and implosives both have glottalic initiation (respectively [+egr] and [−egr]), pulmonic segments have a source at the lungs, and clicks a velaric source. So:

*(ii) [±glottalic]. A [+glott] airstream is initiated by a movement (up or down) of a glottal closure; a [−glott] segment has some other initiator.

*(iii) [±velaric]. A [+vel] airstream is initiated by a movement (forwards or backwards – though only the latter seems to be used linguistically) of a velar closure; a [−vel] airstream has some other source. So:

| (5.20) | Pulmonic stop | Click | Implosive | Ejective |
|---|---|---|---|---|
| Egressive | + | − | − | + |
| Glottalic | − | − | + | + |
| Velaric | − | + | − | − |

## 5.4 Features in phonological description: first steps

A feature system, as a 'universal phonetic alphabet', should allow us to characterize, among other things, the componential structure of segments (distinctive or not), the form of rules (allophonic, MP, fast speech), and historical changes. In this section we will look at a few major conventions that enable us to do this, and give some elementary examples of the applicability of feature notation to real-language data.

### 5.4.1 Segment inventories

The phoneme inventory of a language may be assumed to be a set of bundles of feature specifications (though this does not make segments as independent entities invalid: see §10.1). These can serve as the basis for making all (or at least the bulk of) statements about its (morpho)phonology. Consider for example this possible inventory for modern German:

(5.21)  (A) Vowels

|       | iː | ɪ | yː | ʏ | eː | ɛ | øː | œ | a | uː | ʊ | oː | ɔ | ɑː |
|-------|----|---|----|---|----|---|----|---|---|----|---|----|---|----|
| Obs   | −  | − | −  | − | −  | − | −  | − | − | −  | − | −  | − | −  |
| Cons  | −  | − | −  | − | −  | − | −  | − | − | −  | − | −  | − | −  |
| High  | +  | + | +  | + | +  | − | +  | − | − | +  | + | +  | − | −  |
| Mid   | −  | + | −  | + | +  | + | +  | + | − | −  | + | +  | + | −  |
| Back  | −  | − | −  | − | −  | − | −  | − | − | +  | + | +  | + | +  |
| Round | −  | − | +  | + | −  | − | +  | + | − | +  | + | +  | + | −  |
| ~~Long~~ Tense | + | − | + | − | + | − | + | − | − | + | − | + | − | + |

(B) Consonants

|       | p | b | t | d | k | g | f | v | s | z | ʃ | x | pf | ts | tʃ | m | n | ŋ | r | l | j | h |
|-------|---|---|---|---|---|---|---|---|---|---|---|---|----|----|----|---|---|---|---|---|---|---|
| Obs   | + | + | + | + | + | + | + | + | + | + | + | + | +  | +  | +  | − | − | − | − | − | − | + |
| Cons  | + | + | + | + | + | + | + | + | + | + | + | + | +  | +  | +  | + | + | + | + | + | + | + |
| Oral  | + | + | + | + | + | + | + | + | + | + | + | + | +  | +  | +  | + | + | + | + | + | + | − |
| Ant   | + | + | + | + | − | − | + | + | + | + | − | + | +  | −  | +  | + | + | − | + | + | − | − |
| Cor   | − | − | + | + | − | − | − | − | + | + | + | − | −  | +  | +  | − | + | − | + | + | − | − |
| High  | − | − | − | − | + | + | − | − | − | − | + | + | −  | −  | +  | − | − | + | − | − | + | − |
| Low   | − | − | − | − | − | − | − | − | − | − | − | − | −  | −  | −  | − | − | − | − | − | − | − |
| Back  | − | − | − | − | + | + | − | − | − | − | − | + | −  | −  | −  | − | − | + | − | − | − | − |
| Round | − | − | − | − | − | − | − | − | − | − | − | − | −  | −  | −  | − | − | − | − | − | − | − |
| Nas   | − | − | − | − | − | − | − | − | − | − | − | − | −  | −  | −  | + | + | + | − | − | − | − |
| Lat   | − | − | − | − | − | − | − | − | − | − | − | − | −  | −  | −  | − | − | − | − | + | − | − |
| Strid | − | − | − | − | − | − | + | + | + | + | + | − | +  | +  | +  | − | − | − | − | − | − | − |
| Voice | − | + | − | + | − | + | − | + | − | + | − | − | −  | −  | −  | + | + | + | + | + | + | − |
| Cont  | − | − | − | − | − | − | + | + | + | + | + | + | −  | −  | −  | − | − | − | − | + | + | + |

Note the extent of redundancy of feature specification: some redundancies are clearly universal (e.g. [−obs] predicts [−strid]); others are clearly language-specific, i.e. not necessary, but arbitrary properties of this system, and relevant for the formulation of generalizations about German in particular. Some of the more important of these, stated in the form of 'if-then' conditions, are:

(5.22)   *If:*   [+obs]   [−obs]   [+cons]   $\begin{bmatrix} +obs \\ -ant \\ -cor \end{bmatrix}$
　　　　　　　↓　　　↓　　　↓　　　　　　↓

　　　*Then:*  $\begin{bmatrix} -nas \\ -lat \end{bmatrix}$   [+voice]   [−low]   [+back]

$$\textit{If:} \qquad \begin{bmatrix} -\text{cons} \\ -\text{high} \\ -\text{mid} \end{bmatrix} \qquad \begin{bmatrix} -\text{cons} \\ -\text{long} \end{bmatrix}$$
$$\qquad\qquad\quad \downarrow \qquad\qquad\quad \downarrow$$
$$\textit{Then:} \qquad [-\text{round}] \qquad [-\text{high}]$$

Such redundancies are important – at least from a formal point of view – since any specification entirely predictable from some other(s) in the same matrix does not have to be mentioned in the statement of a rule.

### 5.4.2 *Phonological rules*

Let us take an introductory look at how some aspects of German phonology might be formulated in terms of features, using the material in §5.4.1 as a basis. We will use as examples two rules we have already met in other connections: final obstruent devoicing (the 'rule of permitted finals', §4.3) and the [x] ~ [ç] alternation (§2.11). First, final obstruents. In a Bloomfield-type process-phronology (or modern generative phonology) we characterize inflected forms of the paradigm types [raːt] ~ [raːdəs] as having underlying voiced finals, with a rule to devoice them before a boundary. If we stated this in terms of segments, we'd need one rule for each obstruent: /b/ → [p]/___#, /z/ → [s]/___#, etc. But the only thing that really counts is that the segment in question is an obstruent; we can factor out all other features and write:

(5.23) $\qquad [+\text{obs}] \rightarrow [-\text{voice}] \; / \underline{\quad\quad} \#$

In a rule format of this kind, the items to the left of the arrow and the right of the environment-bar make up the **structural description** (SD), and the material between the arrow and environment-bar the **structural change** (SC). The SD is the set of conditions to be met (the 'if'), and the SC the change effected (the 'then'). The SD is also called the **proper analysis**.

Note further that we do not have to specify [+voice] in the SD; if the input to the rule were already [−voice], this would satisfy the SC automatically. In such a case a rule is said to **apply vacuously**, i.e. all obstruents are in fact voiceless before a word boundary – whether this voicelessness is original or derived (on the original vs. derived contrast see §4.5).

95

So no features have to be mentioned in a rule except those that (for a given language) uniquely define the class of segments affected, and the change(s) effected. A maximally economical statement of a rule includes no features predictable from those necessary for correct statement – either language-specifically or universally; e.g. if all obstruents are [+ cons], this need not be mentioned, etc.

Now to a more complex rule, that for the [x] ~ [ç] alternation. Recall the facts: in an analysis with no phonemic /ç/, /x/ is realized as [ç] (a) after a non-low front vowel; (b) after a consonant; and (c) after a boundary; otherwise it is [x]. So, inspecting the consonant inventory (5.21B), we see that /x/ can be uniquely specified as [+ obs, + back, + cont]; there are no other back fricatives. Thus we can state the rule as:

$$(5.24) \quad \begin{bmatrix} + \text{obs} \\ + \text{back} \\ + \text{cont} \end{bmatrix} \longrightarrow [-\text{back}] / \left\{ \begin{bmatrix} - \text{cons} \\ - \text{back} \\ - \text{low} \end{bmatrix} \right\} \underline{\quad\quad}$$

$$\left. \begin{matrix} [+ \text{cons}] \\ \# \end{matrix} \right\}$$

Note that we don't have to specify anything other than [– back] in the SC; this is because of the convention that nothing changes except what's specified as changing.

That is: the SC effects its particular alteration, but 'carries along' the rest of the features. What (5.24) really does is this (including for clarity a number of features that don't have to be specified, and remain unchanged):

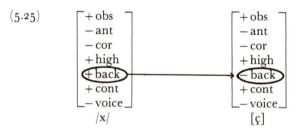

$$(5.25)$$

Thus there is – in our framework – only a one-feature difference between velars and palatals; and changing the value of that one feature 'produces a new segment', or 'changes /x/ into [ç]'. (On the problems raised by 'changing' things see §§8.1, 10.2.)

## 5.5  Capturing natural classes: the role of acoustic features

If some group of segments persistently figures in phonological processes (either synchronic or historical), especially in unrelated languages, an adequate feature system should specify it in a natural way. I will illustrate this point with one particular class; and this will help us focus on the problem of adequacy, and suggest that even a wide-ranging feature framework like the one in §5.3 may be inadequate, if restricted solely to articulatory parameters.

Consider the class consisting of labials and velars. In the *SPE* system this can be specified in one of two ways, depending on the membership of the consonant inventory in which the two occur. Take the two stop-systems below:

(5.26)

| | p | t | k | | | p | t | c | k |
|---|---|---|---|---|---|---|---|---|---|
| Ant | + | + | − | | Ant | + | + | − | − |
| Cor | − | + | − | | Cor | − | + | − | − |
| Back | − | − | + | | Back | − | − | − | + |

(a)                      (b)

In (5.27a), /p k/ can be distinguished as a class as [− cor]; but in (5.27b) they require a **disjunction** (an 'either-or' statement):

(5.27)

$$[-\text{cor}] \qquad \begin{bmatrix} -\text{cor} \\ \begin{Bmatrix} [+\text{ant}] \\ [+\text{back}] \end{Bmatrix} \end{bmatrix}$$

(a)                 (b)

((5.27b) reads: '[− cor], and either [+ ant] or [+ back]', thus excluding [− cor, − back], the palatal. The unbracketed specification within the larger segment-bracket means that whatever else the segment may be, it is [− cor].)

What (5.27b) virtually tells us is that we're dealing with a 'non-class'. But even the simple specification [− cor] isn't really very good, because the class it specifies – in terms of its POTENTIAL membership – is rather peculiar: palatals, velars, uvulars, pharyngeals, and vowels. One would expect to find the class [+ cor] implicated in some process, since it comprises a number of types with the same active articulator, i.e. its formal simplicity has an empirical interpretation. But [− cor] includes the lower lip, the front and dorsum of the tongue, the tongue root, and even the epiglottis (for pharyngeals). One would be hard put to imagine any process involving this motley collection, or any arbitrary subset of it. This suggests that though the positive and negative values for a given feature may be equally 'simple', their LINGUISTIC CONTENT may be quite different: thus [ + cor] is a natural class both formally (see the definition in §5.2), and in terms of content; but [ − cor] is 'natural' only in the mechanically formal sense. 'Simplicity' (insofar as it equates with 'naturalness') is not merely a matter of feature-counting, but is QUALITATIVE (see §8.6).

Yet despite this, the class labials/velars is a common one. Consider the following, for example:

(i) In Old English, which had the voiced stop system /b d g/, /b g/ had fricative allophones between vowels, but not /d/.

(ii) In the Uralic languages, the class is involved in at least two sound changes: (a) Proto-Uralic initial */p k/ become /f h/ in Hungarian, while */t/ remains unaltered; (b) in Ostyak, intervocalic */p k/ become /w g/ but */t/ remains. (In historical discussions, * signifies a reconstructed item.)

(iii) In Middle Korean, (a) /ɯ/ → /u/ before /m p pʰ k kʰ/; (b) back vowels become front before an /i/ in the following syllable, but only if there is an intervening consonant which is either a labial or a velar.

In the Jakobsonian acoustic framework, unlike the *SPE* articulatory one, labials and velars are an easily specified class: they are [ + grave], i.e. their second formants are closer to the first formant than the third. To put it less technically, they are segments with 'low tonality' – though not precisely the same kind as that described under [ + flat] (§5.1.1). We can see the difference in statement using [ + grave], if we take a labial/velar process in a language that has palatals, like Korean. The rule (iiib) above is given below in two formulations: one using only the *SPE* features, and the other using [ + grave] for the consonantal class:

(5.28)  (a) $\begin{bmatrix} --\text{cons} \\ +\text{back} \end{bmatrix} \rightarrow [-\text{back}]/\underline{\quad} \begin{bmatrix} +\text{cons} \\ -\text{cor} \\ \left\{\begin{matrix} [+\text{ant}] \\ [+\text{back}] \end{matrix}\right\} \end{bmatrix} \begin{bmatrix} -\text{cons} \\ +\text{high} \\ -\text{back} \end{bmatrix}$

(b) $\begin{bmatrix} -\text{cons} \\ +\text{back} \end{bmatrix} \rightarrow [-\text{back}]/\underline{\quad} \begin{bmatrix} +\text{cons} \\ +\text{grave} \end{bmatrix} \begin{bmatrix} -\text{cons} \\ +\text{high} \\ -\text{back} \end{bmatrix}$

The specification of the environment is simpler; but there is still more we can do to make the process look even more natural. In the Jakobsonian system, the acoustic properties that make back consonants [+grave] do the same for back vowels, while front vowels are [−grave]. If we use [±grave] for both the vowels and consonants, then what's going on looks rather different:

(5.29)

$$\begin{bmatrix} -\text{cons} \\ +\text{grave} \end{bmatrix} \rightarrow [-\text{grave}]/\underline{\hspace{2em}} \begin{bmatrix} +\text{cons} \\ +\text{grave} \end{bmatrix} \begin{bmatrix} -\text{cons} \\ -\text{grave} \\ +\text{high} \end{bmatrix}$$

That is: while in both (5.28a) and (5.28b) it is clear that the left-hand vowel is becoming more like the right-hand one (or **assimilating**: see §8.2), in (5.29) the formulation of the rule allows us to observe something new: a constraint against sequences of [+grave] segments. Here a different feature framework actually tells us something quite different about the process we're formalizing; and it is clear that the choice of notation does this, as the information is simply not available in (5.28).

Does this mean that features are more or less freely available, so we can do anything we want to? The answer is no, if we restrict ourselves to definitions of features IN TERMS OF OBSERVABLE PROPERTIES. There is no doubt that we can tell whether a segment is grave or high or whatever; but whether a feature that is based on an observable property deserves a place in the universal inventory is another question. The evidence we've been looking at suggests that [±grave] is indeed such a feature: a measurable or empirically definable property that also happens to be utilized by languages in their assignments of segments to classes.

The moral is that articulatory and acoustic features are both necessary: not surprisingly, since any segment must have both articulatory and acoustic properties. You can't make noises without a physical configuration to produce them, and the noises produced by physical configurations have acoustic properties. The two sets of features are **complementary**, and different languages may apparently use either articulatory or acoustic features (or both) in grouping their segments into classes (or we as linguists may profitably use both in trying to describe what we find in languages). We might suggest that as long as a feature represents a real property – either articulatory or acoustic – it is a candidate for linguistic use as a label for a class of segments. Whether any given potential label actually gets used is a matter for empirical investigation.

## NOTES AND REFERENCES

5.1.1 On the development of feature theory, *Fischer-Jørgensen (1975: ch. 8, ch. 9, §§9.29–37) and her references; two major books are **Jakobson *et al.* (1951), *Jakobson & Halle (1956). For more theoretical discussion, *Halle (1962, 1964), and the critical remarks in McCawley (1967).

   If the notion of retroflection, pharyngealization and rounding having similar properties is obscure, try the following: produce a fairly long [s], and then retroflex it, then pharyngealize it, then round it. In all three cases the perceived pitch of the modified segment will be markedly lower. The Arabic argument is after McCawley (1967).

5.1.2 Redundancy is a highly technical matter, and I won't treat it here in detail. See Harms (1968: ch. 8), *SPE* (ch. 4), and **Stanley (1967). For further discussion, **Brown (1970).

5.3 For details of the first modern articulatory feature system, ***SPE* (ch. 7). For critical discussion and revision (though still in the *SPE* spirit), Lass & Anderson (1975: Preliminaries). For more radical criticism, **Lass (1976a: chs. 1, 6–7), **Brown (1970, 1972).

5.3.1 On 'phonological' or 'functional' definitions of features: in many Scots dialects, to take one case, stops, fricatives, affricates and /r/ devoice finally, but /l/ and nasals don't. Here we could treat /r/ as an obstruent, in which case we have the simple generalization that all obstruents devoice. /r/ also patterns with voiced fricatives, not other sonorants, in causing vowel lengthening (§2.9).

   On (5.11), compare *SPE*:

|             | Obstruents | Nasals | Liquids | Vowels | Glides |
|-------------|:----------:|:------:|:-------:|:------:|:------:|
| Sonorant    | −          | +      | +       | +      | −      |
| Consonantal | +          | +      | +       | −      | −      |
| Vocalic     | −          | −      | +       | +      | −      |

It is worth noting that the whole enterprise of constructing a 'universal phonetic alphabet' is considered by some scholars to be misconceived: see **Sampson (1974).

5.3.2 On the so-called 'neutral position', see *Lass (1976a: ch. 1, Appendix).

5.3.2.3 On [±mid], Wang (1968), Kiparsky (1968b).

5.3.4 On Swedish /ʉ/, Lass (1976a: ch. 2).

5.3.6 The definition of 'nasality' here is phonetically oversimplified, if traditional. See **Laver (1980: §2.3), which considers the possibilities for auditory nasalization without 'nasality' in the usual sense. Phonologically, however, [±nas] can probably stand. On the possibility that languages may use more than one degree of nasality contrastively, Ladefoged (1971: 34f).

5.3.8 The discussion of 'voice' is grossly oversimplified. As correctives **Catford (1977a: ch. 6); and Ladefoged (1971: ch. 2) on glottal states.

5.3.9 On aspiration and timing, Lisker & Abramson (1971). On the 'lenis'/'fortis' problem, Catford (1977a: 111ff).

5.3.10 On 'tenseness', *Lass (1976a: ch. 1, Appendix) and *Catford (1977a: 199ff). Catford and I agree that there is no real evidence for tenseness as a property of vowels, but see **Wood (1975a) for some counter-arguments.

5.4 The formalism sketched here was developed within a particular theoretical model ('generative phonology': see ch. 9), which is a formal theory of (essentially) morphophonemic description. But its conventions are now widely used in other contexts, and have become something of a 'common language'.

5.4.1 The specifications in (5.21) are abbreviated: e.g. I assume that there's no need to specify airstreams other than pulmonic egressive or glottal states other than [±voice] for languages that don't use these parameters distinctively. I also omit universally redundant specifications for vowels like those for [±ant, ±lat], etc.

　　The analysis proposed for German follows the phonetics rather closely, in not taking /iː ɪ/, /uː ʊ/, /oː ɔ/ etc. as 'long and short of the same vowel'. The diphthongs /ae ao ɔʏ/ can be taken as clusters of the component short vowels; if one wanted to notate them as monophonemic, we could use some system like that in §6.4. For consonants I assume phonemic /ŋ/ (but see §9.2), and alveolar /r/.

5.5 On the subject of this section see **Lass (1976a: 197–207), where the arguments sketched here are given in full. See also Lass & Anderson (1975: ch. v), Hyman (1973a), Davidsen-Nielsen & Ørum (1978).

　　Formants are bands of resonance whose position is determined by vocal-tract configuration. For introductory discussion see *Ladefoged (1975: ch. 8). The tonality properties of the consonantal types involved here can be observed by producing long fricatives: try [f θ x] in that order, and note the lower pitch of the labial and velar compared to the dental.

# 6

# 'Ultimate constituents', 2: non-binary features and internal segment structure

## 6.1 The homogeneity assumption

Chapter 5 ended with an implicit question and a negative answer: to the question of whether all phonological features have to be (potentially) articulatory we were drawn to answer no by the existence of natural classes like labials/velars that share no common articulators, but nonetheless ought to be captured in a respectable feature system. This looks like the thin end of a wedge; the way is now open in principle to ask: do all features have to be binary?

Note that questions like this are loaded: why should we ask if ALL features ought to be anything? My own judgement, as §5.4 indicates is that we shouldn't; there's no empirical reason why we should expect the 'best' feature system to be homogeneous, with all features of only one type or another. But there is a kind of *a priori* reason why linguists often want or expect feature systems to be homogeneous, or insist that they're defective if they're not; and this boils down in the end to a matter of aesthetic preference plus philosophical commitment (occasionally masquerading as 'scientific conscience'). The assumption that systems of primitives ought to be formally homogeneous is the result of what I like to call 'the atomic fallacy': the view that – when we get down to a basic enough level – the primitive elements of whatever universe we're concerned with will turn out to be of one type only. (See Plato's notion – put forth in the *Timaeus* – that the ultimate constituents of the world are geometrical forms, or the Pythagorean idea that the ultimate constituents are numbers.) But there is no particular evidence that this ought to be the way we look at things outside of the natural sciences.

This is a difficult and philosophically problematical issue, and a textbook like this is no place to push it very far. But I would be failing in a fairly elementary pedagogical duty if I didn't at least raise it, since it has important implications for the interpretation of theoretical claims. And one of my purposes here is to help the reader become aware of basic methodological issues, as a background for critical reading of the professional literature.

To return to the question of preference: this is not always harmless, because it tends to intersect – for many linguists anyhow, especially those of the Chomskyan persuasion – with matters of 'belief'. Specifically, with what philosophers call **ontology**: the 'status' of theoretical entities, in the particular sense of whether they are presumed to have 'real existence' somewhere in the extratheoretical world, whether physical or mental. The proponents of the two major feature theories (Jakobson and his co-workers, and Chomsky & Halle) start with what might be called a 'cognitive' or 'psychologistic' bias: they assume some kind of direct connection between the constructs of a phonological theory and the units of human linguistic perception (Jakobson) or perception/production (Chomsky & Halle). So that phonological elements have their 'real' existence as basic units of some kind of 'mental structure' (whatever that means: see §§ 9.4–5).

Now if features in a linguistic theory have extralinguistic reference, questions like whether a given set is 'the correct one' are in principle intelligible. (Though of course in our present state of ignorance we can't establish whether this is or isn't the case.) But there's no reason I can see – other than this particular bias – why features should be presumed to have such a reference, why their 'real existence' should lie anywhere outside linguistic theory. Is a feature theory, for instance, a theory of linguistic structure, or a theory of psychology? For linguists like Chomsky, for whom linguistics is 'a branch of cognitive psychology' (1972: 1), the latter is the case; but for others for whom the equation of 'linguistic' with 'psychological' or 'mental' isn't self-evident, there's no obvious reason why a feature theory should be anything but a notational framework that yields satisfactory descriptions, and helps us understand the data we're interested in. For my money, the most sensible position is this: the 'best' system is the one that yields the 'best' descriptions. Assuming, that is, some pre-existing definition of 'best', like 'permitting the most elegant statement of (chosen) generalizations'; or 'giving the greatest coverage of (chosen) phenomena'; or 'yielding the maximum number of (unexpected)

103

further discoveries of structure and relations'; or 'giving the account of the data best fitting in with what we take to be the rest of our established knowledge of relevant matters' – or all of these.

Given that linguistics isn't physics or chemistry or even biology (and that it's only a prejudice that says it ought to be, or even be similar), there's no reason to expect that this 'best' framework – if we ever find it or invent it – will be based on formally homogeneous elements (like cells, protein molecules, elementary particles). Neither is there any reason to believe that the elements in the theory will correspond to things in 'the real world'. The difficulty here is that many linguists would like to have their efforts identified with those of workers in the prestigious 'hard sciences' – even though they are probably engaged in quite a different kind of activity. At the moment, the *a priori* imposition of a condition like formal homogeneity is at least premature and unhelpful – if not arbitrary and unjustifiable. We are still ignorant enough to be constantly surprised by things; we ought not to short-circuit our ability to be surprised by being too rigorous at the beginning; especially by producing theories that are powerful enough to hide their shortcomings by being able to accommodate the data – somehow. At the moment the evidence suggests that we need several complementary kinds of primitives. This chapter outlines some of the arguments.

### 6.2 Dissolving binarity: arguments from vowel height

Even in rigorously binary theories, like that of *SPE*, there is some provision for non-binary elements. These may be actual 'special' features like stress (not treated in *SPE*, ch. 7, which deals only with 'segmental' features), or the lower-level phonetic correlates of the binary features themselves. The second of these possibilities will lead into our arguments here.

Chomsky & Halle suggest that the classificatory binary features ultimately (at the physical level) represent 'poles' of continuous physical scales; at some point in a derivation, 'the phonological rules ... will gradually convert these specifications to integers' (*SPE*: 65). For instance, while an underlying /i/ will be [ +high], it may turn out that allophonically /i/ will be slightly lower before nasals than before voiceless stops. While both instances of /i/ will be systematically ('phonologically') [ +high], at the phonetic level the first might be [3 high] and the second [4 high], or whatever. In their phonetic function, that is, features will be n-ary, not binary; a higher-level (classificatory) specification like [+high] will cover a RANGE of physical values or locations on the height continuum. And there is presumably some cut-off point or 'threshold value', i.e. a place where the continuum of numerical values is segmented, so that say [+high] is no longer appropriate, and [−high] takes over.

Given this possibility, we might ask whether a property like vowel height, for example, isn't better treated from the beginning as a continuum, rather than a set of discrete binary oppositions. And indeed there are generalizations of a fairly obvious kind that can't be comfortably treated in terms of binary height-features.

Here is a case in point. In Middle English (14th century), there was a sound change which is usually called 'lengthening in open syllables'. The input system was:

(6.1)    iː    i    u    uː
         eː    e    o    oː
         ɛː             ɔː
         aː    a

In terms of the features in ch. 5, this may be represented as:

(6.2)

|        | iː | i | eː | e | ɛː | aː | a | uː | u | oː | o | ɔː |
|--------|----|----|----|----|----|----|----|----|----|----|----|----|
| High   | +  | +  | +  | +  | −  | −  | −  | +  | +  | +  | +  | −  |
| Mid    | −  | −  | +  | +  | +  | −  | −  | −  | −  | +  | +  | +  |
| Back   | −  | −  | −  | −  | −  | −  | −  | +  | +  | +  | +  | +  |
| Long   | +  | −  | +  | −  | +  | +  | −  | +  | −  | +  | −  | +  |

What happened was this: in general, a short vowel in the first open syllable of a disyllabic word lengthened; and if it was non-low, it lowered. Thus /i/ → [eː], /e/ → [ɛː], /u/ → [oː], /o/ → [ɔː], but /a/ → [aː]. In terms of (6.2), these changes would be stated as:

(6.3)  (a)  $\begin{bmatrix} V \\ + \text{high} \\ - \text{mid} \\ - \text{long} \end{bmatrix} \rightarrow \begin{bmatrix} + \text{mid} \\ + \text{long} \end{bmatrix} /\#C_0\_\_\_\_CVC_0\#$  (/i u/ → [eː oː])

     (b)  $\begin{bmatrix} V \\ + \text{high} \\ + \text{mid} \\ - \text{long} \end{bmatrix} \rightarrow \begin{bmatrix} - \text{high} \\ + \text{long} \end{bmatrix} /\#C_0\_\_\_\_CVC_0\#$  (/e o/ → [ɛː ɔː])

     (c)  $\begin{bmatrix} V \\ - \text{high} \\ - \text{mid} \\ - \text{long} \end{bmatrix} \rightarrow [+ \text{long}] \quad /\#C_0\_\_\_\_CVC_0\#$  (/a/ → [aː])

105

(Where $C_0$ = 'zero or more consonants'.)

Note the lack of generalization, i.e. the apparent unrelatedness of the SDs of the three subrules of the change.

If we look only at the height alterations, we get:

(6.4)　　　(a)　$\begin{bmatrix} +\text{high} \\ -\text{mid} \end{bmatrix} \rightarrow [+\text{mid}]$

　　　　　(b)　$\begin{bmatrix} +\text{high} \\ +\text{mid} \end{bmatrix} \rightarrow [-\text{high}]$

The rules, that is, do not capture the generalization that is easily stated in an informal prose description (which should of course not be the case). Compare the arbitrary grouping of unrelated changes in (6.3) with:

(6.5)　　　In the environment $\#C_0\_\_\_CVC_0\#$, any non-low vowel LOWERS
　　　　　BY ONE HEIGHT and lengthens; low vowels only lengthen.

This captures the clearly unitary process that can be diagrammed as:

(6.6)　　iː ⟵ i　　　u ⟶ uː
　　　　eː ⟵ e　　　o ⟶ oː
　　　　ɛː ⟵ 　　　　 ⟶ ɔː
　　　　aː ⟵ a

This suggests that the primary parameter is not the individual heights, or the features specifying them, but HEIGHT ITSELF as a scale or continuum. This would allow us to give each height a numerical coefficient:

(6.7)　　i　u　4 | Height
　　　　e　o　3
　　　　ɛ　ɔ　2
　　　　a　ɑ　1 ↓

Feature specifications would then be [4 high], [2 high] etc.; and we could use notations like [n high] $\rightarrow$ [n − 1 high], where n is a **variable** ranging over the values 1–4. This would capture 'lowering by one height' very neatly; open syllable lengthening would now be:

(6.8)　　$\begin{bmatrix} V \\ n\ \text{high} \\ -\text{long} \end{bmatrix} \rightarrow \begin{bmatrix} n-1\ \text{high} \\ +\text{long} \end{bmatrix} / \#C_0\_\_\_CVC_0\#$

We add the condition that no height < 1 exists: thus the fact that /a/ only lengthens and doesn't lower is predicted by a stipulation that

[1 high] is the lowest height; this notational system amounts to a reinterpretation of the notion 'gradual opposition' (§3.2).

A synchronic example of the applicability of this way of looking at height is the diphthongization pattern for long vowels in Malmö Swedish:

(6.9)  /iː/ → [ei]        /yː/ → [øy]        /uː/ → [eu]
       /eː/ → [ɛe]        /øː/ → [œø]        /oː/ → [ɛo]
       /ɛː/ → [æɛ]                           /ɑː/ → [æɑ]

The generalization is clear in a numerical system: in prose, 'insert a vowel to the left of the vowel being diphthongized, one height lower, and front; if the vowel is front rounded, the inserted vowel is rounded; otherwise it is unround'. Since there is nothing below [1 high] /ɑː/ → [æɑ] is predicted in the same way as the ME lengthening /a/ → [aː]. If we interpret the long vowels as clusters /ii yy uu/ etc., the same description applies, except that instead of 'insert a vowel . . .' we have 'lower the first element . . .'.

The same approach could be used for the back/front dimension as well: backness could be taken as (at least) three-valued, so that it would intersect with height like this:

(6.10)
```
              1    2    3     Back
     | 4      i    ɨ    u
     | 3      e
     | 2      ɛ
     ↓ 1      a
     High
```

Evidence for this is harder to come by; I am not aware of any linear shifts where (say) /u/ → [ɨ] and /i/ → [ɨ], but the option should be left open.

## 6.3  Non-binary consonantal features

It is clear that the sequence labial–dental–alveolar–palatal–velar–uvular–pharyngeal could be treated in principle as a numerical continuum, like height or backness; though the motivation for this is not obvious (see however the argument at the end of this section). In a sense this is not unexpected, since we are dealing not just with 'places' on a scale, but with different articulators as well (e.g. the tongue is not involved in labials, only its root in pharyngeals, and so on). But there are cases where the properties of consonants seem to merit treatment, if not in terms of a positional continuum, still in terms of more than two values per feature. I will sketch out some arguments here, based mainly on Ladefoged (1971). The first issue, carefully avoided in §5.3, is the problem of 'r'-types: how do we distinguish taps/flaps from trills, and these from stops?

Ladefoged argues this way: it is important, in setting up a feature system, to be able to indicate 'similarity' or 'relationship' of segment types. For example, we want to state generalizations like: (a) affricates are somewhere 'in between' stops and fricatives (as borne out by historical sequences of the type [k] → [kx] → [x], e.g. in the 'High German Sound Shift': the stages are represented by Dutch /maːkən/, Swiss German /maːkxən/, German /maːxən/ 'to make'; and see §8.3.1). And (b) there are clear relations between trills and taps (older Scots [r], newer [ɾ]) and stops and taps and flaps (see the U.S. English material in §2.8).

Ladefoged proposes to handle these relationships with a set of new features, some binary and some n-ary. First, two binary features [stop] and [fricative], with the possible values [o, 1], defined as follows:

(6.11)

[o stop]: no complete closure
[1 stop]: complete closure
[o fricative]: no turbulence
[1 fricative]: maximum turbulence

Thus stops, affricates and fricatives are:

| (6.12) | | Stop | Affricate | Fricative |
|---|---|---|---|---|
| | [Stop] | 1 | 1 | o |
| | [Fricative] | o | 1 | 1 |

(Note that in Ladefoged's system these features are not sequential in affricates; the fact that the friction is an offset would have to be specified by convention: see §6.4.)

The relation between stops and flaps, and trills and taps, is handled as follows: assume another binary feature, [vibration], where [1 vibration] is the **ballistic** movement associated with trills and taps ('throwing' the tongue against a passive articulator), and [o vibration] is the lack of such movement. Then assume an n-ary feature [rate], defined as a function of the time occupied by a segment. Here we have a positive/negative value-scale: [o rate] is a notional 'normal' value for a segment, positive values are shorter than normal, and negative values longer. This feature can be extended naturally (if necessary) to cover all quantitative phenomena; we can now characterize trill vs. tap as normal vs. overshort, vowel vs. semivowel as normal vs. overshort (though syllabicity might be a better criterion here); and short vowel vs. long vowel as normal vs. overlong. For languages like Estonian, with three degrees of length, we have short vs. long vs. overlong, with the latter two specified as [− 1 rate] and [− 2 rate] respectively, as opposed to the [0 rate] short vowel. (The same of course holds for consonantal length: but see the discussion in §10.3.2ff for an indication that at least in some languages there is a more convincing account of length in terms of segments.)

To clarify, the rate scale will look like this:

(6.13)   + 1 tap, flap, semivowel
     0 stop, trill, short C, short V
    − 1 long C, long V
    − 2 overlong C, overlong V

So for a number of major articulation types, we can specify as follows (using specific symbols for the various types):

(6.14)

|      | j  | i | iː | iːː | ʈ  | ɾ  | r | z | dz | d | dː | dːː |
|------|----|---|----|-----|----|----|---|---|----|---|----|-----|
| Stop | 0  | 0 | 0  | 0   | 1  | 1  | 1 | 0 | 1  | 1 | 1  | 1   |
| Fric | 0  | 0 | 0  | 0   | 0  | 0  | 0 | 1 | 1  | 0 | 0  | 0   |
| Vib  | 0  | 0 | 0  | 0   | 0  | 1  | 1 | 0 | 0  | 0 | 0  | 0   |
| Rate | +1 | 0 | −1 | −2  | +1 | +1 | 0 | 0 | 0  | 0 | −1 | −2  |

([ʈ] is a postalveolar flap, [iːː], [dːː] are overlong.)

This multivalued approach to (some) consonantal features, together with the approach to vowel height in the preceding section, raises another possibility: could vowel height and consonantal stricture perhaps BOTH be taken as values of a single parameter, say [stricture]? This is provoked by the reflection that certain types of vowels and consonants can be said to be 'related' in a natural way. For instance, palatal consonants and close front vowels, velar consonants and close back vowels – as suggested by characteristic changes such as palatal(ized) consonants becoming the second element of [i]-diphthongs through loss of consonantal articulation, and velar(ized) consonants becoming in the same way the second elements of [u]-diphthongs. (For example in forms like [mɪiən] 'million', [mɪuk] 'milk' in many U.S. dialects, where [ɪi] is from [ɪl] and [ɪu] is from [ɪɫ].)

109

So we could assume a feature [stricture], which in combination with features for place of articulation would yield vowels as the opener members of a continuous series, from stops as the closest to low vowels as the openest. Considering processes like those cited above, we might suggest these scales:

(6.15)

| | Palatal | | Velar | |
|---|---|---|---|---|
| ⋀6 | ᴊ | | g | 6 ⋀ |
| 5 | j | | ɣ | 5 |
| 4 | i | | u | 4 |
| 3 | e | | o | 3 |
| 2 | ɛ | | ɔ | 2 |
| I | a | | ɑ | I |

Other places of articulation can be brought into the picture as well: for central vowels we might define place as 'palato-velar' (the result of raising [ɨ] is an advanced velar fricative [ɣ̟] ). The difficulty here is that languages don't, in general, seem to use palato-velar as a distinctive point of articulation for consonants (although many U.S. dialects have a palato-velar /r/).

We can also add uvular and pharyngeal to the places, and get a more accurate (if complex) schema like this:

(6.16)

| | Palatal | | | Palato-Velar | | | Velar | | | | | | | |
|---|---|---|---|---|---|---|---|---|---|---|---|---|---|---|
| | 6 | ᴊ ⋀ | | 6 | g̟ ⋀ | | 6 | g ⋀ | | | | | | |
| | 5 | j | | 5 | ɣ̟ | | 5 | ɣ | | | | | | |
| | 4 | i | | 4 | ɨ | | 4 | u | | | | | | |
| | 3 | e | | 3 | ɘ | | 3 | o | ɔ | ʁ | G | | | |
| | 2 | ɛ | | 2 | ɛ | | | | 4 | 5 | 6 | *Uvular* | | |
| | I | a | | I | ɐ | | | ɑ | ʕ | | | | | |
| | | 2 | | | 3 | | | | 4 | 5 | *Pharyngeal* | | | |

( [ɘ] is specifically a half-close central vowel, not the 'generalized' **schwa** [ə]; there is no pharyngeal stop, as these seem not to exist.) Since open vowels (even [a æ]) usually involve pharyngeal constriction, we might take [a] as 'palato-pharyngeal', and include it in both classes.

Something like (6.16) is complementary to an analysis in terms of [high] as a uniquely vocalic dimension (as in (6.7)); it has its uses in describing relations more naturally stated in terms of consonant/ vowel relations than heights alone. For [uvular] and [pharyngeal] we could instance the characteristic replacement of [ə] by [ɔ] before [ʁ] in Tyneside English, e.g. in [feːðɔʁ] 'father', as well as the equally typical [ɔ:(ʁ) ] in *first, fern, work,* which more often have [ɜ:] in other English dialects. These could be taken as shifts from palato-velar to uvular before uvulars. Similarly, the historical change from [æ] to [ɑ] before a pharyngealized /r/ in U.S. English can be taken as a shift from palatal to pharyngeal before a pharyngeal ( [æ] cannot appear before /r/ in the same syllable: [æ] in *cat, mat,* but [ɑ(:) ] in *cart, mart:* all with 17th-century [æ] ).

These proposals are very preliminary; they merely suggest what kinds of generalizations can emerge from different ways of thinking about the componential make-up of segments. But it is clear that there is a germ of something interesting and phonologically relevant in (6.16), and that as it stands it's exceedingly crude. There's a lot more work needed before we know it's going to be fruitful.

### 6.4 Internal segment structure, 1: sequential values

Recall the argument in §2.6, where we adduced evidence for analysing English affricates as units rather than clusters. And recall as well Ladefoged's features [stop] and [fricative], and their possible relevance to the specification of affricates (§6.3). In the feature system outlined in §5.3, we could handle affricates as either stops marked [ + del rel], or (in English) [ + strid]; in Ladefoged's system they would be [1 stop, 1 fricative]. In *SPE,* the relationship between the stop and fricative portions is given by definition in the term 'release'. If either [+strid] or Ladefoged's analysis is used, we need some sequential information: which end of the affricate does the stridency/turbulence come on?

The problem may be a bit clearer if we consider the two sets of representations below:

(6.17)          [ɬ]                                    [tʃ]

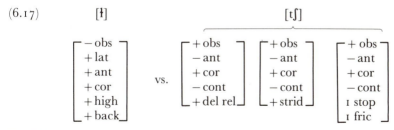

For [ɬ], all the specifications are temporally unambiguous (primary vs. secondary stricture, both simultaneous); for [tʃ], at least one of the specifications must mean '[ʃ] – but after [t]'. Though only the name of the feature in the [+del rel] matrix even suggests this. In the other two matrices there is no information about where the [+strid] or [1 fric] specification ought to go – before or after the stop. Thus this kind of representation makes the (false) claim that release features and secondary strictures are the same kind of animal.

So the 'complexity' of complex segments can be two kinds: simultaneous (in the case of secondary articulations) and sequential (in the case of offsets – and onsets and middles – as we'll see below). The general point is that it may be necessary to specify not only feature-COMPOSITION, but feature-SEQUENCE as well: a single segment might be looked on, in certain cases, as having more than one value for a single feature.

There is a clear example of the need for this kind of treatment in Icelandic. Here there is a general constraint on vowel length: vowels are long before single consonants or finally, and (with certain exceptions that don't concern us here) short before long consonants and clusters. This is no problem for ordinary short and long vowels; but the same conditions apply to diphthongs as well. Now if it were the case that – as in English generally – diphthongs in 'long' or 'short' environments had the length assigned to ONE element, things would be straightforward. But in Icelandic we get short diphthongs where the two elements together more or less equal one short vowel in length, and long diphthongs where both elements together more or less equal one long vowel. The situation can be diagrammed this way (where the subscripts i, j indicate differing vowels):

(6.18)  Short vowel $\underline{\quad V_i \quad}$   Long vowel $\underline{\quad V_i \mid V_i \quad}$

Short diphthong $\underline{\quad V_i \mid V_j \quad}$ Long diphthong $\underline{\quad V_i \mid V_j \quad}$

Comparing long and short diphthongs we get:

(6.19)   $\underline{\quad V_i \quad \mid \quad V_j \quad}$
   $\underline{\quad V_i \mid V_j \mid}$

This suggests that in Icelandic short vowels as well as long vowels must be of two types: those where (for a given time span) the feature specifications remain stable, and those where they shift. Thus the traditional transcriptions are misleading: the common and neuter forms of *læs* 'literate' are usually given as [lai:s] and [laist], but the length is not in fact on the [i]. In this case, a more accurate representation of the /ai/ diphthongs would be:

(6.20)

$$
\text{Short} \qquad\qquad \text{Long}
$$

$$
\begin{bmatrix} -\text{cons} \\ -\text{back} \\ +\text{low} \; +\text{high} \\ \text{o rate} \end{bmatrix} \qquad \begin{bmatrix} -\text{cons} \\ -\text{back} \\ +\text{low} \; +\text{high} \\ -\text{1 rate} \end{bmatrix}
$$

That is, with two contradictory (but sequential) specifications. (See further §§10.3.2–4.) A similar treatment would work with [±continuant] or [stop] and [fricative] for affricates.

A final piece of evidence in favour of sequential features rather than features specifying (say) mode of release comes from some data analysed by Anderson (1976). Anderson shows that there exist in natural languages at least five types of stop, differentially specifiable with respect to nasality. That is: (a) oral stops; (b) prenasalized oral stops (i.e. with a nasal onset); (c) medionasalized stops (i.e. with a nasal onset and offset, and a non-nasal stretch in between); (d) postnasalized stops (nasal offset); and (e) fully nasal stops (i.e. what we normally call ('nasals'). The point about the three middle types is that languages can apparently be found in which each one patterns not as a cluster but as a single segment.

Anderson's material suggests the need for sequential specifications for [±nasal] within the segment: the possibility arises then of not only [+nas] and [−nas], but [+nas/−nas], [−nas/+nas], and even [−nas/+nas/−nas]. This is clearly superior to a set of features like [prenasal], [postnasal], etc., since what is at issue is not 'different features', but 'facts about intra-segmental timing and structure' (Anderson: p. 33). There is one parameter [nasal], which can shift values within the segment.

## 6.5 **Internal segment structure, 2: the concept of 'gesture'**

As we have seen repeatedly, one goal of any phonological formalism is to specify explicitly and in a 'natural' way – within a given theoretical framework – what would otherwise merely be intuitive generalizations. The term 'natural' can be overused; but the sense I intend here is 'without strain' (i.e. over-complication or 'ad-hockery'), and as close as possible to simple derivation from phonetic properties (see §8.6).

We have assumed that even though there is some kind of classificatory feature hierarchy (e.g. [±obs], [±cons] are 'higher-order' and more general than [±back], [±round]), segments are unstructured collections or 'bundles' of features. The first difficulty for this view appeared in §6.4, when we saw that features may be sequentially ordered within segments. Now we will see that there can be simultaneous as well as sequential structuring.

Consider the interchange of voiceless stops and [ʔ] in English (see §2.7). In many varieties of Scots, the glottal-stop rule works roughly like this: /p t k/ → [ʔ] after a stressed vowel (with an optional intervening nasal or liquid), before an unstressed vowel, a syllabic nasal, or a word boundary:

(6.21)  käʔ     'cap'    kɑːrʔrëdʒ   'cartridge'   oʔm     'open'
        bäʔ     'bat'    wɛnʔʌr      'winter'      bʌʔn̩    'button'
        bäʔ     'back'   fʌɫʔʌr      'filter'      broʔŋ̩   'broken'

The rule might be written like this:

(6.22)

$$
\begin{bmatrix} +\text{obs} \\ +\text{oral} \\ -\text{cont} \\ -\text{voice} \end{bmatrix} \rightarrow [-\text{oral}]/ \begin{bmatrix} V \\ +\text{stress} \end{bmatrix} \left( \begin{bmatrix} C \\ -\text{obs} \end{bmatrix} \right) - \left\{ \begin{matrix} \begin{bmatrix} \# \\ V \\ -\text{stress} \end{bmatrix} \\ \begin{bmatrix} C \\ +\text{nas} \\ +\text{syll} \end{bmatrix} \end{matrix} \right\}
$$

(An item in ( ) is optional: see §8.5).

But is this adequate? In particular, why don't segments other than /p t k/ participate? The answer involves an argument from four directions:

(i) There is another (lexically restricted) substitution rule in these dialects, involving [+oral] → [−oral]: /θ/ → [h] in certain positions, as in [hãŋks] 'thanks', [aˑe hẽŋk] 'I think', [evrehẽŋ] 'everything'.

(ii) Postvocalic voiceless stops are often glottalized, i.e. [kaʔt] ∼ [kaʔ] ∼ [katʰ].

(iii) The segments substituted for by [ʔ] are voiceless stops, and the one substituted for by [h] is a voiceless fricative.

(iv) In order to produce [h], the glottis must be open; for [ʔ] it must be closed. In summary, [+oral] voiceless stops are replaced by a (the only, as it happens) [−oral] voiceless stop, and the same for the replaced voiceless fricative. (Some phoneticians reserve 'voiceless' for just those segments with an open glottis, but this is unhelpful; if there is no periodic vocal fold vibration, we can define the acoustic effect as voicelessness.)

Another description of this is that replacement or substitution involves DELETION of all articulation above the glottis, with only a laryngeal 'basic type' remaining, i.e. the **maximally undifferentiated** voiceless stop and fricative, respectively. We might imagine the structure of say /p/ and /θ/ as:

(6.23)

$$
\begin{array}{ccc}
 & /p/ & /θ/ \\
\text{Supraglottal} & \begin{bmatrix} [p] \\ [ʔ] \end{bmatrix} & \begin{bmatrix} [θ] \\ [h] \end{bmatrix} \\
\text{Laryngeal} & &
\end{array}
$$

Or, in terms of features:

(6.24)

$$
\begin{array}{cc}
 & /p/ \\
\text{Supraglottal} & \left[ \begin{array}{l} +\,\text{ant} \\ -\,\text{cor} \\ -\,\text{cont} \\ \left[ \begin{array}{l} -\,\text{cont} \\ -\,\text{voice} \end{array} \right] \end{array} \right] \\
\text{Laryngeal} &
\end{array}
\qquad
\begin{array}{c}
/θ/ \\
\left[ \begin{array}{l} +\,\text{ant} \\ +\,\text{cor} \\ +\,\text{cont} \\ \left[ \begin{array}{l} +\,\text{cont} \\ -\,\text{voice} \end{array} \right] \end{array} \right]
\end{array}
$$

This puts the values for [±voice] in a 'laryngeal gesture' that necessarily accompanies all pulmonic egressive, and glottalic egressive and ingressive segments (the larynx – strictly speaking – is irrelevant for velaric ingressives).

Let us say then that any segment is a hierarchized set of **submatrices** (partial matrices, or matrices within matrices), comprising at least an **oral gesture** and a **laryngeal gesture**. The first contains all supraglottal specifications (place, manner, etc.), and the second is mainly phonation. Each submatrix is an independent whole, capable of being acted on independently by rules. Assuming representations like (6.24), the /p t k/ → [ʔ] or /θ/ → [h] rules consist, not in a switching of values for [±oral], but in deletion of the entire oral (or articulatory) gesture. If a segment is

(6.25)

$$
\begin{bmatrix} [\text{oral}] \\ [\text{laryn}] \end{bmatrix}
$$

then a rule deleting the oral submatrix would have the effect:

(6.26)

$$
\begin{bmatrix} [\text{oral}] \\ [\text{laryn}] \end{bmatrix} \rightarrow \begin{bmatrix} \varnothing \\ [\text{laryn}] \end{bmatrix}
$$

This general schema would apply to both the Scots rules: the format and processes are the same, the variables being the articulatory content of [oral], and the continuancy specification of [laryn] – plus of course the context. One thing to note, however, is that if (6.25) represents a 'full' or 'normal' segment, the result of (6.26) is **defective**: this formalizes the special status of [− oral] segments, which we will return to in §8.3.1.

As it stands, this is a rather blunt weapon; more independent gestures undoubtedly need to be specified, e.g. for initiating airstreams, and the like (see ch. 11). But there is a descriptive gain in assuming that segments have at least this much structure.

One more example will illustrate the different kinds of generalization this approach allows, as well as introducing an important formalism. Recall the Kannaḍa nasals (§3.3): the only nasal + stop clusters in Kannaḍa are homorganic, i.e. [mp mb], [nt nd], etc. If we assume that the specification of nasals before stops consists essentially in the 'filling-in' of blank specifications in an archisegment marked only [+ nas], we could formulate the following set of rules:

$$(6.27) \quad \text{(a)} \ [+\text{nas}] \rightarrow \begin{bmatrix} +\text{ant} \\ -\text{cor} \\ -\text{back} \end{bmatrix} / \_\_\_ \begin{bmatrix} +\text{obs} \\ +\text{ant} \\ -\text{cor} \\ -\text{back} \end{bmatrix}$$

$$\text{(b)} \ [+\text{nas}] \rightarrow \begin{bmatrix} +\text{ant} \\ +\text{cor} \\ -\text{back} \end{bmatrix} / \_\_\_ \begin{bmatrix} +\text{obs} \\ +\text{ant} \\ +\text{cor} \\ -\text{back} \end{bmatrix}$$

$$\text{(c)} \ [+\text{nas}] \rightarrow \begin{bmatrix} -\text{ant} \\ +\text{cor} \\ -\text{back} \end{bmatrix} / \_\_\_ \begin{bmatrix} +\text{obs} \\ -\text{ant} \\ +\text{cor} \\ -\text{back} \end{bmatrix}$$

$$\text{(d)} \ [+\text{nas}] \rightarrow \begin{bmatrix} -\text{ant} \\ -\text{cor} \\ -\text{back} \end{bmatrix} / \_\_\_ \begin{bmatrix} +\text{obs} \\ -\text{ant} \\ -\text{cor} \\ -\text{back} \end{bmatrix}$$

$$\text{(e)} \ [+\text{nas}] \rightarrow \begin{bmatrix} -\text{ant} \\ -\text{cor} \\ +\text{back} \end{bmatrix} / \_\_\_ \begin{bmatrix} +\text{obs} \\ -\text{ant} \\ -\text{cor} \\ +\text{back} \end{bmatrix}$$

But a careful inspection of (6.27) shows that while the formalization is correct, it misses a generalization: what counts is the ABSOLUTE MATCHING of all features other than [±obs], [±nas]. That is, the coefficients for [±ant, ±cor, ±back] (and we could add [±distrib, ±high, ...]) are the same in the SD and SC of the rule. We are dealing with **feature agreement**. The standard notation for this involves so-called **Greek-letter variables** – early letters of the Greek alphabet used as variable coefficients, i.e. ranging over the values '+', '–' for any feature. Thus a variable in one part of a rule stands for a value matched elsewhere; variables always come in pairs.

Using the variables α, β, γ, etc., we can collapse the set of rules in (6.27) into one abbreviated schema:

$$(6.28) \qquad [+ \text{nas}] \rightarrow \left\{ \begin{bmatrix} \alpha \text{ ant} \\ \beta \text{ cor} \\ \gamma \text{ back} \end{bmatrix} \right. / \underline{\qquad} \begin{bmatrix} + \text{obs} \\ \alpha \text{ ant} \\ \beta \text{ cor} \\ \gamma \text{ back} \end{bmatrix}$$

(where [α ant] ... [α ant] stands for [+ ant] ... [+ ant] or [– ant] ... [– ant] etc.).

But stating the rule in this (standard) way, we still miss an important point. Homorganicity is not about PAIRWISE feature agreements, but about identity of articulation for segments AS WHOLES. We can capture this by extending the formalism so that a variable can range over not a feature but a whole submatrix, covering any combination of feature values within it – so long as they agree with those of some other whole submatrix in the rule, covered by the same variable. We can also indicate disagreeing features within the submatrix, as we did in (6.28), by differential specifications for [±nas], etc.

We use a variable standing outside the submatrix brackets, so that the general formula for a homorganic stop + nasal cluster is:

$$(6.29) \qquad \begin{bmatrix} \alpha \begin{bmatrix} \text{oral} \\ + \text{nas} \end{bmatrix} \end{bmatrix} \quad \begin{bmatrix} \alpha \begin{bmatrix} \text{oral} \\ - \text{nas} \\ - \text{cont} \end{bmatrix} \end{bmatrix}$$

Here the [laryn] submatrix is unspecified, since the value for voice is irrelevant.

Building this kind of notation into phonological rules, we can restate the Kannaḍa homorganicity condition as:

$$(6.30) \qquad [+\text{nas}] \rightarrow [\alpha[\text{oral}]] / \underline{\qquad} \begin{bmatrix} \alpha \begin{bmatrix} \text{oral} \\ - \text{nas} \\ - \text{cont} \end{bmatrix} \end{bmatrix}$$

This further predicts – as a formulation specifying place features does not – that if some new type of stop were to arise, by historical change, this too would automatically produce the appropriate nasal to go with it. (6.30) thus serves as a generalized schema or **metarule** (rule-controlling rule) for this TYPE of process, of which individual language-specific conditions can be seen as exponents. (For yet another inter-pretation, see §10.2.1.)

### 6.6 **A problem: auditory/articulatory asymmetry in vowels**

Let us reconsider the status of the traditional terms for vowel characterization, like 'high', 'mid', 'back', etc. The usual assumption is that these are (roughly) names for points on physical (articulatory) scales; I have been assuming this all along, e.g. in the treatments of height and backness in §§5.3 and 6.2. But a serious and interesting problem arises from the often striking asymmetry between auditory perception and articulatory behaviour, which suggests we have been oversimplifying. The usual display of the 'vowel space', and the auditory judgements we make (or are trained to make) about it, often do not correspond to articulation.

The standard characterization of vowel height, for instance, rests on a notional location of 'maximum stricture' or 'highest point of the tongue' at some place on the front/back axis: and the well known and indispensable system of Cardinal Vowels is based on the idea of 'auditorily equidistant' vowel qualities being mapped on to (supposedly) physically equidistant points in articulatory space. Thus the standard display below is assumed to 'represent tongue height':

(6.31)  i   u
       e   o
       ɛ   ɔ
       a   ɑ

The 'rectangular' arrangement is obviously idealized: the 'vowel space' is not really this shape. But even if we were to tilt and deform (6.31) to make it closer to the actual shape, it would still not correspond very well to articulatory facts. Consider for instance the locations of maximal strictures in a set of X-rays of the Cardinal Vowels as shown in (6.32).

(6.32)

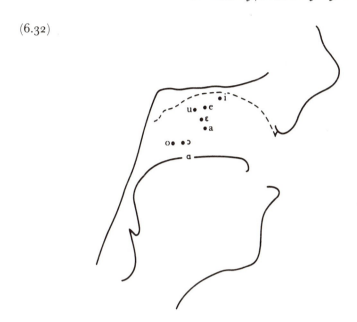

The auditory impression does not match the articulation: while the front series [i e ɛ a] is not too bad, the back series seems wildly out of order, with a large gap between [u] and [o], much larger than that between [ɔ] and [ɑ]; and worse, with the 'half-close' [o] just a bit OPENER than the 'half-open' [ɔ], and so on. Yet nobody hearing the recording that represents the auditory side of this data would have any doubt about a 'descending' scale of vowels in the back series.

If we look at some data from X-rays of vowel heights in different languages, we find the following correlations (after Lindau *et al.* 1972):

(6.33)

| Akan | Ateso | German |
|------|-------|--------|
| i | i u | i |
| ɪ | ɪ | ɪ e |
| u | ʊ | ɛ |
| o ʊ | o | o |
| e ɛ ɔ | e ɔ | ɔ |
| | ɛ | ʊ |

(These represent, of course, RELATIVE positions; for a more detailed matching see Lindau 1975: 5.)

Of the three languages, only Akan shows anything like the expected correlations of tongue height and quality; the others are strikingly out of line.

119

To make things worse, even different speakers of the same language will show gross dissimilarities of tongue height for what are auditorily 'the same' vowels. A study by Ladefoged *et al.* (1972) for instance, examining the vowels /ɪ ɛ æ/ in English, showed the following possible relative tongue heights:

| (6.34) | Relative height of | ɪ | ɪ | ɛ | ɪ, æ |
|---|---|---|---|---|---|
| | maximal stricture | ɛ | ɛ, æ | æ | ɛ |
| | | æ | ɪ | | |

(Abstracted from diagrams in Lindau 1975: 6.)

This kind of data leads Lindau to suggest (1975: 4) 'that a speaker has several possible gestures available for producing a certain point in a basic vowel space, and ... different speakers ... make use of all available mechanisms to achieve the same acoustic result'.

The problem is rather similar with backness (see the X-ray tracings in (6.32)). Here again there does not seem to be a very good correlation between location of maximal stricture and perceived auditory quality.

Interestingly, however, treating the problem ACOUSTICALLY gives results much more like the traditional ARTICULATORY diagram. If we define 'height' in terms of the first formant ($F_1$) of a vowel, and 'backness' as the difference between the values of the second and first formants ($F_2 - F_1$), the vowels arrange themselves in a figure that looks quite like the familiar 'vowel quadrilateral', with a front-to-back slope for the front vowels, and a relatively vertical high-to-low line in back vowels. Compare the idealized quadrilateral (6.35a) with a figure produced by graphing $F_1$ against $F_2 - F_1$ (6.35b).

(6.35)

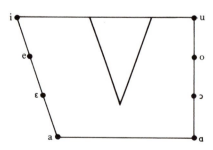

(a) Traditional vowel quadrilateral

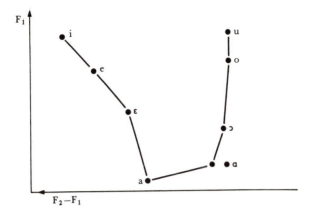

(b) Plot of $F_1$ against $F_2 - F_1$

What are we to make of this? Should we discard the notions 'height' and 'backness'? The answer is clearly no, since these parameters – or whatever corresponds to them – are phonologically relevant, even if phonetically problematical. Obviously the closer phonology is to its phonetic base the better, since this discourages irresponsible idealization, and manipulation of symbols as if they were entirely abstract units, rather than phonetic objects. But phonology can and does operate, apparently, in a rather 'abstract' way at times; at least in the sense of imposing on its material an organization that is neither simple nor articulatorily transparent.

I don't believe that in the end there are really any totally non-phonetic parameters in phonology; only 'phonetic' is a complex notion, involving at least articulation and perception. There is at any rate no doubt that it makes sense to talk of classes like 'high vowels', 'back vowels', etc., and that these labels correspond to at least partly articulatory properties. And whatever they are, processes and classifications in natural languages continually and unproblematically operate in terms of them. (See §6.2 and the discussion of the English Vowel Shift in §7.2.)

What we seem to be dealing with is **multi-parametric** concepts, with a 'pseudo-articulatory' space, or an acoustic, a perceptual, and an articulatory space, with intersecting definitions. This should not be a cause for despair: the concepts, however complex and opaque at the moment, are still workable. But it should make us realize how dimly understood the 'phonetic basis' of phonology is, and that it has both perceptual/articulatory and (apparently) purely 'linguistic' organizing principles. For vowel height, the Jakobsonian ideas seem righter in some ways than *SPE*; but once again the crucial thing is COMPLEMENTARITY.

## NOTES AND REFERENCES

6.1 For detailed discussion of the issues raised here, Lass (1976a: ch. 7).

6.2 For full details of the analysis here, Lass (1974). Standard accounts may be found in any history of English or ME grammar. The changes in (6.3) may be examplified by: /wikə/ → [weːkə] 'week', /metə/ → [mɛːtə] 'meat', /durə/ → /[doːrə] 'door', /nozə/ → [nɔːzə] 'nose', /samə/ → [saːmə] 'same'. The modern pronunciations result from loss of [ə] and a set of changes called the Great Vowel Shift (§7.2).

On notations of the type $C_0$, etc. Any notation $S_m^n$ = 'not less than m or more than n segments'. An unspecified upper limit = 'as many as can occur in the language in this structure', an unspecified lower limit = 'at least one'. If both are unspecified, 'one and only one'. So $C_2^4$ = 'at least two and no more than four consonants', etc. This is an abbreviatory notation or **schema** that can collapse any number of rules: $X → Y/\_\_\_\_ C^2$ collapses $X → Y\_\_\_\_ CC, X → Y/\_\_\_\_ C$.

Rule (6.8): note that this too is an abbreviated schema: [4 high] → [3 high], [3 high] → [2 high], [1 high] → [1 high]. As formulated, it allows for [2 high] → [1 high] as well; but since there are no /ɛ ɔ/ this subrule applies vacuously, i.e. it is simply a language-specific fact that [2 high] for short vowels is 'unoccupied' in ME (see §7.2 on the notion 'occupied slot'). But the formulation includes the (reasonable) 'prediction' that if ME had /ɛ ɔ/, these would have lowered as well.

Another general problem: there is a question whether the numerical labels stand for 'definite points', or 'moveable' (language-specifically variable) ones. Thus in a language whose lowest vowel is the not fully open /æ/, should this be [1 high]? It may be relevant that (as far as I know) no language has the contrast /a/ : /æ/. Perhaps a label like [1 high] should mean 'lowest V in the system – within a specified range', i.e. /æ/ is all right as [1 high], but if /ɛ/ is the lowest it's [2 high].

On the argument of §6.2 in general: claiming that SOME features aren't binary doesn't mean that ALL aren't. Features like laterality or velaric suction may never need to be anything but binary at the phonological level: though all features at the detailed phonetic level probably require n-ary values.

6.3 For the arguments see Ladefoged (1971: 55ff). There is a problem in Ladefoged's groupings flap/stop, tap/trill, with no tap/stop relation. He assumes that in U.S. English one usually gets a flap for intervocalic /t d/, thus relating flaps by rate to stops. But in my own dialect, and many others, the result here is a tap; and similarly, intervocalic /t/ in RP is often a voiceless tap [t̥]. The relationship is thus more complex, and both taps and flaps ought to be naturally derivable from stops. (I don't know whether there are any clear trill/flap relations that would make the whole thing symmetrical.)

On (6.16): for a similar proposal see Catford (1977a: 184f). For a more sophisticated theory of vowels as having places of articulation, **Wood (1974, 1979). The difficulty in (6.16) is partly notational, partly theoretical – at least insofar as notations can be said to embody theoretical claims. That is, we could counter the temporal ambiguity in [tʃ] by *ad hoc* conditions, like '[+strid] on a stop = stridency on release'. But this is indirect, and misses the point that affricates – whether strident or not – are a special kind of distinctive segment.

6.4 The Icelandic material should be contrasted with the situation in my variety of English, where /äi/ is short before /p t k/ and long before /b d g/ (*right* vs. *ride*, etc.), phonetically [äɪ] vs. [ɑ˙ɪ̟]. The first element lengthens, but the second remains short.

Further to Anderson's analysis of nasality, see the discussion of the converse – features 'spreading' over more than one segment – in §§10.2ff.

6.5 The basic arguments behind this section were sketched in Lass & Anderson (1975: Appendix II), and worked out in detail in **Lass (1976a: ch. 6). For further developments of the concept of 'gesture' see §§11.4–6.

The Scots [ʔ]-rule is simplified here; one important set of controls is omitted. While /p t k/ all → [ʔ] finally or before a syllabic nasal, only /t/ commonly does intervocalically – [ʌʔʌr] 'upper' is much rarer than [bʌʔʌr] 'butter' – and /k/ is more frequently involved than /p/, but less so than /t/. On this kind of variation see §12.4. Rule (6.22) is low-level phonetic, depending on a rule 'creating' syllabic nasals (these are derived, not underlying, as there are variants [opʌn], etc.). For discussion of ordering relations in a similar rule sequence in another variety of English, see §12.3.

On variables, Harms (1968: ch. 7), *SPE* (pp. 350ff). Specification of different features with different variables allows them either to agree or disagree within the segment. Thus [α ant, β cor, γ back] stands for any combination of values. If a segment were marked [α ant, α cor], however, this would mean 'agreeing in anterior and coronal', i.e. [+ant, +cor] or [−ant, −cor]. For **feature disagreement** we prefix a '−' to the variable: [α ant, −α cor] = [+ant, −cor] or [−ant, +cor]. On the concept 'metarule' Lass (1976a: ch. 2).

6.6 This section digests a considerable amount of literature. The relation of tongue-shape to vowel-quality is a long-standing problem; for the history and critical remarks on the 'tongue-arching model' see **Wood (1975b). Other important studies are Ladefoged *et al.* (1972), Lindau (1975), and **Wood (1974, 1979). The X-ray tracing is after Ladefoged (1975: 98); the dotted line is a conjectural restoration of parts of the vocal tract unclear in the originals, which are in S. Jones (1929). For further discussions of 'height' and 'backness' see Ladefoged (1971: ch. 8), Catford (1977a: ch. 9). It's worth noting that most auditory/ articulatory parameters are more complex than they seem, even simple ones like 'rounding': some RP speakers, for instance, produce a vowel of unmistakeable [ɒ]-quality in *hot*, etc. with neutral or spread lips. The effect here is produced by a hollowing or **sulcalization** of the tongue-body.

# 7
# Phonological systems

## 7.1  The status of systems

One justification for having a construct in a theory is 'instrumental': if the desired generalizations can be stated better with it than without it, this is a *prima facie* (but criticizable and provisional) justification. So if some phenomenon P seems inexplicable without a construct C; and if C is not implausible or impossible with respect to the rest of our reasonably well-established knowledge (or better, follows from it); then there is a case for C as a provisional theoretical term. Even better: if C allows us to predict some further phenomena P', P'', or proves applicable to phenomena it was not devised for, this gives it further substance. But the argument from inexplicability alone isn't compelling; it's the quality of the explication that counts.

We have mentioned systems without defining them or establishing their theoretical status. Simplistically, it's obvious that given notions like 'phoneme', 'distinctiveness', etc. one must conclude that languages have segment-inventories, phonological and phonetic. The question is whether these *de facto* inventories are mere trivial lists, or (a) whether they have general, cross-linguistically definable properties (can any old assembly of segments be a system?), (b) whether they have any internal structure, and (c) whether they function as wholes in any interesting way.

There are two basic approaches to these matters, leading to rather different uses of 'system'. One is descriptive or **typological**: do (phonemic) segment-inventories fall into reasonably natural types, and is there anything interesting to say about languages from this point of view? One offshoot of this is the area characterized as the study of **universals** (§§7.4ff); are there 'laws' governing the content and/or structure of phonological systems?

The second is the 'dynamic' or 'process' approach: are there phenomena best stated (or apparently only statable) in terms of systems-as-wholes (ideally, derivable from them) – rather than in terms of rules acting on mere units not 'embedded' in a larger structure?

I begin with some arguments designed to show that (at least some types of) systems have interesting properties that do not derive merely from the elements they happen to contain, but from the structures the elements occur in, and conditions on the whole. With this basis, we can proceed to a typological overview of phonological systems, not exhaustive, but sufficient to give an idea of what kinds occur and the constraints on their composition.

### 7.2 **The English Vowel Shift: the argument from non-participation**

One of the major events in the history of English is the so-called 'Great Vowel Shift' (GVS) – a radical transformation of the long-vowel system that began in the 15th century. Its overall effects were:

(7.1)

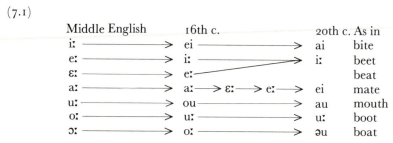

The part of this complex development that concerns us is the ME → 16th century transition. It is clear from the values in (7.1) that what happened, overall, was this:

(7.2)

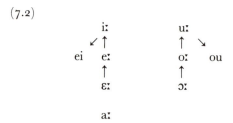

That is, non-low long vowels raise one height; high vowels diphthongize.

126

This can be seen as a **chain**: a series of changes each of which in some way entails the next. Assuming the propriety of describing (7.2) this way, there are two possible chain-interpretations. One, that the high vowels diphthongize, leaving 'empty slots', and the half-close ones 'move up' into the vacated positions, leaving slots behind them, which the half-open ones move up to fill:

(7.3)

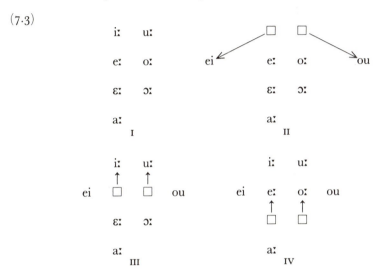

This is called a **drag chain**.

Alternatively, retaining the chain metaphor, we could have the movement begin from below, each vowel 'pushing' the next one up out of place. The high vowels, having no higher height to raise to, diphthongize. This is a **push chain**, and can be visualized by reading (7.2) from /ɛː ɔː/ up. Here there are no empty slots, but a uniform chain progression, each raising entailing the one above. (Otherwise one vowel would merge with the next higher.)

Still a third possibility is that there was a mixture: say a push chain beginning with /eː oː/, and then a drag chain involving /ɛː ɔː/. For reasons not relevant here, no one has seriously entertained the push chain alone; the serious competitors have been either an overall drag chain or a push/drag mechanism starting with the half-close vowels. The problem is that the historical evidence itself does not tell us what the sequence was.

But there is a solution, with interesting theoretical implications. It

127

hinges on range of data: one solution accounts neatly for an important discontinuity in the English dialect picture, and the other doesn't. The discontinuity is this: the most local forms of English descending from northern Middle English have one feature in common: ME /uː/ does not diphthongize. These dialects typically have [uː] in *house*, *mouth* etc. in England, and [u] or a fronted variant in Scotland.

Consider some typical **reflexes** (historical developments) of four of the ME long vowels in northern and non-northern dialect types:

| | Northern: Lowick, Northumber- | Northern: Morebattle, Roxburgh- | Southern: |
|---|---|---|---|
| ME | land | shire | RP |
| iː | ε̆ɪ | ε̆i | aɪ |
| eː | iː | i | iː |
| uː | uː | u | aʊ |
| oː | iː | ø | uː |

(7.4)

An interesting implicational relation is apparent here (and is borne out by further data): any dialect that has an undiphthongized ME /uː/ has a front reflex of ME /oː/. Why should this be, and what does it mean?

The answer involves a connection between the GVS and another well-known change. In the ME dialects ancestral to modern northern English, in the 14th century, /oː/ fronted to /øː/ (later raised to /yː/ in England, hence modern /iː/). The effect can be seen by comparing the systems before and after this fronting:

(7.5)

| iː | uː | | iː | uː |
|---|---|---|---|---|
| eː | oː | | eː, øː | □ |
| ɛː | ɔː | | ɛː | ɔː |
| aː | | | aː | |
| Before | | | After | |

The 'after' system is input to the GVS.

In addition to the implicational relationship between unshifted ME /uː/ and front ME /oː/, we can add the following: no dialect shifted ME /eː/ 'out of place' (i.e. leaving an empty slot for /eː/ like that for /oː/ after the fronting); and no dialect has undiphthongized ME /iː/. The correlation looks too neat to be accidental, and makes sense in a chain model. If the GVS began with a push chain from /eː oː/, then in the north there is nothing to do the pushing, so /uː/ remains.

The condition on diphthongization can be stated this way:

(7.6)    A high vowel diphthongizes unless the slot below it in the same
series (front, back) is empty.

Diphthongization of /uː/, that is, can be predicted from the shape of
the system it appears in. If this is 'complete' (the top two heights
filled), then raising of the half-close vowel will initiate a push chain
(as in all dialects for the front series); if there is an empty slot at
half-close, then the high vowel is unaffected. This suggests that the
GVS can be visualized as a kind of general 'instruction' (or metarule)
to the non-low vowels in the system to raise; coupled with another
general condition that in the basic shift no phonemic distinctions are
to be lost. Such a programme of shifting is best visualized in terms
of a whole system as a structural primitive, with the behaviour of
individual elements determined, not just by their own content, but
by their place as well.

### 7.3    The argument from cyclical shifts

From the preceding we get the idea of a vowel system as
a kind of 'spatial' inventory, where relations like 'above', 'below', etc.
are phonologically relevant. Certainly there is a gain in descriptive
and predictive precision if we think of processes like the GVS as
operating in a **phonological space** (to use the common term). This
also illustrates nicely the point that despite the articulatory/acoustic
asymmetry in vowel characterization (§6.6), the parameters we are
calling height and backness do have some phonological reality: processes can apparently utilize them in a clearcut way, regardless of
their physical implementation. The GVS treats the system as a set
of positions in a two-dimensional space, where [n height] in front is
'the same' as [n height] in back, etc. From now on I will use the
traditional terms without apology, as before §6.6.

Consonant systems as well exhibit patterns of dynamic coherence
under chain shifting, which suggests the same 'systemic integrity' we
saw above for vowel systems. Or at least one could say that there
are many attested phonological processes implying systems-as-whole
– as it were 'predefined' – being among the terms in which language
evolution operates.

Perhaps the point can be made more clearly this way: the best
motivation for a concept of system (in the 'dynamic' sense) is the
existence of 'global' mutations where a statement in terms only of
rules operating on individual segments or segment classes appears to

129

be non-generalizing, but one in terms of **constraints** or **conditions** on whole systems captures the obvious generalizations. We saw this to some extent with the GVS: however one might formulate the individual raisings and diphthongizations, the change as a whole HAS A SHAPE, and this is best described in terms of the system it occurs in. For example, 'All non-low vowels raise one height; any high vowel with a raisable vowel below it diphthongizes.'

Another illustration is a famous global consonant shift, the so-called 'First Consonant Shift' or **Grimm's Law**. This defines the transition from the parent Indo-European protolanguage to the ancestor of Germanic, and involves a change in articulatory type of every member of the obstruent system except /s/ – but no change in the number of distinctive entities or oppositions. (One might say – in terms of contrast – that nothing happened: see §13.1.)

Phonetically, the shift was:

(7.7)

| | Proto-IE | | | | | Proto-Germanic | | |
|---|---|---|---|---|---|---|---|---|
| p | t | k | $k^w$ | | f | θ | x | $x^w$ |
| b | d | g | $g^w$ | $\longrightarrow$ | p | t | k | $k^w$ |
| ḅ | ḍ | g̣ | $g̣^w$ | | b | d | g | $g^w$ |
| | s | | | | | s | | |

(/ḅ/ etc. are breathy-voiced stops, traditionally 'voiced aspirates' /bh/, etc.)

The overall pattern is something like the diagram in (7.8).

(7.8)

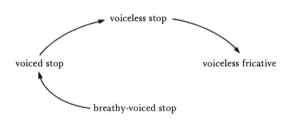

Leaving aside the stable /s/, one category (breathy-voiced stop) vanishes at one end, and a new category (voiceless fricative) emerges at the other. The system of oppositions remains unaltered, and two of the original three non-sibilant types remain: but with different sources. These 'musical chairs' phenomena are common, and seem

130

to be best treated in terms of predefined or pre-existent systems of contrasts, with variable membership of distinctive 'places'.

## 7.4 **Phonological universals and markedness**

Two strands of inquiry tend to be grouped under the heading of 'universals' research: (a) the attempt to discover the (absolute) defining properties of natural languages (**absolute universals**), and (b) the rather different attempt to sort languages into types on the basis of their possession or not of certain (not obligatory) properties. Thus under (a) the search for universals comes up with statements like:

(7.9)   (a)  All languages use a pulmonic egressive airstream.
        (b)  All languages have at least one high vowel.
        (c)  All languages have consonants and vowels.

While under (b), one would be concerned with statements like:

(7.10)  (a)  Some languages also use a glottalic egressive airstream.
        (b)  Some languages have systems with only one low vowel.
        (c)  Some languages have consonant systems with no voice contrast, and some have vowel systems with no rounding contrast.

But there is a point where absolute universals and typology intersect, in so-called **implicational universals**. These are statements of the form '$P_i \supset P_j$', i.e. 'possession of property $P_i$ implies possession of $P_j$ – but not vice versa'. (7.9a) and (7.10a) in fact are parts of such a universal: here $P_i$ is glottalic egressive, and $P_j$ pulmonic. Implicational universals in effect define minimal or obligatory properties of phonological systems, as well as opening up the options: a natural language is by definition an object that contains at least $P_j$, and may be an object containing $P_i \ldots$, etc. It is uncertain whether a large and interesting set of such statements can be made; steps have been taken, but we're nowhere near knowing yet if the goal is attainable.

There is one interesting and problematic area at the universal/typological interface: the existence of what might be called **statistical universals**. These have the form '$p(P_i \supset P_j) = n$', where $n < 1, > 0.5$; i.e. languages with $P_i$ will have $P_j$ with a sample frequency exceeding (often greatly) what would be expected as a result of chance. (If the only choice is presence vs. absence of a property, a random distribution should be roughly 50% with and 50% without for a reasonably large sample, i.e. p = 0.5.) There are also non-implicational statistical universals of the type: $P_j$ occurs in nearly all (or a very high percentage of) languages, but $P_i$ is very rare (even if there's no implicational relation). Examples of statistical (or pseudo-statistical, since we don't really have precise figures) universals: (i) a front rounded vowel at a given height implies a back rounded one at the same height; (ii) voiced obstruents imply voiceless ones (both implicational); (iii) if a language has one front rounded vowel it will be /y/; (iv) no language has more than three front rounded vowels (non-implicational).

The problem is what these mean. They have been known for a long time, and for some (perhaps the majority) of linguists they are an important fact about languages, usually treated (following Prague terminology) under the heading of 'markedness'. According to the many divergent positions that can be grouped roughly under the heading of **markedness theory**, an important distinction can be made between two types of segments, **marked** and **unmarked**.

For any minimally distinct segment-pair, marked and unmarked are defined according to these criteria: a marked segment is (i) less common cross-linguistically than its unmarked counterpart; (ii) tends not to appear in positions of neutralization; (iii) generally has lower text-frequency; (iv) is later in appearing during language-acquisition; (v) tends in cases of phonemic merger (coalescence) to be absorbed into the unmarked category; (vi) tends to be less stable historically; (vii) tends to imply the existence of its unmarked counterpart.

This could be merely definitional or circular, were it not that for a given pair it is normally the same member that fairly consistently meets at least conditions (i, ii, iv) anyhow; the evidence with regard to (iii) is unclear, and (vi, vii) seem not to be true (see Lass 1975). For example, voiceless obstruents, front unrounded vowels, and stops are relatively 'unmarked' in this sense *vis-à-vis* voiced obstruents, front rounded vowels, and fricatives.

It is debatable, however, if these observations can be pushed much further, i.e. given a non-formal, non-statistical interpretation, and used as the basis for an explanatory (predictive) theory. The view that they can is widespread: e.g. markedness is interpreted as 'complexity' (psychological, perceptual, articulatory), and is built into procedures to 'evaluate' grammars or language states in terms of 'cost' or 'non-optimality' (see §8.6). But it is not clear that the predictive power of any form of markedness theory is enough to make it interesting – as anything but a set of inductive generalizations about the distributions of properties in the world's languages. In particular there seems to be no good way of accounting for the 'failures' of markedness predictions.

The difficult cases (really quite common) are those where a system goes from an unmarked to a marked state, and yet the new segments show high stability. Thus the advent of *i*-umlaut (§8.2.1) in the Germanic languages added the segments [y ø] to what were otherwise fairly unmarked systems; and even though some of the dialects (e.g. Southern English) have lost all traces of these vowel types, most of the others have kept them, and even added new ones. Now the original umlaut was a very 'natural' assimilatory process whereby back vowels fronted before a following /i j/: thus pre-OE */muːs/ 'mouse', */muːsi-/ 'mice' → [muːs], [myːsi]. The new [yː] becomes phonemic when the final /i/ is later lost (see §§13.1–2).

But cases where front rounded vowels arise **context-free** (i.e. without conditioning environments) are more troublesome: e.g. there are unconditioned frontings of [u] to [y] in Ancient Greek, Albanian, French, Dutch, Icelandic, and Scottish English. In some of these cases (Greek, French, Dutch) the 'lost' [u] is restored by other changes; in others, like Scots, it is not. Thus the history of some varieties of Scots, from pre-OE times to the present, shows the pattern:

(7.11)

| | | | | | | | | |
|---|---|---|---|---|---|---|---|---|
| i | u | i | y | u | i | u | i | y |
| I | | II | | | III | | IV | |

Between stages III and IV there has been an unconditioned merger to a marked category: /y/ and /u/ have fallen together in /y/ (hence /y/ in *house*, *loose*). In terms of overall markedness (with U 'unmarked' and M 'marked'), the transitions are U → M, M → U, U → M. And the last stage has been stable for several centuries. Thus markedness theory predicts II → III, and counter-predicts I → II, III → IV. Not to mention the fact that the system at stage IV violates a supposed implicational universal.

Data like this focusses on an important methodological problem: the status of so-called 'explanation by tendency'. Many linguists see overall statistical tendencies like those embodied in the concept of markedness as explanations of changes or synchronic states: the transition II → III occurred to 'minimize markedness'. But what about I → II, III → IV? The problem with 'tends to' statements is that they

133

explain nothing because they predict everything (i.e. they predict nothing in particular). If the aim of an explanation is to account for some given SINGLE event, i.e. by predicting its occurrence, markedness seems to be empty, since it allows for all possible outcomes. No single event can refute a claim about the marked or unmarked status of a category. If any given event is – in the larger picture – compatible with a segment being unmarked or marked, then what is the content of 'marked'? (This critique will be slightly tempered in §7.6.3.)

### 7.5  System typology, I: vowel systems

7.5.1  *Introduction: what phonemes does a language 'have'?*

The aim of a typology is to reduce the bewildering array of items in the universe of discourse to a tractable number of classes, on the basis of (significant) shared properties. The size of the data-base, and the number of analytical options available have so far prevented any fully satisfactory classifications. I won't attempt another here; but I will consider some basic problems in system typology, and take a critical look at what has been proposed. Then I will look at a sample of the data these attempts have rested on, and some of the generalizations that emerge. This will give some idea of what remains to be done, and the often important issues that come into focus when you try to do it. Above all, this chapter will give some indication of what phonological systems in general are like.

To begin with, just about everybody agrees that system typology is based on arrays of distinctive segments, organized (for vowels) along the primary axes of height and backness, intersected by rounding, diphthongization, length, nasalization, etc. But the construction of vowel systems is not simply the random choice of items on these parameters: some system types are apparently impossible, others common, and others rare; and almost all seem to be built along certain very basic lines. But before we get to this, we have to discuss two basic problems: the choice of items to represent the phonemes of a language, and the status of long vowels and diphthongs (§7.5.2).

What do we mean by saying 'Language L has phoneme X'? For example, everyone would agree that many varieties of English 'have /æ/': but this symbol stands, in any given dialect, for a spread of allophones. In my own, for instance, '/æ/' subsumes a short peripheral [æ], (*cat*), a short nasalized [æ̃] (*manner*), a long centralized and raised [ǣ:] (*bad, fast*), a nasalized version [ǣ̃:] (*hand*), and a short retracted and lowered [ǽ] (*carry*). So /æ/ stands for an AREA in the vowel space, not a point, as shown in (7.12).

(7.12)

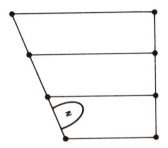

In choosing a symbol for a category, we typically select something like the 'centre' of an allophonic range: if not 'geometrical', a 'phonetic centre', i.e. the least modified form, not the one appearing in perceptually noisy environments (e.g. before /r/ or nasals). Or the one least subject to conditioned modifications (here, lengthening before voiced segments and the like). Failing clearcut applicability of these criteria, one can take the most widely distributed allophone as basic.

But how am I so sure that short [æ] is basic, rather than a shortened version of a long vowel? The answer illustrates a typical argument, and ties in with the next topic. The determining factor is the structure of the phonology as a whole: in my dialect, the long vowels and diphthongs (except for [æ:]) have certain distributional properties, notably the ability to appear in stressed final open syllables (*bee, boo, law*, etc.). No short vowels appear in this position, and the only long quality missing is [æ:]. Therefore we assign the basic quality [æ] to the short series, and represent the category in question as /æ/.

### 7.5.2 *Long vowels and diphthongs*

Specification of systems with a length contrast and/or phonemic diphthongs has been treated most unsatisfactorily, and the difficulties are interesting. If we take a vowel system as a two-dimensional array, then in the simple case of a language with long and short vowels of (at least roughly) the same quality, we can fit them in as pairs:

(7.13) iː i   u uː
    eː e   o oː
    aː a

We could call this (say '5-V + length', and it then qualifies as a 'type'. Classical Latin may have been like this, as is Maltese. But what about a language with the same number of segments, but the following phonetic character?

(7.14) iː      uː
    eː ɪ   ʊ oː
      ɛ   ɔ
      a   ɑː

(A similar system probably characterized 17th-century London English; with the addition of /yː ʏ øː œ/ this would be standard German.) Is this still just '5-V + length'? Or a separate (sub)type, with length and quality not matched? The difficulty is that there is a tendency in much of the literature to 'normalize' systems like (7.14) into (7.13), and treat them as 'alike' for typology.

Here is a concrete example, as a warning. Hockett (1955: 76f) gives the Fox vowel system as /iː i eː e äː ä oː o/ (Notation altered to conform with the practice in this book: /ä/ is open central.) These are 'the phonemes': their characteristic allophones, he tells us, are [iː ɪ æ ɛ ʌ äː oː ʊ], where [ʌ] is central. If we line the two representations up in a 'phonetic space', we get:

(7.15) Phonemic      Phonetic
    iː i       iː
    eː e  oː o   ɪ   ʊ oː
      äː ä      ɛ  ʌ
            æː   äː

Yet Hockett tells us (p. 76) that 'the proper pairing is quite obvious', i.e. 'two of the shorts are high, and two low; two of them front, and two back; and the same classifications apply to the longs'. Fox thus becomes an example of a simple '2 + 2' system (with length extracted – see below), representable as:

(7.16) i   o
    e   a

Obviously we have to ask how much normalization is allowable, and what it means to call a segment 'phonemically high' when its closest realization is half-close. Wouldn't we be better representing Fox as

(7.17)     i
        e        o
            a

(even at the expense of the neat 2 × 2 symmetry)? This way, we can see that Fox uses three heights (even if not distinctively in any one series), as opposed to a language like Amuesha which apparently has /e o/ as its closest vowels, and a low central one, and thus only uses two heights. Equating 'highest vowel in a system' with 'high vowel' enables us, if we're not careful, to come up with 'universals' of the type that all languages have /i u/ (see Crothers 1978: 115). Crothers, even knowing of languages like Amuesha, takes /o/ in such systems as 'reasonably close to' /u/ – thus in fact defining typology in terms of an *a priori* notion of what a natural language ought to contain. I will return to Crothers later on.

This kind of normalization is perhaps the major problem for a reader first embarking on the literature on system classification; Hockett (1955) and Sedlak (1969) are particularly dangerous in this regard – especially when one does not have access to phonetic data from the language being discussed. Crothers escapes this problem in a way, by at least presenting phonetically rather precise examples of his types, so that one has the data for quarrelling with him (see §7.5.3).

Leaving aside normalization, there are further problems with long vowels and diphthongs. While both of these types are usually listed in displays of vowel systems in individual language descriptions, the major tradition of typological studies is ambiguous about length, and nearly unanimous in excluding diphthongs. This latter exclusion – if we take it as a serious theoretical claim – has paradoxical consequences. Such a position would claim implicitly that when ME /iː uː/ diphthongized in the Great Vowel Shift (§7.2), they somehow 'left' the vowel system; but when, as in some Southern U.S. dialects, /ai/ from ME /iː/ (as in *white*) monophthongized to /aː/, it 'returned'. (Needless to say no one has said this explicitly; but if diphthongs are not members of vowel systems it follows.)

Hockett (1955) manages to exclude both length and diphthongization in a rather interesting way. He divides the syllable **nuclei** in a language into **simple** and **complex peaks**, so that the 'basic' vowel system (THE system proper) is always a set of short mono-phthongs. Long vowels and diphthongs are then simple nuclei cluster-ing with either a '**co-vowel**' of length /ː/, or a 'semivowel' /j w/, etc. This in effect reduces anything but short monophthongs to the status of 'tactical' arrangements or clusters, so that (say) 'the English vowel system' no more includes the phonemes /ai au/ as members than 'the consonant system' includes /st fr/, etc.

Phonologically, however, this position is shaky. At least in some languages diphthongs and long vowels must be taken – whatever their phonetic structure – as 'units' in precisely the same way as short monophthongs: and this suggests the need for a classificatory frame-work including them both.

For instance: in Icelandic, diphthongs behave exactly like simple vowels with respect to the assignment of length. In environments where monophthongs are long, diphthongs are as well: thus /i/ is long in *ís* 'ice' (nom sg) and short in *íss* (gen sg), and /ai/ is long in *læs* 'literate' (non-neuter) and short in *læst* (neuter): length is controlled by the following consonantism, with monophthongal or diphthongal nuclei short before long consonants or clusters and long before single consonants.

Or consider English, where diphthongs participate as units, parallel to long and short vowels, in MP alternations. Thus *div*[aɪ]*n* ~ *div*[ɪ]*nity*, *ser*[iː]*n* ~ *ser*[ɛ]*nity*, *hum*[eɪ]*n* ~ *hum*[æ]*nity*, *prof*[aʊ]*nd* ~ *prof*[ʌ]*ndity*, etc. Here one position is always occupied by a long vowel OR a diphthong, and the other by a short monophthong. So long vowels and diphthongs are on a par; if we admit one, we admit the other. And their behaviour parallels that of the short vowels, with which they alternate, so that unit status for one of the three entails the same for the others.

The primary problem with diphthongs, of course, is that there is no obvious 'place' for them in the typical height vs. backness system display. Assuming the independence of diphthongs, where do they go? Should we take say /ei/ as a member of a front vowel system, and /ou/ as back? And what about diphthongs with two backness values, like /oi/? The usual solution in descriptive work is simply to put diphthongs 'somewhere else': cf. the Yiddish system in (2.11), which is a fairly typical way of fudging the issue. The question at the moment is insoluble, and diphthongs remain in a kind of systemic limbo.

An alternative would be to accept an abstract analysis like that of

*SPE*, where [+tense] marks underlying vowels that surface as long or diphthongal, and [−tense] marks the others. This however can't serve as a basis for typology, because the constraints in manipulating 'underlying' systems are too loose. Anything can pass for a system, pretty much, regardless of the phonetics (see §9.3). For example in *SPE*, the underlying nucleus of *boy* is /ɶ/ (low front round tense) and that of *cue* is /ɨ/ (high back unround tense) – neither of which ever appear phonetically. Such representations are artifacts of a certain kind of MP analysis, and not a data-base for the study of systems: it seems close to lunacy to characterize any variety of English as 'having' a low front round vowel. 'Systems' here will refer to something like sets of phonetic norms for distinctively opposed entities, based on some sort of 'classical' phonemic analysis.

### 7.5.3 *Basic vowel system types*

Leaving aside the vexed question of where to put diphthongs, we can look at some of the basic monophthongal system types in the world's languages. There have been three major approaches to vowel-system classification, exemplified by Trubetzkoy (1939), Hockett (1955), and Crothers (1978). Trubetzkoy bases his primarily on what we might call 'axes of contrast': systems are built along the parameters of **degree of aperture** or **sonority** (=height), and **localization** or **timbre** ('clear' vs. 'dark'), with the latter apparently the intersection of backness and rounding ([y] is a 'dark' [i]). This leads to a classification of systems as **linear** (with only aperture contrasts, and no backness or rounding oppositions), **quadrangular** (all vowels opposed in height and backness) and **triangular** (all vowels opposed in aperture, and all but the openest distinct in timbre, the open vowel alone being 'unpartnered').

To illustrate:

(7.18)

| | | | | | |
|---|---|---|---|---|---|
| ɨ | | i | u | i | u |
| ə | | e | o | e | o |
| a | | a | ɑ | | ɑ |

| Linear | Quadrangular | Triangular |
|---|---|---|
| (Adyghe) | (Montenegran) | (Northern Ostyak) |

Systems can be further divided according to the number of timbre classes: so 'two-degree, three-class quadrangular' K'üri:

(7.19)   i       y       u
         e               ɑ

((7.18) from Hockett (Adyghe) and Trubetzkoy; (7.19) Trubetzkoy.) The equation of heights /e/ = /ɑ/ reflects Trubetzkoy's concern with opposition numbers ('degrees') rather than phonetic exponents: cf. Hockett on Fox (§7.5.2).

In Hockett's scheme, the number of distinctions in particular dimensions is primary; thus types are identified by numbers, indicating how many vowels there are at a given height:

(7.20)        i        u              ɨ               i        u
                                      ə                        ə
              a                       a               a
            2 + 1                 1 + 1 + 1         2 + 1 + 1
             Cree                  Adyghe            Ilocano

And so on. This is not too different from Trubetzkoy: his basic types can be read off the code-numbers for the lowest height for triangular or quadrangular systems (1 and 2 respectively), or off all heights for linear.

Both these classifications are fairly insensitive to phonetic detail – or they treat it as irrelevant. (This makes Hockett's extreme normalization a bit less reprehensible, given his purpose.) The one scheme so far that has really attempted to come to grips with quality – so as to be able to state implications between vowel types – is Crothers (1978). He also includes long vowels (if only by the back door – see below), though he does not allow for diphthongs. His scheme is worth looking at (even though it has problems, and in the end probably can't be accepted), because of the way it combines auditory and articulatory information, and attempts to furnish a basis for a theory of universals.

Crothers begins with the (apparent) observation that the smallest known systems (aside from the 'linear' Caucasian ones, which he calls 'reduced') tend to contain only high and low vowels, in certain quality ranges: they are of the type /i u a/, etc. Then he notes that perceptually, front rounded and non-low back unrounded vowels tend to sound more central than their oppositely rounded counterparts: rounded back vowels are 'backer', unrounded front vowels 'fronter' than their opposites. So [y ø] are acoustically closer to [ɨ ə] than to [i e], and to [ɯ ɣ] than [u o]. Thus we get a classification as in (7.21).

(7.21)

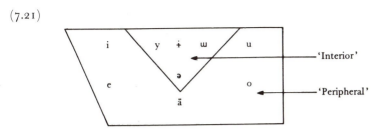

(Slightly modified from Crothers' original.) Because of their perceptual salience, etc., peripheral vowels are 'unmarked', and 'primary'. This leads to a classification which assigns a language a binomial label x.y, where x = the total number of vowel qualities, and y the number of interior vowels. So:

(7.22)      i      ʊ          i      u
            ɛ      ɑ          ə
                              ä

            4.0               4.1
            Cayapa            Margi

But there are some inconsistencies in his application of (7.21), which raise familiar problems. For a number of languages, /ɯ/, which ought to be interior, is taken as peripheral (e.g. in a system /i ä ɯ/, with no /u/, /ɯ/ is 'a kind of /u/': so this, like /i ä u/, is 3.0 instead of 3.1. In fact he gives no examples of 3.1, though he lists what I would take to be 3.1 as 3.0). Further, a language with a system /i a ɯ o/, also with no /u/, is called 4.1: i.e. HERE /ɯ/ counts as interior, with /o/ as the peripheral 'high' vowel. I find it hard to see how the same quality type can legitimately – at this level of system typology – be counted as interior and peripheral in different languages. At the very least, by forcing languages to conform to a scheme where all must have /i u/, we miss out some empirically attested possibilities, and sweep inconveniences under a procedural rug.

Another problem is that while Crothers lists both long and nasalized vowels for the languages in his sample, he types them only by short vowels: it doesn't seem helpful to call both a language with /i a u/ and one with /iː i aː a uː u/ 3.0, and lump them together as 'the same'.

With these taxonomies as a background, I will not attempt a firm classification, but look in a general way at some of the major basic shapes available for vowel systems, on an essentially numerical basis.

141

We can take the building of vowel systems as a partially non-random selection from the inventory of possible vowels. Aside from the 'linear' systems, whose status is problematical (see §7.7), we can specify the construction of a minimal system as follows: take one vowel in the range [i–ɪ–e], one from [ɯ–u–ʊ–o], and one low vowel from [a/æ–ä–ɑ]. Typical minimal systems of this kind are:

(7.23)      i      u          i          u
                ä               a
            Aleut              Moroccan Arabic

The 'point' seems to be maximal dispersion of vowel-quality towards the corners of the vowel space; languages like this (not surprisingly) often have very wide ranges of allophonic variation (see §7.7). With length as an added dimension:

(7.24)   i  u │ iː  uː     e  o │ eː  oː     i  ɯ │ iː  ɯː
            ä │    äː          ä │    äː          ä │    äː
       Alaskan Eskimo         Amuesha           Jaqaru

These are all essentially 'high/low' systems; mid vowels, when they appear, do not function as third terms in a height opposition (which tends to justify Hockett's normalizing procedure: though one still ought to note the flexibility of 'high' in this systemic sense).

The next step up is 4-quality systems, which usually have a high : mid opposition. Sometimes – but rarely – there is no high/mid contrast in any one series, but high/low in one and either high or mid in the other two (Chacobo below):

(7.25)   i                    i    u              i    ɨ
           e    o                ə                           ɔ
             ä                   ä                   ä
           Campa                Margi               Chacobo

In the examples that follow, I will represent /i ɪ/, /e ɛ/, /o ɔ/, /u ʊ/ as 'the same height', if they function as SOLE members of a high or mid range in a given series; front/back asymmetries in systems with one mid or high vowel in a series are not uncommon.

With length added, the strategy still seems similar: though the long systems may be structurally rather different:

(7.26)    i    u  |  e:   o:      i   ɯ  |  i:
          ɛ       |  ɛ:              o  |      o:
          ɒ       |      ɒ:        ä     |    ä:
          Wichita                  Adzera

With nasalization, and nasalization + length:

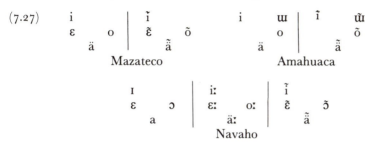

(7.27)    i           |  ĩ               i   ɯ  |  ĩ      ũ
          ɛ    o      |  ɛ̃    õ             o  |        õ
             ä        |     ä̃              ä     |     ä̃
              Mazateco                     Amahuaca

          ɪ           |  i:               ĩ
          ɛ    ɔ      |  ɛ:   o:          ɛ̃     ɔ̃
             a        |     ä:              ä̃
                        Navaho

Even with 4-quality systems we still get (rarely) two-dimensional
high/low types, as in Wapishana:

(7.28)    i  ɨ  u  |  i:  ɨ:  u:  |  ĩ  ɨ̃  ũ
             ä     |      ä:      |     ä̃

5-vowel systems are the commonest: the most typical contrast two
heights in front and back with a low central vowel, though there are
variants with three heights in front, or two central:

(7.29)    i    u      i   ʊ        ɪ      ʊ      i   ʉ
          ɛ    o      ɛ   ɔ        ɛ      ɔ      ɛ      o
             ä           a            ä             ä
          Ainu      Georgian      Yiddish        Garo
                           i   y   u
                                 ɣ
                              ä
                           Mandarin

Mandarin is unusual, for a system this small, in that it has vowels of
the same height and backness contrasting only in rounding. According
to Crothers' sample, and my own experience, front rounded vowels
seem not to occur in systems with fewer than five qualities; there
appears to be a statistical preference for the unrounded types /ɯ ɨ ə/ as

143

'extras' in the smaller systems. Front rounded vowels are in any case areally and genetically restricted: the bulk of examples seen to be Western Indo-European (especially Germanic), Uralic, Altaic, and Sino-Tibetan, with scattered instances elsewhere.

5-V with either length or nasalization or both:

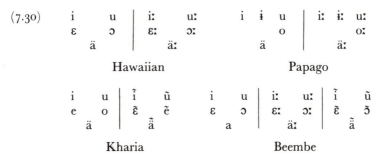

(7.30)

| | | | | | | | | | | |
|---|---|---|---|---|---|---|---|---|---|---|
| i | u | iː | uː | | i | ɨ | u | iː | ɨː | uː |
| ɛ | ɔ | ɛː | ɔː | | | o | | | | oː |
| | ä | | äː | | | ä | | | äː | |

Hawaiian          Papago

| | | | | | | | | | |
|---|---|---|---|---|---|---|---|---|---|
| i | u | ĩ | ũ | i | u | iː | uː | ĩ | ũ |
| e | o | ɛ̃ | ẽ | ɛ | ɔ | ɛː | ɔː | ɛ̃ | ɔ̃ |
| | ä | | ã̈ | | a | | äː | | ã̈ |

Kharia          Beembe

6-V systems show more variety: some use three heights in one or both series, others have rounding contrasts at one height in a series:

(7.31)

| | | | | | | | | | | | |
|---|---|---|---|---|---|---|---|---|---|---|---|
| i | u | | i | u | | i | y | ɯ | u | i | ɨ | u |
| e | o | | ɛ | ə | ɔ | | ɛ | | | | e | | o |
| | a | ɑ | | | ä | | | ɑ | | | | ä | |

Persian     Chuckchi     Chuvash     Itonama

With length (and nasalization):

(7.32)

| | | | | | | | | | |
|---|---|---|---|---|---|---|---|---|---|
| i | ʊ | iː | uː | | ɪ | ʊ | iː | | uː |
| ɛ | ɔ | eː | oː | | ɛ | ʌ | | ɜː | ɔː |
| a | ɑ | aː | ɑː | | æ | ɒ | | | ɑː |

Lithuanian          English (RP)

| | | | | | | |
|---|---|---|---|---|---|---|
| i | u | iː | uː | | ĩ | ũ |
| e | o | | | | | |
| ɛ | | ɛː | | | ɛ̃ | |
| | ä | | äː | | | ã̈ |

Chipewyan

Up to now, no system appears to use more than three heights distinctively; 4-height oppositions seem to appear at 7-V, and are not uncommon above that. Two other points to note: (a) long and short vowels do not have to match in either number or quality; (b) the number of nasalized vowels is often smaller than, and never larger than, the number of oral ones.

144

7-V systems:

(7.33)

| i | u | | i | y | | u | | i | ɨ | u | | i | ɯ | u |
|---|---|---|---|---|---|---|---|---|---|---|---|---|---|---|
| e | o | | | | | | | | | | | | | |
| ɛ | ɔ | | ɛ | | ə | ɔ | | ɛ | ə | o | | ɛ | ə | ɔ |
| | a | | | | ɑ | | | | ä | | | | ä | |

Italian        Albanian        Sundanese        Naga

Note the wide disparities in 'density', from the rather condensed Italian to the dispersion of Albanian; given the high–low 'anchor points', there seem to be few constraints on filling in the rest of the places.

More spatial distribution types occur with length; aside from neatly symmetrical matching systems, we find the common type where (at least some) shorts are lower and/or more central than longs, and the long and short low vowels have opposite backness:

(7.34)

| i | u | i: | u: | | I | Y | ʊ | | i: | y: | u: |
|---|---|---|---|---|---|---|---|---|---|---|---|
| e | o | e: | o: | | | | | | e: | ø: | o: |
| ɛ | ɔ | ɛ: | ɔ: | | ɛ | œ | ɔ | | | | |
| | ä | | ä: | | | a | | | | ɑ: | |

Nengone          German

| i | y | | ʊ | i: | y: | | u: |
|---|---|---|---|---|---|---|---|
| ɛ | œ | | ɔ | e: | ø: | | o: |
| | | ɒ | | | | ä: | |

Hungarian

7-V with nasalization and length:

(7.35)

| i | u | i | õ | | i | u | i: | u: | | ĩ | | ũ |
|---|---|---|---|---|---|---|---|---|---|---|---|---|
| e | o | | | | I | ʊ | I: | ʊ: | | ẽ | | õ |
| ɛ | ɔ | | | | ɛ | ɔ | ɛ: | ɔ: | | ɛ̃ | | ɔ̃ |
| | ä | | ã̃ | | | ä | | ä: | | | ã̃ | |

Burmese                    Kpelle

8-V systems show still more variety:

(7.36)

| i | | u | | i | y | ɯ | u | | i | y | u | | i: | y: | u: |
|---|---|---|---|---|---|---|---|---|---|---|---|---|---|---|---|
| e | | o | | | | | | | e | ø | o | | e: | ø: | o: |
| ɛ | ə | ɔ | | ɛ | œ | | ɔ | | æ | | ɑ | | æ: | | ɑ: |
| | a | | | | | ɑ | | | | | | | | | |

Javanese          Turkish          Finnish

Above this size, systems become somewhat less common. For 9-V
we have:

(7.37)
```
    i  ɨ  u        i  y  ɯ  ʊ         i      ɯ  u
    e     o           ø     o
    ɛ  ə  ɔ           ɛ                ɛ  œ      ɔ
       ä              a        ɑ       a        ɑ
```
      Cham           Azerbaijani          Ostyak

```
        i      u    │   ĩ      ũ
        e      o    │   ẽ      õ
        ɛ  ə  ɔ  ʌ  │      ɔ̃
           ä        │      ã
```
                Mazahua

10-V without and with length:

(7.38)
```
    i     ɯ  u        i     ʉ
    e  ø     o        e     ë     o
    ɛ     ə  ɔ        ɛ     ë̈  ɔ  ʌ
       ä              ä
```
         Akha          Scots (Fife)

```
        i  y     u  │  iː       uː
        e        o  │  eː       oː
        ɛ  œ     ɔ  │  ɛː œː    ɔː
        a     ä     │  aː    äː
```
               Iai

For 11-V:

(7.39)
```
    i  y  u │              i  y     u   │  iː yː   uː
    e  ø  o │              ɪ  ʏ     ʊ   │  ɪː ʏː   ʊː
    ɛ  œ  ɔ │  ɛ̃  œ̃  ɔ̃    ɛ  œ     ɔ   │  ɛː œː   ɔː
    a     ɑ │      ɑ̃       æ     ä      │  æː
```
       French           Swiss German (Bärndüütsch)

Systems much larger than this present analytical difficulties, and
most seem to be controversial; I will end this survey with about the
largest monophthongal system I know of, an Alsatian German type
with ten short and eleven long vowels, which can also be loosely
interpreted as having a five-height front series:

(7.40)

| | | | | | | |
|---|---|---|---|---|---|---|
| i | y | | | iː | yː | |
| ɪ | | ʊ | | ɪː | | ʊː |
| e | ø | o | | eː | øː | oː |
| | œ | | | ɛː | œː | |
| a | | ɑ | | aː | | ɒː |

## 7.6 System typology, II: consonant systems

### 7.6.1 *Obstruents, 1: stops*

The classification problem with consonants is obviously greater than with vowels. Aside from the enormously greater range of inventory sizes (Hawaiian with 8 to Ubykh with 80), there are more parameters of contrast. Compared with say four or five vowel heights, three degrees of backness, two lip attitudes, length, diphthongization, and nasalization, here we have the primary opposition obstruent vs. sonorant, at least three degrees of stricture, two release types, aspiration, (conservatively) twelve places of articulation, apical vs. laminal, secondary and double articulations, at least four glottal states and four airstreams, nasality, laterality, trill vs. tap vs. flap ... and so on. And these interact in such complex ways, and the range of choice is so great, that even relatively crude classificatory schemes like those in §7.5.3 are virtually unworkable.

We can however outline something of a 'choice' procedure for constructing consonant systems, from minimal to maximal, and look at some of the generalizations that emerge.

All languages have obstruents. The minimal system normally involves at least two pulmonic oral stops from the 'cardinal' set /p t k/, with the third either one of this set or /ʔ/. Thus the simplest known are of the type:

(7.41)

| | | | | |
|---|---|---|---|---|
| Hawaiian | p | | k | ʔ |
| Maori | p | t | k | |

The next option is adding one 'intermediate' place, usually palatal or palato-alveolar (the latter typically an affricate), as in:

(7.42)

| | | | | |
|---|---|---|---|---|
| Burera | p | t | c | k |
| Ainu | p | t | tʃ | k |

At this point, using Hockett's (1955) term, we are dealing with 'affricates as positions': /tʃ/ clearly belongs 'between /t/ and /k/'. The

147

picture is not so clear when the stop onset of an affricate is at the same place as a non-affricated stop already in the system. If a language has /t/ and /ts/, is the latter a 'position' or a 'manner'? In the examples below, when /ts/ contrasts with /t̪/, we will take it as a position (alveolar); in a type with /t/ and /ts/, we will take the affricate as belonging to a different subsystem (compare Greenlandic (7.43) with German (7.47)).

The next expansion – five voiceless types – can add retroflex, uvular, a dental/alveolar contrast, /ʔ/ or /ts/:

```
(7.43)   Ao              p   t        c   k      ʔ
         Amahuaca        p   t    tʃ      k      ʔ
         Western Desert  p ʈ t  ʈ        k
         Greenlandic     p ʈ ts           k   q
```

Larger systems with only voiceless stops are rarer, but we do have:

```
(7.44)   Nunggubuyu      p ʈ t  ʈ   c   k
         Chuckchi        p   t          k   q   ʔ
                             ts
```

Beyond six we normally get some other parameter, most often voice; though we can also get non-pulmonic airstreams, secondary strictures, and aspiration. There are also systems with only one series, but voiced; these are restricted, as far as I know, to Australian languages. A typical example is Yidiɲ, which has:

```
(7.45)              b   d   ɖ   g
```
         (where /ɖ/ is a palatalized lamino-alveolar).

There are also some with a voiceless/aspirated contrast only, though these analyses are for the most part controversial. One language not usually analysed this way, but which ought to be, is Icelandic, which should probably be represented as:

```
(7.46)   p    t    c    k
         pʰ   tʰ   cʰ   kʰ
```

In the literature, the unaspirated set is usually given as /b̥ d̥/, etc. (i.e. 'lenis' voiceless stops: but they sound plain voiceless to me). This is probably an orthographic prejudice, as well as a reflex of the notion that aspiration contrasts do not occur in Germanic: it is worth noting that the unaspirated series is written *b, d, gj, g*.

With a simple voice contrast, the number of possibilities is enormous.

We have symmetrical and asymmetrical systems of various sizes – in the latter case with one or more voiced segments missing more often than voiceless ones. A few types:

(7.47)

| | p | t | k | | p | t | k | | | t | k |
|---|---|---|---|---|---|---|---|---|---|---|---|
| | | d | | | | | g | | b | d | |

      Sentani           Rotokas        Chuave

| | p | ʈ | k | | p | t | tʃ | k | | p | t | tʃ | k |
|---|---|---|---|---|---|---|---|---|---|---|---|---|---|
| | b | ɖ | g | | p | t | dʒ | g | | pf | ts | | |
| | | | | | | | | | | b | d | | g |

     French         English    German (standard)

| | p | t | k | ʔ | | p | t | tʃ | k | q | | p | ʈ | | tʃ | k | ʔ |
|---|---|---|---|---|---|---|---|---|---|---|---|---|---|---|---|---|---|
| | | ts | | | | b | d | ɟ | g | | | b | ɖ | ɖ | ʥ | g | |
| | | dz | | | | | | | | | | | | | | | |
| | b | d | g | | | | | | | | | | | | | | |

    Chamoro        Yugakhir       Papago

We can also add aspiration, or aspiration and breathy voice:

(7.48)

| | p | t | tʃ | k | | p | t | ʈ | tʃ | k |
|---|---|---|---|---|---|---|---|---|---|---|
| | b | d | dʒ | g | | b | d | ɖ | dʒ | g |
| | pʰ | tʰ | tʃʰ | kʰ | | pʰ | tʰ | ʈʰ | tʃʰ | kʰ |
| | | | | | | b̤ | d̤ | ɖ̤ | dʒ | g̈ |

     Burmese         Bengali

And larger systems may add some other airstream type, e.g. Sindhi, with the above plus an implosive series:

(7.49)

| | p | t | ʈ | tɕ | k |
|---|---|---|---|---|---|
| | b | d | ɖ | dʐ | g |
| | pʰ | tʰ | ʈʰ | tɕʰ | kʰ |
| | b̤ | d̤ | ɖ̤ | dʐ | g̈ |
| | ɓ | | ɗ | dʐ | ɠ |

(/tɕ dʐ/ are alveopalatal affricates, i.e. palatals with alveolar coarticulation.)

Aspiration – without voice – is combined with a glottalic egressive airstream in Eastern Armenian:

(7.50)

| | p | t | tʃ | k |
|---|---|---|---|---|
| | | ts | | |
| | pʰ | tʰ | tʃʰ | kʰ |
| | pʼ | tʼ | tʃʼ | kʼ |
| | | tsʼ | | |

Further modifications may include double stop articulations, prenasalization, and velaric ingressives (clicks), which themselves may be
subject to secondary modifications, e.g. aspiration, simultaneous stop
closures, breathy voice, and so on. To illustrate the latter, Zulu has
three basic click types: lamino-dental/ǀ/, apical postalveolar /ǃ/, and
alveolar lateral /ǁ/, which can be voiced, voiceless, aspirated, nasal,
and nasal/breathy-voiced:

(7.51)

| p | | t | | k |
|---|---|---|---|---|
| b | | d | | g |
| | ǀ | ǃ | ŋǁ | |
| | ǀʰ | ǃʰ | ǁʰ | |
| | g̃ǀ | g̃ǃ | g̃ǁ | |
| | ŋ̃ǀ | ŋ̃ǃ | ŋ̃ǁ | |
| | ŋ̤ǀ | ŋ̤ǃ | ŋ̤ǁ | |

A further dimension of contrast is length: we find it, for instance,
with aspiration and breathy voice in Brahmin dialects of Kannaḍa:

(7.52)

| p | t | ṭ | tɕ | k |
|---|---|---|---|---|
| b | d | ḍ | dʑ | g |
| pʰ | tʰ | ṭʰ | tɕʰ | kʰ |
| b̤ | d̤ | ḍ̤ | dʑ̤ | g̈ |
| pː | tː | ṭː | tɕː | kː |
| bː | dː | ḍː | dʑː | gː |

A very large system, including the rare contrast of long vs. short
ejectives and a laterally exploded affricate is Avar:

(7.53)

| p | t | | | k | q | ʔ |
|---|---|---|---|---|---|---|
| b | d | | | g | | |
| | ts | tʃ | | | | |
| | | | | kː | | |
| | tsː | tʃː | | | | |
| p' | t' | | | k' | q' | |
| | ts' | tʃ' | | | | |
| | tsː' | tʃː' | | | | |
| | tɬː' | | | | | |

And we can add secondary strictures; the most common are labialization and palatalization, though pharyngealization, uvularization,
etc. also occur. Both palatalization and labialization are used in
Abkhaz:

(7.54)

| p | t | ts | tʃ | tɕ | k | | |
| | tʷ | | | | kʷ | qʷ | |
| | | | | | kʲ | qʲ | |
| b | d | dz | dʒ | dʐ | g | | |
| | dʷ | dzʷ | | | gʷ | | |
| p' | t' | ts' | tʃ' | tɕ' | | | |
| | tw' | tsʷ' | | | | | |

All the systems so far, whatever their shape, contained labials. Systems without them do occur, though they are rare, and genetically and geographically restricted. The most typical occur in languages of the north-western U.S., e.g.

(7.55)

| t | tʃ | k | q | | ts | tʃ | tɬ | k | q |
| ts | tɬ | | | | ts' | tʃ' | tɬ' | k' | q' |
| | | kʷ | qʷ | | | | | | |

        Tlingit                              Tillamook

This brief survey by no means exhausts the possibilities; for more details it is worth looking closely at Hockett and Nartey.

### 7.6.2 *Obstruents, 2: fricatives*

Implicationally, fricatives are a 'secondary' category: a sample studied by Nartey (1979) gives twenty-one languages with none at all. There are usually fewer fricatives in a system – often many fewer – than stops: e.g. Klamath with sixteen stops and /s/, and Adzera with nine and /fs/.

If only one fricative is to be added to a basic stop system, there is a strong cross-linguistic preference for some kind of /s/; of Nartey's 36 one-fricative languages, 30 have /s/, and 2 each have only /β/, only /f/, or only /ɣ/. Of systems with more than one, only a handful lack /s/, e.g. Abipon with /x ħ/, Koiani with /f ð/, and Lakkia with /f θ ɬ/. So the 'basic' fricative type is an anterior, coronal sibilant. We now have something like a minimal 'archetype' for an obstruent system, i.e. /p t k s/.

We can get some idea of the relations between stop and fricative systems if we look at the fricatives correlating with the stop inventories in the previous section. Of the systems there, Burera, Western Desert and Nunggubuyu have no fricatives at all, Maori and Sentani only /f/, Rotokas only /β/, and Hawaiian only /h/ (see (7.41–4), (7.47)). All the rest have /s/ plus one or more others – with no particular correlation between stop and fricative numbers except that the stops outnumber the fricatives, or between places of articulation. Some systems are highly symmetrical, others quite asymmetrical (French vs. Icelandic in (7.57) below).

Taking some of the simpler ones as examples, with the stops and fricatives together, to show some possible patterns, we find:

(7.56)

| | | | | | | | | | | | | |
|---|---|---|---|---|---|---|---|---|---|---|---|---|
| p | | k | ʔ | | | p | t | k | | | p | t | tʃ | k |
| | | h | | | | f | | | h | | | | s |

Hawaiian          Maori          Ainu

Ainu is something like an 'average' small system; no real fricative/stop symmetry, four places for stops, and /s/ alone.

As systems increase in size, the patterns become more complex; we find fricatives in positions unmatched by stops, and the kind of voiced/voiceless asymmetries or 'gaps' we saw with stops:

(7.57)

Icelandic
```
p   t           c       k
pʰ  tʰ          cʰ      kʰ
f   θ   s               h
v       j
```

German
```
p   t           tʃ  k
pf  ts
b   d
f   s           ʃ   x   h
v   z
```

French
```
p   ʈ           k
b   ɖ           g
f       s   ʃ
v       z   ʒ
```

Papago
```
p   ʈ           tʃ  k   ʔ
b   ɖ   ɖ   dʒ  g
        s   ʂ
```

Secondary articulations, length contrasts, and alternative airstreams are also available for fricatives. These do not usually occur in the smaller systems, but the large Caucasian ones are quite striking. Thus Avar:

(7.58)
```
p   t           k   q       ʔ
b   d           g
    ts  tʃ
                kː
    tsː tʃː
p'  t'          k'  q'
    ts' tʃ'
    tsː' tʃː'
    tɬː'
```

    s    ʃ    x    χ    ħ    h
    ɬ
    sː   ʃː   xː   χː
    ɬː
  v   z   ʒ      ʁ   ʕ

Here, with fricatives added, a new place previously unrepresented: pharyngeal, with voiced and voiceless /ʕ ħ/. Even without secondary articulation, this brings the fricative inventory to seventeen. But with secondary strictures and length we get this, in Abkhaz:

(7.59)    p   t   ts   tʃ   tɕ   k
            tʷ                 kʷ   qʷ
                                kʲ   qʲ
    b   d   dz   dʒ   dʑ   g
            dʷ  dzʷ              gʷ
    p'  t'  ts'  tʃ'  tɕ'
          tʷ  tsʷ
    f   s       ʃ              χ   ħ
                                  χʷ  ħʷ
                                  χʲ
                     ɕʷː
    v   z       ʒ             ʁ
                                 ʁʷ
                                 ʁʲ
                    zʷː

For aspiration and other airstreams in fricatives, we can turn to Burmese with the sibilant series /s sʰ z/, and Amharic with /s s'/.

### 7.6.3   *Some generalizations about obstruents*

On the basis of the material so far, and the rest of the languages in Nartey's survey, we can derive a set of probabilistic (largely implicational) statements about the structure of obstruent systems. The most important are these, based loosely on Nartey's 'Universals':

(i) Languages usually have at least three simple oral stops, most likely /p t k/.

(ii) If a language has an affricate it most likely also has at least three plain stops.

(iii) If there is only one affricate, it is most likely /tʃ/.

(iv) The number of voiceless stops is usually greater than the number of voiced, or equal.

(v) The number of affricates is less than the number of plain stops (but cf. Tillamook, (7.55)).

(vi) A language is highly unlikely to have 'secondary' stops (i.e. coarticulated, double, non-pulmonic, aspirated, etc.) unless it has 'primary' (voiceless or voiced) plain stops.

(vii) A language is highly likely to have at least one primary (in the sense of (vi)) fricative.

(viii) If a language has only one, it is most likely /s/, next most likely /f/.

(ix) The number of voiceless fricatives is likely to be greater than that of voiced; and there is likely to be an implicational relation between a voiced fricative and its voiceless cognate. The second statement is more weakly predictive than the first, and truer for fricatives than for stops.

(x) The number of fricatives is unlikely to be greater than that of stops.

(xi) No language has secondary fricatives unless it has primary; and primary normally outnumber secondary.

There are also cross-linguistic frequency hierarchies for place of articulation for stops (different for affricates and plain stops) and fricatives. According to Nartey's figures, they seem to be as follows (X > Y = 'X is more frequent across languages than Y'):

(7.60)      Obstruent frequency hierarchies
      *Stops:* Dental/Alveolar > Labial > Velar > Palatal > Uvular
      *Affricates:* Palatal > Dental/Alveolar > Labial > Velar
      *Fricatives:* Dental/Alveolar (central) > Labial > Palatal >
                Velar > Uvular/Pharyngeal >
                Dental/Alveolar (lateral) > Retroflex
      (Glottal stops and fricatives are excluded, since they do not figure in Nartey's survey; 'palatal' for affricates and fricatives probably conflates palatal and palato-alveolar at least; and 'dental/ alveolar' for fricatives conflates various sorts of /s/ and the rare /θ ð/. As an offhand guess, I would think /ʔ/ might be about as common as uvular stops, and glottal fricatives somewhat more common than retroflex: but this needs testing.)

These observations suggest that cross-linguistically:

(i) The dental/alveolar region is 'preferred' (except for affricates), in that if a language has only one place of articulation for a given obstruent type this is what it is most likely to be. (This appears not to hold for implosives.)

(ii) Voicelessness is preferred for obstruents in the same sense; the majority in any language are likely to be voiceless, and there is a tendency for voiced ⊃ voiceless.

The notions 'preferred' and 'likely' need some explication: what do they mean? From one point of view, the greatest value of these statistical 'universals' is to enable us to set up something like a language-general '**index of oddity**', where e.g. Ainu with its /p t tʃ k s/ is distinctly 'normal' or 'basic', and Avar and Abkhaz are 'odd'. Such judgements serve in part to sharpen our expectations when we meet new languages. Remembering that these are phonemic – not phonetic – 'normalcy statements', we can be justified in suspecting that, for instance, if a language has a pharyngeal fricative or uvular stop phonetically, it is more likely than not to be better characterized as an allophone of something else than a primary allophone. (For example, many varieties of English have uvular allophones of velar stops before low back vowels, and pharyngeal allophones of /h/ in the same context; but one would not want to characterize any variety of English as having /q G ħ/.) In addition, the frequency distributions can serve as a partial check on the reconstruction of unattested language-states: the 'odder' the system we reconstruct, the more argumentative support it needs.

But there is an important *caveat*: 'likely' must be used with genetic and areal 'tact'. That is, many cross-linguistic distributions conceal very strong anti-tendential local clusterings. For instance, while pharyngeals are rare overall, there is a very high concentration in Semitic, Caucasian, and some Amerindian languages; while breathy-voiced are rare in general, they are common in the Indo-European languages of India, and in upper-caste dialects of Dravidian languages that have borrowed extensively. In fact, one characteristic of areal and genetic groups is the way they often concentrate 'oddities': a particularly striking example is the virtual restriction of phonemic clicks to a portion of southern Africa. So what's rare universally may actually be the NORM for a family or area: we may have '**family universals**'.

### 7.6.4 *Sonorants, 1: nasals*

The preference for dental/alveolar articulation is even more striking for sonorants than for obstruents; but the voicing preference is reversed. This might be a cross-linguistic definition of the feature

[± obs]: segment types showing a clear statistical preference for voice-lessness are obstruents, those with a preference for voice are sonorants. This would tend, for instance, to classify lateral fricatives as obstruents (as we did, following Nartey and Hockett): /ɬ/ is much commoner than /ɮ/.

For nasals, the most complete survey is again Nartey (1979). According to his data, nearly all languages have 'primary' nasals – non-coarticulated voiced pulmonic nasal stops. There are eight in his sample with none, covering a fairly wide geographical and genetic range, including Quileute from North America, Rotokas from the South Pacific, and Apinayé from South America. Hockett adds Duwamish and Snoqualmie (also Coast Salishan, like Quileute); but remarks (p. 119) that these languages once had nasals and have now lost them. (I don't know if this is the case for Rotokas and Apinayé.) If all languages without nasals can be shown to have had them, this may be a rather bizarre case of an 'extinct universal' – a property that once was obligatory for natural languages but is no longer.

Aside from a few odd cases, then, languages normally have at least one nasal, most likely /n/. If there are two, the second is most likely /m/ (see the basic fricative distributions: /s/, /f s/); though /ŋ/ occurs as well. For three, the dominant pattern is /m n ŋ/ (cf. oral stops), though we get others as well. Some 1, 2, and 3-nasal systems:

(7.61)

| n | ŋ | m |
|---|---|---|
| Chipewyan | Mixtec | Taoripi |

| m n | m ɲ | |
|---|---|---|
| Ainu | Wapishana | |

| m n ŋ | m n ɳ | m ɳ ɲ |
|---|---|---|
| English | Pashto | Papago |

4-N and larger systems spread the contrasts out in much the same way as for stops and fricatives:

(7.62)

| m ɳ ɲ ŋ | m ɳ n ɲ | m n ŋ N |
|---|---|---|
| Yiddish | Diegueño | West Greenlandic |

| m ɳ n ɲ ŋ | m n ɳ ɲ ŋ |
|---|---|
| Araucanian | Ostyak |

Nasals can also have secondary articulations, voice contrasts (though phonemic voiceless nasals are rare), as well as length and double articulation contrasts:

(7.63)

| m | n | ŋ | | m | m | ɳ | | | m | n |
|---|---|---|---|---|---|---|---|---|---|---|
| m̥ | n̥ | ŋ̊ | | mː | nː | ɳ | | | mʲ | nʲ |

     Aleut             Kannaḍa         Bulgarian

| m | n | ɲ | ŋ | | m | m | ɳ | n | ŋ |
|---|---|---|---|---|---|---|---|---|---|
| m̥ | n̥ | | ŋ̊ | | m̥ | n̥ | ŋ̊ | ɳ̥ | ŋ̊ |
| | | | ŋʷ | | | | | | ŋ͡m |
| | | | | | | | | | ŋ͡m̥ |

     Hopi                     Iai

The cross-linguistic implications are the same type as for obstruents: in general, complex implies simple, voiceless implies voiced. The frequency hierarchy is:

(7.64)      Dental/Alveolar > Labial > Velar > Palatal > Retroflex > Uvular

### 7.6.5 *Sonorants, 2: 'liquids'*

'Liquids' covers a disparate set of segments, primarily lateral approximants and '*r*', i.e. alveolar and post-alveolar trills, taps, and approximants, and occasionally fricatives, and some uvular and velar trills, fricatives and approximants. (Whether a fricative 'counts as' an obstruent or a liquid is a matter of phonological analysis: German /ʁ/ counts as a liquid with /l/ because of its distribution and other phonological behaviour.)

The widest-ranging survey of liquid types is Maddieson (1980a). This is unfortunately (for our purposes) largely a statistical exercise, with little citation of anything but cross-linguistic frequencies, and few particular descriptions. But the sample is large (321 languages), and the findings of interest. I will sketch his results, and illustrate the major types – including some he doesn't mention – from other sources.

Virtually all languages (95% in the sample) have at least one liquid, and 72% have more than one. The largest systems appear to have seven, but these are rare (1%). Of the total, 79% have one or more laterals, and 76% one or more *r*-types. Overall, the preference is for simple segments, voiced as for nasals. Place for liquids is predominantly denti-alveolar, both for laterals and non-laterals; the manner preference for non-laterals appears to be for trills. The frequency hierarchies are:

(7.65)   *Laterals:*   Dental/Alveolar > Retroflex > Palatal > Velar

    *Non-laterals:* ⎰ *Place:*   Dental/Alveolar > Retroflex > Velar > Uvular

           ⎱ *Manner:* Trill > Tap/Flap > Approximant

Some relatively simple liquid systems:

(7.66)

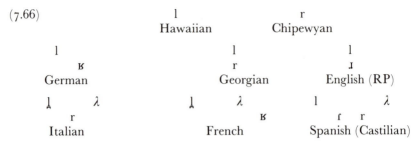

|  |  |
|---|---|
| l | r |
| Hawaiian | Chipewyan |

| l | l | l |
|---|---|---|
| ʁ | r | ɹ |
| German | Georgian | English (RP) |

| ḻ | λ | ḻ | λ | l | λ |
|---|---|---|---|---|---|
| r |  |  | ʁ | ɾ | r |
| Italian |  | French |  | Spanish (Castilian) | |

The simple vs. complex implication doesn't hold for all liquid systems; some have only liquids with secondary strictures in one or both categories (not mentioned by Maddieson):

(7.67)    ḷ    ḻ        ḻ
                ʁ    ᵼ⁺
          Yiddish    English (New York)

The symbol /ᵼ⁺/ is a pharyngealized palato-velar approximant, the New York '/r/'.

More complex systems add length or further place contrasts. Two Dravidian examples illustrate alternative strategies:

(7.68)       r    ɾ              ⁺r    r̄    ɭ
                l    ɭ              l    ɭ
                lː   ɭː            lː   ɭː
             Kannaḍa          Malayalam

> (/r̟/ is an advanced alveolar trill, /r̄/ is a retracted one; /ɭ/ is a retroflex approximant.) Other languages add voice contrasts, e.g. Burmese with /l̥/.

Maddieson's data gives the following main generalizations:

(i) Languages with two or more liquids are likely to have at least one lateral, and a lateral/non-lateral contrast.

(ii) A language with one or more laterals has a voiced lateral approximant.

(iii) Languages with two or more laterals may contrast them either in manner or voice, but not both (e.g. a language will not have a voiced lateral flap vs. voiceless approximant).

(iv) Languages with two or more r-types are unlikely to restrict the contrast to place alone (unlike laterals).

(v) A liquid with both lateral and non-lateral allophones is the likeliest candidate for the single liquid in a system (e.g. Nasioi with an alveolar tap realized as [l] before /u o/).

### 7.6.6 Sonorants, 3: 'semivowels' ('glides', vocoid approximants)

These terms refer to the familiar /j w/ types that appear in so many languages, as well as the less common labial-palatal approximant /ɥ/, the labiodental /ʋ/, and the velar, / ɰ /. Except for /ʋ/, these can be characterized as 'raised high vowels' in consonantal function. A recent survey (Maddieson 1980b), while producing the same problems as his (1980a), nonetheless comes up with some interesting generalizations. The most important seem to be:

(i) 90% of the sample languages have one or more vocoid approximants. Among the rare languages lacking them are Chipewyan, Crow, Samoan.

(ii) The vast majority (86%) have /j/; a smaller majority (75%) have /w/.

(iii) There is no apparent implicational relationship between /j/ and /w/, though 71% of the sample have both.

(iv) The other types are rare.

The preference hierarchy is notably different from those for all other segment types:

(7.69)      Palatal > Labial-Velar > Labial-Palatal > Velar

(I'm not sure where labiodental /ʋ/ fits in; I suspect that at least some reported '/w/' are in fact /ʋ/ – as in some varieties of Scottish English – and it may be somewhat less common than /w/ and more common than /ɥ/.) Here are some characteristic systems:

(7.70)

| | | | |
|---|---|---|---|
| j | w | j w | j ɥ |
| Navaho | Hawaiian | English | Polish |

| | | |
|---|---|---|
| w ɥ j | | ʋ j |
| French | | Kannaḍa |

Contrasts in voicing and glottal state can be added as well:

(7.71)

| | | | |
|---|---|---|---|
| w | j | w | j |
| w̥ | | w̥ | |
| | | w̰ | j̰ |
| Scots | | Margi | |

(where /w̰ j̰/ have 'laryngealized voicing', i.e. creaky voice).

159

### 7.7 What phonemes does a language 'have'? revisited

In discussing phonemic norms for vowel symbols (§7.5.1), we specified something like the 'centre' of a range of phonetic variation as basic – what the language 'really has' – and the rest of the allophonic range as 'derived' from that. Thus the typical allophonic statement is a rule operating on a PHONETICALLY SPECIFIED 'underlying representation' of some kind, and producing a set of 'surface' phonetic entities. In this respect the Unique Underlier Condition (§4.4) that was suggested as a condition on MP analyses seems to hold for phoneme–allophone relations as well. And it is usually assumed to hold in the same terms: the 'base form' of a phoneme is taken as having PHONETIC CONTENT (see the discussion of binary vs. n-ary feature specifications in §6.2). But there are difficulties with this view, which suggest alternative ways of approaching the concepts 'phoneme' and 'phonemic system', and a new dimension for typology.

Consider a rather extreme case: the 'linear' vowel systems of the NW Caucasian languages (Abkhaz, Abaza, Adyghe, Kabardian, and Ubykh). These languages all have phonemically minimal systems, varying apparently between two and three distinctive units. The problem is that the allophonic spread is so enormous that the units expounded by the qualities have to be specified quite abstractly. Thus Kabardian has the vowel phones:

(7.72)   i           ɨ      ü    u
         e      ɪ           ʊ    o
              ɛ̈      ə      ö    ʌ
         a                      ɑ

But (for instance) [iɪ] appear only in the vicinity of /j/, the rounded vowels only near labialized consonants or /w/, etc. Given the usual criteria for phonemic analysis, we arrive at three large-scale units, which might be specified this way:

(7.73)   /'Close'/ ⟶ [i ɪ ɨ ʊ ü u ...]
         /'Mid'/   ⟶ [e ɛ̈ ʌ ö ...]
         /'Open'/  ⟶ [a ɑ ...]

The 'units' here are not phonetically specifiable in the normal sense; should they even be called 'phonemes' at all? It seems quite arbitrary to assign a phonetic symbol (with the implication of some underlying phonetic representation) to one of these monster phonemes. Though one has to do something, and we typically get displays in the literature like the /ɨ ə ä/ cited earlier for Adyghe, and assumed by Trubetzkoy's term 'linear'.

The best one can say about languages like this is that they are difficult, and do not fit in a satisfying way into the usual analytical framework. (After all, /ɨ ə ä/ is really no less arbitrary than /i e a/ or /u o ɑ/, is it? The central symbols are, to be sure, graphically in the 'middle' of the range: but this doesn't make them phonetically 'basic' in any realistic sense.)

But this difficulty appears in a number of much less exotic system types as well, and suggests a new analytical strategy. Consider a language which – on a traditional analysis – is often said to 'have no fricatives or voiced stops': Tamil. The distribution of obstruent phones in native Tamil words is:

| (7.74) | # _____ | V ___ V | VN ___ V |
|---|---|---|---|
| | p | v | b |
| | t | ð | d |
| | – | ḍ | ḍ |
| | tʃ | s | dʒ |
| | k | x | g |

With this kind of distribution, a phonemic analysis would be built on the fact that voiceless stops (including [tʃ]) are in complementary distribution with both fricatives (voiced and voiceless) and voiced stops (the missing [t] is an 'accidental' gap in distribution, but is what we'd expect). Given this, and given that the environments where the fricatives and voiced stops occur are precisely those where one would expect these 'weaker' segment types (see §8.3 for discussion of 'strength'), it seems reasonable to take the voiceless stops as basic. Thus the Tamil obstruent system is /p t ṭ tʃ k/, and belongs to the simple type with no voice contrast.

But does complementary distribution like this force a choice of detailed phonetic representation? That is, just because we have the possibility of predicting say intervocalic [x] from a 'basic' /k/, do we have to make a choice of phonetic specification with respect to continuancy and/or voice in 'underlying' ( = non-phonetic or non-realized) representations? Granted, to make NO commitment to a basic representation would miss an obvious generalization; (7.74) looks like the precursor to a structural statement. There is clearly some kind of patterning or organization here. But given the phonetic inventory, fully-specified 'phonemes' of the usual sort may, as in Kabardian, be an unmotivated choice.

The choice problem resolves itself to this: motivating a **direction of derivation**, i.e. what justifies a direction /t/ → [ð], rather than the reverse? Characteristically such judgements are made (though rarely explicitly) on the basis of intuitions about typological 'naturalness' (there seem to be no languages with systems of only fricatives and voiced stops), and characteristic directions of historical change (see §8.3). But do these considerations dictate the analysis of a synchronic system? My judgement is that there is no necessary connection between these two sets of criteria and the analysis of a phonemic system – or at least no one seems to have demonstrated one. In this case, perhaps we ought to refrain from detailed specification of underlying forms, except for obstruency and place? Then Tamil too would have rather 'abstract' phonemes, not as bad as Kabardian, but still nothing as precise as /t/, etc.

Perhaps the best approach is to say that what Tamil has is not /p t k/, etc., but merely an obstruent system, underlyingly UNSPECIFIED for voice or continuancy; in other words, obstruents with only place features, and a set of 'strengths' or 'grades'. Thus we would have [obs, lab], [obs, dent], and so on, with no particular realization type given any special status as 'primary'. This avoids arbitrary (and ultimately redundant) underlying specification for voice or continuancy – since these features are predictable in ALL cases by word-position, and no particular value is – overall – 'characteristic' (unlike the case of, say, English /p t k/). This is in fact the real generalization that emerges from (7.74). We might envision a structure like this:

| (7.75) | *Place* | *Grade I* | *Grade II* | *Grade III* |
|---|---|---|---|---|
| | Labial | p | b | v |
| | Dental | t | d | ð |
| | Retroflex | – | ɖ | ɖ |
| | Palatal | tʃ | dʒ | s |
| | Velar | k | g | x |

Or we could use something like archiphonemic symbols, e.g. /P T K/, and so on, to show that this is a system with all features but place non-distinctive.

This is not the place to spell out the arguments in detail; but it is worth noting that the same data, under different theoretical requirements, yields very different systemic organizations. And this last view (which is essentially my own, and in no way 'standard') raises the possibility of a new dimension in system typology.

For instance: under the standard phonemic interpretation, Tamil with its /p t t tʃ k/ would appear to belong to the same type as Maranungku with /p t c k/ or Western Desert with /p ʈ t ̪ k/ – a language with only voiceless stops and no fricatives. Yet the Australian languages apparently do not show the same kind of realizational variation as Tamil: voicing, for instance, if it occurs, is restricted and usually optional. Thus the inventories – on the 'basic phoneme' interpretation, with 'directional' realization rules – show the languages as similar in type. Provided, that is, 'type' is defined within such a 'base-and-derivation' theory. But given a theory where languages may either have or lack 'full' underlying specification for particular features, Tamil comes out as belonging to quite a different category.

Thus we might propose a typological framework enriched by categories like 'place language' as opposed to 'phoneme language', or 'minimally-specified-phoneme language' vs. 'fully-specified-phoneme language'. These terms are *ad hoc* coinages; I merely want to suggest that there's room for a lot more research into the bases of a respectable theory of phonological typology. If this turns out to be a fruitful direction, we may want to say that the phoneme (as a fully-specified distinctive segment) is not a universal; that there are different language types at a level of description that has not been taken seriously, since all typologies to date have been phonemic in a more or less standard sense.

## 7.8 **Polysystematicity and neutralization**

Let us ask a question we have not asked, since we've been taking a positive answer for granted: is it always legitimate to identify a phone type in one position in a word with the same type in another position (aside from obvious cases like phonemic overlap)? Or, on a phonemic level, if a language has [m] vs. [n] in initial and final positions, are these phones to be referred to the phonemes /m/ and /n/ in both cases, as members of a single phonological system? Most theories implicitly answer yes; but at least one major phonological school (the 'Firthian' or 'prosodic' – see §§10.2ff for details) has made the premises explicit, and answered no. And under the conditions imposed by this negative answer, a new view of systems emerges, and an old problem – neutralization and how to characterize it – disappears.

In a pioneering paper of 1935, J. R. Firth treated the distribution of nasals in Marathi, which has a set-up rather similar to Kannaḍa (§3.3). In Marathi, only [m] and [n] occur initially, and [n ɲ] finally; but medially there are eight nasal phones, [m ɱ w̃ ɳ n ɳ ɲ ŋ]. Firth remarks that in transcriptions he uses the symbol [n] for all alveolar nasal phones, i.e. the initial [n] that contrasts with [m] only, the final one which 'functions in a three-term alternance', and the pre-consonantal one before [ts t d]. But he does not identify all these [n]'s 'as linguistically or functionally the same unit' (1935a [1957]: 51). 'Surely', he says, 'we are free to use the same letter without being compelled to concoct a rationalized "derivation" from the letter in the shape of a phoneme theory. Similarity of sound is no safe guide to functional identity'. (Up to a point, of course, this is obvious: in a Praguian account initial and final [t] in German are not 'the same' either – but Firth carries this much further. It is also worth noting that he raises the question of a distinction between notational practice and a theory of linguistic 'realities': we will return to this important notion in §8.5.)

Here (without saying so) Firth is in fact being more Praguian than the Praguians: if systems of oppositions ('three-term alternances', etc.) are what count, then Marathi has three nasal systems, not one: an [n] in the system {[n] vs. [m]} is just not the same thing as an [n] in {[n] vs. [ɲ] vs. [m]}, and so on. 'Sameness' is in phonology a **relational** concept, not a phonetic one. But note that the 'different-ness' of the two [n]'s here is not the same as the difference between the 'non-derived' [k] in Latin [priːnkeps] and the 'derived' [k] in [reːks] (see §4.5): the distinction is functional and 'static' (in terms of place in a system of oppositions), not a matter of morphophonology or derivation; the concepts 'underlying' and 'superficial' don't come into it.

This leads to a theoretical view of languages as at least potentially **polysystemic**, not **monosystemic** as in most classical phonological analysis. Languages may have different systems for different word-positions, different accentual conditions, even different morpho-syntactic or lexical categories. Let us look again at the German obstruents (see §5.4) through this polysystemic telescope, i.e. not considering the distribution of phones to be the deployment of elements of a single system:

(7.76)
| | (1) # _____ | | (2) V _____ V̇ | | (3) _____ # |
|---|---|---|---|---|---|
| | p | b | p | b | p |
| | t | d | t | d | t |
| | k | g | k | g | k |
| | | z | | z | s |
| | ʃ | | ʃ | | ʃ |
| | x | | x | | x |

Each segment in context (1) participates in a 9-way opposition; each one in (2) in a 10-way one; and each one in (3) in a 6-way. Further, systems (1) and (2) are characterized by a voice contrast, but system (3) belongs to a different 'language type' (though Firth would not have put it this way, and indeed was not concerned with typology). On this interpretation, we don't talk about 'the German stop system', but 'the German initial/medial/final stop systems', and so on.

If we adopt this view, of course, the problem of neutralization vanishes, because in final position there's no /p/–/b/ contrast to BE neutralized, and final /p/ is not a member of the initial or medial /p b/ systems. (In effect we reduce neutralization to something that looks like defective distribution – though even this concept is out here, since we can't identify initial and final [p] as exponents of one category.)

In a similar way, and perhaps more insightfully, the Old English vowel-neutralization discussed in §3.4 can be resolved not into neutralization of particular oppositions, but into a matter of the different content of separate systems. Compare the neutralization analysis in (3.17) above (repeated below as 'monosystemic') with a polysystemic analysis:

(7.77)

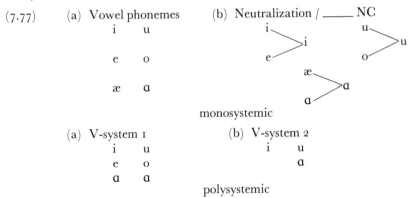

(a) Vowel phonemes

|   |   |
|---|---|
| i | u |
| e | o |
| æ | ɑ |

(b) Neutralization / _____ NC

monosystemic

(a) V-system 1

|   |   |
|---|---|
| i | u |
| e | o |
| ɑ | ɑ |

(b) V-system 2

|   |   |
|---|---|
| i | u |
| | ɑ |

polysystemic

The /u/ in system 1 is not identified with that in 2, because its function is utterly different.

What do we achieve with this approach? We solve the problem of what phone represents what archiphoneme very simply – since the question can't be asked. It is in fact a legitimate – if occasionally dangerous – move to dispose of questions by letting your theory make them unaskable. (For example, our cosmology doesn't allow us to ask 'Which god makes the crops come up in the spring?') The problem is, as always, whether in the long run we gain or lose by the exclusion.

In the OE vowel case, we do gain; with the German obstruents we lose. That is, since neutralization of gradual oppositions like vowel height leads to indeterminate or arbitrary results, a neutralization-free polysystemic account captures the facts better. But in a case like German, where the initial/medial pairs and the final singles are systematically related in a way that can be stated once and for all, and has a clear phonetic characterization, this seems to be more significant than the mere brute fact that the inventories are different. And – if we want to admit this – since the morphophonology shows a relation between the voiced and voiceless members of each pair, any account that makes the two systems unrelated is less revealing.

It looks as if we ought not to make either monosystemic or poly-systemic analyses binding in advance, but let the totality of facts about the language make the decision for us – if we can. And this decision may well be different for different (sub)systems in different languages. Complementarity yet again (see §§5.5, 7.7).

## NOTES AND REFERENCES

7.1 Theoretical constructs: there is a philosophical position called **instrumentalism** which in its crude form claims that theories are neither true nor false, but only more or less satisfactory devices for calculation, prediction, or description. It is opposed to **realism**, which in ITS crude form claims that theories are either true or false, and that theoretical objects have potential existence in the real world (see §6.1). Galileo, for instance, was not, as the popular mythology has it, condemned by the Inquisition for teaching Copernican astronomy *per se*; but rather for insisting it was a true picture of the world, that the earth REALLY moved around the sun – instead of saying that the phenomena were most elegantly treated AS IF this were so. The position taken in this book is often ambiguous between the two. (If you find this sort of thing interesting – and it is relevant to linguistics or any other theoretical subject – a good introduction to the philosophical discussion can be found in Chalmers 1978: chs. 10–11.)

7.2 For the GVS in detail, see any history of English; for the argument sketched here, Lass (1976a: ch. 2). On push and drag chains, Martinet (1955). On chain shifts in general, Labov *et al.* (1972).

7.3 On Grimm's Law, any standard Germanic handbook; the best treatment in English (if a bit dated now) is Prokosch (1938). The picture here is oversimplified, and bypasses various allophonic and other complications.

7.4 There is an enormous literature on 'universals', beginning with the important collection edited by Greenberg (1963). Of particular interest are the papers by Ferguson, Saporta, and Greenberg. Much important work in this area appears in the working papers of the *Stanford Universals Project* and the most recent large-scale effort is the four volumes edited by Greenberg, of which vol. 2** (Greenberg *et al.*, 1978) is devoted to phonology. For some very clear discussion of typology in general, *Comrie (1981a: ch. 1).

On markedness theory in this sense see **Postal (1968: ch. 8), **Chomsky & Halle (1968: ch. 9), Greenberg (1966a, b), Gamkrelidze (1978) and his references. The extremely negative position I take on the markedness issue is perhaps eccentric: compare the material cited above with my own extended arguments (**Lass 1975, **Lass 1980: ch. 2), and see §8.6 below.

On the universals (i)–(iv) given in this section, it is worth noting that they are generally taken as absolute, but aren't. For example, (i) is falsified by varieties of Scottish English with /y/ but no /u/; (ii) by Australian languages (see §7.6.1) with voiced obstruents but no voiceless ones; (iii) by varieties of English with /øː/ (e.g. [bøːmɪŋəm] 'Birmingham' in that city) but no /yː/; (iv) by Austrian dialects with /y ø œ Œ/. The chances are that nearly all absolute universals are artifacts, due to defects in the data-base; no one knows everything. And any specialist in a language family is likely to have data (often unpublished material from his own field notes or from specialist colleagues) that others know nothing about, and that 'generalist' theoreticians have no access to.

Thus the counter-examples to (i) and (iii) come from simple observation in the course of my own work; (ii) is the result of happening to pick up Dixon (1977) on impulse; and (iv) comes from a colleague's field notes. This just suggests something of what a genuine universals project has to cope with. There are also problems in deciding what 'counts' as an instance of a particular category, and this also destroys some supposed universals (§7.5).

7.5.1 On the general problems of typology, with a good literature survey, see Thrane *et al.* (1980: chs. 4–5). The most noteworthy attempts at vowel-system typology are **Trubetzkoy (1939), **Hockett (1955), Sedlak (1969), and **Crothers (1978). These are all worth reading with care.

7.5.4 The bulk of the material here is based on Crothers (1978: Appendix III), except for Yiddish, RP, German, Scots, Kabardian, and Swiss and Alsatian German (after Keller 1961), and the Hungarian system, which is courtesy of Veronika Kniezsa.

I have altered Crothers' notation to conform more closely to IPA conventions, and have conflated his /ɛ E/, /ɔ O/, where the capitals stand for 'mean mid' values, roughly between half-close and half-open, as /ɛ ɔ/.

One further remark on the consequences of omitting long vowels from Crothers' typological index is in order: he gives English (RP) as a six-V system with no interior vowels on the basis of /ɪ ɛ æ ʌ ʊ ɒ/ (with /ʌ/ interpreted as open central); but it has FIVE long vowels, one of them (his /ɔː/, my /ɜː/) interior. Therefore RP (even if /ʌ/ is allowed as peripheral) should not be grouped with Persian.

7.6 Much of the material here is based on the system-inventories in **Nartey (1979) which is the most complete survey of obstruent systems available (based on a sample of over 300 languages). Germanic and Dravidian systems from my own notes, Caucasian from Catford (1977b), Sindhi, Zulu from Ladefoged (1971), Yidiɲ from Dixon (1977). Nartey's interest is in implicational universals, and he has little to say about symmetry: for a good treatment of this, Hockett (1955). Nartey also omits glottal fricatives (on dubious grounds: he includes /ʔ/ under stops); so data on /h ɦ/ is partly from Hockett, partly from my own notes. Burmese and Amharic fricatives after Ladefoged (1971).

7.6.4 Data on nasals from Nartey (1979), except for West Greenlandic (Rischel 1974), Yiddish and Kannaḍa.

7.6.5 Liquid systems not from Maddieson are Hawaiian, Chipewyan, Georgian (Hockett 1955), Malayalam (Ladefoged 1971), German, English, Italian, Spanish, Kannaḍa (my notes).

7.6.6 Navaho, Hawaiian from Hockett (1955), Margi from Ladefoged (1971); all others my own observation.

7.7 Kabardian after Catford (1977b). There have in fact been attempts to reduce the inventory still further: Kuipers (1960) gives it NO vowels, but only a 'feature of openness', taken as a kind of secondary articulation of consonants. This is pretty well demolished by Halle (1970). See discussion in Catford.

7.8 On polysystemic theory see **Firth (1948), and the elaborate discussion of Thai in Henderson (1951).

# 8
# Phonological processes

## 8.1 The concept of process: terminology, theory, problems

Terms like 'velarization', 'palatalization', etc. are often used ambiguously and rather misleadingly. With years of practice one gets used to this, but it can be troublesome at the beginning. So can the proliferation of terms referring to process types, which are more or less traditional, but hard to trace to a definitive source. This chapter is a rough guide through the labyrinth of concepts and terminology, and an introduction to the nature and formalization of some characteristic inter-segment relations.

First, 'palatalization' and the like. These are used in two basic ways: **statically**, as names for secondary articulations (a palatalized consonant has superimposed [i]-colour), and **dynamically**, as names for processes (to palatalize is to impose such colour). But this isn't as troublesome as the ambiguous use of the process sense: 'to palatalize' can not only be to impose [i]-colouring, but to turn a non-palatal into a palatal. Thus not only [t] → [tʲ], but [t] → [c] or [k] → [c] are palatalizations, as traditionally are [k] → [tʃ], [s] → [ʃ], etc. The same holds for the other '-*ization*' terms.

There's yet a further ambiguity: terms like 'palatalization' can be (and often are) used to refer not only to phenomena that are clearly processes in a pretheoretical sense (see below), but also to ones open to reasonable non-process interpretations. A classic instance is the common interpretation of segmental DISTRIBUTIONS in terms of realizations that can be given process interpretations. Thus the English alternation of front and back velars depending on vocalic environment is often described as 'palatalization before front vowels'. Such an interpretation is highly theory-dependent; it assumes, among other things, a 'base-and-derivation' theory of the phoneme (§7.7), i.e. a belief in 'real' synchronic processes, the change of entities into others

169

in the course of a derivation. If you believe this, then it's legitimate to talk of a process as 'what really lies behind' complementary distributions, say; otherwise it's simply a descriptive metaphor. Under any interpretation it's a fact that there are front and back velars; but whether this involves 'palatalization' in a process sense is a matter of theoretical faith and/or analytical style. The only extra-theoretical 'fact' is the nature and distribution of the segments.

The only case where process terms can be used in a relatively theory-neutral sense is where the relation between input and output is TEMPORAL: i.e. in describing historical change. Take the now familiar voice-alternation in German obstruents; it happens to be a fact about the history of German that a sound change occurred that devoiced final obstruents, so that what is now [raːt]/[raːdəs] was once (roughly) [raːd]/[raːdəs]. The change [d] → [t] was a real event in historical time, and it left traces of itself as a paradigmatic irregularity. In our description of current language states we tend to resolve the 'surface' irregularities by referring them to 'deeper' regularities (§4.5); and thus we invoke processes that often mirror the historical changes that produced the irregularities in the first place. (Whether this is legitimate or not is debatable: see §§9.3ff.)

The problem of the 'genuineness' of processes (or phenomena statable as processes) becomes a bit more subtle when it comes to relations holding between speech tempi. Thus I have a sequence of increasingly casual forms of SENTENCE, [sɛnʔtɨns], [sɛnʔtn̩s], [sɛ̃ʔtn̩s] and [sɛ̃ʔn̩s]. Does this mean that in going from one style to another '[ɛ] turns into [ɛ̃] and [n] deletes', or '[ʔt] becomes [ʔ]'? Or is it just that one particular form is appropriate for/used in one tempo rather than another? (Compare this with the Scots speaker who says *thrapple* in his most locally-marked register and *throat* in his more 'standard' variety. Do we want to say '*thrapple* turns into *throat* ...'? Or that 'the speaker uses *thrapple* ... OR *throat*'?) That is: one possible non-historical interpretation of 'process' is 'substitution relation'.

This said, it's perfectly possible to use process-notations and formalizations without any commitment to 'reality', as they are descriptively useful – so long as we know what we're doing, and keep the theoretical problems in mind. With these *caveats* as a background, I will draw on historical, distributional, and fast-speech phenomena more or less indifferently for illustration, following the (perhaps ultimately harmless) sloppiness of the scholarly tradition.

## 8.2 **Assimilation and dissimilation**

These are catch-all terms: almost any process can count as one or the other, depending on context. Broadly, in **assimilation** one segment becomes more like (or identical to) another (or two become more like each other); **dissimilation** is the converse. Thus if [k] → [x] context-free, this is simply **spirantization**; but if the same thing happens between vowels, this can count as assimilation: the stop takes on the opener stricture of its surroundings. Conversely if [r] → [l] context-free, this is just 'lateralization' (the term is non-traditional); but if it happens in a form containing another [r], this is dissimilation (e.g. L *arbor* → Sp *arbol*). This said, assimilation is so common and important that various types are worth being discussed as such.

### 8.2.1 *Direction and contiguity*

The standard assimilation taxonomy involves **direction**; the assimilating influence may work either to the right or the left. Consider these English tempo variants:

(8.1)

|     |   | Tempo 1 | Tempo 2 |           |
|-----|---|---------|---------|-----------|
| (a) | 1 | əʊpən   | əʊpm̩    | 'open'    |
|     | 2 | sɛvən   | sɛvm̩    | 'seven'   |
| (b) | 1 | aɪm kʰʌmɪŋ | aɪŋ kʰʌmɪŋ | 'I'm coming' |
|     | 2 | aɪm nɒt | aɪm nɒt | 'I'm not' |

In (a) the influence moves from left to right, or forward; in (b) from right to left, or backward. This can be seen more clearly if we reformulate:

(8.2)     (a)  1  n ⟶ m   /p\_\_\_\_
                      ⟶ Direction

          (b)  1  m ⟶ ŋ   /\_\_\_\_k
                      ⟵ Direction

Case (a) is **progressive** or **perseverative assimilation**; (b) is **regressive** or **anticipatory**.

Assimilations may be further categorized according to whether the segments involved are in contact or separated by others. In (8.1) we have **contact assimilation**, but there is also **distant assimilation**, in which, either progressively or regressively, the influence moves across some intervening segment(s).

The most characteristic distant assimilation is **metaphony**: non-contact vowel assimilation. Traditionally there are two types:

(regressive) **umlaut** and (progressive) **vowel harmony** (though some writers use 'vowel harmony') for both. Umlaut can be illustrated by the Germanic *i*-umlaut, in which (in general) back vowels fronted before a following /i/ or /j/, normally with one or more consonants intervening:

(8.3)
$$\begin{bmatrix} u(\text{:}) \\ o(\text{:}) \\ a(\text{:}) \end{bmatrix} \rightarrow \begin{bmatrix} y(\text{:}) \\ ø(\text{:}) \\ æ(\text{:}) \end{bmatrix} / \underline{\quad} C \begin{Bmatrix} i \\ j \end{Bmatrix}$$

Stating it in features, the nature of the assimilation is clear, with the SD being [ + back] ... [ − back] and the SC [ + back] → [ − back].

The commonest metaphonies are assimilatory; but there are dissimilatory ones as well. One striking case is a sequence of umlaut and 'anti-umlaut' in the ancestors of modern Tamil and Kannaḍa, where the following rule-sequence has been reconstructed:

(8.4)

$$\text{Stage I} \quad \begin{bmatrix} i \\ u \end{bmatrix} \rightarrow \begin{bmatrix} e \\ o \end{bmatrix} / \underline{\quad} C_i^1 a$$

$$\text{Stage II} \quad \begin{bmatrix} e \\ o \end{bmatrix} \rightarrow \begin{bmatrix} i \\ u \end{bmatrix} / \underline{\quad} C_i^1 a$$

Curiously, the phone sets [i u] and [e o] are in complementary distribution at both stages in the same environment; only by assimilation to lowness at stage I and dissimilation at stage II.

Vowel harmony as a systematic process can be illustrated from Hungarian. Here, most suffixes have two or more allomorphs, which are conditioned by the vowel(s) of the preceding root-morpheme. In the simplest case, the suffix has two allomorphs, one with a front and one with a back (or non-front) vowel, controlled by the stem:

(8.5)

|  |  | Root-N | 'from inside N' | 'in N' | 'at N' |
|---|---|---|---|---|---|
|  | 'house' | häːz | häːz-boːl | häːz-bɒn | häːz-näːl |
|  | 'garden' | kɛrt | kɛrt-bøːl | kɛrt-bɛn | kɛrt-neːl |

There is also a harmony involving frontness/roundness, as in this three-allomorph suffix:

(8.6)

|  |  | Root-N | 'up to N' |
|---|---|---|---|
|  | 'house' | häːz | häːz-hɔz |
|  | 'garden' | kɛrt | kɛrt-hɛz |
|  | 'squash' | tœk | tœk-hœz |

Disregard for the moment the question of the underlying forms of the suffixes; we will return to this problem in vowel harmony, and other aspects, in §§9.3, 10.2.3. The Hungarian data, though grossly over-simple (a lot of exceptions have been omitted) at least gives the general idea.

Finally, there are 'bi-directional' or **fusional** assimilations, in which a sequence $S_iS_j$ (where S = 'segment') $\rightarrow S_k$ (where k = some combination of features from i, j). A familiar example is English alveolar/palatal sandhi:

(8.7)    hɪt juː       hɪtʃuː       'hit you'
         kʰɪd juː      kʰɪdʒuː      'kid you'
         mɪs juː       mɪʃuː        'miss you'

The output of a fusion is usually a 'compromise' segment: in (8.7) the alveolarity of the first element and the palatality of the second 'meet halfway' in a retracted alveolar with a raised tongue-body (which is what a 'palato-alveolar' really is). A similar if less obvious type of compromise assimilation occurs in Sanskrit vowel sandhi (§4.7, (4.18) ), where /-ɑ + i-/ $\rightarrow$ [-e-], /-ɑ + u-/ $\rightarrow$ [-o-], i.e.

(8.8)

The second element in the sequence controls backness, the first height; but height is assimilated by the second element moving 'one step' toward the height-controller /ɑ/, the result being a single segment combining the backness of one element and the (relative) height of the other.

### 8.2.2  *Basic assimilation and dissimilation types*

There is probably no segmental property that can't be the target of an assimilation or a dissimilation. It may be helpful to look at some major types in terms of the parameters they can be seen as responding to.

(i) *Place.* Examples have already been given of simple cases for consonants (8.1), as well as more complex fusional ones (8.7). If as suggested (§6.3) we extend the term 'place' to cover vowel height and backness, all examples so far except roundness harmony in

173

Hungarian are place assimilations (and this goes for dissimilations as well).

Diphthongization can also be assimilatory; in pre-Old English [u] was inserted between a front vowel and certain back consonants ('breaking' in the handbooks): e.g. /sæx/ 'I saw' → [sæux], /selx/ 'seal' → [seułx]. This can be seen as 'protection' of a front vowel from a back environment; hence the 'transition' vowel [u] is an assimilatory response. Later on, these diphthongs underwent an internal height-assimilation: [æu] → [æɑ], [eu] → [eo].

Under a bi-segmental interpretation (§5.3.10), diphthongization of long vowels and monophthongization of diphthongs are relevant. If [iː] = [ii] and [uː] = [uu], then the diphthongization of ME /iː uː/ in the Great Vowel Shift (§7.2) is dissimilation: /ii/ → /ei/, /uu/ → /ou/. By the same token, the monophthongization of ME /au/ to /ɔː/ in Early Modern English (e.g. *law* /lɔː/ from /lau/) is a mutual assimilation, in principle not unlike the Sanskrit case described earlier; but since both original segments are directly 'represented' in the output here, there has been no fusion: Sanskrit /au/ → /o/ vs. English /au/ → /ɔɔ/.

(ii) *Stricture.* The commonest type is opening of stricture in response to surrounding opener stricture ('weakening', §8.3). So Spanish /b d g/ → [β ð ɣ] between vowels, Proto-Dravidian */c k/ → [s x] inter-vocalically in Tamil. Assimilation to closer stricture ('strengthening') is also attested, if rarely: in some southern U.S. English dialects, /z/ → [d] before /n/ ([bɪdnɪs] 'business', [wʌdn̩t] 'wasn't'), i.e. a fricative becomes a stop before a (nasal) stop.

(iii) *Lip attitude.* The commonest type is rounding (usually anticipatory) of consonants in the vicinity of rounded vowels, e.g. [t̹ʰ] in English *tore, to*. Vowel rounding after rounded segments is also common; in Northumbrian Old English /e/ → [ø] after /w/ (Nhb *woesa* 'to be' vs. *wesan* in other dialects); and a later revival shows up in those varieties of English with /wɒ/ or /wɔ/ for original /wa/, e.g. *watch, wallet, swallow*.

(iv) *Velic attitude.* The commonest instance is anticipatory vowel nasalization before /N(C)/, as in most varieties of English. This is the usual precursor to the development of phonemic nasalized vowels: the deletion of a nasal after it has nasalized a vowel leaves [V]/[Ṽ] as a marker for what used to be [V]/[ṼN], thus phonemicizing vowel nasality. For example, French /fɛ̃/ *fin* vs. /fɛ/ *fait*, from Latin /fin-/, /fakt-/ (plus other changes of course). Progressive nasalization occurs too, if less commonly: Sundanese appears to have a general rule nasalizing any sequence of vowels after a nasal, provided there are no intervening supraglottal articulations or boundaries: [mãro] 'to halve', [ɲãĩãn] 'to wet', [nĩʔĩs] 'to take a holiday'.

(v) *Glottal state.* Assimilatory voicing and devoicing are well attested, the former e.g. in Sanskrit voicing sandhi (§4.7), the latter in English external sandhi, e.g. [hæftuː] 'have to', [hæstuː] 'has to' [juːstuː] 'used to'. These are regressive; progressive voice assimilation occurs in the allomorphy of the English plural, genitive, third person singular present and weak verbal past after obstruents: /s/ in *hawks, hawk's, walks,* /z/ in *bags, bag's, lags,* /t/ in *walked,* /d/ in *lagged.* Intervocalic voicing assimilation is also common, see the neutralization of the English /t/ : /d/ contrast (§2.8).

Voice assimilation occurs in sonorants as well, with, in general, devoicing in response to voiceless obstruents. Thus Icelandic has progressive devoicing of /r l n/ after /h/ as in [hr̥iːva] 'rake', [hl̥øypʰa] 'run', [hn̥iːvʏr] 'knife', as well as regressive devoicing of these and /m/ before (most) voiceless stops, as in [hɛm̥ˑpa] 'cassock', [vɛr̥ˑpʰa] 'throw', [ɛl̥ˑtʰa] 'pursue'; and progressive devoicing in final position after stops: [fʏkˑl̥] 'bird', [vɔhpn̥] 'weapon'.

Glottal state dissimilation is rare, but there is an example in Maxakali nasal sandhi: [mĩnnĩ] 'black', [kõnnɨ̃ŋ] 'macaw', but [kõnnɨ̃ŋ m̃ĩnnĩ] 'black macaw'.

(vi) *Complex assimilations.* More than one parameter may be involved in assimilation; such processes characteristically result in the formation of geminates or identical clusters from sequences of dissimilar consonants. Perhaps the most familiar examples are Latin preposition + verb compounds, like *afferō, attulī, allātum* 'carry to' (pres 1 sg, perf 1 sg, past part), from *ad-ferō, ad-tulī, ad-lātum,* or *colligō* 'tie together' from *con-ligō.* A rather different case, involving nasals devoicing and becoming obstruents, occurred in early Scandinavian, where [-ŋk-] → [-kk-], [-nt-] → [-tt-], [-mp-] → [-pp-]: Old Norse *drekka* 'drink', *batt* 'bound', *kappi* 'warrior' (original structures visible in OE *drincan, band, cempa*).

### 8.2.3 *Acoustic assimilation*

Assimilation is normally thought of as articulatory adjustment (anticipation or persistence of vocal-tract configurations). But the concept can be usefully extended to cases where the trigger is an acoustic property, mediated via auditory perception. Since we have already allowed for acoustic features anyhow (§5.5), it is a simple matter to extend this to assimilation.

The following sound change occurred in some dialects of Austrian German:

(8.9) $\quad \begin{bmatrix} i(:) \\ e(:) \end{bmatrix} \rightarrow \begin{bmatrix} y(:) \\ ø(:) \end{bmatrix} \; / \underline{\hspace{1cm}} ł$

i.e. unrounded front vowels round before velarized /l/. An articulatory feature analysis would show no connection between rounding and any property of [ł]; the change looks arbitrary. But acoustic analysis reveals a different picture: velars (and velarized segments) have general 'low tonality' (specifically, low second and third formants); and the acoustic effect of rounding is to lower these formants as well.

If a segment with a low $F_2$, say, follows one with a high $F_2$, the transition between them will show a 'flattening' or 'downshifting' of this formant. Imagine a speaker 'misreading' this downshift BETWEEN two segments, and locating the lower value in the first segment; and then altering the articulation of that segment to square with the perceived effect. Schematically:

(8.10)

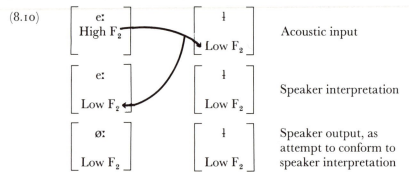

| | |
|---|---|
| $\begin{bmatrix} e{:} \\ \text{High } F_2 \end{bmatrix} \quad \begin{bmatrix} ł \\ \text{Low } F_2 \end{bmatrix}$ | Acoustic input |
| $\begin{bmatrix} e{:} \\ \text{Low } F_2 \end{bmatrix} \quad \begin{bmatrix} ł \\ \text{Low } F_2 \end{bmatrix}$ | Speaker interpretation |
| $\begin{bmatrix} ø{:} \\ \text{Low } F_2 \end{bmatrix} \quad \begin{bmatrix} ł \\ \text{Low } F_2 \end{bmatrix}$ | Speaker output, as attempt to conform to speaker interpretation |

(Retraction of [e:] to a central or back vowel would also be a reasonable response to the same acoustic input; on the indeterminacy of assimilatory response see §8.6.)

A similar instance occurs in many dialects of English, where non-low vowels lower before a pharyngealized palato-velar /r/: here the tongue position is in fact HIGH, but the transition is interpreted as a lower articulation of the preceding vowel, due to the high $F_1$ value associated with pre-pharyngeal transition. These transition effects, of course, are maximized and extended in the course of time; what starts as a minimal coarticulation effect is often sharpened or focussed ('phoneticized') into a perceptually more salient effect, often leading to gross phonetic or phonemic change.

Thus it looks as if assimilation is **bi-modal**: there is the same 'choice' with regard to assimilation as there is with other phonological generalizations: we can respond either to articulatory or acoustic properties.

## 8.3 **Phonological strength**

### 8.3.1 *Lenition and fortition*

Both synchronic and historical phonologies show frequent processes involving change both in stricture and glottal state. For various (not entirely obvious) reasons these are customarily grouped together, as follows: any movement to the right along the hierarchies in (8.11) below is **lenition** or **weakening**; any movement to the left is **fortition** or **strengthening**:

(8.11)    (a)  Stop > Fricative > Approximant > Zero
          (b)  Voiceless > Voiced

The motivation is clear for (a): each step to the right increases the permeability of the vocal tract to airflow. That for (b) is not immediately clear; but the frequency with which the change voiceless → voiced is a precursor to opening of stricture argues for an essential similarity; as do the coexistence of (a)-type and (b)-type changes as exponents of 'the same' process in languages. A case in point is the **initial mutations** in Celtic languages, where in similar contexts (now morphosyntactic, once phonological), we have the following: (i) voiceless stops become voiced; (ii) voiced stops become fricatives; (iii) voiceless lateral fricatives (a) lose their friction, and (b) become voiced. Consider the isolative forms vs. masculine possessives of these nouns in North Welsh:

(8.12)              Root N     His N
         (i)   pɛn        i bɛn        'head'
         (ii)  braud      i vraud      'brother'
         (iii) ɬɔŋ        i lɔŋ        'ship'

Each initial goes one step down whatever hierarchy it's on; and /ɬ/ goes from voiceless to voiced on (b) and fricative to approximant on (a). So phonologically the two are connected; though the phonetic connection is obscure. (For a possible interpretation, see §§11.4, 11.7.)

But the traditional hierarchy (8.11) needs expansion: we ought to include affrication and aspiration as forms of weakening as well, since they both involve opening of stricture in the release phase of a stop.

Perhaps the best way to look at lenition/fortition overall is in terms of two strength scales, one of **openness** and one of **sonority**: movement down the first involves decreased resistance to airflow, movement down the second an increase in the output of periodic acoustic energy. And a segment can, as we'll see, move from one hierarchy to another. So:

(8.13)

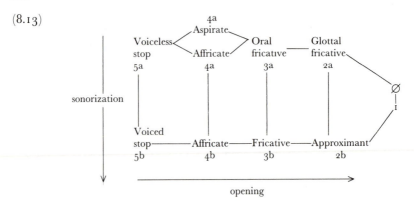

(8.13) defines a set of coordinates for strength-changes: down and/or right is lenition, up and/or left is fortition.

Taking a voiceless stop as the strongest segment type, we have two simple routes to zero: via opening alone, or via sonorization plus opening (or opening plus later sonorization). In general, movement to the right and down is commoner (more 'natural') than the opposite; and once (say over a language history) a segment has started on a path of lenition, it rarely appears to restrengthen. (This is not, as it may seem, a matter of lenition being 'cumulative' or 'directional': a segment does not know where it came from, and if lenition is generally more probable than fortition, the odds are that any segment at any point on its hierarchy will weaken, if it does anything.)

So input can be made at any point, and transfer can occur between sub-hierarchies, more or less at any point, e.g. a voiceless fricative can voice, and then continue down the opening scale at the (b) level. Conversely, a segment may strengthen by moving from (b) to (a), and then weaken (e.g. final [g] → [k] in German, and then in some dialects final [k] → [ç] after front vowels). The one place, however, from which fortition in the strict sense can't occur is zero: if a deleted segment is replaced by something, this is not a matter of strength any more.

A word is in order on the sequence 3a → 2a in (8.13), which assigns a special status to glottal fricatives. This is in keeping with the claim in §6.5 that non-oral segments are 'defective', i.e. one submatrix short. There is strong evidence for this not only from synchronic processes like the Scots /θ/ → [h] rule, but from the sources of /h/ in many languages. Perhaps the majority of /h/ in present-day languages can be traced back to the lenition of other obstruents; to take a few examples, all Germanic /h/ are from /x/ from Indo-European /k/; Armenian /h/ is from earlier /p/; Latin /h/ is from earlier /g/; Greek (Classical) /h/ from /s/; in Uralic, Ostyak, Hungarian, Yurak /h/ from /k/; in Dravidian, Kannaḍa /h/ from /p/, Pengo, Kuvi /h/ from /c/; Manda, Kui /h/ from /k/; and so on. In none of these families can we reconstruct an original /h/.

We further find that /h/ is particularly prone to loss; so much so that it can be regarded as a natural 'way-station' from obstruent to zero. On this basis we can set up a two-phase progressive lenition schema for obstruents, divided into what we can call 'feature change' and 'matrix change' (after Lass 1976a: 163):

(8.14)                    Progressive obstruent weakening

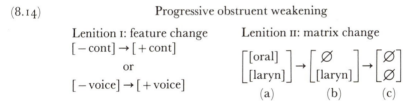

Lenition I: feature change       Lenition II: matrix change

Stage (c) of Lenition II may be called **de-oralization**, or **de-articulation** and produces a matrix type particular prone to loss.

On the question of whether segments can 'skip' stages on the hierarchies, the evidence is ambiguous. Languages certainly exhibit ALTERNATIONS that look like progressions that skip steps (e.g. many forms of Northern English have [tʰ] or [ts] ~ [ɹ], as in [ʃʊtsʊʔp] ~ [ʃʊɹʊʔp] 'shut up' and the like); but it is unclear whether these substitution relations should be interpreted as processes in themselves, or as the relics of former historical processes, some of whose intermediate stages happen to be missing from the record. In the case above, that would mean that there ought to have been either a voiced stop or fricative stage between the input and [ɹ].

But keeping this issue on one side, we can illustrate various movements along the hierarchies, just to show the sorts of relations that come under the general heading of strength changes, and to illustrate the pervasiveness of the patterns. As in previous sections of this chapter, I will use a rather unsorted mix of historical and synchronic examples. (In the material below, '5a > 4a', etc. refer to the strength stages in (8.13).)

A *Lenition*

(i) **Opening alone**

(1) 5a < 4a/4a′: English /t/ → [tʰ]/[ts] (depending on dialect) initially; pre-Old High German /p t/ → [pf ts] in certain environments (cf. *Pfund, Herz* vs. *pound, heart*).

(2) 5a > 3a > 2a: IE *\*/k/ → Germanic /x/ → /h/: IE *\*/kerd-/ 'heart' → Proto-Gmc *\*/xert-/ → later /hert/ (E *heart*, G *Herz*); 2a > 1 pre-consonantally in English, *\*/nokt-/ 'night', OE *niht* [nixt], 16th-century [neiht], Mod [nait].

(3) 3a > 2a > 1: Latin /f/ → Old Spanish /h/ → Mod /∅/ (*filius* → *hijo* /ixo/, initial /h/ in 16th century).

(ii) **Sonorization alone**

(1) 5a > 5b: Proto-Dravidian *\*/t k/ → Kannaḍa /d g/ between vowels: /odagu/ 'help' from *\*/utaku/.

(2) 3a > 3b: Old English /f θ s/ → [v ð z] between vowels; Welsh initial mutation of voiceless stops (see above).

(iii) **Sonorization + opening**

(1) 5a > 5b > 3b > 2b: Latin /k/ → Old Spanish /g/ → Mod Sp [ɣ] → Puerto Rican Spanish /w/: L *aqua* → Sp *agua* → PR /awa/.

(2) 5a > (5b?) > 3b: Proto-Dravidian medial *\*/t/ → Tamil [ð]: [uðirɯ] 'drop off' from *\*/utir-/.

B *Fortition*

(i) **Desonorization**

(1) 5b > 5a/ 3b > 3a: final devoicing of obstruents in German. The scale (8.13) does not have distinct places for voiceless nasals and approximants (indeed the status of nasals is uncertain, since they do not typically weaken to anything except nasality on vowels, if that's what that is): but with a suitable revision, the Icelandic devoicings in §8.2.2 (v) would come under this heading as well.

(2) 3b > 3a: devoicing of /v z ɣ/ in Amsterdam Dutch: /friːs/ for *Fries, Vries* (/friːs/ vs. /vriːs/ in the south), /sɛin/ *zijn* 'his', /χʊt/ *goed* 'good'.

(ii) **Closing**

(1) 2b > (3b?) > 4b: Latin /-j-/ → Italian /ʤ/ (L *maior*, It *maggiore*); 2b > 3b in French, *majeur* /maʒœr/.

(2) 3b > 5b: Southern U.S. /z/ → [d] ([bɪdnɪs] 'business', etc.).

(3) 2b > 5b (intermediate stages uncertain): IE */-ww-, -jj-/ → /-gg-, -dd-/ in some Germanic dialects: Old High German *triuwa* 'troth', *zweiio* 'of two' vs. Old Norse *tryggva, tveggja*. (See any handbook of comparative Germanic under 'Holtzmann's Law'.)

8.3.2 *Preferential environments and 'protection'*

In a rather general way we can characterize particular environments as 'preferred' for certain strength changes. The notion of preference (just as in the choice of system elements, see ch. 7) is PROBABILISTIC: no environment is exclusively or predictably of one type or another, but certain processes occur so often in certain places that we can say 'X is a preferred weakening environment', etc. Judgements like this are basically inductive, i.e. they arise on the basis of extensive observation, though in some cases there is also a 'phonetic explanation' of sorts (see §8.6).

For instance, V ___ V is a prime weakening environment: all things being equal, we expect lenition here. Thus the set of developments of Latin intervocalic /b d g/ in the modern Romance dialects follows the expected picture of descent down the scales:

(8.15)

| | Latin | Italian | French | Spanish |
|---|---|---|---|---|
| | -b- | -v- | -v- | -β- |
| | -d- | -d- | ∅ | ∅ |
| | -g- | -ʤ- | ∅ | ∅ |

(L *habēre* 'have', It *avere*, Fr *avoir*, Sp *haber*; L *crēdere* 'believe', *credere, croire, creer*; L *legere* 'read', *leggere, lire, leer*.) Not all segments have weakened, and the weakenings haven't gone the same distance in all the languages (see §8.3.3). But the pattern is clear. And on the basis of many such observations we would be entitled to assume – even in the absence of any other evidence, such as the actually attested 'parent' language, Latin – that Italian was the most 'primitive' of the three modern dialects, in the sense of being closest to an 'original' condition.

The special status of intervocalic position – and indeed something else about the nature of strength – is suggested by the development of stops in different positions in Uralic. Consider the reflexes of (a) initial */p t k/, (b) intervocalic */p t k/, and (c) intervocalic */pp tt kk/ in four Uralic dialects:

(8.16)

| Proto-Uralic | Finnish | Hungarian | Vogul | Ostyak |
|---|---|---|---|---|
| *p- | p- | f- | p- | p- |
| *-p- | -p- | -v- | -p- | -w- |
| *-pp- | -pp- | -p- | -p- | -p- |
| *t- | t- | t- | t- | t- |
| *-t- | -t- | -z- | -t- | -t- |
| *-tt- | -tt- | -t- | -t- | -t- |
| *k- | k- | -h- | -h- | -k- |
| *-k- | -k- | -k- | -g- | -g- |
| *-kk- | -kk- | -k- | -k- | -k- |

Regardless of the failures of lenition, we notice the following: (a) if a stop weakens in initial position, it seems to prefer opening to sonorization; (b) if a single stop weakens intervocalically, sonorization is usual, and opening frequent; (c) the double stops never undergo either sonorization or opening, though they may shorten. Thus, if this material is representative, it suggests that both syllable-initial and intervocalic are weakening contexts, but that the preferred modalities for lenition are opening initially and sonorization intervocalically.

This in itself is not surprising, considering that if lenition is sometimes at least an assimilatory response, V ＿＿ V should be more effective as a trigger than ＿＿ V ('two vowels are more vocalic than one'). This is further borne out by the resistance of /pp/ etc. to weakening: here one might say that two consonants are more consonantal than one, and hence double the resistance. Thus ＿＿ C is a **protected** environment, i.e. consonants are not so prone to lenition if protected by another consonant as they are standing alone. And this shows up in other, apparently unrelated cases, which can be made to fall together under a single generalization about protection. First, the failure of aspiration in most dialects of English for /p t k/ in clusters with /s/ ([stæk] vs. [tʰæk]; in those dialects that do aspirate after /s/, the aspiration is usually shorter and less pronounced). Second, the failure of IE */p t k/ to become Germanic /f θ x/ if in clusters with another obstruent: L *spuō* 'vomit', English *spew*, L *stella*, E *star*, L *captus* 'captured', OE *hæft* 'captive' (here the protection works in one direction only – a preceding obstruent protects but is not itself protected, hence OE /ft/ corresponding to Latin /pt/). Third, in Greek /s/ fails to become /h/ in clusters: *hépta* '7' (cf. L *septem*) as expected, but *estí* 'he is' not *ehtí* (cf. L *est*).

### 8.3.3  More on strength hierarchies

The Uralic data in (8.16) shows another interesting pattern. If you look at which segments weaken in particular languages, you note that there doesn't seem to be – in any position – an across-the-board lenition: certain place categories are 'weak' or 'strong', and they vary from language to language:

(8.17)

|         |        | Hungarian      | Vogul          | Ostyak                |
|---------|--------|----------------|----------------|-----------------------|
| Initial | Weak   | Labial, velar  | Velar          | —                     |
|         | Strong | Dental         | Labial, dental | Labial, dental, velar |
| Medial  | Weak   | Labial, dental | Velar          | Labial, velar         |
|         | Strong | Velar          | Labial, dental | Dental                |

The strength classes also seem to be determined by different features: Hungarian has [ + grave] as the weak initial class, [ + anterior] as the weak medial; while [ + grave] is the medial weak class in Ostyak, and the strong initial in Vogul, etc. Data like this refutes the claim of some writers (e.g. Foley 1977) that certain places are universally weaker than others (i.e. more prone to lenition), and that there are implicational hierarchies such that if one class lenites it will be velars, and lenition of dentals implies that of velars, etc.

What is true, however, is that if at a given time a language has a weakening process, there is a strong tendency for certain place categories to be weak and others strong, in a given position. We can add to the above the spirantization of intervocalic grave voiced stops in Old English (§5.5), the U.S. English weakening of /t d/, the spirantization of /t d k g/ but not /p b/ in Liverpool English, and so on. At least for place, strength hierarchies are language-specific, not universal.

We can see the interaction of universal and particular strength relations in a study by Zwicky (1972); he looked at the susceptibility to deletion (as an index of weakness) of segments in one dialect of English, and came up with the following ranking:

(8.18)     Stops > Fricatives > ŋ > m > n > l > r > h > w > j > Vowels

The types follow (8.13), to a large extent; but the positions are independent. In the latter case, 'strength' is a more arbitrary, less phonetic concept than it is for the larger classes.

## 8.4  **Whole-segment processes: insertion, deletion, reordering**

Up to now we have looked mostly at alteration of segmental

features; we have not been concerned in detail with the creation, deletion, or linear transposition of whole segments. But processes with segment-size domains are common and important.

### 8.4.1 *Insertion*

New segments may appear 'from zero' in formerly unoccupied marginal positions in the word or morpheme, or between two previously abutting segments. The general term for such insertion is **epenthesis**, Two types are worth defining separately, as the processes they denote often have special theoretical status.

(i) **Prothesis** is the insertion of an initial segment, normally a vowel – usually with a phonotactic motivation. Thus in the transition between late Latin and Old French, initial /sp st sk/ clusters became illegal, and were destroyed by prothetic /e/: L *spiritus* 'spirit', *stella* 'star', *scala* 'ladder', Fr *esprit, étoile, échelle* (the two latter with later loss of /s/).

(ii) **Anaptyxis** is the insertion of a vowel between two consonants, most usually sonorants, or an obs + son or son + obs cluster. This is often the sequel to syllabification of a sonorant: so in varieties of English with [fıləm] 'film', [æθəliːt] 'athlete', the anaptyctic [ə] may derive from earlier [fılm̩], etc. Anaptyctic vowels are also referred to as **parasite vowels** or by the Sanskrit term **svarabhakti**.

There are also more 'general' epentheses that belong to neither of these types: vowel epenthesis can occur in the form of diphthongization of short vowels, or (on a bi-segmental interpretation), lengthening of short vowels. Such epentheses may be assimilatory (as in [i]-insertion after non-high vowels before palatals and velars in some U.S. dialects: S. Indiana [bæig] 'bag', [bʊiʃ] 'bush', [bɛiɲtʃ] 'bench'); or non-assimilatory, as in the shift of earlier /æ/ to /æə/ in certain forms of RP.

Consonant epenthesis is equally common: one frequent type stems from a timing lag between a nasal consonant and a following oral, where the velum closes before the 'target' post-nasal oral closure is formed. The result is an epenthetic oral stop, homorganic to the nasal, but (usually) with the voicing value of the non-nasal. A familiar English example is the epenthesis of [t] in /n___s/, [p] in /m___θ/, and [k] in /n___θ/, as in [pɹɪnts] 'prince/prints', [dɹɛmpt] 'dreamt', [sʌmpθɪŋ] 'something', [lɛŋkθ] 'length'.

Since all epentheses can be interpreted as 'replacement of zero' by something, the standard formalization is '$\emptyset \rightarrow X$'. Thus French /e/-

prothesis and English [ə]-anaptyxis before sonorants could be stated respectively as:

(8.19)   (a)  $\emptyset \rightarrow e /$ _____ sC

(b)  $\emptyset \rightarrow \mathrm{ə} / C$ _____ $\begin{bmatrix} C \\ -\,obs \end{bmatrix}$

This 'works'; but stating the two in the same way rather misses the point, as does stating post-nasal stop epenthesis in the same format, e.g.

(8.20)

$$\emptyset \rightarrow / \begin{bmatrix} +\,obs \\ -\,cont \\ \alpha[artic] \\ \beta[phon] \end{bmatrix} / \begin{bmatrix} +\,nas \\ \alpha[artic] \end{bmatrix} - \begin{bmatrix} +\,obs \\ \beta[phon] \end{bmatrix}$$

(The conventions for agreement in place and phonation build on the discussion in §6.5; [α[artic]] is a variable over all possible values for place features, and [β[phon]] is equivalent to a variable over the laryngeal gesture: i.e. the epenthetic stop agrees with the nasal in place and the following obstruent in phonation.)

The point is that a process like (8.19a) has a rather 'abstract' motivation, in terms of a change in syllable structure conditions; it is not phonetically motivated. Whereas in (8.19b) and (8.20) there is a 'source' for the inserted segment. To clarify: anaptyxis typically occurs before or after sonorants, which (*vis-à-vis* obstruents) are relatively more 'vocalic' or 'vowel-like'. From this we could argue for a feature [+vocalic] shared by all sonorants with vowels. Then we can interpret anaptyxis as **segmentalization** or **linearization**: movement of a feature specification from a position in a vertical column to a new place in a horizontal sequence. So for /æθliːt/ → [æθəliːt]:

(8.21)  $\begin{bmatrix} \theta \\ +\,obs \\ +\,cons \\ -\,voc \\ \vdots \end{bmatrix} \begin{bmatrix} l \\ -\,obs \\ +\,cons \\ +\,voc \\ \vdots \end{bmatrix} \rightarrow \begin{bmatrix} \theta \\ +\,obs \\ +\,cons \\ -\,voc \\ \vdots \end{bmatrix} [+\,voc] \leftarrow \begin{bmatrix} l \\ -\,obs \\ +\,cons \\ -\,voc \\ \vdots \end{bmatrix}$

That is, rather than 'zero becoming a vowel', a vocalic component is copied out and moved one place to the left. We can then assume that this moved component develops a '**carrier**', i.e. it is coordinated with some appropriate set of place features, derived either from the segment it's extracted from (see below), or from general conditions in the language defining a 'minimal' or 'neutral' vowel ([+voc] can't stand alone without other features to 'embody' it).

This can be supported by languages in which anaptyctic vowels are qualitatively dependent on features of consonants they can be said to derive from. In some varieties of Scots there is parasiting after /l/ and /r/ before another sonorant, as in *film, farm*, but the inserted vowel is not a 'neutral' [ə]; after /l/ (which is velarized) it is rather back, and after the alveolar /r/ it is rather front: [fɪɫʌm], [fɛrëm]. Vocalicity and a (modified) place specification have been extracted. We might formalize this using the format typically used for syntactic transformations (SD = structural description, SC = structure change; the numbers identify items):

(8.22)

$$
\text{SD:} \quad \begin{bmatrix} -\text{obs} \\ +\text{cons} \\ +\text{voc} \\ \alpha\,\text{back} \end{bmatrix}_{1} \quad \begin{bmatrix} -\text{obs} \\ +\text{cons} \end{bmatrix}_{2} \quad \text{SC:} \quad 1 \quad \begin{bmatrix} +\text{voc} \\ \alpha\,\text{back} \end{bmatrix} \quad 2
$$

Similarly, [i]-insertion before palatals and velars in English could be seen as copying out of [+high] which develops a vocalic carrier, here not responsive to place. And using the same framework, we can interpret the complex stop-epenthesis between nasals and obstruents as a double copying, moving in two directions: (8.20) is really:

(8.23)

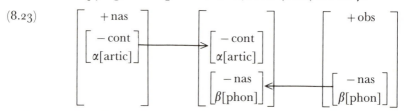

Thus we can distinguish phonotactically or non-phonetically motivated processes as genuine instances of 'segment from zero', from spurious epenthesis or feature-segmentalization.

### 8.4.2 *Deletion*

If segments can emerge from zero, they can also merge with it, i.e. delete. So the standard format for deletion rules is the mirror-image of that for epenthesis, i.e. 'X = ∅'. As with epenthesis, there is a more specific traditional terminology:

(i) **Aphaeresis** is initial deletion: as in English *I am* → *I'm*, *I have* → *I've*, German *wie geht es* → *wie geht's* 'how goes it', or the historical loss of initial /k/ before /n/ in English *knife, knight*.

(ii) **Syncope (syncopation)** is formative-internal deletion: the term is most frequently used for vowel loss, but some writers extend it to consonants as well. We can see the results of syncopations in comparisons of American and British forms of certain words: /sɛkrɪtɛri/ vs. /sɛkrɪtrɪ/ 'secretary', /dɪkʃənɛri/ vs. /dɪkʃn̩rɪ/ 'dictionary', etc. It may also show up as a systematic MP process, as in a class of sonorant-final nouns in Swedish: *tempel* 'temple' vs. *templet* 'the temple', *läger/lägret* 'camp', *sägen/sägnen* 'legend'.

(iii) **Apocope (apocopation)** is loss of a final element. To take Swedish again, in sandhi the final vowel of a nominal stem deletes before the plural suffix: *flicka* 'girl', *flickor* 'girls', *gubbe/gubbar* 'old man/men' (see §4.7). Apocope of consonants is also quite common: in many varieties of English, for instance, final /t/ deletes before a word beginning with another consonant, as in [læstʰaɪm] 'last time'; low-stress words may also lose their finals, as in *and, of*.

Historically, deletions are frequently (as (8.13) suggests) the last stages of lenitions; the weaker a segment is – in general – the more prone it is to deletion. Thus consonants will increase in deletability as they move right along the strength scale, unstressed vowels (which, generally having lower amplitude and/or perceptual salience than stressed ones, may be 'weak' in a slightly different sense) are more deletable than stressed ones; and, to a slight extent, high vowels tend to be weaker than low, perhaps because of their inherent relative shortness.

But deletion is not always phonetically motivated; many deletions are morphophonemic, or phonotactic, or both. This is clear for instance in Swedish vowel sandhi: there is a general constraint against two-vowel sequences across a boundary, but it is instantiated in different ways depending on the syntactic categories involved. The stem-final vowel of a noun deletes before the plural ending (see §4.7, (4.20)), while the initial vowel of the definite article deletes after a vowel-final noun: *flicka/flickor, flicka/flickan*. So a **negative condition** ∗/V + V/ operates as a kind of **filter** to block ill-formed strings that would otherwise arise in the course of derivation; but this restriction may have either apocope or aphaeresis as its exponents. The two processes may be said to be involved in a '**conspiracy**' to block /V + V/:

(8.24)     Filter: $*/V + V/$

Exponents:

$$V \rightarrow \varnothing \, / \left\{ \begin{array}{c} \underline{\phantom{xx}}]_n + \quad V]_{pl} \\ V]_n + \underline{\phantom{xx}}]_{art} \end{array} \right\}$$

### 8.4.3 *Reordering*

**Metathesis** or transposition of segments is much less common than deletion or epenthesis, but occurs with some frequency as a historical change, and is occasionally found as an MP process. Most metatheses are sporadic (but see below for a systematic example). For instance, there have been a number of apparent metatheses in the history of English: thus in Old English we find interchanges of /p/ and /s/, as shown in spelling variants: /ps/ → /sp/ in *wæpse* ~ *wæspe* 'wasp', /sp/ → /ps/ in *æpse* ~ *æspe* 'aspen', *cosp* ~ *cops* 'copse', *wlisp* ~ *wlips* 'lisping'. (Note that the metathesized forms *wasp, copse* are now standard; though some dialects show *wopse*.) Another metathesis, of uncertain age, involves nasal sequences, particularly /m/ and /n/: *emnity* for *enmity* is quite frequent, and *anenome* for *anemone* seems to be developing near-standard status (judging from the frequency with which one hears even gardening experts using it). Note that these cases are all lexeme-specific, which is very common with metathesis: I have never heard *\*phomene, \*phenonemon, \*anemity, \*amaenia.*

A curious formal problem arises in the treatment of metathesis: should we interpret, say, /ps/ → /sp/ as an 'interchange', or as a movement of one segment 'over the other'? And in the latter case, which one moves? Consider the possibilities:

(8.25)            Original state                    Metathesis

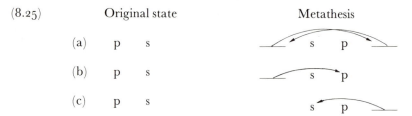

That is, /p/ can move to the right of /s/ as in (b), /s/ can move to the left of /p/ as in (c), or both as in (a). As far as I know there is no solution to this. The standard formulation for metathesis fudges the issue by not making a commitment. Thus the change above would be stated:

(8.26)     SD:     p     s               SC:     2     1
                   1     2

The formalism simply embodies the result, without telling us how we got there.

Now for an example of systematic (morphophonemic) metathesis, where a segment interchange is part of a complex morphosyntactic process, interacting with other rules. Consider plural formation in Papago:

(8.27)     Singular                Plural
           bana                    baːbana       'coyote'
           toːna                   toːtona       'knee'
           čïho                    čïčhïo        'cave'
           bahi                    baːbhai       'tail'

There are at least three processes going on here: (a) **reduplication** of the initial syllable of the noun stem; (b) lengthening of the vowel in the reduplicated syllable if the original is short, and shortening of the stem vowel if the original is long; (c) metathesis of /h/ after the reduplicated syllable.

First, reduplication: is this to be stated as 'syllable epenthesis'? Clearly not, since the motivation is morphological: the reduplicated sequence should probably be taken as a realization of a plural morpheme, a phonological 'spelling' of an abstract category. So:

(8.28)     SD:   Pl  +  C $\left\{\begin{matrix} V \\ V: \end{matrix}\right\}$          SC:   1 → 3   4
                 1      2     3     4

We can then adjust the quantity of the reduplicated syllable with two rules:

(8.29)     (a)   SD:   C   V   +   C   V          SC:   2 → V:
                       1   2   3   4   5

           (b)   SD:   C   V   +   C   V:         SC:   5 → V
                       1   2   3   4   5

Metathesis of /h/ is then:

(8.30)     SD:   C   V   +   C   V   h   V      SC:   5   6 → 6   5
                 1   2   3   4   5   6   7

Finally, a case of spurious metathesis, as a complement to the spurious epenthesis discussed in §8.4.1. The modern English forms *bright, fright* are the result of an apparent metathesis of /r/ and /x/ (OE *h*), as suggested by forms like early OE *be(o)rht, fyrhto, forhtiga* 'frighten', later *breht, fryht, frohtiga*. Or they would be, if not for some interesting spellings actually attested. That is, we find variants that can be arranged in an interesting sequence, like this:

(8.31)

| | | | |
|---|---|---|---|
| berht | — | breht | 'bright' |
| — | geberehtniga | gebrehtniga | 'brighten' |
| fyrhto | fyrihto | fryht | 'fright' |
| forhtiga | forohtiga | frohtiga | 'frighten' |

The /-Vrx-/ forms are historically older: cf. Gothic *baírhts, faúrhts, faúrhtjan*, which represent an older stratum of Germanic.

What does (8.31) suggest? I think it suggests first of all that for the two missing forms, we can fill in *\*bereht, \*geberhtniga*. That is, the apparent metathesis, judging from the other forms, was preceded by anaptyxis of a (more or less) matching vowel after the /r/. A reasonable scenario would be: (a) vowel-copy; (b) transfer of stress to the copied vowel (no direct evidence, but the rest falls out neatly; we know that the vowel before /r/ was originally stressed); (c) deletion of the original, now unstressed vowel. That is:

(8.32)  $C\acute{V}rxC \rightarrow C\acute{V}rVxC \rightarrow CVr\acute{V}xC \rightarrow Cr\acute{V}xC$

$\quad\quad\quad 1 \quad\quad\quad 2 \quad\quad\quad 3 \quad\quad\quad 4$

Given only 1 and 4, we have metathesis; given 1 and a spelling representing either 2 or 3 (stress was not marked in Old English), we have anaptyxis and syncope and (inferred) stress-shift, with 'metathesis' as a sort of accidental side-effect.

## 8.5 Complex processes and abbreviatory notations

Any phonology involving processes will require notations that generalize over partly similar ones, and allow the formal unification of intuitively unified sets of sub-processes. The development of phonological theory over the past two decades has been marked by, among other things, an increasing interest in such complex processes and their formalization, and the evolution of special formalisms for them. We have already introduced a number of these; in this section we will look at a few more relatively standard notations.

The status of notations is controversial: are they basic elements of the theory, standing for 'realities' of some sort? Or are they simply expository devices, ways of enabling us to get down on paper the kinds of statements we want to make, in the clearest way possible, with no particular theoretical status? If the former, then every notation is bound to its theory, and we have no right to use a notation outside its original framework, or with no reference to a particular theoretical context; if the latter, we're entitled to use anything we need in order to express the descriptive generalizations we're after.

I take the position that it is – at this stage anyhow – rather silly to claim that a notation is anything more than a visual metaphor, that it represents 'mental structure' or some aspect of an innate *faculté de langage*. Notational devices are distinct from theories about what the notations may involve. The important point is that notations enable us to sharpen our perceptions of matters like rule-relatedness, and often to state (and even discover) generalizations that would be obscure or invisible without them (see §10.2).

Phonological descriptions ideally aim for 'economy' – i.e. the avoidance of repetition, and the expression of generalizations in the simplest form. So for instance where rules involve partially similar structures, the notation should group the similarities together and throw the dissimilarities into relief. Current practice provides us with a host of notations that try to do just this.

But it is important to note that – however useful they are – their empirical foundation is obscure. Let us return briefly to the question of 'real' properties of language being reflected in notations. One view is that particular abbreviatory devices that are applicable to linguistic data (obviously only a small subset of all conceivable ones) say something about the 'nature of language': a natural language is an object containing rules that can be abbreviated in certain ways, but not others. If we adhere to a strongly 'realist'/'mentalist' view, then it should be the case that the generalizations expressible in our notations are just those that speakers 'make use of' in language-learning, processing, etc. (so Chomsky 1965). This does not appear to be an empirical issue.

It is in fact not possible to produce a principled, non-intuitive justification for abbreviatory devices like Greek-letter variables, braces, etc.; there is some marginal evidence from language history that rules MAY evolve so as to maximize abbreviability, but this is sparse (see Kiparsky 1968b). For now, however, we can simply take it as a procedural imperative that within a process-phonology, abbreviation is desirable, and failure to use it where technically possible is a failure of analysis, 'missing a generalization'.

The principle behind all abbreviation is primarily the avoidance of restatement; this leads to **conflation**, i.e. grouping of related rules into a **schema**, of which they are **subrules** or **expansions**. Let us take an example in detail. In my speech, stressed vowels are nasalized before /NC/, and before a final nasal: [kʰæ̃ːnˀt] 'can't', [kʰæ̃n] 'can'. So there are two partly identical rules:

(8.33)
(a) $\begin{bmatrix} V \\ +\text{stress} \end{bmatrix} \rightarrow [+\text{nas}] / \underline{\hspace{1em}} \begin{bmatrix} C \\ +\text{nas} \end{bmatrix} C$

(b) $\begin{bmatrix} V \\ +\text{stress} \end{bmatrix} \rightarrow [+\text{nas}] / \underline{\hspace{1em}} \begin{bmatrix} C \\ +\text{nas} \end{bmatrix} \#$

Factoring out similarities and enclosing the rest in braces:

(8.34)
$\begin{bmatrix} V \\ +\text{stress} \end{bmatrix} \rightarrow [+\text{nas}] / \underline{\hspace{1em}} \begin{bmatrix} C \\ +\text{nas} \end{bmatrix} \begin{Bmatrix} C \\ \# \end{Bmatrix}$

(8.34) would informally be called a 'nasalization rule' – but it is in fact two rules conflated, i.e. a generalization over two processes that we want to claim are a 'unit'. What braces express, of course, is disjunction (see §5.5); but it is clear that we wouldn't really want to speak of 'two nasalization rules' here.

Braces can also be used in more complex ways, 'nested' within each other, e.g. when a process affects a scatter of only partly related items. They allow extraction of relevant contexts out of a larger whole. Thus the rule for lengthening of /æ/ in New York English runs (in part) this way:

(8.35)     /æ/ lengthens before: voiced stops, all fricatives, all sonorants except /ŋ/ and /l/

A standard formulation would be:

(8.36)
$\begin{bmatrix} V \\ -\text{back} \\ +\text{low} \end{bmatrix} \rightarrow [+\text{long}] / \underline{\hspace{1em}} \begin{Bmatrix} \begin{bmatrix} \begin{Bmatrix} \begin{bmatrix} +\text{obs} \\ -\text{cont} \\ +\text{voice} \end{bmatrix} \\ [+\text{cont}] \end{Bmatrix} \end{bmatrix} \text{(a)} \\ \begin{bmatrix} \begin{Bmatrix} \begin{bmatrix} -\text{obs} \\ +\text{nas} \\ +\text{ant} \end{bmatrix} \\ [-\text{lat}] \end{Bmatrix} \end{bmatrix} \text{(b)} \end{Bmatrix}$

From the top down: a low non-back V lengthens before EITHER$_1$ (a) an obstruent which is EITHER$_2$ [− cont, + voice] OR$_2$ [+ cont]; OR$_1$ before (b) a sonorant which is EITHER$_3$ [+ nas, + ant] OR$_3$ [− lat]. The unbracketed specifications in each larger matrix hold for the disjoined bracketed ones inside; each set of braces (as the subscripts above suggest) indicates another level of disjunction.

Another form of disjunction allows insertion of subsidiary 'if-then' clauses inside larger ones (all rules, obviously, are in one sense 'if-then' clauses). Consider the Old English sound change 'breaking', which can somewhat oversimply be stated as:

(8.37)   (a) Insert a [u] between a front vowel and a back continuant consonant.
(b) But if the back continuant is a sonorant, another C must follow.

(For example /æ/ → [æu] before /x/ alone, but before /rC lC/, not /r l/ alone: /r l/ were probably velar(ized).)

So the two subrules are:

(8.38)

(a) $\varnothing \rightarrow \begin{bmatrix} V \\ + \text{high} \\ + \text{back} \end{bmatrix}$ / $\begin{bmatrix} V \\ - \text{back} \end{bmatrix}$ _____ $\begin{bmatrix} C \\ + \text{cont} \\ + \text{back} \end{bmatrix}$

(b) $\varnothing \rightarrow \begin{bmatrix} V \\ + \text{high} \\ + \text{back} \end{bmatrix}$ / $\begin{bmatrix} V \\ - \text{back} \end{bmatrix}$ _____ $\begin{bmatrix} C \\ - \text{obs} \\ + \text{cont} \\ + \text{back} \end{bmatrix}$ C

We note one thing at the outset: the subrules must NOT apply in the order (a, b). If this happened, then (a), which is more general (including all back continuants) would allow [u]-insertion before both obstruents and sonorants without a following C. We must have (b) apply first, since this is the more specific environment; then (a) can apply to what's left, which will be [+ obs].

We can handle this by abbreviating (8.38) in a particular way, with a LONGEST-FIRST convention on expansions. The subsidiary 'if-then' (8.38b) is expressed within angled brackets ⟨ ⟩ .. ⟨ ⟩, the first incorporating 'but if', the second 'then'. Thus:

(8.39)

$\varnothing \rightarrow \begin{bmatrix} V \\ + \text{high} \\ + \text{back} \end{bmatrix}$ / $\begin{bmatrix} V \\ - \text{back} \end{bmatrix}$ _____ $\begin{bmatrix} C \\ + \text{back} \\ + \text{cont} \\ \langle - \text{obs} \rangle \end{bmatrix}$ <C>

The longest-expansion-first convention ensures the order of application (8.38b–a).

Another case where abbreviatory notations appear to unify otherwise disparate processes involves a special use of parentheses, along with an ordering condition as for angled brackets, and another, special one. Consider the basic rules for Latin accentuation:

(8.40)     (a) Accent the antepenultimate vowel if the penultimate vowel is (i) short, (ii) in an open syllable: *hóminis, denárius, régibus*.
(b) Otherwise accent the penultimate vowel, regardless of length: *amámus* (penult long), *témplum* (penult closed).
(c) Accent the single vowel in a monosyllable: *híc, hás*.

Since these three rules determine the location of all accents, there's a *prima facie* case for generalizing: but how do we do it? First, to formalize the subrules:

(8.41)     (a) $V \rightarrow [+acc] /$ ____ $C_o \begin{bmatrix} V \\ -long \end{bmatrix} \$ C_o V C_o \#$

(b) $V \rightarrow [+acc] /$ ____ $C_o V C_o \#$
(c) $V \rightarrow [+acc] /$ ____ $C_o \#$

$\$ =$ syllable boundary: see §10.3.5)

These can be collapsed with parentheses as follows:

(8.42)     $V \rightarrow [+acc] /$ ____ $(( C_o \begin{bmatrix} V \\ -long \end{bmatrix} \$ ) C_o V ) C_o \#$

Taking the longest expansion first (not excluding any material in round brackets) we get (8.41a); taking the second (excluding material in the inner parentheses), we get (8.41b); and excluding all material in parentheses, (8.41c). Thus:

(8.43)     (a)     d     e     n     ā     r     i     u     s
                                    ____     C     V̌     \$     V     C_o     #
                                     ↓
                                     á́

(b)     a     m     ā     m     u     s
                         ____     C     V     C     #
                          ↓
                          á́

(c)          h     i     c
                    ____     C     #
                     ↓
                     í

A schema like this requires a condition of **disjunctive ordering**: i.e. once a subrule has applied to a given string, no other subrule may apply, even if its SD is met by the remaining string. To see why this is so, consider *denārius*: if subrules could apply wherever their SDs were met, we'd get:

(8.44)　　(a)　denárius (by (8.41a))
　　　　　(b)　denáríus (by (8.41b))
　　　　　(c)　denáríús (by (8.41c))

One further example of an abbreviatory notation: the case of **mirror-image environments**. These are sequences where one SD is the reverse of another, e.g. $X \to Y / \underline{\quad} A$, $X \to Y / A \underline{\quad}$. Thus some varieties of Scots have an allophonic rule where /ɛ̆/ (*fish, hit*) becomes [ʌ] (identical to /ʌ/ in *but*) either before or after /l/, which is [ɫ]. So [hʌɫ] = *hull/hill*, but the two vowels are distinct elsewhere. Collapsing with braces in the usual way, we would get:

(8.45)
$$
\begin{bmatrix} V \\ -\text{front} \\ -\text{back} \\ 3\ \text{high} \end{bmatrix} \to [+\text{back}] / \begin{Bmatrix} [+\text{lat}] \underline{\quad} \\ \underline{\quad} [+\text{lat}] \end{Bmatrix}
$$

We can generalize this by suppressing the environment-bar:

(8.46)
$$
\begin{bmatrix} V \\ -\text{front} \\ -\text{back} \\ 3\ \text{high} \end{bmatrix} \to [+\text{back}] / [+\text{lat}]
$$

(Features based on Scots system in (7.38).) Not a very 'explanatory' rule as it stands: though if we assume that $[+\text{lat}] \to [+\text{back}]$ by redundancy rule, the FORM of (8.46) makes the point that it's the presence of [ɫ] contiguous to a vowel – not its position – that counts.

## 8.6　Natural processes, evaluation measures, and explanation

Consider these two rules:

(8.47)　　(a)　$V \to [+\text{nas}] / \underline{\quad} \begin{bmatrix} C \\ +\text{nas} \end{bmatrix} \#$
　　　　　(b)　$V \to [+\text{nas}] / \underline{\quad} \#$

There is a clear difference: (8.47a) is 'reasonable' or expectable, (8.47b) 'arbitrary'. Or, pre-nasal nasalization is **phonetically motivated**, final nasalization **unmotivated**. Phonetically motivated rules are generally – if loosely – referred to as **natural**, unmotivated ones as **unnatural**.

In one strand of contemporary theory, the concept of naturalness (either as such, or in the form of markedness) has been seen to interact with simplicity or economy, as follows: a notation should be so designed that it SELECTS as simple, abbreviable, etc. just those aspects of phonology that are – in some sense – natural. And conversely, it should 'punish' (rather than 'reward') unnatural phenomena by making them harder to capture, more complex, etc.

Now this can't be done by simple feature-counting (as had once been thought): in these terms, say, (8.47b) is 'simpler' than (8.47a). And we saw other instances of this in our discussion of natural classes (§§5.2, 5.5) – i.e. there are distinctly non-natural classes, like [ − cor], that are formally simple.

But why should one want to quantify the notion of naturalness, and 'reward' and 'punish' analyses anyhow? It is not universally accepted that one ought to, but such attempts have been made, and their failures are theoretically interesting. In the tradition of generative grammar, one strand, stemming from discussions in Chomsky (1965) and elsewhere, has been the assumption that it is possible to construct, for a formalized theory, an **evaluation measure**: a mechanical procedure that will judge grammatical descriptions in such a way that a 'cost' is assigned to certain items, while others are 'free'. Thus any set of competing formulations can be judged as more or less 'costly', and the ideal is the 'cheapest' possible.

In *SPE* an attempt was made to bring together considerations of markedness and evaluation so that systems and rules could be assigned a cost on the basis of a set of **marking conventions**. I will not go into detail on this matter, but just give an example of how the system is supposed to work.

Taking the general criteria for markedness set out in §7.4, we can say that the unmarked values for roundness on vowels are: (a) [ − round] for front and low back vowels; (b) [ + round] for non-low back vowels. Using u (unmarked) as a coefficient, we can say:

(8.48)

$$[\text{u round}] \rightarrow \left\{ \begin{array}{l} [\alpha \text{ round}] \; / \; \left[ \begin{array}{c} \overline{\alpha \text{ back}} \\ -\text{low} \end{array} \right] \\[2em] [-\text{round}] \; / \; [\overline{+\text{low}}] \end{array} \right\}$$

(Where '____' inside a segment indicates a **simultaneous context**, i.e. what is [u round] is a vowel that is [α round, α back, − low] or [− round, + low].)

We add the stipulation that in any rule or system display, an m (marked) value for a feature has (say) a cost of 1, and a u is cost-free. Thus given the systems /i u ɑ/ and /i y u ɑ/, the first is free, and the second has a cost of 1. (There are also costs for mid vowels, non-back low vowels, etc.)

But now observe this problem: it is apparently possible for a rule with a marked output to be simpler than one without:

(8.49)

(a) $\left[ \begin{array}{c} V \\ -\text{back} \\ +\text{high} \\ -\text{round} \end{array} \right] \rightarrow [+\text{back}] \; (i \rightarrow ɯ)$

(b) $\left[ \begin{array}{c} V \\ -\text{back} \\ +\text{high} \\ -\text{round} \end{array} \right] \rightarrow \left[ \begin{array}{c} +\text{back} \\ +\text{round} \end{array} \right] (i \rightarrow u)$

The *SPE* solution is to propose a concept of **linking**, whereby when a feature changes in a rule, all other features whose markedness-values depend on the changed feature take on their unmarked values with no cost. Thus since [+ round] is linked to [+ back, + high], (8.49b) costs nothing – though formally it is more complex than (8.49a).

This is all very well, and effects the desired economy. The problem is that it appears, for all its ingenuity, to have no empirical consequences. That is: if there are cheap and expensive rules and systems, there ought to be some non-formal correlates to them, of the type suggested in §7.4. Take for instance the Germanic *i*-umlaut in (8.3): this anticipatory metaphony ought to be 'costly', since when /u o/ umlaut, they go to [y ø], thus incurring a cost of 2; linking would predict the favoured output to be [i e], which would have no cost. And not only is the rule costly, but so is the resulting system – at least after the marked vowels are **phonologized** (become phonemic, no longer allophones of /u o/: see §13.1). Assuming, that is, that markedness values are computed on a phonological, not a phonetic level. Here we have a costly rule that overrides linking, and ultimately a costly system: yet in the majority of the Germanic dialects, these marked vowels have remained stable for nearly a millennium and a half.

Examples like this can be multiplied *ad libitum*. The problem is, simply, that if an evaluation measure evaluates anything real (rather than simply reflecting an irrational cross-linguistic distribution), there ought to be consequences assignable to marked states: instability, difficulty in learning, etc. And there is no real evidence that any such consequences exist.

In fact, neither the idea of a formal evaluation measure in general, nor a quantifiable notion of naturalness/markedness have made any really enlightening contributions – other than to the construction of an 'index of oddity' (see §7.6.3). Nor do they tell us anything we don't already know – though they do tell us things we don't want to know, because they're either untrue or unintelligible.

Is the whole idea of naturalness then a dead end? Not necessarily, if we put it into a reasonable perspective. Leaving aside a purely statistical notion like markedness, let's return to phonetic naturalness of a more transparent kind. It's clear that phonetically natural processes are 'privileged' in a rather obvious way: (a) given a choice of a natural vs. an unnatural process, the natural is much more likely; (b) given the choice of no process vs. a natural one, there's a greater likelihood of the natural process than no process (though (b) is a much weaker predictor than (a)).

The question of LIKELIHOOD is the conceptual problem that bedevils all forms of theory which have a strong naturalness component. If both the natural and the unnatural occur, about the best you can say is that an instance of a natural process is an occasion for lack of surprise, and contrariwise for an unnatural one. But this doesn't rob the concept of content: it makes it more subtle and complex, and less straight-forwardly 'explanatory'.

A naturalness judgement is an answer to a 'why?'-question about something. Why is (8.47a) natural? Because nasalization – all things being equal – is expectable before a nasal. Why? Because the velum is up for an oral vowel and down for a nasal, and it's natural to anticipate an articulation. Why? Because speakers tend – overall – to PREFER certain articulatory configurations to others.

Now if we examine these preferred types, it becomes apparent that many of them share a component which can (crudely but tradition-ally) be called '**ease of articulation**'. That is, perhaps the largest number of natural processes are assimilatory: they tend in effect to prolong particular gestures over larger stretches of phonic substance, or minimize the number of independent gestures in a sequence.

This is where naturalness can become interesting. If a process is frequent, or a system configuration 'unmarked', noting this is only the first step in exploring its significance. The motivation (if any – see below) will generally turn out to be either articulatory or perceptual; so markedness/naturalness are not explanations, but things to be explained.

But – and this is crucial – it is a mistake to say that once you have discovered the motivation for a process, you have explained why the process occurs. You haven't: you've just said what it is about the process that makes it attractive to speakers who happen to 'want to achieve' the goal implied by the motivation.

A simple example will clarify: one of the commonest 'natural processes' is nasal assimilation to following obstruents. The motivation is transparent: a cluster [nk], say, requires two gesture-shifts: one for the velum and one for the tongue-body, while [ŋk] requires only a shift of the velum. Therefore it's not surprising that if a speaker wants to minimize the 'effort' involved in /NC/ clusters, he will simply make the nasal homorganic with the stop.

But, on the other hand, he could do one of two other things: (a) make the stop homorganic to the nasal, i.e. [nk] → [nt]; (b) change the nasality and place values on the nasal, so that [nk] → [kk]; or (c) he could do a third thing, which is nothing at all. Option (a) seems virtually unattested; (b) and (c) are both common.

So we now have some new questions: (a) why are both [nk] → [ŋk] and [nk] → [kk] possible strategies for 'resolving' **heterorganic** (non-homorganic) /NC/, but not [nk] → [nt]? And why are there cases where [nk] is left alone? These are at present unanswerable, but some interesting considerations arise from them. First, assimilation or any other natural process is subject to two problematical options:

(i) '**Multiple strategy**'. Given a potential assimilation, there is always more than one way to effect a motivated change.

199

(ii) **'Null strategy'**. Given a potential assimilation, it is perfectly possible to do nothing about it.

That (ii) is the case should be clear from the simple fact that natural processes still occur; if natural resolutions of marked sequences were NECESSARY, they would already have happened in all possible environments, and the marked inputs would never occur. Therefore no assimilation or other natural process is ever necessary; therefore none is predictable; therefore the relation between input and output is never cause-and-effect, but rather MOTIVATED CHOICE: a much looser and less explanatory principle.

The /NC/ phenomena discussed above bring out another interesting fact, which relates to our consideration of 'strength' (§8.3). There is another, more relativistic definition, which has to do not so much with airflow or stricture as IDENTITY. Under this definition, a segment $S_i$, is weaker than $S_j$ if in assimilation it is $S_i$ that becomes more like $S_j$, or 'yields' or 'loses features' to $S_j$. Thus in /NC/ it is /N/ that is weaker: it picks up either place or place + obstruency from /C/.

Overall, sonorants are weaker in this sense than obstruents (which ties in with the hierarchy obs > son > $\emptyset$). It is more often than not the cases, both in /NC/ and /CN/, that /N/ assimilates: thus in addition to Kannaḍa nasal assimilation (§3.3), and the virtually exclusive homorganicity condition in Dravidian, Romance, Bantu, and many other families, we have assimilation in /CN/: e.g. German casual forms like [zaːgŋ] *sagen* 'to say', [haːbm̩] *haben* 'to have' and the English progressive assimilations in (8.1).

Only rarely do obstruents assimilate to sonorants: for obstruents and nasals we have processes like /gn/ → [ŋn] in Latin (*agnus* 'lamb' [aŋnus]) and Swedish (*vagn* 'wagon' [vaŋn]); a /kl gl/ → /tl dl/ change in Cumberland English (/tliːn/ 'clean', /dlʊv/ 'glove'); and a scatter of others, like the /kn/ → /tn/ rule in some forms of Southern U.S. English (/tɛtnɪkəl/ 'technical'). It's worth noting that all of these are multiple-strategy cases; for null strategy compare the many cases of non-assimilation (German *Amt* 'office', Swedish *samt* 'together', Polish *bank* [baŋk] 'bank', and so on).

The best we can say is that there is such a thing as **natural context-sensitivity**: if a particular context tends to elicit a particular process, the nature of the elicited process will probably be deducible from some property of the context.

NOTES AND REFERENCES

8.1 The issue of process vs. non-process has not been widely discussed in the literature: the usual assumption is that 'process' is an unambiguous and intuitively plausible notion. For some dissenting voices see Allen (1951), and the discussion in §10.2.1.

8.2.1 Taxonomy by direction is usually restricted to assimilation, but the terms apply as well to dissimilation. Perhaps the restriction is due to the relative rarity of dissimilation, and its generally unsystematic nature. On Germanic *i*-umlaut see any handbook of Germanic. The Dravidian material is after Bright (1966), Hungarian after Makkai (1972b). On fusion, Sigurd (1975).

8.2.2 On OE breaking, Lass & Anderson (1975: ch. III and refs.); for Sundanese nasalization, here oversimplified, S. Anderson (1974: 148ff). Final devoicing in German, etc. has been argued – perhaps unwisely – to be voice assimilation, with word boundaries interpreted as (equivalent to) voiceless obstruents (Lass & Anderson 1975: ch. v). For Icelandic devoicing, see Einarsson (1945: 12ff); on Old Norse assimilations, Gordon (1957: 282ff).

8.2.3 On acoustic assimilation, J. Ohala (1974), Lass (1976a: ch. 7); on Austrian rounding, Keller (1961), Chen (1974).

8.3.1 The general theory of strength here derives largely from Lass & Anderson (1975: ch. v) and Lass (1976a: ch. 6). For a critique, Dekeyser (1978). The hierarchies are fairly uncontroversial, except for the idea of aspiration and affrication as weakening, which goes against the widely held view that aspiration at least is associated with 'strong' or 'fortis' articulation. For a defence of aspiration/affrication as strengthening, and a quite different theory of strength, based on functional rather than articulatory categories, **Drachman (1977), also *Hyman (1975: §5.3.4). For a completely 'abstract' (non-phonetic) theory of strength, Foley (1977). I find both of these frameworks unconvincing, but they are worth looking at.

For details on sources of /h/, Lass (1976a: ch. 6). On the question of 'missing links' or intermediate stages in historical development, §13.4.4.

8.3.2 For more discussion of the Uralic material, Lass & Anderson (1975: ch. v).

8.3.3 On positional strength hierarchies, Foley (1977).

8.4.1 On the notion of a moved vocalic component developing a 'carrier', cf. the use of *do* in English as a carrier for tense/number in questions and negatives without a lexical auxiliary: *Does he/did he sing? He doesn't/didn't sing* vs. *Can he/Could he, He can't/couldn't.* This could be treated as seg-mentalizing a feature-complex out of the auxiliary component, and attaching it to a relatively 'empty' lexical carrier (*do* might be called an 'empty verb' in much the same way as [ə] can be an 'empty vowel'). For more on linearization, Sigurd (1975).

8.4.2 On 'conspiracies', Kisseberth (1970), Lass (1974).

8.4.3 Papago data after Langacker (1972). For discussion of the OE meta-theses, Lass (1978). An interesting case of putative vowel metathesis is discussed in detail in *SPE* (358ff).

8.5 On the question of the 'reality' of notations see *SPE* (ch. 1) vs. Robins (1957). The claim that abbreviatory notations reflect real properties of language (and hence, by a rather devious argument, of 'mind') is made explicitly in Chomsky (1965: ch. 1); for a sceptical discussion of this, and an interesting treatment of the notion 'significant generalization', Hurford (1977). On abbreviatory notations in general, **Harms (1968: ch. 7), **SPE* (ch. 8). For disjunctive ordering, *SPE* (340ff). The dis-cussion here has merely scratched the surface of a very complex topic.

8.6 For a detailed exposition of the issues raised here, *Hyman (1975: ch. 5). For the first modern markedness theory, ***SPE* (ch. 9). For a detailed critique of markedness, **Lass (1975); for a philosophical treatment of the issues, including the problem of naturalness and explanation, **Lass (1980: ch. 2). On naturalness see further the **Dressler/Lass exchange in Thrane *et al.* (1980: 75–102). On general properties of natural rules, Schane (1972).

There is a school of thought called 'natural phonology' (e.g. Stampe 1969, 1973, Donegan & Stampe 1977) which makes rule naturalness the prime consideration in theory, to the point of making a distinction between (innate) 'natural processes' and (learned) 'rules'. Their general view is that children are born with a set of processes, and language learning consists at least partly of 'unlearning' these wired-in processes (like obstruent devoicing, vowel nasalization before nasals, etc.). For a critical view of this movement, J. Ohala (1974), Householder (1977). This is not, by the way, to be confused with 'Natural generative phonology', which is a different theoretical approach (§9.6 below).

# 9

# The limits of abstraction: generative phonology

## 9.1 The conceptual core: 'relation by mediation'

We return in this chapter to more 'theoretical' concerns than those that occupied us in chs. 5–8: further away, anyhow, from phenomena that could (pretheoretically) be said to 'occur', and toward apparently deeper questions of theoretical interpretation. We will be concerned with unobservables: items whose existence and nature are detectable only through the traces they leave, or inferrable by complex strategies of argument.

The focus is a fundamental debate about the nature of phonological representations – and hence about the properties of the rule systems that relate them to phonetics. And this in turn brings us to the central issue: the accountability of phonology. Exactly what is it about, and where are the boundaries between it and other aspects of linguistic structure?

These questions (already implicit in our discussion of Bloomfieldian process morphophonemics and the UUC, §§4.3–6), can now be put more precisely: how far ought we to let ('deep') phonological representations diverge from ('surface') phonetic ones? And how far (if at all) should morphophonemics rather than allophonics determine the shape of a phonological description? Such questions are relevant particularly with respect to the specification of underlying forms, the segments we allow to appear in them, and the length, complexity, and ordering properties of the chains of rules relating phonology to phonetics. What segments, morpheme-shapes, etc. does a language 'really have' (see §§7.5.1, 7.7), and where do they appear?

These issues, though implicit in all forms of 'process phonology', have been most clearly focussed in the phonological theory evolved in the last 20 years or so in association with transformational grammar: so-called **generative phonology** (GP). This is a developing set of approaches, not a monolithic theory; but all branches have enough in common to let us use GP as a cover term.

GP was originally developed as the phonological aspect of what was intended as a unified or 'integrated' theory of grammar, whose syntactic side was first brought into prominence in Chomsky's *Syntactic structures* (1957). Two important strands of earlier theory, however, form the technical basis: a binary feature-theory (originally Jakobsonian, later articulatory), and neo-Bloomfieldian process morphophonemics, incorporating a very strong form of the UUC. GP, in other words, is essentially a theory of morphophonemic structure, with phonetics as a 'last stage' – as we'll see.

I will not go into great technical detail, as there are good introductory treatments of the theory as a whole (see notes); and because many of the issues that have been and are being debated are ephemeral, or likely to become so shortly. I will rather be concerned with those basic ones whose clarification we owe to GP debates.

The central concept in GP (and transformational grammar in general) is the **mediated relation**: surface exponents of underlying linguistic units are related to each other not directly, but via common underliers, or as I like to call them, **mediators**. A set of forms felt (on whatever grounds) to be related have this expressed by a **common source** – not by rules mapping between the forms themselves. The linguist's task is 'discovering' these mediators, and the rules mapping them on to the surface forms.

The syntactic paradigm case is a transformational relation posited among members of a **paraphrase class**: a set of cognitively synonymous sentences differing in word order or minor lexical material, etc. Take (a) *I consider that she is beautiful*, (b) *I consider her to be beautiful*, (c) *I consider her beautiful*. The TG claim is that their synonymy and structural differences can be best expressed, not by taking one surface sentence as 'basic' and the others 'derived', but by deriving all three from an 'abstract' source that codes all the relevant relations. Say this is something like [I consider [COMP she PRES be beautiful]]: then (a) involves attaching *that* to the complementizer node, (b) 'raising' of *she* to object position in the main clause, neutralization of tense, etc.; and (c) is (b) plus deletion of *be* (exact details are irrelevant).

The principle of mediation holds for allophonic, morphophonemic, and syntactic description in parallel:

(9.1)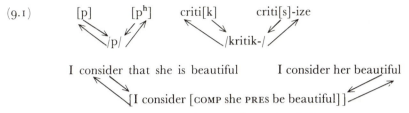

The surface forms in any paradigm (phonetic, MP, syntactic) are always related, not TO each other, but BY a 'third party'. Alternations thus reflect 'deeper' unities, and all grammatical components are formally parallel.

On the face of it, a reasonable position. But incorporated into a very powerful theory, allowing rule ordering and virtually unlimited use of mutation rules, it creates some serious and interesting problems.

As an introductory statement, we can abstract from the literature an explicit version of the often implicit assumptions that guide work in standard GP. The basic aim is: MINIMIZE SUPPLETION. This is achieved in a number of ways, the most important of which are:

(i) *Generality and mileage.* The best rules are those that do the most work, i.e. affect the greatest number of forms. 'Regularity' is the aim: dissolve irregularity where possible, make it only 'apparent' (§4.5). So in order to get maximum mileage out of rules (which is the other side of minimizing suppletion), it is permissible to alter underliers – often in unexpected ways – to make otherwise general rules more general (§§9.3–4).

(ii) *Rule-dominance.* Since we want to make as much alternation and (apparent) 'irregularity' as possible 'regular', we should derive all we can from common underliers and general rules. This means: avoid idiosyncratic marking of lexical items, make the lexicon a last resort, and value phonological conditioning over morphosyntactic. This can be put as a directive: MINIMIZE STORAGE; MAXIMIZE COMPUTATION. That is, let forms take 'free rides' (§4.5) on rules you already need, and let the rules do the work.

I will illustrate these procedural principles, and the problems they raise, with two examples.

### 9.2 Abstract analysis: the German velar nasal

We have already looked at an 'abstract analysis' of a GP type (without calling it that) in connection with the Latin consonant-

205

stems (§4.5). The one we will consider here, while not dissimilar, will focus on some other major argument types and analytical concepts.

Consider the distribution of [m n ŋ] in Standard German:

| (9.2) | #___ | V__V | ___Obs | Vr___# | Vl___# | ___# |
|-------|------|------|--------|--------|--------|------|
|       | m    | m    | m      | m      | m      | m    |
|       | n    | n    | n      | n      | n      | n    |
|       | —    | ŋ    | ŋ      | —      | —      | ŋ    |

So far, nothing curious except the missing initial [ŋ], and its absence from liquid clusters. And all three nasals appear to be phonemic: [ram] 'ram' vs. [ran] 'ran' vs. [raŋ] 'twisted'. But there's an oddity: while [ŋk] is common, [ŋg] is virtually unattested except in loans ([taŋgo] 'tango', [ʊŋgarn] 'Hungary'). We can say that it's not a legal native German cluster. This is strange for a freely-clustering language (cf. the freedom in English: *sing, sink, finger*).

Is this just defective distribution, or something deeper? A possible insight comes from the morphophonemics of a class of nasal-stem strong verbs (compare verbs in -N with those in -NC):

| (9.3) | | | Infinitive | Pret I Sg | Past participle | |
|-------|---|-----|-----------|-----------|-----------------|---|
| (a) | i   | ʃvɪmən | ʃvam | gə-ʃvɔmən | 'swim' |
|     | ii  | rɪnən  | ran  | gə-rɔnən  | 'run'  |
|     | iii | zɪŋən  | zaŋ  | gə-zʊŋən  | 'sing' |
| (b) | i   | fɪndən | fant | gə-fʊndən | 'find' |
|     | ii  | zɪŋkən | zaŋk | gə-zʊŋkən | 'sink' |

Leaving aside (a iii) for the moment, the general rule for vowel quality seems to be: if the stem is in /-N/, the alternations are /ɪ ~ a ~ ɔ/; if the stem is in /-NC/, then /ɪ ~ a ~ ʊ/. The odd man out is /-ŋ/, which has the vocalism appropriate to /-NC/.

Perhaps a change of status is in order? If /ŋ/ behaves like /NC/, why not MAKE it /NC/? There is that missing [ŋg]; and if we analyse [zɪŋən] as /zɪŋgən/, we can capture (a) the distributional gap, and (b) the aberrant vocalism of verbs in [-ŋ] in the same generalization. We do this as follows: take ALL [ŋ] as deriving from assimilation of /n/ to a velar (there's no *[nk]); then have a rule deleting /g/ after [ŋ] (a 'rescue rule': §4.5):

(9.4)  (a) n → ŋ/___ $\left\{ \begin{array}{c} g \\ k \end{array} \right\}$

(b) g → Ø/ŋ___

So [zɪŋən] is /zɪngən/, and goes into verb class (9.3b), which presumably has a raising rule operating in the past participle before /NC/. Its vocalism is now 'normal'. Not only do we clear away an irregularity, we reduce the phoneme inventory: the pair [zɪŋ] 'sing!':[zɪn] 'sense' is no longer a 'true' minimal pair, since the real contrast is /zɪng/:/zɪn/ (another linearity violation: see §2.8). There's no phonemic /ŋ/; phonetic [ŋ] is always the result of one or both of the rules in (9.4). And this also tells us why there's no initial [ŋ]: German phonotactics disallow /#NC/, so it COULDN'T occur; and the same for final /r____#/, /l____#/, since neither /rNC#/ nor /lNC#/ are allowed.

We might note here the problem of **trading-relations**: removing /ŋ/ simplifies the phoneme system, but at the cost of two rules and a dissymmetry. On a 'concrete' analysis we have two fewer rules, as well as /m n ŋ/ paralleling /p b t d k g/ and /f s x/; on an 'abstract' analysis we have a complex derivation and a gap in the nasals. But the implicit assumption is that if you trade off symmetry and fewer rules against coverage, the latter wins.

Yet another phenomenon falls into place on this analysis: the existence of dialects with 'intrusive [k]'. Most forms of standard German have final [ŋ] in forms spelled *-ng*: thus the singular and plural forms of *Ding* 'thing' are [dɪŋ], [dɪŋə]. But there are (northern) dialects that have [dɪŋk], [dɪŋə]. If the base form is /ding/ we can account for the [k] by using a rule we need anyhow: final obstruent devoicing) §§ 4.3, 5.4.2). So:

| (9.5) | | [k]-dialect | | Standard | | |
|---|---|---|---|---|---|---|
| | Input | dɪng | dɪngə | Input | dɪng . | dɪngə |
| | 9.4a | dɪŋg | dɪŋgə | 9.4a | dɪŋg | dɪŋgə |
| | Devoicing | dɪŋk | — | 9.4b | dɪŋ | dɪŋə |
| | 9.4b | — | — | Devoicing | — | — |

Note that the devoicing rule (which both dialects need for the [raːt] ~ [raːdəs] type alternations) must be ordered differently in the two with respect to *g*-deletion: in the [k]-dialect it must precede, and in the standard it must NOT. Leaving this aside for the moment, we can claim to have done two things: (a) captured the 'core' of [ŋ]-phonology with the /ng/ analysis, and (b) shown that the two dialects are 'the same' underlyingly, the only difference being the ordering of two rules. But we've opened a Pandora's box, as we'll see.

Let's look a bit further at this question of rule order. All dialects require a devoicing rule, but in some it must be prevented from applying to certain forms, even though they meet its SD. And it looks as if the way to do this is by CONTROLLING the order of application so that devoicing applies in the standard at a point where it 'does no damage' – i.e. after the [g] that it WOULD devoice is safely deleted.

This device – placement of rules at a particular point in the ordering even though their SDs are met elsewhere – is called **extrinsic ordering**; as opposed to **intrinsic ordering**, where applicational sequence is determined by the rules themselves, not imposed. (For example, *g*-deletion intrinsically follows assimilation, since its SD requires the [ŋ] solely produced by the former rule.)

The availability of extrinsic ordering is crucial for an abstract analysis of this kind; without it there would be a considerable loss of freedom in the manipulation of underliers, since it is a powerful device for introducing rescue rules. In the next section we will see a more striking example of this.

### 9.3 'Abstract segments' and absolute neutralization: Hungarian vowel harmony

Recall the basic facts about vowel harmony in Hungarian suffixes (§8.2, (8.5–6)): non-front root vowels trigger non-front suffix allomorphs, front trigger front. Just as a reminder:

| (9.6) | | Root-N | 'from inside N' | 'in N' | 'at N' | 'to N' |
|---|---|---|---|---|---|---|
| | 'house' | häːz | häːz-boːl | häːz-bɒn | häːz-näːl | häːz-nɒk |
| | 'garden' | kɛrt | kɛrt-bøːl | kɛrt-bɛn | kɛrt-neːl | kɛrt-nɛk |

This is the basic system; but there are exceptions, which create difficulties. First, the vowels /i iː ɛ eː/ are called **'neutral'**, because of the odd way they interact with the normal V(owel) H(armony) rule. If they co-occur in a stem with 'normal' or non-neutral vowels, they seem not to 'count' as controllers of VH; thus

| (9.7) | | Root-N | 'from inside N' | 'in N' | 'at N' | 'to N' |
|---|---|---|---|---|---|---|
| | 'coach' | kɔtʃi | kɔtʃi-boːl | kɔtʃi-bɒn | kɔtʃi-näːl | kɔtʃi-nɒk |

(A stem of this sort also overrides another aspect of VH, which we will look at later – stem-internal harmony, §10.2.3; but this is not to the point here.)

This neutrality itself is not a problem; the VH rule can be so constructed that it ignores neutral vowels, and the last non-neutral vowel in the stem controls VH. The trouble comes with stems containing ONLY neutral vowels; here the VH system appears to break down, and harmonization looks random:

(9.8)

| | | Root-N | 'from inside N' | 'in N' | 'at N' | 'to N' |
|---|---|---|---|---|---|---|
| (a) | 'water' | viːz | -bøːl | -bɛn | -neːl | -nɛk |
| | 'knife' | keːʃ | -bøːl | -bɛn | -neːl | -nɛk |
| (b) | 'torture' | kiːn | -boːl | -bɒn | -näːl | -nɒk |
| | 'target' | tseːl | -boːl | -bɒn | -näːl | -nɒk |

The neutral (a)-roots show phonetically expectable front harmony; the (b)-roots show back harmony. How do we interpret this?

There are two basic approaches: one is to mark these aberrant items in the lexicon with some **rule feature**, e.g. [+back VH], which overrides the 'normal' (assimilatory) VH rule. The other is to use a form of 'as-if' argument, based on the notion that BEHAVIOUR is what counts, not 'surface' phonetics.

We argue this way:

(i) Some /iː eː/ behave harmonically like front vowels, and some like back vowels.

(ii) Purely phonological solutions are preferable to morphological or lexical ones (minimize suppletion: §9.1).

(iii) Therefore the non-harmonic /iː eː/ must be underlyingly different from the harmonic ones; they are 'not really' front.

(iv) We cannot represent them as (say) /uː oː/, because these vowels are phonemically distinct, and we'd never be able to distinguish /uː/ that surface as [uː] from those that surface as [iː], except by some special marking, which we want to avoid.

(v) Therefore we represent them as back vowels which do NOT appear on the surface, i.e. /ɯː ɤː/.

(vi) This makes all applications of VH regular: we save the phonetic naturalness of the rule.

(vii) All we need now is a rule to get rid of /ɯː ɤː/ after they've done their work, i.e. ordered after VH; let's call this RR ('rescue rule').

I won't get into the problem of the underlying forms (if any) of the suffixes; they could obviously be front, back, or unspecified. I will assume for the sake of the illustration that the suffix 'in N' is underlyingly /-bɛn/ (see Vago 1973 for arguments) – though nothing rides on that decision. Then we have the following derivations:

(9.9)

|        | 'Regular' | | | 'Irregular' | |
|--------|-----------|---------|----------|-------------|---------|
| Input  | viːz-bɛn  | keːʃ-bɛn | häːz-bɛn | kɯːn-bɛn   | tsyːl-bɛn |
| VH     | —         | —       | -bɒn     | -bɒn        | -bɒn    |
| RR     | —         | —       | —        | kiːn-       | tseːl-  |
| Output | viːz-bɛn  | keːʃ-bɛn | häːz-bɒn | kiːn-bɒn   | tseːl-bɒn |

What we have here is an UNDERLYING CONTRAST THAT NEVER SURFACES, but manifests itself only as differential MP behaviour of phonetically surface-identical segments. This move – using an underlying contrast to trigger differential behaviour, and then getting rid of it at a pre-surface stage of derivation – is called **absolute neutralization**. That is, it is context-free, unlike 'classical' neutralization, which is always context-determined (ch. 3). The situation can be represented this way:

(9.10)

Underlying long high/mid system

| iː | yː | ɯː | uː |
|----|----|----|----|
| eː | øː | ɣː | oː |

Surface long high/mid system

| iː | yː | uː |
|----|----|----|
| eː | øː | oː |

Neutralizing rule

$$\begin{bmatrix} \text{ɯː} \\ \text{ɣː} \end{bmatrix} \rightarrow \begin{bmatrix} \text{iː} \\ \text{eː} \end{bmatrix}$$

Effect

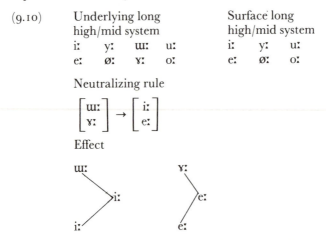

Assuming a purely 'instrumental' view of analytical devices (§7.1), this very powerful solution does its job; above all it 'justifies' our intuition that VH is a phonetically natural process, by taking recalcitrant examples and showing that despite appearances they are after all instances of a deeper regularity. And indeed, this sort of procedure can be seen as a quite reasonable extension of the UUC, and the commitment to minimizing suppletion and maximizing regularity (in the sense of rule-governed-ness).

But this is a pretty unconstrained theory, and in principle might allow you to do almost anything to get the right results. And note that 'the right results' doesn't just refer to the right OUTPUT: this could be obtained with morphological marking as well. What it refers to is correct output PLUS maximization of 'significant generalization' ( = 'phonological solution').

## 9.4  Some arguments against abstract solutions

Absolute neutralization, then, grows out of the desire to get rid of suppletion, plus two devices that phonologists have allowed for some considerable time: extrinsic ordering, and underliers that differ from surface forms. It seems – on one interpretation – only a matter of degree to move from underliers that differ from surface forms in having segments that appear elsewhere on the surface (if not in the exponents of THESE particular underliers) to underliers with segments that don't appear on the surface at all. So long, that is, as these can be motivated by arguments analogous to the less extreme ones. This is important, because it makes attempts to constrain phonological theory that much harder. Since absolute neutralization grows naturally out of less powerful devices, it's hard to see how one might outlaw it (if one wanted to) on a principled basis. The problem is drawing lines, as usual.

But why would we want to outlaw it? Is it *per se* objectionable? To some linguists it is, and the following criticisms can be levelled against it and the whole 'abstract' approach.

(i) *Excessive power*. The more powerful a theory is, the less responsive to empirical checks. How would you test (let alone falsify) the claim that Hungarian 'has' underlying /ɯː ɣː/? Any testing must be done on grounds external to the analysis (§9.5); given only the internal argument, and the criteria leading to it, all you can argue about is whether those criteria have been optimally met. As for 'power' itself, in the extreme case, if anything can be anything, then you end up with nothing. One might equate the argument 'If non-harmonic /iː/ is really /ɯː/, then VH can be made phonetically natural' with 'If my aunt had wheels, she'd be a bicycle'.

(ii) *Dubious criteria*. In cases like this there appears to be a conflict between 'simplicity' and 'strength'. That is, if we don't choose an abstract solution, we get a more complex picture, e.g. by having to use rule features or lexical marking. This assumes that a feature like [ + back VH] in the lexicon for a phonemic /tseːl/ 'costs more' than a phonemic /tsɣːl/ with no rule feature: even though this involves both an extra phoneme (and a 'marked' one at that) and an extra (extrinsically ordered) rule. So to get a 'simpler' solution we need

211

more complex machinery ('trading-relations' again). And it is unclear what the motivation is for making additional 'computation' relatively cheap, and lexical marking expensive. Aesthetically it's fairly obvious; empirically it's questionable (see (v) below).

(iii) *Loss of discrimination.* The usual claim is that a solution like the one offered for Hungarian is 'explanatory' in that it 'tells why' there are apparent hitches in an otherwise regular system. This rests on an assumption that 'beneath the surface' things are more likely than not to be regular. But there's an easy counter-claim: the abstract analysis really produces a blurred picture of the language, by fudging the obvious 'regular'/'irregular' distinction. Thus we get a neat account of what in reality is rather a mess; and we lose the ability to discriminate regularity from irregularity because we have the (excessive) power to resolve irregularity into apparent regularity. We create a false picture by making the fact of non-harmonic vowels into a pseudo-fact.

(iv) *Misplaced naturalness.* The standard justification of abstract analyses is that the rules involved are 'phonetically natural'; and indeed the VH rule in the abstract account is just that, whereas rule features aren't. If we value phonetic motivation highly, and penalize descriptions for morphological 'arbitrariness', this counts as a plus for abstractness. But what does 'phonetic naturalness' mean at a PREPHONETIC point in a derivation? If naturalness is a matter of coarticulatory or perceptual effect (see §8.6), how can these essentially physical properties be relevant in a non-physical arena – which must, on a 'realist' interpretation, be where this is all taking place? This has never been satisfactorily answered but there is an answer of a sort available within the GP framework (see (v) below).

(v) *Psychological implausibility.* GP analyses are normally set in the context of a strong realist and 'mentalist' position. Thus Vago (1973: 597), one of the sources of the Hungarian analysis: 'The job of linguistic theory is to provide a set of principles which automatically evaluates competing analyses, and designates one as the internalized generalization of the idealized speaker-hearer'. Vague as this is, the import is clear: some kind of mapping is assumed between a 'selected' analysis and a speaker's 'internalized generalization'. If we take this seriously, it makes extraordinary claims about the representational powers of naïve speakers. In any such theory (see Chomsky 1965: ch. 1), the crucial events are those of language-acquisition: since underlying representations (and rules) are obviously acquired during the child's interaction with linguistic data.

If we take this all at face value, and connect our description with language-acquisition, we get a scenario like this:

(a) The child, when he has enough input, observes that while VH is a general and overall phonetically natural process, there are classes of forms that appear not to follow it.

(b) Since phonological solutions to problems of this sort are preferred to morphological (i.e. the linguist's METHODOLOGICAL criteria are imputed to the child as PSYCHOLOGICAL ones), the child produces some 'alternative hypothesis' to account for the facts.

(c) One of the 'irregular' classes can be eliminated by reformulating the VH rule so that it ignores neutral vowels in stems that also contain non-neutral ones.

(d) But the remaining irregularities must be accounted for by restructuring the underlying representation so that VH works out correctly for as many forms as possible, see (b) above.

(e) Therefore the child posits underlying 'abstract vowels' /ɯː ɤː/ – which he can never have encountered in his linguistic experience; as well as a rule to neutralize them on the surface when they've done their work.

This means that the child must be 'pre-programmed' with an extremely rich set of 'universals'; he comes into the world with 'knowledge' of all possible segment-types occurring in the world's languages. In principle, then, every child must 'have /ɯ/ available', whether he's ever heard it or not. One could view this either as 'bold speculation' or an unforgiveable confusion of children and linguists.

(vi) *Recapitulation of history.* As even convinced abstract phonologists will admit (e.g. Vago 1973), the situations where absolute neutralization or other very abstract strategies are needed typically result from 'deformation' of regularities by historical change. The neutral /iː eː/ in Hungarian seem to have been historical back vowels, which fronted after the modern VH system was established. Thus (crudely) the facts laid out in (9.10) may represent an episode in the history of Hungarian.

If this is so, ought the same facts ALSO to be attributed – in this form – to the speaker's 'knowledge'? Or is the (apparent) synchronic analysis really a disguised version of the history of the language, projected on to the speaker, with no real justification? Methodo-

213

logically, at least, this 'coincidence' between history and synchrony is suspicious; why furnish two separate 'explanations' for the aberrant behaviour of certain vowels when one will do? In Geoffrey Sampson's formulation (1975), 'one fact needs one explanation'.

Behind this attribution to the speaker lies of course the set of assumptions in §9.1; especially the claim (or prejudice?) that languages are basically 'regular'. One could argue instead that languages are regular unless history (as it is well known to do) interferes with their regularity; and one could counter the assertion that speakers prefer to minimize storage with the assertion that they prefer to maximize it. At the moment there's not much evidence one way or the other. From the point of view of method, however (and perhaps of common sense, though that can't be pushed too far), the messier picture of the speaker, which neither attributes to him the powers of the linguist, nor recapitulates history, might be preferable.

(vii) *'Diacritic' use of phonological features*. Retreating from psychology and similar non-linguistic concerns, perhaps the most damning criticism of the abstract approach is that the 'phonological solution' is really a fake. Phonological specifications (here the conjunction [+back, −low, −round]) are being used as mere notational variants of purely morphological specifications. An abstract /ɯː/ where the surface shows [iː] is nothing more than a shorthand for '[iː] that is harmonically back'; the 'vowel' is really a **diacritic** marking, like [+back VH], and only LOOKS, because of the notation, like a 'segment'.

## 9.5 Testing abstract analyses: the role of external evidence

It's clear from the assortment of possible arguments against extreme abstractness in §9.4 that there exists no canon of argument and evidence types that can force a decision; a lot seems to depend on how seriously you take any of those arguments, and this may ultimately be a subjective matter. But it seems reasonable to ask if we can develop some more refined approaches to the question.

The 'classical' GP claim is that procedural or description-internal criteria lead to 'psychologically real' analyses: i.e. that the maximally general, simple etc. description coincides with what the speaker favours. This has been criticized as 'armchair psychology'; and indeed one striking (and unsurprising) feature of the GP tradition is its relative lack of interest in psychological testing, amounting almost to an anti-experimental bias. This is of course only a problem if one's goal is description of 'speakers' minds', not merely of language structure; in the latter case we are not dealing with empirical issues in the same sense.

Given such a non-mentalist, 'structural' view of what phonology is about, one can criticize abstract analyses on methodological grounds: arguments (i, ii, iii, vi) in §9.4 would be relevant. If one makes psychologistic claims, however, then arguments (iv, v) are crucial. In any case, if a theory makes what purport to be empirical claims about what speakers 'know', its proponents are obliged either to test them, or state them in such a way that it's clear how they might be either supported or falsified.

In other words, we need some **external** or **substantive** criteria for justification. If we want to make a serious decision about how a speaker might 'represent' a linguistic form (rather than how WE might best describe it), we must draw upon independent criteria: evidence from areas such as typology, language history, casual speech, child language, language pathology, and the like. Or at least there's a respectable tradition that claims that this is how we ought to go about it.

As Royal Skousen says in an important study (1975: 14), 'although generative phonologists account for phonetically plausible regularities in morphological data, the significant question is whether speakers . . . can actually capture these regularities'. There are many POSSIBLE analyses for any set of data; GP in its 'classical' form (e.g. *SPE*) appears to claim that there's an *a priori* way of deciding which one the speaker 'prefers' – without consulting him. But as Skousen points out, a simple analysis is better than a complex one (in this context) only if speakers actually account for the data by using it. Both sides, of course, beg an important question: what justifies the assumption that all speakers of a given language make the same generalizations, or that they are equally competent, i.e. 'know their language' equally well, or have comparable (unconscious) 'theories' about its organization?

Overall, the literature on testing abstract analyses by external as well as internal evidence shows two main results: roughly (a) that you can't predict from the FORM of an analysis whether external evidence will support or disconfirm it (i.e. every analysis must be tested individually: we'll see two examples of this here); (b) the more abstract the analysis, the less likely external evidence will be to support it. If it's abstract enough, it will probably be impossible to find any external evidence that will be relevant (e.g. in the case of absolute neutralization of a contrast one of whose members never appears in the language). Such analyses can probably be dismissed as empirically vacuous.

But many do lend themselves to testing. Let's consider first the account of German [ŋ] as /ng/ (§9.2). In one of the most extensive and painstaking attempts at external justification in the literature, Wolfgang Dressler (1981) surveys the basic types of evidence, and explores their interaction with this analysis. I will take a critical look at Dressler's account here.

(i) *Typological.* How does the analysis square with the facts about systems and low-level, easily justifiable rules? Here the evidence is balanced: systems with /m n/ and with /m n ŋ/ are both common (§7.6.4), and many languages have /m n/ with [ŋ] only before velars. The *g*-deletion rule is more of a problem though the outlawing of *[ŋg] at least finally is widespread in Germanic. The /ng/ solution is typologically acceptable, but not 'correct'.

(ii) *Historical.* Is there anything about the history of German, or language history in general, that speaks either way? Take the historical derivation of [dɪŋ]/[dɪŋə]. In standard German, the phonetic developments are:

(9.11)

| | V ___ V | ___ # |
|---|---|---|
| I | dɪŋgə | dɪŋg |
| II | dɪŋgə | dɪŋk |
| III | dɪŋŋə | dɪŋk |
| IV | dɪŋə | dɪŋk |
| V | dɪŋə | dɪŋ |

Assuming this history, the /g/ → $\emptyset$ rule is a case of '**rule telescoping**', i.e.

(9.12)    Historical:    -ŋg-   →   -ŋŋ-   →   -ŋ-
          Synchronic:    -ŋg-   ⟶   -ŋ-

The derivation is shortened, and we omit [$C_1C_1$] clusters, which are illegal on the surface. Of course [ŋg] is too; but we assume that a violation of a TYPE of phonotactic constraint is worse than a mere segmental violation where the type is allowed. There's no argument at all for [ŋŋ] in modern German, but some for [ŋg].

From (9.11) it's clear that the northern [dɪŋk] dialects show the original sequence, and the standard has either (a) **reordered** the devoicing rule to come after *g*-deletion, or (b) extended the [-ŋ] forms analogically (see §13.3) to regularize the paradigm. Reordering of course assumes extrinsic ordering; but assimilation and *g*-deletion are intrinsically ordered, so if you don't want extrinsic ordering, analogy is a better solution.

But note that this argument ASSUMES rules and derivations, and the possibility of abstract underliers; if you accept this in principle, then the /ng/ analysis is legal, and the historical evidence gives no more than very weak support, because of all the assumptions involved.

(iii) *Dialect evidence.* Aside from the [k]-dialects, there is evidence from the Viennese standard which can be taken to support /ng/. Consider:

(9.13)

| Viennese | Standard German | |
|----------|-----------------|------|
| aŋkst | aŋst | 'anxiety' |
| hɛŋkst | hɛŋst | 'stallion' |
| laŋksam | laŋzaːm | 'slow(ly)' |
| sɪŋkt | zɪŋt | 'he sings' |
| sɪŋkst | zɪŋst | 'thou singest' |
| ɛŋə | | 'narrow' |

So Viennese has a paradigmatic alternation [sɪŋən] ~ [sɪŋkst] ~ [sɪŋkt].

Dressler argues that the Viennese forms clearly show the cluster-devoicing one would expect, given /sɪŋgt/ → [sɪŋgt]; but there's an alternative interpretation: the 'inserted' [k] is merely the result of a timing lag between velic closure and devoicing, as in English [sʌmpθɪŋ], [strɛŋkθ], [drɛmpt], etc. (see §8.4.1). Would anyone want to derive these from UNDERLYING /sʌmpθɪŋ/, /strɛŋkθ/, etc.? (I.e. this may be merely a fact about the low-level phonetics of Viennese, not its phonology.)

But, says Dressler, what about the fact that educated Viennese speakers shift easily between Viennese and standard German? Given a concrete analysis, Viennese might have /ng/ and the standard /ŋ/: so dialect-switching (an everyday affair) involves switching of underlying forms and phonological systems. Given the ease of this switching, should the two dialects really be that different underlyingly?

One might add: how (except within a framework of untestable

assumptions about the extent to which bi-dialectal speakers really can have 'different' underlying systems) can you tell? Dressler doesn't go into this, though he obviously assumes that the best analysis keeps dialects as similar as possible except at more superficial levels.

(iv) *Phonostylistic/sociophonological.* Does evidence from various speech tempi and styles have any bearing? Here the arguments become more interesting and potentially convincing. Considering that rule (9.4a) is an assimilation, and (9.4b) an 'articulatory shortening rule', we might expect that as speech becomes more casual, the rules would extend their domains: more applications in more contexts (see §§12.2–3).

And indeed, going through a series of increasingly casual styles, we find the assimilation – originally tied to positions within the morpheme – extending across morpheme and word boundaries. Thus *anklagen* 'to accuse', structurally /an + klaːg + ən/: formal style [ánklaːgən], in faster speech [áŋklaːgən], [áŋklaːgŋ] (note the reverse assimilation in the last syllable). And in still faster speech, *mein Gero* 'my G.' /maen # geːrɔ #/, formal [maen geːrɔ], comes out as [maeŋ geːrɔ]. Thus the rule extends itself over both types of boundaries with increasing casualness (or the boundaries are suppressed: see §12.3). So on a fairly 'concrete' level we have evidence for (9.4a) anyhow; i.e. the rule is attested for speakers of German, and extends as predicted. (This then supports surface [ŋk] as coming from [nk], rather than /ŋk/.)

But what about (9.4b)? For North German speakers, the reduction-sequence for *angeklagt* 'accused' (underlying /an + gə + klaːg + t/: cf. *anklagen*) is: [áŋgəklaːkt] → [áŋgəklaːkt] → [áŋəklaːkt]. So *g*-deletion is also attested, if only in the sequence [-ŋgə-]. The import of these forms is that (assumed) input [ng], intermediate [ŋg], and output [ŋ] are observable IN THE SAME SPEAKER, in transition from one style to another. In Dressler's view, no 'reasonable analysis' could avoid rules of the (9.4) type, and describe adequately the range of casual speech phenomena.

Still, how do you get from this to underlying /ng/ in [dɪŋ]? Dressler argues this way:

> If a speaker has to derive [ŋ] in casual styles from underlying /ng/, then WE MAY ASSUME [emphasis mine: RL – but may we?] that there exists a very strong psychological motive for him to derive the occurrences of [ŋ] in formal styles from /ng/ . . . as well . . . And since in Middle High German /ng/ and /n/ were the underlying form anyway, why should the speakers have restructured these inputs at all (i.e. only for the most formal styles)?

Problem: at the level of consciousness where such 'judgements' would be made (if they are made at all), or such 'pressures' could be felt, how can we tell what's motivating the speaker? There seems to be no way into this at all, save speculation.

(v) *Loanwords.* The historical development of some loans shows a sequence very like that for casual speech. In all loans, (9.4a) apparently applies, outlawing *[ng nk] within the morpheme. As loans become more familiar, they get 'nativized' (i.e. 'more German'), and show *g*-deletion as well as weakening of unstressed vowels to [ə] (the environment for [-aŋgə-] → [-aŋə-]):

(9.14)

| | 'Foreign' | 'Nativized' | |
|---|---|---|---|
| | áŋgɛla | áŋəla | 'Angela' |
| | ǵaŋgɛs | ǵáŋəs | 'Ganges' |
| | táŋgɛns | táŋəns | 'tangent' |
| | taŋganíːka | taŋəníːka | 'Tanganyika' |

Once more, evidence for both rules.

(vi) *Child language.* Dressler offers some anecdotal evidence from his daughter's speech around the ages 3–4. He notes that she tended to substitute /g/ for /d/, especially after /n/, e.g. [vɪndi] ∼ [vɪŋgi], diminutive of *Windel* 'nappy'. This argues for the possibility in early stages of /ng/ as her representation. In other cases, e.g. *Mandarine* 'mandarin orange', she got [maŋgaríːnə] ∼ [maŋəríːnə] (see (9.14)). Such forms would presuppose velar substitution, followed by (9.14a–b).

(vii) *Speech pathology.* In some forms of aphasia, patients seem to show substitution behaviour where [ŋ] parallels /mb nd/, e.g. using [ŋg] for [nd] or [mb]. Some patients also produce (unassimilated) [ng] in forms with normal [ŋ].

These last two kinds of evidence are problematical: can we really assert that child language (in process of acquisition) tells us anything about adult representation (rather than about children's learning)? And does grossly abnormal behaviour necessarily tell us anything about the underlying structure of normal behaviour? Such views are often assumed to be valid, but really need much more argument.

Criteria (i–vi) are at least 'permissive' for /ng/; (iv–vi) can be taken as supportive, and (vi–vii) perhaps weakly so. As against this, there is a scatter of facts that seem to speak against /ng/:

(viii) *Speech errors.* In English, there is some evidence from slips of the tongue that [ŋ] might derive from /ng/; Fromkin (1971: 34) cites errors like [sɪg] *for the* [mæŋ] 'sing for the man', [kʌnt] *the* [strɪg] 'cut the string', etc. She argues that these could involve movement of a nasal from before /g/. A survey of similar work in German seems to offer no relevant examples.

(ix) *Child language.* Dressler's daughter also showed some substitution of [ŋ] for single /n/, e.g. [váŋə] for *Wanne* 'basin'. But there is no evidence of [n] for [ŋ], whereas /n/ and /m/ do substitute for each other.

(x) *Poetic usage.* [m n ŋ] form permissible half-rhymes in good German verse (e.g. *drin*: *Schwing*), whereas [n nd] etc. are either impermissible or at least poor. Thus in rhyme [ŋ] behaves like the other nasal 'units', not like a cluster.

So different types of evidence move in different directions, with one area (child language) supplying arguments pro and con. Dressler's view is that overall the support for /ng/ is good enough for it to be accepted. One could say that IF you're prepared to accept synchronic processes at all, and at least the degree of abstraction that allows for some distinction between underlying and surface forms, this one is well-supported. The best evidence, I think, is (iv) and (v), which shows that there are some cases where both [ng] and [ŋg] do surface, and that these can be naturally related to [ŋ].

My second example is simpler, and involves less evidence; it also gives a less equivocal answer, which leads on to our next topic. Consider these active and passive verbs in Maori:

(9.15)

| Active | Passive | |
|--------|---------|------|
| awhi | awhitia | 'embrace' |
| hopu | hopukia | 'catch' |
| aru | arumia | 'follow' |
| tohu | tohuŋia | 'point out' |
| mau | mauria | 'carry' |
| wero | werohia | 'stab' |
| kite | kitea | 'see' |

This could be subject to two possible solutions:

(a) Morphological. Seven verb classes, with passives of the form /-Cia/ or /-a/, where in /-Cia/ forms the C is predictable only from the lexical identity of the stem, and the same for /-a/. Thus a 'conjugation' solution, where Maori simply has seven verb classes.

(b) Phonological. Passive has one underlying form, /-ia/, and all allomorphy is totally phonologically conditioned.

The trick is how you segment. If you go by the active forms, then (a) comes out, i.e. /awhi + tia/, /mau + ria/, /kite + a/. But if you segment /awhit + ia/, /maur + ia/ (and of course still /kite + a/: but see below), then you get (b).

That is, take the underlying form of {passive} as /-ia/, with two rules: (a) C-deletion in final position, and (b) /i/-deletion if the preceding stem ends in a vowel:

(9.16)    (a) $C \rightarrow \varnothing /$ ___ #
          (b) $i \rightarrow \varnothing / V +$ ___ a

Rule (9.16a) is further justified by the fact that Maori words never end phonetically in -C: i.e. the rule leads to a true generalization about surface forms (like final obstruent devoicing in German). This gives derivations like:

(9.17)

|        | Act    | Pass        | Act    | Pass        | Act    | Pass       |
|--------|--------|-------------|--------|-------------|--------|------------|
| Input  | awhit# | awhit + ia# | maur#  | maur + ia#  | kite#  | kite + ia# |
| C-del  | awhi#  | —           | mau#   | —           | —      | —          |
| i-del  | —      | —           | —      | —           | —      | kite + a#  |
| Output | awhi   | awhitia     | mau    | mauria      | kite   | kitea      |

Very neat, infinitely preferable to seven lexically controlled allomorphs, and no generalization at all.

But if we go beyond the paradigmatic material presented as a 'problem' to be solved by finding the most economical and insightful combination of underliers and rules, our preference is reversed. A study by Kenneth Hale (1973) reveals the following:

(i) Nominal stems can be used as verbs in spontaneous conversation; when these 'new' verbs are created, they always take /-tia/ in the passive.

(ii) Derived causative verbs, which are formed from actives with the prefix *whaka-*, always take /-tia/ as their passive: *mau ~ mauria*, but *whaka-mau ~ whaka-mautia*, not *\*whaka-mauria*.

(iii) Borrowed verbs from English, even unassimilated ones that retain their original final C, always take /-tia/.

(iv) When speakers forget the traditional passive for a verb, they can substitute /-tia/.

So the 'undesirable' solution, listing separate verb classes according to their (arbitrary) passives, is in fact the speakers' solution; though it does look as if we're on the way to a new kind of conjugation, with an invariable /-tia/. The C-deletion rule, as we might suspect, is a fact about the history of Maori and other Polynesian languages – as is the tendency to regularize conjugation by 'detaching' one passive ending (incorporating the historical stem-final C) and using this for all verbs. This is complete in Hawaiian, which has /-ˀia/ (old*/-kia/) for all passives.

So we can see that in order to justify an analysis, we have to go beyond the phonetic data; and indeed, there's no reason to assume that a system will necessarily be stable or structurally unified: it all depends on whether we catch it at rest or in process of change (see chs. 12–13). At any rate there's no evidence that speakers perceive the initial consonants of passive suffixes as belonging to the verb stems. The 'highly valued' abstract solution, while 'capturing the facts' from a paradigm-internal point of view, cannot be 'designated' as what the speaker does. Contrary to expectations (at least those built into the theory) the speaker appears to be quite happy to maximize storage and minimize computation; he seems to operate on concrete word-forms, not abstract morphemes (see §9.6).

## 9.6 **Constraining the theory**

Given this sort of evidence, Hale suggests a principle for controlling the abstractness of underlying forms. C-deletion is a relic of Maori history – the origin of the current mess, not part of its synchronic structure. Hale suggests that C-deletion produced restructuring: the boundaries shift, and we pass from the phonological solution (b) above (which was valid as long as there were phonetic consonant-finals) to the morphological solution (a). Thus old /#awhit+ia#/ is now /#awhi+tia#/. Assume that speakers have no access to anything but surface phonetic organization; then there's no way to posit an underlier like */#awhit#/, since the speaker has no experience of phonetic [-C#]. So he suggests a general condition making it illegal for conditions on word- or morpheme-structure to differ between underlying and surface levels: we disallow any underlying representation that violates a universal surface canonical pattern (i.e. one that is phonetically exceptionless within the language in native forms).

Such a proposal has profound implications. It means in effect scrapping many (if not most) of the 'best' analyses, and going back to a less 'economical' and 'unified' phonological model. On the other hand, such a move could be seen not as a loss of generalizing power, but as a refinement: it allows a more discriminating and sharply differentiated classification of rule- and alternation-types, and a more complex (and hence realistic?) picture of phonology. No longer a seamless web from morphophonemic to allophonic transcription, but a congeries of rule and representation types, in complex and ultimately unstable interaction. Above all, it sets the phonology/morphology boundary in a different place, as well as untangling history and synchrony, and giving us perhaps a better perspective on both (see below and ch. 13).

There is an enormous literature on the subject of constraints on abstractness, ranging from mild attempts to tinker with the strongest bits of machinery to radical recastings of the whole apparatus. I will not go into the history of the debate here, but merely single out some important types of proposals.

It's clear that there are three main offenders conspiring to produce excessive power:

(i) *Unity*. The assumption that there is only one type of rule, and that sequences of these rules carry representations from the MP (or as it's sometimes called **systematic phonemic**) level to the surface (or **systematic phonetic**), and that MP and allophonic rules are no different in principle.

(ii) *Extrinsic ordering*. Without this power, many types of abstract analysis are impossible, i.e. those where ill-formed underliers or inter-mediate representations must be destroyed by a properly placed rescue rule.

(iii) *Abstract underliers*. If underliers can differ nearly without limit from surface forms, this deprives the actual 'data' of significance, and – in cooperation with (ii) – vastly increases the number of possible solutions for any set of data.

So the principal strategies of attack may focus on one or another of these aspects, but to be successful they must ultimately take on all three. The most interesting counter-theories tend to work by (i) reclassifying rules into a number of distinct types with restricted domains; (ii) disallowing extrinsic order; and (iii) severely constrain-ing possible underliers.

One approach, under the general heading of **Natural Generative Phonology** (NGP), introduced by Vennemann and Hooper among others (see notes), starts with a series of methodological postulates and a model of the lexicon that treats MP alternations in a different (and more selective) way from GP. Hooper (1976) suggests three primary constraints:

I **True generalization condition.** '... the rules speakers formulate are based directly on surface forms and ... relate one surface form to another, rather than relating underlying to surface form' (1976: 13). Under this condition all rules are 'surface-true', and no rule can refer to a 'nonexistent segment' ('existence' ≡ (is equivalent to) 'surface occurrence').

II **No ordering condition.** All ordering relations between rules are intrinsic, or determined by universal principles of rule-application (e.g. all rules apply wherever their SDs are met, but certain SDs take applicational precedence – in all languages – over others: see notes).

III 'No phonological features appear in the lexical representation of a morpheme except those that occur in SOME [my emphasis, RL] surface representation of that morpheme' (p. 20). This would exclude *SPE*'s /bɔ̃e/ for *boy*, /rixt/ for *right*, but not /sign/ in *sign/signify*; it would also exclude Hungarian /kɯːn/, German /zɪng/.

These conditions lead eventually to the establishment of a taxonomy of rule types, according to domain and function:

(i) **P-rules** (phonological rules proper). Purely phonetically conditioned, may not refer to any morphosyntactic information (not even boundaries).

(ii) **Sandhi rules.** These refer to boundaries, either word or morpheme.

(iii) **MP rules.** These include all morphosyntactically conditioned rules, producing 'phonological' (MP, not allophonic) alternations.

(iv) **Syllable rules**. These specify the allowable shapes of syllables, and hence are conditions on morpheme and word structure.

(v) **Morphological spell-out/word-formation rules.** These assign phonological shapes to abstract morphemes like {plural}, etc., or define processes of derivational morphology.

(vi) **Via-rules.** These are statements of relationship between related morphemes or MP alternants: e.g. *divine/divinity* would be 'linked' by a rule /ai/ ⟷ /ɪ/: though each form would be listed individually in the lexicon.

Among other things, this repartitioning of the rule-component allows a distinction to be made between forms that are (vaguely) 'related', and genuine MP alternations, and separates both of these from allophonic alternations. We can see how this works by looking briefly at one of Hooper's arguments: a criticism of a semi-abstract analysis of certain Spanish alternations by Harris (1969).

Consider *leche* /letʃe/ 'milk' vs. *lactar* /laktar/ 'to lactate', *láctico* /laktiko/ 'lactic'. In Harris' GP analysis, these forms are presumed to contain 'the same morpheme', hence require a common underlier, and [tʃ] ∼ [kt] is produced by a rule-sequence acting on this underlier: for Harris, /lakt/. However, since not all forms with this underlier undergo the rules, they are partly 'arbitrary', i.e. to be marked with a diacritic, which he calls [+S]. This triggers the following derivation:

(9.18)
$$\begin{bmatrix} \text{/lakte/} \\ +S \end{bmatrix}$$

     Rule:                                             Effect:

(a) $k \rightarrow j / \underline{\quad} \begin{Bmatrix} t \\ s \end{Bmatrix}$              lajte

(b) $t \rightarrow tʃ / j \underline{\quad}$            lajtʃe

(c) $a \rightarrow e / \underline{\quad} j$             lejtʃe

(d) $j \rightarrow \varnothing / \underline{\quad} t$             letʃe

(The arguments for these particular rules are immaterial: within the GP framework we can take them as motivated.)

Clearly /lakte/ isn't impermissibly abstract: cf. /laktar/ – so condition III won't disallow it automatically. And the rules are not extrinsically ordered. But there are problems: (a) the amount of 'garbage' (ill-formed, non-surface intermediate forms) between input and output; (b) some historical evidence which suggests that we are not dealing with an MP relation proper, but something far more distant. The historical evidence is of particular interest, since it constitutes a good argument against the likelihood of any rule-sequence relating [k] and [tʃ].

Unsurprisingly, the alternation is a historical product; but the history is surprising from the GP point of view. First, *lactar, láctico* are re-borrowings (and late ones at that) from Latin (the ancestor of Spanish). Early direct historical developments show uniform /tʃ/: *lechoso* 'milky', *lechar* 'to milk'. Second, when the first re-borrowings from Latin took place in the 13th century, /kt/ showed up not as /tʃ/ but as /ut/: *actus* 'act' → *auto*. Thus the /kt/ → /tʃ/ rule which is the source of the /tʃ/ in *leche* (L /lakt-/) was ALREADY NON-PRODUCTIVE over half a millennium ago.

The claim then that /lakte/ underlies *leche* is dubious. The NGP solution is that there is a relation, certainly, but a lexical, not an MP one. That is, *leche, lactar* are both in the lexicon, and there is a via-rule connecting them, /kt/ ↔ /tʃ/; but no derivation, no mediated relation, no direction of derivation, hence no alternation proper.

The relation thus has no 'common third party' at all: it's simply a survivor from the earlier history of Spanish, whose status is clarified by a consideration of that history. (Similarly, English *vine* is an early borrowing from French which has gone through the GVS, but *machine* is a later one, that hasn't: otherwise it would be \**mach*[ai]*ne*.)

This discussion highlights a distinction often not made: true MP alternation (involving inflectional and derivational paradigms) vs. **etymological relations**. The latter are unsystematic, unproductive, and often involve specialized or 'learnèd' vocabulary, since they are by definition due to borrowing: whether from related languages as in *star* (English); *stellar* (Latin); *aster* (Greek); or from the earlier history of one's own, as in *leche*:*lactar*; as well as normally being quite unknown to the speaker without 'inside information'. Such distinctions aren't always hard-and-fast: there may be degrees of relatedness. Thus any speaker of English will presumably relate *sit*:*sat* (OE *sittan, sæt*), and perhaps *seat* as well; when we get to *settle, set*, the relation is more remote (*set* is historically the causative of *sit*); it requires a knowledge of Latin to relate *sedate, sedentary, sediment*; and of Indo-European comparative linguistics to put *nest* (from \*/ni-sd-os/ 'a place to sit', /sd/ representing the root /s_d/ 'sit') in the same group. So the NGP focus on paradigmatic relations enables us to separate things that GP would conflate. Presumably once you know the etymologies, you can 'have' a via-rule: *heart*:*cardiac*:*cordial, five*:*pentad*:*quintuplet, whale*:*baleen, quick*:*vivid*:*biology* etc. are related. See any etymological dictionary and acquire via-rules.

How does NGP deal with MP rules proper? The key here is the lexicon: rather than containing invariant underliers, the lexical entry itself codes the alternants. Thus in German we might have (9.19a) below for /raːt/ ~ /raːdəs/, (9.14b) for non-alternating /raːt/, and a rule like (9.14c) for the former:

(9.19)  $/raː\begin{Bmatrix} t \\ d \end{Bmatrix}/$  $/raːt/$  $\begin{Bmatrix} t \\ d \end{Bmatrix} \rightarrow \begin{Bmatrix} d/ \underline{\quad} + V \\ t \end{Bmatrix}$

(a)  (b)  (c)

But isn't this where we came in? In §4.1 we argued against precisely this treatment for German /t/ ∼ /d/ because it failed to distinguish systematic alternation from suppletion. And Bloomfield argued half a century ago that any alternative to a base-and-derivation model was equivalent to mere lexical listing of alternating and non-alternating morphemes; and that THEREFORE we need underlying /raːd/ and should conflate MP and phonological levels. NGP appears to claim that (9.19a) is preferable BECAUSE it involves lexical listing.

So the argument is turned around: earlier we rejected special MP symbols for alternations because they were equivalent to suppletion, now we recommend them for the same reason: /raːt/ ∼ /raːdəs/, despite their systematicity and phonological stability, are no different (or only marginally different) from *good ∼ better*. Let's look at the argument in more depth, before we decide.

What's the real difference between the two? Really only (a) phonetic specifiability (with a connection to phonotactics) and (b) the number of examples. There are lots of voice alternations, and only one lexeme of the 'good' type. But this apparently retrograde step comes to grips with an issue skirted by Bloomfield and GP: how many instances make a 'regularity'? We have only an intuitive sense (if that) of how many examples are needed to justify positing a base-form + rule(s): so perhaps the honest solution is to refer all non-transparent alternations to the lexicon, i.e. shift them into morphology.

And there's more: in the end, of course, even underlying /raːd/ + devoicing may be equivalent to (9.19a) anyhow; is that /d/ a 'real' /d/, or – since *[raːd] is impossible – a diacritic to trigger an alternation? After all, there's nothing IN any token of [raːt] to allow you to infer which lexeme it represents. And in the child's acquisition, he must have at least one instance of alternation and one of non-alternation before he can establish paradigms. And this could just as easily be done by entering the fact of alternation – and its type – for each lexeme ('the one that means "cycle" takes /d/'). Perhaps the best solution is to take /t/ ∼ /d/ as the product of an MP rule interacting with the phonotactic restriction against final voiced obstruents.

This is a characteristic example of a kind of cyclicity in linguistic thinking: NGP is really (though in a more sophisticated way, based on arguments that can only have arisen from the GP experiment) going back to the kind of thinking that motivated the proponents of a separate MP level; though the justification now is, if anything, more solid. A case of *reculer pour mieux sauter*?

The NGP attempt is not entirely successful: it both over-differentiates (by separating rules referring to boundaries from other P-rules and syllable-structure rules) and under-differentiates, by lumping all of the phonotactics under syllable structure. In the latter case, for instance, we lose sight of the possibility that syllable structure may be conditioned by word-position: e.g. in Kannaḍa closed syllables are allowed, but only in non-final position, and all final syllables are open. This framework also takes no account of rules that operate in connected and casual speech (see below and ch. 12).

A rather more realistic and insightful approach is proposed by Linell (1979): this seems to me overall the best set of distinctions yet suggested, and provides a subtle and highly differentiated model of the various aspects of 'phonological competence'. For Linell, phonology is 'language-specific phonetics' (p. 31), and MP alternations are products of history, 'synchronically unmotivated complications' of paradigms (p. 135). Because of this, there are no underlying forms in the usual sense (base morphemes underlying paradigms); the basic representation is a **phonetic plan**: a more or less redundancy-free representation that serves as a plan for pronunciation. Such a representation must be 'executable', and is 'described in terms of the agent's know-how' – i.e. it is a directive for performance. So it is not a conflation of parts of allomorphs, and contains no surface-illegal segments or sequences: i.e. it's always a word-form or an affix.

To take an example: consider Finnish nouns of the type *käsi* 'hand', gen sg *käden*, partitive *kättä*, essive *kätenä* (similarly *vesi* 'water', *vuosi* 'year'). These are opposed to the type *lasi* 'glass' (*lasin, lasia, lasina*). GP analyses usually assign *käsi* a base /kæte/, with rules /e/ → [i] /___#, and /t/ → [s] /___/i/. This alternation, however, is not fully productive (though some new words may enter this class). Linell proposes that – in general – we take the speakers' 'citation form' as the base, and provide 'morphophonological markings' to generate the oblique forms. (For example, if you ask a Finnish speaker the word for 'hand', the answer is *käsi*, not an oblique form, or a stem or other 'abstract' item: this is *prima facie* evidence for storage of a 'paradigm head' as representative of an alternation-set.) The entry for 'hand' is then ( ⸩ indicates variants, just like the horizontal ∼ ):

(9.20)     /k    æ    s    i/
                     ‹    ‹
                     t    e
                     ‹
                     d

with unitary 'morphological operations' that will produce the non-basic forms where they are morphologically and phonotactically permissible. Such a representation will interact with the rest of the rules of the grammar, e.g. /s/ will be substituted by [d] if the next syllable is short and closed (as in gen sg), etc. This is close to Hooper's model: but there is no 'morphophoneme' or anything of the sort to represent the sets [s ~ t ~ d], or [i ~ e]; the whole paradigm is derived from what is essentially a phonemic representation of one word-form. Note: this is in no way an 'underlying form', but a WORD on the basis of which other words can be constructed.

This model distinguishes the following main rule types:

(i) **Phonotactic rules (PhtRs).** Conditions on the structure of phonetic plans and 'careful pronunciations' (i.e. citation forms: see §12.2). They represent in a way speakers' assumptions about 'pronounceability': i.e. the PhtRs of English disallow initial /fn/, even though this cluster may appear as a result of vowel-deletion in casual speech ([fnɛtɪks] for *phonetics*, etc.): yet it's surely right to say that [fn] is an 'effect', rather than a 'fact about English consonant clusters'. These rules will be largely in terms of if:then conditions, e.g. (a simple example) the distribution of voice in German obstruents:

(9.21)     If:          [ + obs] #
                          ↓
          Then:       [ − voice]

Other rules, which Linell doesn't specify formally, will presumably list permissible syllable structures and cluster configurations, etc.

(ii) **Perceptual redundancy rules (PRRs).** These are the traditional allophonic rules; Linell gives them this name because 'perception (which is categorical) extracts certain features of phonetic strings as superordinate ("phonemic"), thus leaving out other subordinate, predictable features' (p. 171). For example, aspiration in English, vowel-lengthening before /r v ð z #/ in Scots, etc. In principle, PhtRs are conceived of as stating redundancies over features ALREADY PRESENT in a string, while PRRs are BLANK-FILLING; e.g. every final obstruent in German is specified for voice, and (9.21) is a filter; whereas initial /p t k/ in English have a blank for aspiration, which is filled in during the specification of articulatory commands. So aspiration would be controlled by (at least) two PRRs, of the type (not Linell's examples):

(9.22)　　If:　　$s \begin{bmatrix} +\text{obs} \\ -\text{cont} \end{bmatrix}$　　　　$\$ \begin{bmatrix} +\text{obs} \\ -\text{cont} \end{bmatrix} \acute{V}$

　　　　　　　　↓　　　　　　　　　↓

　　　Then:　　$[-\text{asp}]$　　　　$[+\text{asp}]$

(iii) **Articulatory reduction rules (ARRs).** These control the range of possible pronunciations in different speech styles and tempi, or 'variation in articulatory accuracy'. They may be presumed to operate on the output of the PRRs. For example, the rule producing, in some varieties of English, a nasalized tap [ɾ̃] in an input sequence /-V́ntV-/, as in [wɪ̃ɾ̃ər] for *winter*. This category contains rules such as deletions of cluster members and unstressed vowels, non-citation-form assimilations, etc. For discussion see ch. 12.

(iv) **Morphophonological rules proper (MRPs).** These are 'such *not*-phonotactically motivated rules as are needed to account for morphophonological alternations' (p. 172f; emphasis in original). The point about lack of phonotactic motivation is that in general 'wrong' versions of MP alternants are fully pronounceable, and not abnormal in the language. Take *serene* ~ *serenity*; there's nothing wrong with */sərí:nɪtɪ/ (though it happens not to exist): cf. *obesity*. In other words, there nothing about /əCí:CVCV/ that's illegal: it's a fact about *serene* that its -*ity* derivative has /ɛ/, and this is part of its lexical specification. Similarly for *electri*[k] ~ *electri*[ʃ]*ian*: there's nothing wrong with *electri*[k]*ian* (cf. *chicken*) – it's a matter of morphology.

Some properties of these various rule types are worth discussing, as they tend to support the distinctions, especially in setting off (i–iii) vs. (iv).

(i) Type of conditioning. It might seem that the obvious distinction is that PhtRs and PRRs are phonetically conditioned and 'automatic' (applying wherever their SDs are met); but this is oversimple, and one of the main reasons for rejecting Hooper's absolute separation of purely phonetically conditioned rules and others. While the majority of both types are sensitive to nothing more abstract than their segmental surroundings and word-termini, there are others that are sensitive to more abstract information, including morpheme boundaries as well (e.g. the phonotactics of complex forms may be different from the phonotactics of simplices, even if the segmental structures are the same). A case in point is the Swedish constraint against sequence ending in /Vnt/, if V is unstressed and preceded by a stressed vowel and there is a morpheme boundary between /n/ and /t/. That is, in essence /-Vnt#/ is legal unless /n/ is the final C of a disyllabic adjective and /t/ is the neuter morph. So *mógen* 'ripe', neuter *móget* (expected *\*mógent*), *váken* 'awake', neuter *váket* (*\*vákent*), but *fin* 'fine', neuter *fint* (*\*fin*), and *fórint* 'Hungarian coin', names like *Créscent*, *Víncent*, etc. (Linell p. 132). The rule would be:

(9.23)

$$\text{If:} \qquad X \begin{bmatrix} V \\ -\text{stress} \end{bmatrix} \underset{\downarrow}{n} + t \#$$

Then: $\qquad\qquad\qquad\qquad \varnothing$

Condition: X contains a stressed syllable

Even ARRs may be partly conditioned by higher-level considerations; many forms of English delete final /t d/ differentially in fast speech, so that deletion is less likely if the stop is the sole representative of an inflection (deletion in *mist, told*, but less in *missed, tolled*).

(ii) Generality. All rules may have exceptions: but there are likely to be more for MRPs than the other types – unsurprisingly, considering their lexical-morphological dependence. There are however exceptions to the others as well: cf. the allophonic exceptions discussed in §2.10 (for their origins, §13.4.2); and PhtRs often have exceptions in non-nativized loans. Thus /#ps-/ is not legal in Swedish except in Greek loans like *psykologi* /psykɔlɔgíː/, etc. – though even here one gets doublets in /sy-/. Presumably loan-phonotactics might constitute a separate 'marginal' or 'peripheral' system, not really part of the 'core' phonotactics. So in many varieties of English no citation form has nasalized vowels except for a set of more-or-less nativized French forms like *restaurant*, and frank loans like *raison d'être*.

(iii) Recoverability. One striking difference between PhtRs and PRRs on the one hand, the MRPs on the other, is the extent to which inputs can be inferred or recovered by the speaker from output forms. Given German [raːt], Finnish [kæsi], one cannot tell 'what kind of' [t] or [s] is present just from phonetic information: one must know what word it is, i.e. the phonetic plan of the headword of the paradigm, to know if it belongs to an alternation-set or not.

While this opacity is occasionally the case with ARRs as well (e.g. the homophony of *back* and *bat* as [baˀ] in some forms of English: §2.7), by and large the inputs of the more 'concrete' rule types are easily recoverable, given knowledge of the rules. For example, take nasalised vowels not followed by a nasal in English: [kʰæ̃:ˀp], [kʰæ̃:ˀt], [hæ̃ˀk]. The nasal can be recovered merely from phonetic information plus rules: the ARRs of nasalization and nasal-deletion operate on a structure controlled by a PhtR that specifies nasals as homorganic to following stops within the morpheme: the words are therefore *camp*, *can't*, *hank* (but cf. §12.3). Compare this with French [œ̃], which can be connected either with /m/ or /n/: [œ̃] ~ [yn] 'one' (masc/fem), vs. [paʁfœ̃] ~ [paʁfyme] 'perfume/to perfume'.

This classification partitions those aspects of language related to sound structure in a natural way: PhtRs and PRRs are the fundamental components of 'phonological structure' in the fairly strict (categorical) sense; ARRs relate to the deployment in speech of the structures established by the first two (as well as interacting with physiological and social parameters: ch. 12); and MRPs are the interface between phonology proper and morphology – often being the relics of old PhtRs, PRRs, and ARRs.

## 9.7 **Abstractness: some conclusions**

Insofar as anything in linguistics can be said to be 'conclusive', the past fifteen years or so have established that the GP model is excessively powerful, allows too much latitude both for unbridled imagination and the recovery of history, and has no sound claims to psychological plausibility. The idea that all aspects of sound/ meaning relationship in natural language can be unified by a single set of rules of one formal type, with two and only two 'theoretically significant' levels (systematic phonemic ≡ morphophonemic and systematic phonetic, or phonological and phonetic) has turned out not to be well supported by linguistic data, however attractive it seems at first.

We have not, however, ended up with a new orthodoxy; both NGP and Linell's model (as well as many other 'concrete' theories), while better than what came before, are neither fully justified on grounds of principle nor clearly 'correct'. The latter goal is of course not attainable; the best we can say – on this issue – is that insofar as abstract analyses represent a recovery of historical processes they are not part of synchronic linguistics; and insofar as they don't, they seem at present to represent nothing in particular, except the intersection of data, cleverness, and a set of unjustified and ultimately unjustifiable assumptions about 'good' descriptions, and a set of apparently counter-empirical assumptions about language learning and processing.

Wherever we end up in the future, in the complex matter of the domain of phonology, and the morphology–phonology relation, one thing seems clear (to me at least): the tradition of abstract analysis and phonology/morphophonemics conflation will be seen as an aberrant episode in the history of the discipline, and MP alternations will stay firmly in morphology, where they belong.

## NOTES AND REFERENCES

9.1 For the development of GP and an outline of its main tenets, *Fischer-Jørgensen (1975: ch. 9). A number of important papers from the earlier years are collected in Makkai (1972b: ch. iiib). For textbook treatments of varying degrees of orthodoxy and sophistication, Hyman (1975: chs. 3–4), **Anderson (1974), **Sommerstein (1977: chs. 6–9), *Rubach (1982); the latter is particularly good on motivating argumentation. For the conceptual foundation and some classic analyses, the basic source is **SPE (for theoretical foundations chs. 1, 8). The bulk of post-1968 literature builds in one way or another on positions taken in SPE.

A good entrée to the issues in the professional literature is the controversy between Householder and Chomsky & Halle (**Householder 1965, **Chomsky & Halle 1966, Householder 1966), and the critical commentary on SPE in *Vachek (1964b). It's also worth looking at the arguments against other schools in **Postal (1968) – an intemperate but influential book. See also the early critique in **Botha (1971).

One issue I have not treated here is the GP attempt to do away with the contrast-based phoneme as a primitive; the major source is Halle (1959), and for discussion see Sommerstein (1977: 116ff) and Schane (1971). The strongest attack on contrast is Postal (1968: chs. 1–2).

The GP literature has so dominated the journals in recent years that I won't try for any real coverage; I will single out those works that concentrate on methodological or conceptual issues, not highly technical formal argument or debates about specific analyses.

9.2 The analysis of [ŋ] stems from a pre-GP source (Isačenko 1963), with further arguments from *Vennemann (1970); further discussion and literature in §9.5. For some initial arguments against this treatment, **Vennemann (1974a).

The topic of rule ordering is immensely complex, and perhaps ultimately unrewarding; the need for extrinsic ordering is strictly a function of abstract analysis, which has been (see §§9.4ff), if not discredited, certainly rendered suspect. Nonetheless the topic is of at least historical interest, and has been at the centre of theoretical debate. The 'classical' position is that while all phonological rules are not (necessarily) linearly ordered, at least some are, and the relations may be extrinsic. This was first challenged in a series of papers by Koutsoudas and others (**Koutsoudas 1972, **Koutsoudas *et al.* 1974). These initiated a debate (not only in phonology) on the ordering properties of rules, with a movement towards what is now called the UDRA (Universally Determined Rule Application) hypothesis. The idea is that the need for extrinsic order can be obviated by a strong universal theory predicting the applicational interactions of rules on the basis of aspects of their formal relations: e.g. notions like 'Proper-Inclusion Precedence', which claims that a rule whose SD properly includes that of another necessarily takes precedence, etc. In a theory of this kind, all rules are essentially 'unordered' (i.e. intrinsically ordered, or applying wherever they can), since principles of the metatheory – not language-particular facts – dictate applicational sequence.

For an introductory survey of the issues, **Sommerstein (1977: ch. 7); for other contributions, the papers in **Koutsoudas (1975), Goyvaerts (1980: 51ff), and Pullum (1978).

9.3 Hungarian data from Makkai (1972b). The solution is loosely based on Vago (1973), an important justification of analyses of this type. There is some controversy over whether Hungarian did indeed have /ɯ ɤ/-types in its earlier history (Comrie 1981b: §2.2), but the standard treatments reconstruct them and connect them with neutral VH.

9.4 The literature on the 'abstractness controversy' is enormous, and relevant to the following sections as well. For an accessible summary up to the mid 1970s, *Hyman (1975: 3.3.5); see also Sommerstein (1977: ch. 9), Goyvaerts (1980: Part 1). The most important papers in the early stages of the debate are **Kiparsky (1968a), **(1971), **Hyman (1970), **Harms (1973), **Hyman (1973b). The last three should be read as a sequence. For further discussion, Schane (1974), Kaye (1981), Eliasson (1981). The issue is taken up in other frameworks as well; see notes to next sections.

9.5 For examples of testing of abstract analyses, see *Steinberg & Krohn (1975), *M. Ohala (1974), J. Ohala (1974). The 'psychological reality' problem is treated extensively in **Derwing (1973: esp. chs. 4–6); on the general problem of testing, Cohen & Wirth (1975).

For more on the Maori data, Kiparsky (1971), Linell (1979). The idea that substantive as well as formal evidence is needed has been around at least since Kiparsky (1971), and is foreshadowed in Kiparsky (1968b). The most important monograph in this area is still **Skousen (1975). For another detailed attempt to justify a solution, using both formal and external evidence, **Zwicky (1975b) on the English -*s* and -*ed* endings.

9.6 For NGP and its precursors, **Vennemann (1974a, b), **Hooper (1976), and the discussion in Goyvaerts (1980, Part 1, Appendix 2). Many of the papers in Bruck *et al.* (1974) also fall within this general approach. There are many other kinds of more 'concrete' theories as well; aside from Linell (1979), see Eliasson (1981). For a recent critical study of rule types in NGP see Clayton (1981).

To assess the current state of play on the GP paradigm, one can sample three collections of partly critical, partly 'revisionist' and partly 'orthodox' essays: **Goyvaerts & Pullum (1975), which is specifically a collection of responses to issues raised in *SPE*; second, **Dinnsen (1977), which illustrates contemporary approaches growing for the most part out of classical GP; and finally **Goyvaerts (1981), an uneven but commendably eclectic book, which is a state-of-the-art report on phonology in the 1970s (misleadingly entitled *Phonology in the 1980s*, but originally to have been published in the late 70s).

Many scholars still defend an abstract approach, and work goes on in this direction. Perhaps the most spirited and challenging recent defence is **Gussmann (1978), with data mainly from Polish and English; see also the work in 'cyclical phonology' in Rubach (1980). And for a recent critical summary, with special attention to the structure of argument and the kinds of claims actually being made, see the elegant discussion of GP approaches to French in **Love (1981).

# 10

# Beyond the segment: prosodies, syllables, and quantity

## 10.1 'Reduction': how primitive are primitives?

So far we've assumed (without argument) that the segment is somehow 'privileged', the central primitive element in phonology. With the bulk of linguistic tradition we've taken it as the upper bound of primitiveness, with the feature as a lower bound. Indeed, the thrust of the argument in chs. 3, 5–6 was a move from the apparently self-evident segment to its less obvious – but no less important – sub-segmental components.

But what have we actually done? The process of argument involved is common to both the natural and social sciences, and is called **reduction**: the attempt to interpret higher-level entities as constellations of lower-level ('smaller') ones. And one striking form of progress in science has been a continuous and fairly successful programme of reduction: e.g. of previously indivisible atoms (Gr *a-tómos* 'uncuttable') to smaller 'elementary' particles like electrons and protons, and these to even more 'elementary' ones like quarks; of genes to nucleotide sequences, and so on.

It's vital however that we don't misinterpret reduction: 'reducing' an entity to its components doesn't make it disappear. Higher-level constructs typically retain their identities under reduction. For example: say what the liver does as a whole is reducible without residue to the sum of the metabolic activities of its component cells, and these to coded instructions from the cells' DNA to manufacture certain proteins, etc. There would still be a significant sense in which 'liver-function' as a whole is an irreducible component of a physiological system, along with 'kidney-function' (which has a reducible componential structure as well). That is, the body has a 'detoxification system', which is a functional whole, a primitive, on the level

236

of 'whole-body metabolism'; and ITS primitives are the functional wholes of liver, kidneys, etc.

Similarly, if we reduce segments to feature-complexes, this doesn't make segments go away, or turn them into MERELY informal abbreviations for feature-complexes. As is clear from deletion, insertion and metathesis, for instance, there is a level at which the componential make-up of segments is essentially irrelevant, and they function as wholes. And similarly syllables (§10.3) which at one level are segment-sequences, have their own unique identity as well.

So componentiality doesn't entail reduction to the extent that the 'compositional' products of the components vanish or become theoretically invalid. Rather we should see reducible elements, in a term introduced by Arthur Koestler, as **holons**. A holon is an entity which, regardless of its lower-level structure or place in a hierarchy, functions as a unique whole, a unit. The crucial concept is not 'primitiveness' or 'divisibility', but PRIMITIVENESS WITH RESPECT TO A GIVEN LEVEL of analysis.

Holons, as Koestler says, are 'Janus-faced': like the Roman god of doorways they face in two directions at once, as components themselves with respect to higher levels, and wholes with respect to lower. To illustrate, consider the primitiveness of the category 'NP' in a tree like this:

(10.1)

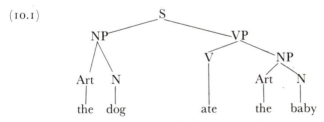

From the 'point of view of S', NP is a (linear) component, along with – on its level – VP; from the point of view of VP, NP has the same status along with V. But from the point of view of Art and N, NP is a higher-order whole. And grammatical processes can treat NP in either way: componentially, e.g. by allowing the insertion of adjectives between Art and N; as a whole, e.g. by permuting NP regardless of its constituents. The point is nearly obvious, but in the light of the emphasis I've been putting on complementarity, and the arguments to follow, it's important: what something is depends on which end you look at it from.

All this is by way of re-establishing the legitimacy of segments, as a prelude to an anti-reduction argument in the opposite direction. Whatever the undoubted 'reality', usefulness, etc. of segment-sized chunks of phonetic substance, there are levels of organization at which they are the 'lower' faces of holons, of a quite different nature.

## 10.2 **Prosodic phonology**

### 10.2.1 *A first approach to prosodies*

Let's return yet again to the Kannaḍa nasals (§§3.3, 6.5). Recall the facts: given a sequence NC, where C is some phonemic stop, all place features of N are predictable from those of C: [kempu], [aɲču], [beŋki], etc. Since, as we said, the phonemicity of the stops is unambiguous, the best solution to the problem of the nasal phones [ɲ ŋ], which appear only before some homorganic stop, is via neutralization. We take all nasals in NC clusters as representatives of an archinasal /N/, thus avoiding arbitrary phonemic decisions.

But I fudged the issue a bit, to make a point about neutralization. What after all forced this decision? The answer is a 'segmental prejudice' (segments as upper bounds: §10.1). We wanted (implicitly) a DIRECTION FOR ASSIMILATION, and this involved holding one item (the place of the stop, which seemed independently established) constant, and taking the place of the nasal as a **dependent variable**. Thus we ended up with the statement 'Nasals agree in place with following stops'. But we started with the observation 'All NC clusters are homorganic'; and this can lead us in a different direction. The two statements may seem synonymous, but their implications are not the same.

Let's turn the argument on its head so that the question of 'dependent' status for the nasals disappears. Consider the inventory of NC sequences:

$$(10.2) \qquad m\begin{Bmatrix}p\\b\end{Bmatrix} \qquad n\begin{Bmatrix}t\\d\end{Bmatrix} \qquad \eta\begin{Bmatrix}t\\d\end{Bmatrix} \qquad \mathrm{\textltailn}\begin{Bmatrix}\check{c}\\\check{j}\end{Bmatrix} \qquad \eta\begin{Bmatrix}k\\g\end{Bmatrix}$$

Now we purge ourselves of some preconceptions: (a) that 'assimilation' must be a process with a direction; (b) that single segments and their interactions are the proper domain for stating distributions like (10.2); (c) that a phone in one environment ought to be identified with 'the same' phone elsewhere (the monosystemic prejudice: §7.8).

With our new perspective, (10.2) shows not a set of neutralizations or nasals assimilations, but a CLASS OF SYLLABLE-FINALS: we could state them (with $C_{-v}$, $C_{+v}$ as respectively voiceless, voiced) as:

(10.3)

| Bilabial | Dental | Retroflex | Palatal | Velar |
|---|---|---|---|---|
| $N\left\{{C_{-v}\atop C_{+v}}\right\}$ | $N\left\{{C_{-v}\atop C_{+v}}\right\}$ | $N\left\{{C_{-v}\atop C_{+v}}\right\}$ | $N\left\{{C_{-v}\atop C_{+v}}\right\}$ | $N\left\{{C_{-v}\atop C_{+v}}\right\}$ |

That is: we have a set of five basic NC-syllable-finals, each characterized AS A WHOLE by a place of articulation. The only variable is the voicing value of C. The point-of-articulation features are **unplaced**: they 'ride over' the whole syllable-terminus, and cover everything in their domain. On this interpretation, then, syllable-final [p t ʈ č k] are not instances of 'the phonemes /p t ʈ č k/', but 'exponents of the C-piece' of members of the NC-system.

We can then represent some typical forms in a new way, with the labels P T Ṭ Č K representing the 'spread' places of articulation in (10.3):

(10.4)

| Phonetic representation | (10.3)-representation |
|---|---|
| [kempu] | ke $\overline{\text{NC}_{-v}}$ \| u   (P) |
| [ondu] | o $\overline{\text{NC}_{+v}}$ \| u   (T) |
| [čeṇḍu] | če $\overline{\text{NC}_{+v}}$ \| u   (Ṭ) |
| [aɲču] | a $\overline{\text{NC}_{-v}}$ \| u   (Č) |
| [beŋki] | be $\overline{\text{NC}_{-v}}$ \| i   (K) |

(The downstroke on ‾‾| represents the syllable-terminus.)

Following terminology introduced by J. R. Firth (1948), we will call these larger-than-segment elements **prosodies**. What we have then is a basic homorganic NC syllable-final type, with varying prosodies of place (P, T, etc.); the articulatory features do not inhere in particular segments, but in the sequence. We abstract out the feature(s) common to the sequence elements as a prosody; and this leaves behind less than fully-specified segments (**phonematic units** in Firthian terminology). These are clearly neither the same as classical phonemes, nor as archiphonemes, since there is no question of neutralization.

How does this differ from an analysis in terms of assimilation-as-process? If X assimilates to Y, Y serves as a 'focus' or 'source' from which features 'move to' X: we still abstract a common property, only we distribute it by moving it from one place to another. But a further abstraction lets us bypass movement and direction, at least in a case like this where the 'unassimilated' form doesn't occur. (For example, as opposed to variants like [sɛvən] ~ [sɛvɱ], where there's at least a *prima facie* case for process.) In a prosodic analysis we ask: why invoke the extra 'process' machinery when all that has to be said is that homorganicity is inherent in the sequence? Or, why make one segment distinctive for place, and the place of the other(s) 'derived' or 'secondary', when the sequence as a whole is distinctive? Syllable-finals, in this analysis, are holons: their 'lower' face is a segment-sequence (say from the point of view of a phonetic transcription), and their 'upper' face is a unit with a particular place of articulation.

This kind of insight was developed primarily by British linguists (the 'London School') in the 1950s and 60s, into a very elaborate notational/analytic system (not 'theory', for reasons that will become clear below), usually called **prosodic phonology** or **prosodic analysis**. We will examine the fruitfulness of this approach further in the next sections; but as a prelude it's worth giving an account of its practitioners' intellectual set. This is worthwhile because their methodological ideas furnish an interesting corrective to the extreme realism of GP and similar approaches – even if they may also appear to go off the deep end.

Several basic ideas are shared by most (if not all) of the prosodists:

(i) There are no phonological universals. Thus Robins (1970 [1957]: 190) says that in phonology, 'existence or reality are not predictable of anything other than the actual ... data under observation'. This means that 'terms and concepts used in analysis are in the nature of a set of words, and no more, employed by the analyst to talk about his data'. And this implies further that

(ii) There are no 'true' or 'correct' analyses (or theories). On this it's worth quoting Robins at length (1970: 191):

> No one analysis, or mode of analysis, is the only one accurate or sacrosanct, but any account of the language, in any terms, is an

> adequate statement ... provided that, and to the extent to which, it comprehensively and economically explains what is heard ... in the language ... Questions of truth and falsity, of 'what is there' and 'what is not there', only arise ... at the level of the barest phonetic observation ... before any analysis has taken place.

(Assuming of course that 'observation' without 'analysis' is possible, which is false – cf. §1.3; still the principle is reasonable if we give it a sophisticated interpretation.) Compare this with Vago's claim (§9.4) that linguistic theory provides 'a set of principles which automatically evaluates competing analyses, and designates one as the internalized generalization' of the speaker.

A view like Robins' can be taken as either broadly tolerant or intellectually irresponsible, depending on how far you push it and where your sympathies lie. Certainly it absolves its proponents from any need to make their theoretical claims testable; but since they are not claiming to provide general 'scientific' theories, can we fault them for this, or accuse them of evasion?

This is not of course wholly relevant to the advantages or dis-advantages of the prosodic approach, which could just as easily be taken in a 'realist' sense; I treat it here not as a 'competitor for truth' with classical phonemics or GP or anything else, but as another way of looking at some things. It's important to remember that the value of an analytical technique may be – and quite often is – independent of what its inventor(s) think about it.

(iii) There are no (synchronic) processes. Robins again (p. 196):

> It is an unsuitable metaphor to say that one sound operates at a distance over intervening sounds to exert a force on another sound, and change it from something which in fact it never was (in the words concerned) into something else. It is indeed generally desirable that synchronic description ... should ... avoid the use, even metaphorically, of terms and concepts more appropriate to ... diachronic study ...

Thus prosodic analyses are fundamentally STATIC: the only relation between prosody and phonetics is exponence. Any phonetic string is simultaneously prosodic and segmental; there are no 'rules' (and of course no ordering), no 'intermediate stages' of derivation. There is not, as in process phonologies, an input–output relation between an underlying or abstract representation and the phonetic surface, e.g. the description of [kempu] simply IS:

(10.5)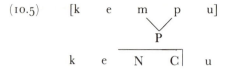

(iv) The syntagmatic dimension is as important as the **paradigmatic**. Most phoneme-based theories are primarily paradigmatic in the sense that their focus of interest is in systems of contrasting (substitutable) items; syntagmatic (linear) structures are of interest, except in phonotactics, primarily insofar as they condition realizations or processes. In prosodic phonology the emphasis is reversed, so that the phonematic units may be nearly empty of distinctive specification, which has been shifted to the prosodies.

This is further shown by the fact that prosodies do not have to be 'phonemic' or distinctive in any way: any phonetic property, regardless of its distinctiveness, may be prosodic. Thus in a dialect of English where all coronals are velarized in syllable-final position, this 'ɯ-prosody' is as much a part of the overall description – and of the same status – as a distinctive syllable-final prosody like Kannaḍa NC.

### 10.2.2 *Types of prosodies*

The idea of prosody has a much greater extension than our simple examples so far suggest. For the Firthians, almost anything CAN count as a prosody, provided the requisite sort of abstraction can be made. Take a dialect of English where (simplifying a bit) all initial voiceless stops are aspirated, all final ones glottalized, and initial and final voiced stops partly voiced and unaspirated. Taking words of the shape CVC as examples, we can interpret all these distinctions prosodically: aspiration is a syllable-initial h-prosody, glottalization a final ʔ-prosody, and voicing a v-prosody of either end. Leaving vowels unspecified, we can take all possible permutations of voiced and voiceless CVC, and represent them as:

(10.6)

| Phonetic | Prosodic |
|----------|----------|
| [pʰVʔp] | ʰPVPʔ |
| [pʰVb] | ʰPVPᵛ |
| [bVʔp] | ᵛPVPʔ |
| [bVb] | ᵛPVPᵛ |

Here P is a phonematic unit whose components are stopness and labiality. We could also take nasality as a prosody:

(10.7)

| | Phonetic | Prosodic |
|---|---|---|
| | [pʰVm] | ʰPVPⁿ |
| | [mVʔp] | ⁿPVPʔ |
| | [bVm] | ᵛPVPⁿ |
| | [mVb] | ⁿPVPᵛ |
| | [mVm] | ⁿPVPⁿ |

The phonetics are described with a set of precise exponence state-ments; to give some flavour of what these would be like, we could specify the prosodies above this way:

(10.8)    *h*: voicelessness during stop closure; release of closure before voice onset on following vowel.

*ʔ*: slight glottal constriction during voicing of preceding vowel ('tight phonation'), followed by glottal stop preceding or simul-taneous with stop closure; relatively short preceding vowel.

*v*: (a) initial: voiceless stop onset, voiced or whispered offset, merging into full voicing on vowel; (b) final: voiced or whispered onset, voiceless offset; relatively long preceding vowel.

*n*: (a) initial: full stop closure with voicing throughout, lowered velum, slight nasalized onset to following vowel; (b) final: full stop closure with voicing, lowered velum, relatively long and nasalized preceding vowel.

We might observe further that we have two rather different kinds of prosody here: *ʔ*, *h* are bound to a particular place in the syllable (they are **markers** of syllable position), while *n*, *v* are free.

How do we decide what counts as a prosody and what as a unit? The procedures haven't been worked out as meticulously as those for phonemic status, but there are enough examples in the literature to give us some good clues. The crucial point seems to be: to qualify as a prosody, some phonetic property or bundle of properties should either (a) extend over more than one segment, or (b) have implications for more than one '**place**' in a structure. 'Place' is a complex notion; it can include not only (sequential) position, but 'place' in a grammatical system: many morphophonemic phenomena can be treated as prosodies of particular grammatical systems. So for example both a segment and its position are 'places', which makes 'syllable-initial stop' a prosodic domain; and 'syllable-initial' and 'masculine possessive' are both places, which makes it possible to treat Welsh initial mutations prosodically (see §8.3.1).

The literature (both implicitly and with a few explicit statements) suggests the following primary prosodic categories:

(i) **Sentence prosodies**: i.e. intonation contours; a subcase of this might be phrasal contours, or prosodies of 'sentence-pieces'.

(ii) **Word prosodies**; features like vowel harmony, characterizing whole words, or portions larger than one syllable.

(iii) **Syllable prosodies**: length, tone, stress, any other features like labialization, velarization, etc. that can characterize whole syllables.

(iv) **Syllable-part prosodies**: features characterizing beginnings, middles or ends, e.g. aspiration and glottalization in English.

In terms of functions, we might make the following further distinctions:

(v) **Junction prosodies**: these are properties of the boundaries between higher-level structural units (words, morphemes). For example, in languages with 'fixed' stress, like Czech and Finnish (initial) or Polish (penultimate), stress can be taken as a prosody with its **focus** on the word boundary (i.e. it belongs to the word as a whole, but not as a phonetic property spread over a number of segments: its function is **demarcating**). In this case although stress would be focussed on a boundary, its phonetic exponent could either be the syllable contiguous to the boundary (Czech) or one a syllable away (Polish). Just as English aspiration signals the beginning of a purely phonological unit ('stressed syllable'), Czech stress signals the beginning of a morphosyntactic unit ('word').

(vi) **Diagnostic prosodies**: in the literature a number of heterogeneous features are generalized as prosodic, but differ from other types in having vaguer and more complex domains. Thus English initial [ð] can be taken as a marker of the category 'deictic/determiner'; [w̥], for those dialects that have it, is a prosody of 'native lexicon', and so on. Even features of particular styles can be characterized as 'style prosodies'. This extension is rather less helpful than other uses: one ought perhaps to distinguish prosodies in the first six senses from these diacritics.

10.2.3   *The prosodic treatment of vowel harmony*

The concept of word prosody suggests that this non-segmental approach might be applicable to **long-domain** phenomena like metaphony (§8.2.1). Could a prosodic treatment help us over some of the difficulties we saw in §9.3, and lead to a relatively 'concrete' and phonetically realistic analysis? It seems clear in principle that we could mark entire words with a harmonic prosody, extending over the whole sequence of vowels: nothing would have to 'turn into' anything else (thus avoiding Robins' 'inappropriate metaphor'); and we could have defectively specified vowels as phonematic units, with their phonetic realizations prosodically determined.

This radical approach seems especially suitable for languages where metaphony is a major aspect of vowel phonology, e.g. Hungarian. Recall that in our earlier treatment (§9.3) we assumed that the suffix vowels had a specific ('underlying') backness value, and that the root vowels were phonemes of the usual type as well, specified for all features. We further assumed that the underlying suffix vowel was affected by that of the root, so that suffixes 'assimilated progressively' to the preceding vowel(s). We were then faced with the problem of the 'neutral' vowels, which were either irrelevant to VH in stems with non-neutral vowels as well, or appeared to be harmonically random. It was the latter property that prompted the 'abstract' analysis of [iː] as /ɯː/, etc.

If we look at VH prosodically, however, a number of earlier problems vanish. If VH is a word prosody, then we don't have to specify segmental underliers; and it is also much easier to deal with an aspect we haven't mentioned yet – VH within the stem. In Hungarian, as in most VH languages, it's not only suffixes that harmonize to stems; stems themselves (with certain exceptions) are also harmonic units. Take some typical disyllabic roots:

| (10.9) | Front-harmonic | Back-harmonic |
|---|---|---|
| | bøːrœnd 'suitcase' | bɔlɔnd 'crazy' |
| | lɛveːl 'letter' | tɒnäːr 'teacher' |
| | kœzeːp 'middle' | kɔmɔλ 'serious' |
| | pynkœst 'Pentecost' | vɒnɒl 'line' |

It's clear that backness (B) and frontness (F) can be extracted as prosodies, and the phonematic units specified only for height (H, M, L), roundness ($\omega$) and length (the latter two could be prosodic as well, but for convenience we will not extract them):

(10.10)  $^F\mathrm{bV}^{\omega}_{\mathrm{M}}\mathrm{rV}^{\omega}_{\mathrm{M}}\mathrm{nd}$  $^B\mathrm{bV}^{\omega}_{\mathrm{M}}\mathrm{lV}^{\omega}_{\mathrm{M}}\mathrm{nd}$

[bøːrœnd]  [bɔlɔnd]

Our first problem (still at root level) is 'mixed harmony' words, i.e.

with both neutral and non-neutral vowels, where the neutral and the non-neutral disagree in backness:

(10.11)    fɒzeːk 'pot'                    veːkɔɲ 'this'
           kɔtʃi 'coach'                   igɒz 'true'

These can be treated as doubly-prosodic, i.e. having prosodies with syllable-length – not word-length – domains:

(10.12)    $^{B}kV_{M}^{\omega}$ $^{F}ʧV_{H}$            $^{F}V_{H}$ $^{B}gV_{L}^{\omega}z$
           [kɔtʃi]                           [igɒz]

But note that [kɔtʃi] (see (9.7)) as a whole is back-harmonic; this suggests that the above treatment, while adequate for the phonetics of the root, will not handle suffix-harmony; this will require a junction prosody of a special kind, and we'll return to this below.

Before we go any further with VH in this framework, it's worth establishing just why we want to talk of word prosodies. The clearest evidence of VH as a marker of word-length pieces is from compounds, where each component is self-harmonic, and the harmony does not cross the boundary:

(10.13)    hɛɟ + ɔldɒl 'hillside'         $^{F}hV_{Mɟ} + {}^{B}V_{M}^{\omega}ldV_{L}^{\omega}l$

           nɒɟ + sivy: 'great-            $^{B}nV_{Lɟ}^{\omega} + {}^{F}sV_{H}vV_{:H}^{\omega}$
                      hearted'

Words with one neutral vowel are di-prosodic, and this seems also a natural treatment for compounds; so in fact the prosodic description already shows up something of an anomaly connected with the phenomenon of neutrality itself, which we will capitalize on below.

Let us now turn to the problematical all-neutral roots (see (9.8)): e.g. [kiːn] and [tseːl], which are back-harmonic. Here the prosodic analysis forces a decision; we must distinguish the harmonic properties of these roots from 'normal' word-harmonic behaviour. That is, we shift our view from phonetic harmony to VH as a LEXICAL property: the aberrant back harmony of front roots belongs to the roots them-selves as wholes, not to the vowels in them – since in our non-process framework we can't distinguish, on a segmental level, between front-harmonizing and back-harmonizing front vowels. A front-prosodic root is just that, and we can say nothing else about it *qua* root.

The obvious solution is to mark the root-terminus with a 'forward-looking' junction prosody to control the suffix vocalism, while the root itself remains prosodically front:

(10.14)  $\text{F}_{\;kV{:}_{H}n}\;+\;^{B}$  $\qquad$  $\text{F}_{\;tsV{:}_{M}l}\;+\;^{B}$
$\qquad\;\;$[ki:n]  $\qquad\qquad\qquad$ [tse:l]

These look pretty ad hoc and sloppy; but we can turn this into a positive advantage. If the 'normal' situation for a Hungarian non-compound word (regardless of morphological complexity) is for it to be harmonic, the 'extra' junction prosody, which attaches to the (prosodically unmarked) suffix is an explicit marker of 'abnormality'. Rather than concealing an irregularity in a 'regular' derivation, as in the GP solution, the notational system here forces an explicit recognition of the deviance. And since we allow no 'depth', but treat all vowel quality as at least syllable-prosodic, the lack of discrimination in the abstract solution (§9.4 (iii)) is neutralized. We can tell by inspection which words are normal (phonetically surface-harmonic) and which aren't. The distinction is coded in their prosodic structure, as in (10.15) below (see (9.8)):

(10.15)  $\qquad\qquad$ 'Normal'  $\qquad\qquad\qquad$ 'Deviant'

$\text{F}_{\;vV{:}_{H}z}\;+\;bV{:}_{M}^{\omega}l$  $\qquad\qquad$  $\text{F}_{\;kV{:}_{H}n}\;+\;^{B}\;bV{:}_{H}^{\omega}l$
$\qquad$ [vi:zbø:l]  $\qquad\qquad\qquad\quad$ [ki:nbo:l]

$\text{F}_{\;kV{:}_{H}\int}\;+\;bV{:}_{M}^{\omega}l$  $\qquad\qquad$  $\text{F}_{\;tsV{:}_{M}l}\;+\;^{B}\;bV{:}_{M}^{\omega}l$
$\qquad$ [ke:ʃbø:l]  $\qquad\qquad\qquad\quad$ [tse:lbo:l]

The 'deviant' forms thus look arbitrary or unmotivated, and are notationally more complex; and the root and suffix are treated like members of a compound, which are non-harmonic.

This also gives us a different way of looking at the historical origin of neutral harmony. In the GP solution, the original back vowels in /kɯ:n/, /tsɣːl/ 'remain' in the underlying representations, and the change consists merely in the addition to the grammar of a neutralizing rule. On the prosodic account, the WORD as a unit has remained harmonically back with respect to its suffix, which has made the harmony lexical, not phonological. The original root prosody has been shifted to a post-radical junction prosody, and been replaced by a front prosody for the root. The neutral roots are thus taken out of the VH system, and form an excrescence, a 'sore thumb' explicitly recognized by the notation: simply a residue left behind by historical change, nothing 'deeper'. Change in this sort of model is more far-reaching than in GP; the latter postpones real change by interpreting the historical shift /ɯː ɣː/ → /iː eː/ as a rescue rule; the prosodic account makes lexical restructuring immediate.

Note by the way that immediate restructuring is not restricted to the prosodic model; the di-prosodic notation is equivalent to a rule feature. The prosodic analysis stands or falls on other grounds, e.g. the non-necessity of specified vowels, and the unitary, non-process interpretation of VH. The only special point is that in prosodic analysis, as in any framework without derivational 'depth', explicit notice of deviance is built into the notation. Or, to put it another way, the notational armoury is sufficiently impoverished to disallow abstractness, whereas in any process phonology at least some abstractness is permitted.

## 10.3 **Syllables**

### 10.3.1 *Preliminaries*

I've used 'syllable' so far in an intuitive way, assuming familiarity; but with no definition or theoretical argument. Everyone knows that 'a syllable is what *syllable* has three of', but we need something better than this. We have to get reasonable answers to three questions: (a) how are syllables defined? (b) are they primitives, or reducible to mere strings of Cs and Vs? (c) assuming satisfactory answers to (a, b), how do we determine syllable boundaries?

We might ask first whether syllables are phonetically definable, as all phonological constructs should be. The first (and for a while most popular) phonetic definition was Stetson's (1928) **motor theory**. This claimed that syllables correlate with bursts of activity of the intercostal muscles ('chest pulses'), the speaker emitting syllables one at a time, as independent muscular gestures. But subsequent experimental work has shown no such simple correlation; whatever syllables are, they are not SIMPLE motor units.

We're still far from any solid phonetic definition, but there are some useful proposals made by J. C. Catford (1977a: ch. 5). Catford suggests that speech is produced in measured bursts of **initiator power**, or **feet**, which are the basic rhythmic units of a language. (The 'initiator' is normally the pulmonic egressive machinery.) In English, for example, each initiator-burst corresponds to a stressed syllable, and the intervals between stressed syllables are (all things being equal) roughly equal. So English is said to be '**stress-timed**', as opposed e.g. to French, where there seems to be one burst per syllable, regardless of accent. So French is **'syllable-timed'**. These are rather gross but workable distinctions.

Each initiator-burst is a power-curve, rising to a peak of emitted acoustic energy, and then tailing off. We can represent English stress-timing by superimposing a schematic curve over a syllable-sequence, as follows ( ´ = main stress):

| (10.16) | (a) | Jóhn bought | twó new | bóoks there | yésterday |
|         | (b) | Jóhn | bóught two | néw books | thére |
|         | (c) | Jóhn saw a | bláckbird | yésterday | |

(Verticals represent foot-divisions.) Whereas the French equivalents of (b, c) would be more like:

| (10.17) | Jean | a | ache | té | deux | livres | hier |
|         | Jean | a | vu | un | merle | hier | |

Each language has its own kind of **isochronism** (rhythm based on roughly equal units); the initiator-power is emitted in 'quanta', which in French generally coincide with syllables in the simple sense, in English with stressed syllables.

So the definition of 'phonetic syllable' seems reasonably straight-forward for a syllable-timed language (assuming this kind of distinction is valid); but for one like English things are a bit more complex: foot boundaries may (but don't have to) coincide with syllables. Consider two possible readings of the letter-sequence A, B, C, D, in one case as four isolated primary stresses, in the other with a trochaic rhythm:

(10.18)

Isolated:

Trochaic:

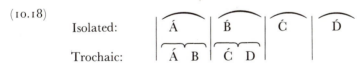

Or, A, B, C in dactylic or anapaestic rhythm:

(10.19)

Dactylic:

Anapaestic:

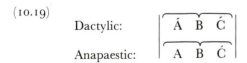

The shapes of the trochaic, dactylic, and anapaestic curves suggest how a single initiator-quantum may contain more than one syllable: the divisions are marked by 'momentary slight retardations of ... initiator movement ... either by articulatory closures [as in the above examples: RL]', or by 'a slight, self-imposed retardation and re-acceleration of the initiator, as in E F [iɛf]' (Catford: p. 89).

A universal phonetic definition (if there is one, and if this is on the right track) will have a rhythmic basis: all languages have an inherent rhythmic organization, based on the emission of timed iniator power-bursts, each burst having a single peak. If the curve is free of retardation, then the syllable ≡ the foot; if not, then there are syllables within the foot. So the syllable is a minimal chunk of initiator activity, bounded by small intra-foot retardations, or by foot boundaries (after Catford: p. 90).

This is a **phonetic syllable**. But there is another construct, more important for our purposes, the **phonological syllable**; and this may or may not be coterminous with the phonetic. At least it will require more precise definition, especially with respect to boundaries and internal structure; note that Catford's definition allows us in principle to locate the peaks of syllables, but does not tell us where the boundaries between one syllable and the next are placed. The phonological syllable might be a kind of minimal phonotactic unit, say with a vowel as a nucleus, flanked by consonantal segments or legal clusterings, or the domain for stating rules of accent, tone, quantity, and the like. The phonetic syllable then is a 'performance' unit, whose entire reality is phonetic; the phonological syllable is a structural (if phonetically based) unit, perhaps with non-phonetic properties as well (see §§10.3.2ff).

10.3.2    *The reality of the syllable: quantity*

If syllables aren't merely 'there' phonetically, but have some theoretical status, what is it? One argument might come from the possibility that they are STRUCTURED strings, not just CV ... sequences, and have a place in phonological description such that some generalizations are better stated with them than without them (see §7.1). Here is one fairly typical (if elaborate) argument, which will introduce some useful terminology and concepts.

We begin, perhaps curiously, with morphology. Consider these forms from various Old English noun declensions (given in orthographic form, with vowel length marked as $\bar{v}$; the declension names are traditional, for reference; $\flat = /\theta/$).

(10.20)   (a)  Neuter *a*-stem, nom pl:

| A | B |
|---|---|
| fæt-u 'vessels' | bǣl 'funeral pyres' |
| hof-u 'dwellings' | wīf 'women' |
| col-u 'coals' | word 'words' |
| lim-u 'limbs' | land 'lands' |

(b)  Neuter *a*-stem disyllables, nom sg vs. gen sg:

| A | B |
|---|---|
| wæter/wæter-es 'water' | ātor/atr-es 'poison' |
| gamen/gamen-es 'game' | tungol/tungl-es 'star' |

(c)  Feminine *o*-stem, nom sg:

| A | B |
|---|---|
| coþ-u 'disease' | ār 'honour' |
| den-u 'valley' | bǣr 'bier' |
| tal-u 'tale' | lind 'linden' |
| far-u 'journey' | scofl 'shovel' |

(d)  Masculine *i*-stem, nom sg:

| A | B |
|---|---|
| win-e 'friend' | glǣm 'gleam' |
| hef-e 'weight' | mǣw 'seagull' |
| hyp-e '(rose)hip' | byrst 'loss' |
| mer-e 'pool' | ent 'giant' |

(e)  Masculine *u*-stem, nom sg:

| A | B |
|---|---|
| sun-u 'son' | gār 'spear' |
| breg-u 'prince' | hād 'rank' |
| lag-u 'sea' | feld 'field' |
| sid-u 'custom' | ford 'ford' |

Consider first the alternation of suffixed 'A' and endingless 'B' forms: is this arbitrary (morphological) or phonological? Examination suggests there is phonological conditioning, of this sort:

(10.21)   (a)  If the stem ends in -VC, there is a suffix;
          (b)  If the stem ends in -VCC or -V̄C, there is no suffix.

And we can get (10.20b) into this as well:

(10.22)    (c)  If the first syllable of a disyllabic sonorant-final noun ends in
-VC, then the next vowel does not syncopate in gen sg;
(d)  If the first syllable (as above) ends in -VCC or -V̆C, then
there is syncopation.

The two seem related, in that -VCC and -V̆C trigger the same sort
of processes; they are clearly a class, but why? Are they a 'natural'
class? If this relation were simply one-off, we could dismiss it; but it
occurs again and again elsewhere in Germanic and Indo-European,
and indeed in other language families; and not only in phonology
proper and morphology, but in metrics as well, in verse traditions as
scattered as Old English, Greek, Latin and Kannaḍa. For example, in
OE verse, certain portions of the line are reserved for -VCC or -V̆C
syllables. So it's worth trying to account for this class, because of its
persistence.

Observe that the prevocalic portion of the stem syllables in (10.23)
is irrelevant; what counts is V and its sequel(s). We can now introduce
some terminology for talking about syllable structure. A syllable
consists of an **onset** (O) and a **rhyme** (R); and the rhyme of a
**peak** (P) and a **coda** (Co). Any of these categories except P may be
empty (e.g. *oh, ah*). This is naturally expressed as a form of
**constituency**: a syllable (σ) can be represented as a BRANCHING TREE:

(10.23)

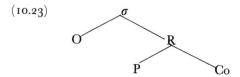

These higher nodes dominate categories like V, C, which in turn
dominate specific segments. Thus for some selected English monosyllables we might have:

(10.24)

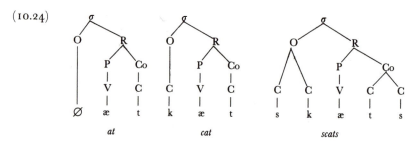

Now look again at the OE data: here are trees for the stems of typical pairs of items from (10.22a, b), first syllables only for (b):

(10.25)     (a)         A                                    B

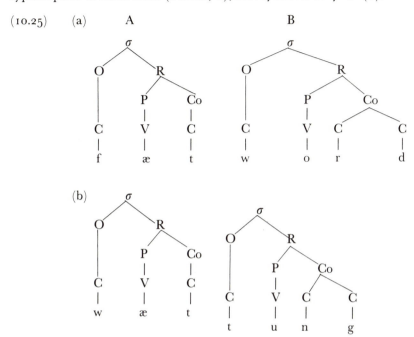

So far, merely another way of expressing the generalization: 'suffixes/ no syncope on -VC stems, no suffixes/ syncope on -VCC'. We will have an improvement only if we can get -V̄C into the same framework in a natural way. Consider: what do we mean by 'long vowel'? Basically, one whose articulation is prolonged beyond some notional 'short' value for the language in question, e.g.[eː] ≡ [e] + [e] with no hiatus, or [ee]. Note in this connection the long vowel/diphthong parallelism discussed in §§5.3.10, 7.5.2: e.g. the alternations in *div* [aɪ] *n* ~ *div*[ɪ]*nity*, *ser*[iː]*n* ~ *ser*[ɛ]*nity*, etc. And further, the fact that in English the two categories pattern together as the only vocalic types that can occur in a stressed final open syllable.

Now diphthongs are uncontroversially VV sequences; the only real difference between a diphthong and a long vowel is that the latter remains qualitatively the same for its whole duration, while the former changes quality. (I omit the special case of 'short' diphthongs, like those in Icelandic, §6.4: I will return to these below.) So a long vowel is $V_1V_1$, and a diphthong $V_1V_2$, i.e. they each consist of two portions or **morae** (sg **mora**), but short vowels have only one; the latter are

**monomoric**, as opposed to the **bimoric** complex nuclei. If we accept this, we can add long vowels to (10.25):

(10.26)

And so on. We now have a formal and inclusive definition of the A-type vs. B-type stems, which gathers the disparate Bs under one natural heading. The key is rhyme structure: for the suffix-less and syncopating B-types, either P or Co BRANCHES; for the A-types, R contains no branching constituent. Following traditional terminology, the A-types (no branching R-constituent) are **short** or **light** syllables, the B-types (at least one branching R-constituent) are **long** or **heavy**. We thus distinguish **length** (a durational property of segments) from **quantity** (a structural property of syllables). And in the OE examples it's clearly the latter that's relevant.

The important point about this argument is that it establishes a structural distinction between syllables-as-units and simple linear strings of Vs and Cs. If 'heaviness' were only a matter of segment-sequence, we should have the equivalence VC ≡ VV; but we don't, since VC counts as light. Syllables then are HIERARCHICAL structures, and (apparently) 'branching' is a structural primitive. This seems to be a clear instance of non-reducibility.

Using this same approach, we can now see why English should have a certain limitation on the form of final stressed syllables. We have established that a VC syllable is a branching R with a non-branching P, Co; and VV is a branching P, while VVC is a branching R with a branching P. The simplest permissible stressed final syllables in English have rhyme structures like this:

(10.27)

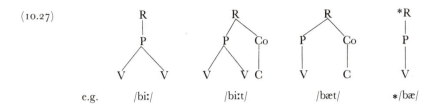

e.g.     /biː/     /biːt/     /bæt/     */bæ/

The phonotactic restriction can be defined this way: no rhyme that does not branch, OR contain at least one branching constituent, may stand in stressed final position. (Note that this is not the same as the definition of heavy syllable, where mere branching of R is insufficient.) The last configuration in (10.27) is in fact a phonotactic filter (see §8.4.2, (8.24)).

A further example of this kind of phonotactic generalization is the distribution of length and syllable quantity in Swedish. This shows us also how consonant length has a natural cluster interpretation, parallel to that of vowel length. In Swedish, every stressed syllable must be heavy; but there is complementary distribution of long and short consonants and vowels, with clusters patterning with long consonants, e.g.

(10.28)

| [Vː] | [VːC] | [VCː] | [VC₁C₂] |
|------|-------|-------|---------|
| viː 'we' | viːt 'white', non-neuter | vitː 'white', neuter | vind 'wind' |
| jɑː 'yes' | dɑːg 'day' | dagː 'dew' | dans 'dance' |
| jeː 'give' | jeːt 'goat' | jɛtː 'given' | jɛst 'gesture' |

If phonetic [Vː], [Cː] are interpreted as [VV], [CC], this gives us the following legal stressed rhyme types (*σ́* = stressed syllable):

(10.29)

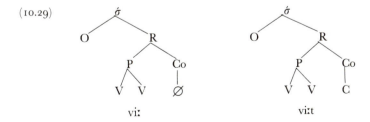

         viː                viːt

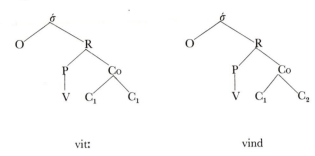

vit:                              vind

So a Swedish stressed syllable must have at least one branching rhyme-constituent, and no more than one; unlike OE, which allowed **overlong** or **hypercharacterized** syllables, with two R-branchings: compare Swedish *ost* 'cheese' and OE *dūst* 'dust':

(10.30)

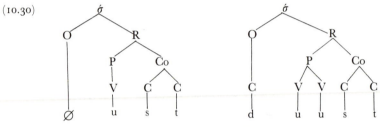

Swedish heavy rhyme          OE hypercharacterized rhyme

While Swedish allows fairly heavy post-peak clustering, as in *spotskt* 'scornful' (neuter), this does not amount to hypercharacterization: the branching is restricted to Co, and the vowel is short. Once again we find a notion naturally characterized in terms of a syllable with internal constituent structure: like length itself, hypercharacterization is a hierarchical, not a linear concept.

Given this essentially 'moric' interpretation of syllable quantity, what do we do with languages with a short-long diphthong distinction (whether phonemic or phonetic is beside the point)? Icelandic has a quantity system very like Swedish, except that the short diphthongs are apparently interpreted as monomoric, i.e. as non-branching peaks, whereas long diphthongs are bimoric. The mora is essentially a higher-level TEMPORAL category: at the level where the rules for quantity are stated, a short diphthong must be a single V, a 'gliding short vowel'. So we might want to posit an additional level or 'tier' of syllabic organization, 'below' the phonotactically relevant, where the internal structure of a monomoric peak is irrelevant. Thus Icelandic [laiːs], [laist], common and neuter of *læs* 'literate' are:

(10.31)

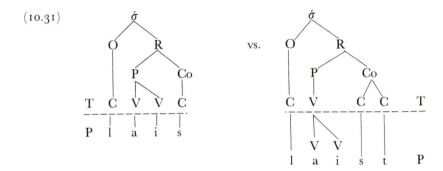

At the 'tactic level' T (above the broken line) the two rhymes are morically distinct, whereas they differ – irrelevantly for quantity – at the phonetic level **P**. This might serve as a crude way into the phonetic syllable/phonological syllable distinction.

10.3.3  *Canonical quantity and 'compensation'*
The Swedish distribution in (10.28) is a post-medieval development from an ancestor that allowed five stressed syllable types (here illustrated from the related – and better attested – Old Icelandic, which was of the same structural type):

(10.32)

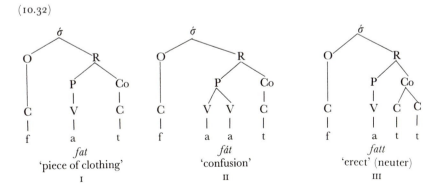

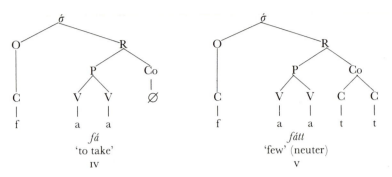

But Swedish, along with the other Scandinavian languages (except Danish), underwent a 'quantity-shift' which restricted stressed rhymes to types II, III, IV, eliminating light I and hypercharacterized V. This can be interpreted in terms of R-branching. For type V with a morph boundary within Co, like *fátt*, the solution was simple: since the last /t/ represents the neuter morph (*fár*, 'few', non-neuter vs. *fátt* from */faːr + t/), the inflection can be saved by simply eliminating a P-branch: thus Swedish *få*/foː/, *fått*/fɔtː/. So we have:

(10.33)

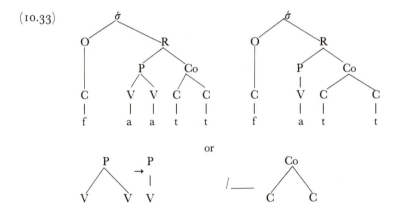

But where the hypercharacterized rhyme did not contain a boundary different dialects handled the problem in different ways. Thus earlier /fleːtːa/ 'to plait' shows up as /flɛtːa/ in Värmland and /fleːta/ in Stockholm. This can be visualized in terms of a metarule (§7.2) with two possible implementations:

258

(10.34)     Hypercharacterization adjustment: only one R-constituent may branch.

Implementation:

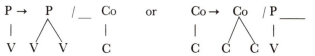

(Värmland)                    (Stockholm)

For VC rhymes, there are also two strategies, that look like (10.35) in reverse; although in some areas, such as Stockholm, both were available. Hence Old Swedish *skip* 'ship' comes down as *skepp* /ʃɛpː/, but *spur* 'mark' as *spår* /spoːr/. Again, a metarule with two implementations:

(10.35)     Canonical stressed rhyme: at least one R-constituent must branch.

Implementation:

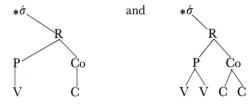

The whole shift may be taken as a response to a stressed rhyme filter, of which (10.33–5) are subcases (a meta-metarule?):

(10.36)     Canonical stressed rhyme filter:

A similar process can be seen in so-called **compensatory lengthening**, where loss of a segment is apparently 'compensated' by a lengthening (= new branching) that restores the affected syllable to its original quantity. Thus proto-West Germanic \*/ɣans/ 'goose', \*/munθ/ 'mouth', \*/finf/ 'five' show up as OE *gōs, mūþ, fīf*. We can visualize this as:

(10.37)

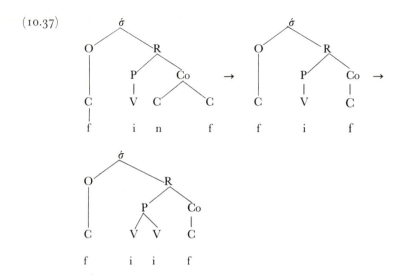

A 'lost' branch is replaced by another branching (in a different R-constituent), keeping the syllable heavy. Note however that this compensatory lengthening is specific to rhymes with the linear structure VNC (where C is a fricative); OE as we have seen did not restrict stress to heavy syllables. Though it is of interest that the same pre-fricative nasal-loss in unstressed syllables did not lead to compensation: e.g. the 3 pl present ending *-aþ* /aθ/, earlier \*/anθ/.

### 10.3.4 *More arguments for the syllable*

We will look briefly at two further arguments for the primitivity of the syllable as a descriptive unit. The first is from stress assignment. Consider Polish, where stress is penultimate in words of more than one syllable, regardless of length or internal structure (and of course final in monosyllables). So *rók* 'year' (nom sg), *rókem* (inst sg), *uwága* 'attention!', *cukieréczek* 'candy', *telefonísta* 'telephonist'. How would this be treated in a non-syllabic notation? In such a system, stress must be assigned to vowels: we could have a stress-assignment rule of any of the three types below:

(10.38)  (a) $V \rightarrow [+stress] /$ ___ $C_o (V) C_o \#$
      (b) $V \rightarrow [+stress] /$ ___ $C_o (VC_o) \#$
      (c) $V \rightarrow [+stress] /$ ___ $(C_oV) C_o \#$

Note that all three bracketings of the sequence are equally arbitrary; and that all three give exactly the same results, i.e. they are equally 'correct'. This in itself is not a major problem, since we have no reason to expect unique solutions all the time – if ever. But the fact that any bracketing will work as well as another leads us to suspect that we might be missing something. Now consider what 'C$_0$' means: it really says that it doesn't matter in the least if there are ANY Cs at all, either before or after the vowel in question. Yet most linguists would agree (see §§5.4.2) that nothing ought to be mentioned in the SD of a rule that is (strictly) irrelevant to its application. But in fact any notation in terms of Cs and Vs without the Cs would imply strings of contiguous Vs, which is not what we want. And if we put in variables between the vowels whose interpretation was 'anything or nothing', we'd STILL be stating the irrelevant.

This problem is an artifact of a system that assigns stress to vowels, not whole syllables. If the syllable is a prime unit, then Polish stress assignment can be stated naturally as:

(10.39)

$$\sigma \rightarrow \acute{\sigma} \mid \underline{\hspace{1cm}} (\sigma) \# \qquad \text{or} \qquad \text{If:} \quad \sigma(\sigma)\# \\ \downarrow \\ \text{Then:} \quad \acute{\sigma}$$

This applies to any syllable-sequence, regardless of length or internal structure, just like (10.38a–c); but it mentions nothing except the relevant items, $\sigma$ as the domain for stress, and its relation to $\#$.

Another argument for the primacy of syllables – as in some sense independent of their nuclei – comes from processes of vowel-deletion and syllabification of consonants. In many languages vowels can be deleted in connected speech, with their syllabicity 'transferred' to consonants: so in German [leːgən] → [leːgn̩] → [leːŋ] *legen* 'to lie', where the first form is divocalic and disyllabic, but the others are monovocalic but still disyllabic. Or take the more complex set of forms in English that can realize *university* [juɪnɪvɜ́ːsɪtɪ] → [juɪn̩vɜ́ːsɪtɪ] → [jun̩vɜ́ːʂtɪ]. Here the vowel-count drops from 5 to 3, but the syllable-count remains at 5: the pattern is $\sigma \, \sigma \, \acute{\sigma} \, \sigma \, \sigma$, regardless of whether the power-peak is a V or a C. It looks again as if we want to take words as – rhythmically – made of syllables, which may have as peaks anything that in a given language can carry syllabicity. In the tree model of the syllable we've been using, the transformations of *university* would be:

(10.40)

Syllabification here involves 'transfer' of a consonant from O to R, where it replaces the original inhabitant of P.

### 10.3.5  *Delimiting syllables*

Assuming the syllable as a primitive, we now face the tricky problem of placing boundaries. So far we've dealt primarily with monosyllabic forms in arguing for primitivity, and we've decided that syllables have internal constituent structure. In cases where poly-syllabic forms were cited, the syllable-divisions were simply assumed. But how do we decide, given a string of syllables, what is the coda of one and the onset of the next? This is not entirely tractable (some scholars have taken this difficulty as evidence against the syllable); but some progress has been made. The question is: can we establish any principled method (either universal or language-specific) for bounding syllables, so that words are not just strings of prominences, with indeterminate stretches of material in between?

There are two basic approaches to this, what we might call the 'universalist' and the 'phonotactic'. The universalist approach (exemplified by Hooper 1972, 1976: ch. 12) begins from a set of assumptions about universally 'optimal' syllable structures, and develops from this a general procedure for inserting boundaries – with, if necessary, language-specific deviations (which count as 'marked') or additions. The argument goes roughly like this (after Hooper 1972):

(i) CV is the minimal, universally attested, and hence 'optimal' syllable; therefore the first rule for boundary placement defines the type:

(10.41)     $\emptyset \rightarrow \$ / [+\text{syll}] \underline{\quad} [-\text{syll}] [+\text{syll}]$

Thus a form like *butter* would be syllabified /bʌ$tər/; I will return to this (problematic) suggestion below.

(ii) The problem of indeterminacy arises with /VCCV/, etc. Where does the boundary go? Hooper decides on division according to the segment types present, e.g.

(a) If -CC- is obs + obs, the boundary goes between: *after* is /æf$tər/, and so on.

(b) If one C is an obstruent (not followed by a nasal), the boundary goes before it, regardless of what else is present: so *party* is /pɑːr$ti/, *content* is /kən$tɛnt/, *refuse* is /rɪ$fjuːz/ (my replacements of Hooper's Spanish examples). This gives a rule:

(10.42)     $\emptyset \rightarrow \$ / [+\text{syll}] [-\text{syll}]_0 \underline{\quad} [+\text{obs}] \begin{bmatrix} -\text{obs} \\ -\text{nas} \end{bmatrix}_0 [+\text{syll}]$

(iii) A problem arises with /sC/ clusters: (10.42) puts the boundary between /s/ and /C/ intervocalically so that /VstV = /Vs$tV/. This Hooper says is 'correct' for Spanish: *estar* 'to be' = /es$tar/; but not for English, where she says the boundary 'appears' to be before /s/ (p. 535): we will see below that /sC/ clusters can be syllabified differently in different words in English. She also suggests that different languages will syllabify /VslV/ and /VsrV/ differently, but gives no evidence for her choices.

(iv) Sonorant clusters: (a) NN, NL (L = liquid), LN, LL all have the boundary between the two: thus *camera* /kæm$rə/, *ulna* /ʌl$nə/, *harness* /hɑːr$nɪs/, *Carla* /kɑːr$lə/ (my examples). (b) If there is one C and a 'glide' (/w j/ following *SPE* she takes as [ − cons]), then the boundary comes before the C: for types of English with /nj/ in *new*, we'd get *anew* /ə$njuː/.

(v) Finally there is a rule that assigns $ at the beginnings and ends of words, so *anew* is finally /$ə$njuː$/. We will take this suggestion up below in looking at a very different way of bounding syllables.

Some of these assignments seem arbitrary: what's the motivation, say, for dividing /nj/ as /$nj/, /ft/ as /f$t/? Here Hooper goes back to a model of the 'ideal' syllable discussed in earlier literature, by linguists like Saussure and Jespersen: according to this, there is an optimal ordering of elements with respect to a syllable-peak, which shows up as a cross-linguistically very common pattern (after Hooper 1976: 196):

(10.43)     Optimal σ-initial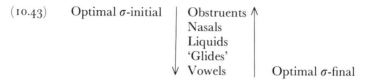

Crudely, onsets are mirror-images of codas. To put it in more detail, taking O, Co as **margins** and P as **nucleus**, we get a 'template' for syllables in which the more **sonorous** or vowel-like elements (those with the greater acoustic output) tend to occur closer to the nucleus, and the least sonorous further away. Schematically:

(10.44)     MARGIN                    NUCLEUS                    MARGIN
            obs > nas > liq > glide > vowel < glide < liq < nas < obs
            Least V-like        >     Most V-like     <     Least V-like

Thus we could expect /pnjVrnt/ as a less 'marked' syllable then /njpVtrn/, etc. The problem of course is that many languages 'violate' this pattern: though it is a common one, and can be used for setting up an 'index of oddity' (see §7.6.3) if nothing else.

Unfortunately, however, DEDUCING syllable boundaries from the class membership of segments tends to fall foul of phonetic reality in many cases, and we find (unsurprisingly) that universalist definitions are both too powerful and too restrictive. In Hooper's approach, the basic evidence for boundary placement in a particular language comes primarily from statistical likelihoods of syllable types in other languages, plus a set of assumptions about 'vowel-like-ness' and the consequences it ought to have. And this can lead to circularity. In particular, this approach fails to take account of the possibility of phonetic and phonotactic evidence for bounding; and, most importantly perhaps, the possibility that a segment does not have to 'belong' uniquely to only one syllable.

Let's look now at another approach, starting from Hooper's (obviously correct) claim that syllable boundaries are universally assigned to the beginnings and ends of words. Given a monosyllable, then, it's clear that syllable and word boundaries must coincide at both ends: *cat* can only be /$kæt$/, *sprats* only /$spræts$/. But what about cases where there's clearly more than one syllable? Can we always assign boundaries correctly according to Hooper's criteria? Consider *butter*, by (10.45) unambiguously /$bʌ$tər$/. For a dialect with phonetic [bʌtər], this seems to work quite well; but what about a variety with [bʌʔtər]? In such dialects, glottalization is characteristically a marker of word-final position (hence syllable-final): thus *but* [bʌʔt] but not *[ʔtʌb] for *tub*. This surely suggests that the correct syllabification is /$bʌt$tər$/, not /$bʌ$tər#/. So syllabifications may vary from dialect to dialect – and here the evidence is language-specific and precise, not deduced from a (relatively unsupported) ideal model. We will see another argument below against Hooper's syllabification.

But first, one more example of the use of phonetic evidence, based again on the coincidence of $ and # in monosyllables. Take aspiration in English, clearly a marker of word-initial( ≡ syllable-initial) position. Many varieties of English, where aspiration does not occur after /s/, nevertheless have apparent [C] : [C$^h$] contrasts between vowels in /sC/ clusters. An example from my own dialect: *discussed* is [dɪskʰəst], contrasting with *disgust* [dɪskə́st] (there is no evidence for /g/ in the latter: neither *[dɪzgə́st] nor *[dɪsgə́st] occur). If aspiration marks syllable-initial position, then we can explain these forms neatly:

(10.45)   *discussed* [dɪskʰə́st]: therefore $dɪs$kəst$
          *disgust*  [dɪskə́st]:  therefore $dɪ$skəst$

Now since allophonic distributions seem to be relevant to syllabification, how about moving on and extending the distributional approach? Let us try assigning boundaries in general on phonotactic grounds. Since we agree on the $/# coincidence in monosyllables, why not project the phonotactics of word-initials/-finals to the bounding of syllables? Take a case like *anger*. Try the possibilities /$æŋ$gər$/, /$æŋg$ər$/, /$æ$ŋgər$/. The first looks good (*hang, grr!*); but the second is out, since final /ŋg/ is illegal (in a dialect with /ŋg/ in *sing*, etc., as in much of the NW of England, this would be the obvious division); and the third is out because there is no monosyllable *\/æ/ (a stressed final rhyme must branch: (10.27)), and no initial /ŋg/. So there might be a basic principle:

(10.46)   No syllabification should yield syllables that are not canonical monosyllables in the language in question.

This will need some refinement, but it's a good start. By (10.46), then, our syllabification of *butter* as /\$bʌt\$ər\$/ is doubly justified: /\$bʌt\$/ (*but*), /\$ər\$/ (*er* . . .), and \*/\$bʌ\$/.

But this approach can lead to indeterminancies of an interesting kind, which suggest that our procedure has been too restrictive. Take a form like *habit*. Following the argument from the illegality of \*/æ/, \*/bʌ/, we would syllabify /\$hæb\$ɪt\$/; but note that not only are /\$hæb\$/ and /\$ɪt\$/ good syllables – so is /\$bɪt\$/. There is in fact (unlike /VtV/ in a glottalizing dialect) no evidence in particular for assigning /b/ exclusively to the first syllable: it has no independent syllable-final properties – nor any syllable-initial ones. Or take *butter* in a dialect that doesn't have [ʔt] in medial position but has the tap [ɾ]; this segment never appears anywhere except between a stressed and an unstressed vowel: so [ɾ] can never have either initial or final properties.

Given cases like this, where there is no strong evidence (either allophonic or phonotactic) for assigning a segment to one or the other of its flanking syllables, we can do one of two things: (a) take an arbitrary, theory-based decision (e.g. assign C to the following V to maximize CV, as Hooper does – even in violation of phonotactics – or let the phonotactics lead and assign it to the preceding V); or (b) we can recognize the arbitrariness and ambiguity. That is, say there are segments that do not belong unambiguously to either of their flanking syllables (we will later extend this to clusters as well). We can then represent *habit* this way:

(10.47)

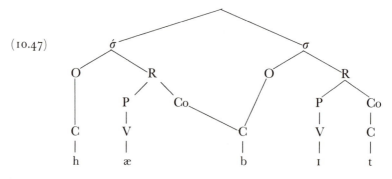

We thus introduce the possibility of **overlap** between syllables. If we

266

represent syllables as bracketed constituents of a word, we then have (for a glottalizing dialect) the following representations for *butter, habit*:

(10.48)   *butter* [bʌʔtər]   [₁bʌt]₁ [₂ər]₂

   *habit* [hǽbɪt]   [₁hæ [₂b]₁ ɪt]₂

We can now explore the implications of this a bit further.

10.3.6   *Interludes*

Let's call a segment or cluster between two peaks an **interlude**. On the basis of the preceding discussion, there appear to be two types: **non-overlapping** or **properly bracketed**, and **overlapping** or **improperly bracketed** (*butter* vs. *habit*). The claim has been advanced in the literature that this distinction is significant, in that (a) there are phonological rules sensitive to it, and (b) there is a tendency for historical processes to treat overlapping interludes as 'optimal', and to produce them where possible. Or at least that there are historical changes that seem otherwise unconnected, but fall into a natural pattern if looked at in these terms.

Thus Anderson & Jones (1974a: 7) propose a universal syllabification principle that suggests that interludes consist of a syllable-final (segment or sequence) preceding a syllable-initial; and that 'precede' includes overlap where possible. Let us examine some evidence for (a) and (b) above.

(a) English stress-assignment. In *SPE*, the stress rule for English non-compound words, the M(ain) S(tress) R(ule), involves a distinction between 'strong' and 'weak' clusters. A strong cluster is basically a long vowel + C, or a short vowel + CC – so far simply the familiar 'heavy' types – while a weak cluster is VC. The importance is that strong clusters tend to attract stress. But there is a curiosity: /VrC/ is strong, and /VCr/ weak: *fratérnal*, with stress before /rC/, but *álgebra* with no stress before /Cr/ (expected *algébra*). In a framework that takes the bracketing of interludes into account, however, the differences fall out naturally:

(10.49)   [₁fræ[₂t]₁ər[₃n]₂əl]₃

   vs.

   [₁æl[₂ʤ]₁ə[₃b]₂rə]₃

That is, /rn/ can be syllable-final, so the syllable it terminates is closed by CC (even if the /n/ belongs to the next syllable as well); whereas /br/ cannot be final but only initial – hence the syllable closes with /b/, and the /r/ belongs to the next: thus it is VC, not VCC. The distinction is not in terms of the elements, but of their bracketing, and the basis of the bracketing is phonotactic.

(b) Maximizing overlap. A number of changes in the histories of languages have been plausibly interpreted as involving a change from non-overlapping to overlapping interludes. For instance, a series of cluster-simplifications in late OE/early ME could all be said to involve this shift, which gives them a formal unity that they don't otherwise have:

(10.50)    Change           e.g. OE → ME

| | | | |
|---|---|---|---|
| -nds- → -ns- | andswerian | → answerie | 'to answer' |
| -dsp- → -sp- | godspell | → gospel | 'gospel' |
| -ds- → -s- | godsib | → gosib | 'gossip' |
| -stm- → -sm- | blostmian | → blosmie | 'to blossom' |

The change in syllable-bracketing is:

(10.51)        [and] [sw...] → [an [s] w...]

                [god] [spel] → [go [s] pel]

                [god] [sib] → [go [s] ib]

                [blost] [m...] → [blo [s] m...]

The fact that otherwise disparate processes, that would simply have to be called 'cluster-simplification', have a unitary interpretation argues for this analysis: it tells us for instance why [ds] goes to [s], but [sp] doesn't go to [s] – since [sp] is a good initial and final cluster.

## NOTES AND REFERENCES

10.1   On the concept of reduction see Waddington (1977: ch. 1). For the holon, Koestler (1978).

10.2.1–2   On prosodic analysis: the foundations are laid in **Firth (1948), a difficult but rewarding paper; on the basic techniques and orientations, the introduction to Palmer (1970) is excellent, as is *Hill (1966). For an introductory treatment, stressing the intellectual background, Sampson (1980: ch. 9). For textbook treatment, Sommerstein (1977: ch. 3).

But the best way in is through actual prosodic analyses, since there's not very much 'theoretical' writing in the field; a good selection would be **Allen (1951), **Carnochan (1951), Palmer (1955, 1966), **Waterson (1956), Bendor-Samuel (1960), and Carnochan (1960) – all in Palmer (1970), which is an indispensable collection of the major prosodic writings. In addition, Firth (1935b) – 'pre-prosodic', but interesting in its anti-process approach to assimilation, Albrow (1966), Asher (1966), Henderson (1966).

10.2.3 The treatment of Hungarian VH here is entirely my own, and perhaps a bit unorthodox – though not I think false to the spirit of prosodic analysis. For a different treatment, extracting prosodies in quite another way, without the word/junction distinction, see Albrow (1975), which also has some interesting remarks on English. For a 'mixed' prosodic/generative approach to VH of a different sort, see Fromkin (1965).

Not all kinds of VH are in fact amenable to strict prosodic treatment; Azerbaijani, for instance, though superficially similar, has an 'iterative' system, where only the preceding vowel determines the harmonic properties of the next one. Thus *söz* 'word', *söz-üm* 'my word' (with the suffix – in prosodic terms – $V_H$); also *söz-lär* 'words', with the plural suffix $V_L$, and rounding neutralized for non-high vowels. But note *söz-lär-im* 'my words', where the plural takes the shape appropriate to a preceding unrounded vowel – thus clearly not influenced by the vowel of *söz*. Cf. the discussion of the typology of vowel-harmony systems in Altaic, Uralic, and Chuckchi in Comrie (1981b: §§2.2, 3.2, 6.1).

The classic prosodic treatment of vowel harmony is Waterson (1956) on Turkish, which uses – unusually for a prosodic study – palatographic evidence to support the phonology. Waterson shows that for Turkish, the prosodies have an interesting empirical correlate, in that not only the vowels, but the consonants as well show harmonic properties: e.g. all the consonants in a front-prosodic word are palatalized, all in a word with lip-rounding labialized, etc. (I don't know if this is true for Hungarian, but I suspect it is, if not so dramatically as for Turkish.) Waterson's paper is a model for the judicious use of theoretical argument and experimental evidence, and has been unjustifiably neglected by writers on VH in general.

A recent approach, 'autosegmental phonology' has also attempted to deal with VH; though it's not clear to me whether it is in fact (despite its formal sophistication) much more than a notational variant of prosodic analysis. For examples, Clements (1977). For an important comparison of prosodic and non-prosodic phonologies, **Lyons (1962).

10.3.1 The syllable is an enormously complex area, and the treatment here deals with only a small selection of the potential issues. For the debate about whether syllables are needed at all, see **Kohler (1966), and the answer in **Anderson (1969). For an attempt to revive Stetson's motor theory in a sophisticated and linguistically useful way, **Allen (1973). Current thinking on the topic as a whole may be sampled in **Bell & Hooper (1978). On syllables in general, see also the early paper by Fudge (1969). On stress- and syllable-timing, see Roach (1982).

10.3.2 On syllable quantity and its importance, **Arnason (1980), a study of the development of quantity in Germanic, particularly Icelandic. The branching tree model of the syllable has been recently developed (along slightly different lines from those taken here) in the framework of 'metrical phonology'; for work in this tradition see e.g. **McCarthy (1979), Kiparsky (1979), S. Anderson (1982). For discussion of various concepts of syllable structure **Ewen (1980: 3.5, 7.1–2); on the length–quantity distinction, Árnason (ch. 6). For more recent treatment along metrical lines of Germanic syllable structure, Lass (1983).

10.3.3 For a rather different account of compensatory lengthening, see de Chene & Anderson (1979).

10.3.4 The argument from Polish stress follows Basbøll (1981).

10.3.5 The boundary problem is clearly not solved, though the attempts described here may be as far as we're likely to get. Aside from Hooper (1972, 1976), see **Anderson & Jones (1974a), Anderson & Jones (1977: ch. IV). On the relation of syllable boundaries to the phonotactics of word-beginnings and endings, Pulgram (1970). The universalist approach has been further developed in Kiparsky (1979), who proposes a 'syllabic template' in which all positions are marked S(trong) or W(eak), in reference to 'sonority hierarchy' of the type shown in (10.45–6). For further proposals, see Basbøll (1977), and the study of Swedish phonotactics in Sigurd (1965); also the critical discussion in Ewen (1980: ch. 7). For some experimental evidence, see Fallows (1981).

10.3.6 The 'overlap' theory of interludes is developed in detail in Anderson & Jones (1974a, 1977); the arguments from English cluster simplification are based on analyses by Charles Jones.

# 11

# Dependency relations

## 11.1   **The concept of dependency**

This chapter introduces a quite different approach to phonological description, where one principle is claimed to be implicated in virtually all aspects of phonological structure. This view has not been widely accepted by 'mainstream' linguists, and has not received, except among a small group of workers, the attention it deserves. It represents an interesting departure from previous frameworks, and manages to make connections that are inapparent in other systems, by unifying apparently disparate phenomena under a single set of notations. But the conceptual basis is complex, and not as intuitively accessible as, say, phoneme theory, or even feature theory in the sense of chs. 5–6. All I will do here is sketch the basic principles, and give a critical account of some of the most important ideas.

So far, concepts and operations in phonology have been defined mostly along the paradigmatic and syntagmatic axes: opposition, contrast vs. non-contrast, inventories (paradigmatic) vs. realizations, redundancies, processes (syntagmatic). Or with the conceptual opposition of (paradigmatic) 'system' vs. (syntagmatic) 'structure', to use Firthian terms. Our concern that is has been largely with statements of the occurrence or non-occurrence of items in syntagmatic association, either linear (segment-sequences, prosodies) or non-linear (features within segments). These concepts will still form the basis even of the rather different and enriched model presented here. But we ought to ask whether the inventory of concepts we have is sufficient, or whether there is a case to be made for a new primitive, and associated new types of structures and operations.

We have already encountered some notions with a bearing on this chapter: hierarchical relations (e.g. in the discussion of 'gestures' and internal segment structure in §6.5), and constituency (§10.3 on

271

syllables). So we now have three basic relations: **precedence** ( = linear sequence); **componentiality** ( = non-linear association of 'atomic' elements in segments); and **constituency** ( = hierarchical bracketing). We now add a fourth: **dependency**. This is a tricky idea, and easier to illustrate than define. We begin with a syntactic example.

Consider the sentence 'the man saw the dog', in three languages with different canonical orders of S(ubject), O(bject), V(erb): SVO English, SOV Kannaḍa, and VSO Welsh, in terms of simple phrase-structure trees:

(11.1)

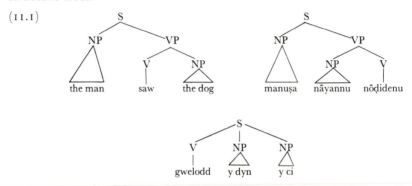

All three show different precedence relations; and at least in a VSO language, different constituency as well, since here there is no evidence for a VP constituent (the predicate is discontinuous, hence syntactically not a 'phrase'). Yet in one sense all three are the same: the relation of the predicator (*saw, nōḍidenu, gwelodd*) to its NP arguments. The verb, that is, is the **head** of the predication, and **governs** its arguments: or they are **dependent** on it. In a logical semantic representation (ignoring sequence and constituency), each sentence is a predication involving a two-place predicate 'saw', and two arguments 'man', 'dog': they could all be represented in logical notation by the formula $P(a,b)$, where $P$ = 'saw' and $a$, $b$ are the arguments. Or, in a dependency-based case grammar, by something like

(11.2)

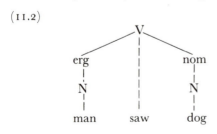

(where erg(ative), nom(inative) are case-labels for the relations contracted by the arguments of V).

To put it another way, V is a 'characteristic' (and normally obligatory) constituent of a predication, as N is of NP, V of VP, etc. To take another example, NPs like *the black dog, le chien noir,* Swedish *den svarta hunden,* though respectively [NP art Adj N], [NP Art N Adj], [NP Art Adj N Art], are 'headed' by a governing N, with Art, Adj as dependents.

Now to phonology. We might naturally apply this notion to the syllable, viewing it as a dependency structure, with a governor and dependents. A syllabic element (V, Ç) 'characterizes' a syllable (as a minimal obligatory component). Thus a monosyllable like *cat* will have its 'marginal' elements (O, Co) dependent on or governed by its syllabic. Graphically:

(11.3)

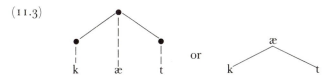

By convention, vertical position in a dependency graph = degree of dependency: the governor is of 'degree zero', /k, t/ of 'degree one', etc.

If a syllabic governs a syllable, then we could argue along the same lines that a stressed syllable governs a sequence of syllables: using the same notational principle, we can graph a disyllabic, initial-stressed word like *habit* as:

(11.4)

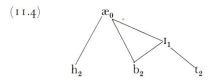

Here peaks occupy two levels of prominence or dependency, and margins a third (indicated by subscripts); note that /b/ is governed by both /æ/ and /ɪ/, i.e. is an overlapping interlude (see §10.3.6). Thus stress-assignment rules can be seen as creating dependency structures out of bracketed strings of syllables. The English Main Stress Rule, for instance, which is responsible for the initial stress of *habit*, would assign governorship to /æ/ and subordinate /ɪ/ to it: a representation like (11.4) would arise this way:

(11.5)     [h ǣ [ b ] ɪ⁰ t]          →          [h ǣ [ b ] ɪ¹ t]

or

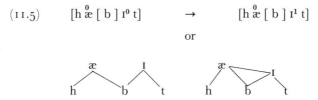

(A word-tree without a unique governor is ill-formed.) On this model, stress-assignment, rather than being the elevation of one syllabic to prominence, is the subordination of one to another.

### 11.2  Intrasegmental dependencies: the structure of vowels

We can extend the notion of dependency structure from syllables to their constituent segments, and claim that that these too have an internal relational structure. Let us begin by introducing the basic relations that will concern us here, and the conventional notations; we will see them in operation as we proceed. There are two basic relation types we will be concerned with: relations of dependency and relations of sequence. To illustrate:

A *Dependency*

(a) **Strict dependency**: a ⇉ b 'a governs b'. (Conversely, b ⇇ a 'b is governed by a'.

(b) **Mutual dependency**: a ⇄ b 'a and b are mutually dependent or co-dependent', i.e. they govern each other.

(c) **Combination**: a,b 'a is in combination with or associated with b', i.e. there is no dependency relation in any strict sense.

B *Sequence*

(a) **Precedence**: a < b 'a precedes b'; b > a 'be is preceded by a'.

(b) **Coincidence**: a = b 'a is coincident with b', i.e. a, b are not in a linear relation.

These relations can be represented graphically in a fairly straight-forward way. To take two examples of combined dependency and sequence relations:

(11.6)     (i)   a ⇉ b, a < b:

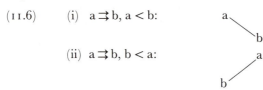

(ii)  a ⇉ b, b < a:

Note that (11.6i) is a fairly natural representation for a long vowel or **'falling' diphthong** (one with a syllabic first element), and (ii) for a **'rising' diphthong** (with a syllabic second element):

(11.7)

e.g. [ai̯] in *bite*          [i̯u] in *butte*

(The diacritic [ ̯ ] indicates non-syllabicity.) So at least complex segments can be reasonably interpreted as structures with governor–dependent relations (and affricates might be similarly represented, as stops governing fricatives: see §11.4).

To give graphic representations of non-sequential relations, we have:

(11.8)    (i)   a ⇉ b, a = b:          a
                                        |
                                        b

          (ii)  a ⇄ b, a = b:          a : b
          (iii) a,b, a = b:            a, b

In cases like (11.8i), the dependent element is said to be **subjoined**; in cases of simple precedence, they are **adjoined**.

Where does all this get us? Let's begin with the characterization of vowels. Recall (§7.5.3) that the simplest 'archetypal' vowel systems tend to consist of three units, /i u/ and a low one. We might argue from this that underlying vocalic organization is a set of three primitive elements, and that all larger systems in some way 'expand' this basic inventory. If this is true, we could claim that e.g. mid vowels, front rounded vowels, etc. are more 'complex' (i.e. non-basic), and ought to show this in their structures.

Dependency theorists claim that we can posit, to begin with, three 'elements' or **primitives**, |i|, |u|, |a| (primitives are given in verticals): these are respectively 'palatality', 'gravity/flatness/round-ness', and 'openness'/'sonority'. The simplest vowel systems would then consist of the three elements alone, uncombined:

(11.9)     i   u     i   u     i   u
            a         a         a

          |i|       |u|
               |a|

(The backness of the one low vowel would be specified either by universal convention or low-level phonetic rules.)

Now consider the descending series [i e ɛ æ]. If |a| stands for pure openness (associated with a back(ish) quality, presumably, in the unmarked case), and |i| for pure palatality, there is a sense in which vowels become more '|a|-like' as they descend. One obvious way of capturing this intuition is in terms not of additional discrete primitives (like features), but CHANGING DEPENDENCY RELATIONS among |i u a|, so that |i| becomes less hierarchically prominent, or increasingly subordinated to |a|. So:

(11.10)    [i] |i|   [e] |i⇉a|   [ɛ] |i⇄a|   [æ] |a⇉i|

                                    or

          [i]        i
          [e]        i
                     |
                     a
          [ɛ]        i:a
          [æ]        a
                     |
                     i

And for back vowels:

(11.11)    [u] |u|   [o] |u⇉a|   [ɔ] |u⇄ɑ|   [ɒ] |a⇉u|   [ɑ] |a|

                                    or

          [u]        u
          [o]        u
                     |
                     a
          [ɔ]        u:a
          [ɒ]        a
                     |
                     u
          [ɑ]        a

This captures the Trubetzkoyan notion of 'gradual opposition' (§3.2) in a formal way: the increase of |a| in descent or of |i|

in ascent characterizes movement along a parameter whose poles are |i| and |a|, i.e. 'graduality'. This is different from an n-ary or scalar system (§6.2), which still represents qualities as discrete, unrelated 'positions'; here they are the result of CHANGING RELATIONS. And the notation also captures the intuitive 'middle' position of half-open vowels: they hold the two polar elements in balance.

More 'complex' vowel types can still be represented with this set of three elements. For example, front rounded vowels, which have a |u| in combination with the ordinary front configurations:

(11.12)    [y] i,u    [ø] i,u    [œ]    i,u:a
                         |
                         a

In fact we need at least one more primitive: |ə| or 'centrality', to characterize both central vowels and centralized back and front vowels. For unrounded central vowels:

(11.13)    [ɨ] i,ə    [ə] ə    [ɜ] ə:a    [ä] a
                                            |
                                            ə

(The two last are not standard in the literature, but follow from the system.)

And centralized front and back vowels of the types [ɪ ʊ] show either |u| or |i| governing, rather than in combination: this is in accord with the fact that these tend to function as basically front or back rather than central:

(11.14)    [ɪ] i        [ʊ] u
               |            |
               ə            ə

Things get a bit difficult with non-low unrounded back vowels, and the notation proposed in the literature is problematical. Anderson & Ewen (1980b) and Ewen (1980) propose representing them as basically ~{i, u}, i.e. 'not-|i| or |u|'. This is notationally adequate for a system with no unrounded central vowels at the same height as any unrounded back one: e.g. no /ɯ/:/ɨ/ contrast. (If there were central vowels, obviously, ~{i, u} would in fact be equivalent to |ə|.) The claim would seem to be that there is a 'place' in a vowel system that can be occupied by /ɯ/ or /ɨ/ – but you can't have both. Thus a language like Naga (7.33), with /ɯ/ and /ə/ but no /ɨ/, would have its

/ə/ specified as |ə| and its /ɯ/ as |i, ə|: i.e. as if it were in fact /ɨ/. This move clearly runs afoul of the objections raised in §7.5.3 against letting X 'count as' Y if there's no Y (regardless, to a large extent, of the phonetics), in order to make the notation conform to supposed universals.

There is another objection, too: all the other vowel-classes have positively specified content. Only /ɯ ɤ ʌ/ are a negative class, defined virtually by what they aren't, i.e. by excluding all others. One ought to be suspicious of notational discontinuities like this. According to the standard notations, then, the specifications (given a non-central interpretation) for close, half-close and half-open unrounded back vowels are:

$$(11.15) \quad [\mathrm{ɯ}] \sim \{i, u\} \quad [\mathrm{ɤ}] \sim \{i, u\} \quad [\mathrm{ʌ}] \quad \sim \{i, u\}{:}a$$
$$\mid$$
$$a$$

So if a given system has central unrounded vowels as well, the back unrounded ones will be treated as in (11.15); otherwise they will have a |ə|-component. This means that e.g. /ɯ/ is 'really' /ɨ/ unless it's /ɯ/, which is to my mind unacceptably relativistic.

Now this technical hitch grows out of the desire to make vowel characterization conform to intuitions (based largely on cross-language distributions) of 'complexity' or 'markedness': rarity = complexity, hence the commonest types should have the simplest descriptions. But it can be remedied, I think, by a more rigorously phonetic approach to the whole vowel space, which disallows any relativistic equations of different vowel types.

Let us see what happens if we revise the system of primitives: I propose introducing |ɯ| 'velarity' and |ω| 'labiality'/'roundness', and dispensing with |u| completely. (|u| seems to conflate too many properties anyhow: see §5.1.1 on [+flat].) And |ω| will never occur in any relation with another primitive except combination, i.e. it is always non-dependent and non-governing.

So the vowel space can be defined by its poles, |i| and |ɯ|, with |ə| for the centre – and with height specified as before. This reverses, note, the 'complexity' relations between [u] and [ɯ]; now [ɯ] is |ɯ| alone, and [u] is |ɯ, ω|. Despite the views of some dependency theorists (cf. Ewen 1980: §§8.1.2, 8.2.1) who value the notion of differential complexity highly, I think we lose little if anything by the reversal (and cf. the arguments in §§7.4, 8.6 here). Overall I think it's a good idea for ALL markedness considerations to be excluded from phonological characterizations: there is no reason for a particular language to code in its own segment specifications what are in essence facts about language-in-general; there is no way for a speaker to have access to such information (save in terms of an absurd degree of 'innate specification': see §9.4). And in any case it is descriptively irrelevant. Segments ought to code only their own properties, not statistics of cross-language distribution.

The proposed revision would then give us representations of these types:

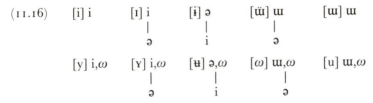

(11.16)    [i] i        [ɪ] i        [ɨ] ə        [ü] ɯ        [ɯ] ɯ
                        |            |            |
                        ə            i            ə

           [y] i,ω      [ʏ] i,ω      [ʉ] ə,ω      [ω] ɯ,ω      [u] ɯ,ω
                        |            |            |
                        ə            i            ə

And so on for the other heights. Thus fronting is |ə|-increase followed by loss of |ɯ| and addition of |i|, etc., and both axes of the vowel space can be given parallel interpretations.

### 11.3    Vocalic processes in a dependency framework

Leaving aside the controversy about back unrounded vowels, we will return here to the standard notation. The system as given in §11.2 does yield satisfying and plausible accounts of a number of process types, in which certain informal notions become formally statable, and 'unity of a process' can be captured in an interesting way. One simple example is the Sanskrit vowel sandhi discussed in §8.2.1. Recall that across a boundary, /ɑ + i/ → [e], /ɑ + u/ → [o]. This was presented as a 'mutual assimilation', with the second V as controller of height. We can now provide a more precise interpretation: if the initial vowels represent the elements |a|, |i|, |u|, then we have a simple shift from a precedence relation to one of dependency:

(11.17)    a < i → i              a < u → u
                   |                      |
                   a                      a

Or, for both processes:

(11.18)     SD: $V_1 < V_2$                 SD: $V_2$
                                                       |
                                                    $V_1$

This is a change of relations only, in this framework, and can be precisely stated as a general schema for both instances. In the more complex case of a non-fusional mutual assimilation like /au/ → [ɔː], we can use a similar representation: first the dependency shift, then a copying of the new first mora thus created:

(11.19)

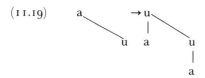

The same shift from precedence to dependency, but with retention of bimoric structure.

The graduality element, plus the operations we've already seen, can be deployed to give an account of *i*-umlaut. Recall the basic outline of the process (§8.2.1); these are the results in Old English:

(11.20)     i  y  ← u

            e  ø  ← o
            ↑
            æ ←——— ɑ

(This occurs if there is a following /i, j/; or for our purposes here, a syllabic or nonsyllabic /i/.) Leaving aside various complications like the umlauts of diphthongs and long vowels, the basic process can be given in a feature notation as:

(11.21)

$$\begin{bmatrix} V \\ \langle -\,back \rangle \end{bmatrix} \rightarrow \begin{bmatrix} -\,back \\ \langle -\,low \rangle \end{bmatrix} / \underline{\quad} C_0 \begin{bmatrix} -\,obs \\ -\,back \\ +\,high \end{bmatrix}$$

(For the ⟨ ⟩ ... ⟨ ⟩ notation, see §8.5.) The rule (11.21) breaks the process in (11.20) into two distinct sub-processes: raising of low front vowels (⟨− back⟩ → ⟨− low⟩) and fronting of back vowels (V → [− back]). Yet it seems clear that 'deep down' there's only one thing happening: each vowel is being 'attracted' towards the upper left-hand corner of the vowel space (or the palatal corner of the whole articulatory space): becoming more |i|-like, in fact. One could think of the whole thing as governed by a metarule (§7.2) like:

(11.22)    V → ['attract'] / ____ C$_0$[i]

So each vowel moves in the |i| direction in an obvious way: back towards front, low towards high. In terms of dependency structures, the transitions are:

(11.23)    [u] → [y]:          u → u,i

          [o] → [ø]:          u → u,i
                           |    |
                           a   a

          [ɑ] → [æ]:          a → a
                              |
                              i

(The results are slightly different in other Germanic dialects, e.g. Old High German; for more on the history of umlaut see §§13.2–3.)

Clearly |i| is being added to the input segments: but why in these particular (seemingly inconsistent) ways? i.e. why should the increase of |i|-prominence be combination for /u o/, subjunction for /ɑ/, and an apparent reversal of dependency for /æ/? Part of the answer is the segments that would result if the mode of increase were the same in all cases. Say we added |i| only in combination:

(11.24)    (a)  u → u,i          (b)  u → u,i
                                   |
                                   a

        (c)  a → *a,i          (d)  a → *a,i
                     |              |
                     i           i

The starred forms simply have no interpretations: there are no segments characterized like (c) and (d). It is just possible that (c) might represent a vowel between [e] and [ɛ] (see (11.10): but there is no evidence for an output of this type in OE, or any Germanic system with three vowels in the [e]–[ɛ] range.

What about uniform subjunction?

(11.25)

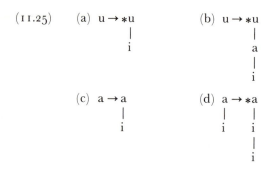

(a) u → *u
　　|
　　i

(b) u → *u
　　|
　　a
　　|
　　i

(c) a → a
　　|
　　i

(d) a → *a
　　| |
　　i i
　　　|
　　　i

Again, (a) has no interpretation; nor do (b), (d); the latter are 'overstrong' in the usual terminology. So one could say that |i| in fact gets into the output segments in the only way consistent with conditions on representations and the structure of the inputs.

But there's one possibility missing: why does |a ⊐ i| → |i ⊐ a|, and not the intermediate |a ⊠ i|, i.e. [ε]? Here the answer is that this would have been a possibility, but there's no evidence that it happened that way. Weak as it sounds, it might just have been a fact about Old English that its canonical vowel system was three-height; the evidence tells us that – at least in attested OE – the *i*-umlaut of original /æ/ fell together with /e/, which was [e] (the lowering to [ε] is much later). The actual historical scenario MIGHT well have been |a ⊐ i| → |a ⊠ i| → |i ⊐ a|, considering the likelihood of vowel change being gradual; but at least [e] is the way things ended up.

## 11.4 The structure of consonants: the categorial gesture

The dependency characterization of segments develops the concept of 'gesture' (§6.5), positing three distinct sub-gestures, as opposed to the original oral vs. laryngeal: **categorial, articulatory,** and **initiatory**. The categorial gesture defines (roughly) the degree of 'consonantality' or 'vocalicity' of a segment, i.e. what in the *SPE* framework would be the 'major class' and 'manner' features (§§5.3.1., 5.3.7). The articulatory gesture consists basically of the traditional 'place' features (e.g. the vocalic components |i u a ə |) – though rather differently interpreted, as well as nasality, laterality, etc.; and the initiatory gesture characterizes airstream and glottal state.

The suggested categorial primitives are |V| 'relatively periodic' and |C| 'relatively occluded'/'non-periodic'. In association, they provide categorial definitions of some major segment types this way:

(11.26)

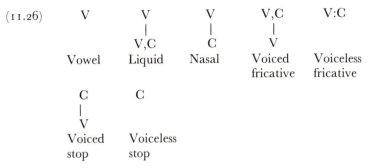

At first the assignments may seem arbitrary; but the motivation is clearer if we rank the types along a scale, starting with voiceless stops:

(11.27)

$$C \to \underset{|}{\overset{}{C}} \to V{:}C \to \underset{|}{\overset{}{V,C}} \to \underset{|}{\overset{}{V}} \to V$$

This looks very like an outline of the segmental strength hierarchy (§8.3.1, (8.13)): nasals are omitted because they don't participate in 'standard' lenition. That is, these characterizations give us a way of explicating lenition in terms of something rather more precise (if at the same time more complex and abstract) than the 'resistance to airflow' criterion suggested earlier. The two end-points of the scale are maximal |V|, |C|; and lenition is the increase in |V|-prominence (whether as periodic vocal-fold output or turbulence with some degree of formant structure) – as well as the demotion and ultimate deletion of |C|. And conversely for fortition.

We see for instance that all sonorants (vocalic or consonantal) have a governing |V|, and obstruents a governing |C|. In this formulation, the two modes of lenition – opening and sonorization – have the same formal basis: only pure opening involves |V| added either as co-dependent with |C| or in combination; and sonorization involves subjunction.

So far, then, we can characterize part of the hierarchy (8.13) in dependency terms:

(11.28)

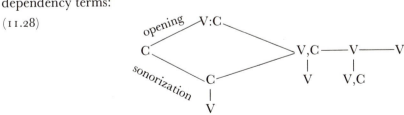

At each step, |C| is demoted or weakened by |V|: e.g. from voiceless fricative to vowel |C| goes from co-dependent to combined, to dependent, to zero. And so on. But this omits affricates and aspirates, as well as [h], and leaves the picture incomplete.

Affricates may be characterized in dependency terms as complex structures with a fricative governed by a stop; but with the whole as a single segment, even though sequence is involved. The suggested representations are:

(11.29)

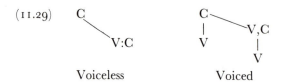

Voiceless          Voiced

At first this appears to claim that affricates are in fact clusters (i.e. temporally two segments long, rather than 'half-stop and half-fricative' in the compass of one segment); that this is not the case is made clear by the relation of the governing stop node to a vocalic nucleus. Compare the categorial representations for *cat*, *scat*, *chat*:

(11.30)

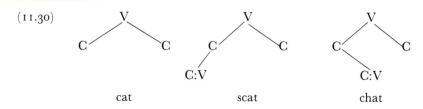

cat          scat          chat

Here the monosegmental status of /tʃ/ is indicated by the closeness of the governor |C| to the syllabic; the /sk/ sequence in *scat* is bi-segmental (a cluster properly speaking), while the affricate shows 'modification' of a single node. So the hierarchy can be expanded:

(11.31)

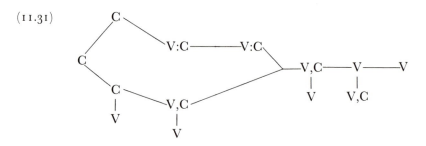

We will introduce aspiration and [h] later, when we come to the initiatory gesture, and give a complete characterization of (8.13).

11.5   **The articulatory gesture**
The strategy so far is reminiscent of Jakobsonian reductionism (§5.1.1): how few primitives will suffice for a natural representation of segment classes? Here the approach is formally richer than the Jakobsonian (or *SPE*) strictly componential method, i.e. it is relational as well: but still reductionist, in that the small set of primitives is combined into segments by means of a very small set of relational operations, and where possible a new relation takes the place of a new primitive. But it's worth noting that even this quite radical reduction does not have 'simplicity' as its result; the final structures are considerably richer and more complex than in a purely componential theory of the segment. And in addition, the phonetic function is as important as the classificatory (as pretty much in *SPE* as well).

The specification of place operates on the same formal principles but introduces some new elements. In addition to the vocalic components, which obviously have a part to play in consonants in any descriptively adequate system, we introduce some with specifically consonantal relevance.

The first is |l| 'linguality': the tongue (body or blade) as active articulator. Uncombined, it represents the larger class dentals/alveolars ($\equiv$ [+cor]); in combination with the 'colouring' elements |i|, |u|, we get palatals and velars. So:

| (11.32) | \|u\| | \|l\| | \|l, i\| | \|l, u\| |
|---|---|---|---|---|
| | Labials | Dentals | Palatals | Velars |

This captures two obvious natural classes: velars and labials (see §5.5) and velars and palatals (see below). So far, this does nothing not done by [+grave] (labials and velars) and *SPE*'s [+high] (palatals and velars). But (11.32) implies that dentals, palatals and velars are also a natural class – and indeed this is the sole justification of |l|. What we need is evidence that this class functions as a unit – e.g. by finding processes that implicate all three members, or subsets other than those that can be captured by [+high] or [+grave]: otherwise |l| is a pseudo-class, nothing more than the disjunction of two specifications. Here are some examples of processes from the history of English, implicating (i) palatals/velars, (ii) dentals/velars, (iii) dentals/palatals, (iv) dentals/palatals/velars:

(i) In late West Saxon OE, the diphthongs /æɑ/, /æːɑ/ monophthongized and raised to /e/, /eː/, (a) before velars and (b) after palatals: (a) *seh* 'he saw', *ēge* 'eye'; (b) *cēs* 'he chose', *scēp* 'sheep', *gēr* 'year', earlier *seah*, *ēage*, *cēas*, *scēap*, *gēar* (*h* = [x], *g* = [g] medially, [j] initially in these examples: *c* here = [ʧ], *sc* = [ʃ], *ea* = [æɑ], *ēa* = [æːɑ]).

(ii) In Middle English *c.* 1200, there was extensive raising before dentals and velars: *brist* 'breast', *linth* 'length', *stynch* 'stench', *sick*, *string*, *wing*, *mingle* (all with historical /e/: only the pre-velar group has survived in the standard dialects). Another raising in the same environment shows up in the 16th century, with *e*-spellings ( = [æ] or [ɛ] ) for expected a /a/: *mesacar* 'massacre', *elexander* 'Alexander', *ectes* 'acts', *exion* 'action'.

(iii) In the 15th century, long before the general raising of ME /a/ to [æ], we find *e*-spellings for historical /a/ before dentals and palatals: *gled* (ME *glad*), *becheler* (Old French *bacheler*).

(iv) Throughout ME, we find sporadic epenthesis of /i/ after /e a/ before palatals, dental nasal + palatal, and velar nasal + velars: e.g. *aische* 'ash' (OE *æsc*), *bleinte* 'blinked' (past of *blenchen*), *leinthe* 'length' (OE *lengðu*). In many U.S. dialects of the southern Midwest, vowels diphthongize before dentals, palatals, and velars, the epenthetic vowel agreeing in backness with the preceding original: [khæ͠ɪnt] 'can't', [lɛ͠ɪmθ] 'length', [fɹiʃ] 'fish', [bʉʊʃ] 'bush', [lɛɪg] 'leg', [hɔʊg] 'hog'.

Assuming then that we want to capture this class, it's clear that the other two available feature systems, *SPE* and the Jakobsonian, each manage to equate only two of the three:

(11.33)

| | *SPE* | | | | Jakobsonian | | |
|---|---|---|---|---|---|---|---|
| | Dental | Palatal | Velar | | Dental | Palatal | Velar |
| Ant | + | − | − | Compact | − | + | + |
| Cor | + | − | − | Grave | − | − | + |
| High | − | + | + | | | | |
| Back | − | − | + | | | | |

| Dependency | | |
|---|---|---|
| Dental | Palatal | Velar |
| \|l\| | \|l,i\| | \|l,u\| |

(Note that this is an argument for an element, not for a dependency treatment *per se*: a feature [lingual] could do the same work.)

So |l| alone ≡ [ + cor]; but there are distinctions within this area that have to be made. The dependency solution involves two other elements, |t| 'apicality' and |d| 'dentality'. These capture two kinds of gradients: those involving the active articulator (degree of involvement of tip vs. blade), and those involving the passive articulator (alveolar vs. dental). For the apical/laminal/retroflex gradient, we have:

(11.34)   Laminal   Apical   Retroflex

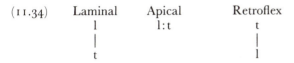

(From here on I will use both these notations and the |l ⇒ t| types, depending on whether or not I want to stress the subordination relation; they are of course equivalent.)

Laminals involve primarily the blade, retroflexes exclusively the tip; apicals, properly speaking, are 'less apical', perhaps, than retroflexes, but 'more apical' than laminals. But the laminal/apical contrast – except for retroflexes – is actually less important than the dental/ alveolar. No language, as far as I know, has a pure laminal/apical contrast at the same place; but many languages have a dental/alveolar contrast either among their obstruents (see Western Desert (7.43), Nunggubuyu (7.44)) or nasals (Diegueño, Araucanian (7.62)).

Consider a language with six contrasting nasals, Malayalam: its system can be represented this way:

(11.35)    u     l,d     l:t        t         l,i      l,u
                                    |
                                    l
          [m]   [n̪]     [n]       [ɳ]       [ɲ]      [ŋ]

So |d| distinguishes /n̪/ uniquely, and two relations of |l| and |t| give us alveolar vs. retroflex. But on the phonetic level, apicality has another role: all Malayalam coronals are phonetically apical, and this has to be specified somewhere. Now dependency components can be added by rule like any others, so we can specify /n̪/ as phonetically apical by a low-level rule adding |t|: even though this has no distinctive function. Thus we get |l,d,t|, i.e. an apico-dental nasal.

The two remaining places, uvular and pharyngeal, involve only one new primitive. Uvulars may be represented quite reasonably as 'lowered' velars (see §6.3, (6.16)), so they are |l,u,a|; pharyngeals, being like labials non-lingual, are characterized by an element |r|, 'tongue-root retraction', perhaps better 'pharyngeal narrowing' and lowness, so they are |r,a|. The major places now have the following representations:

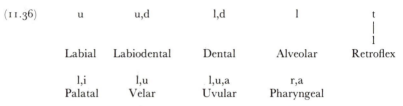

(11.36)

| u | u,d | l,d | l | t |
| | | | | │ |
| | | | | l |
| Labial | Labiodental | Dental | Alveolar | Retroflex |

| l,i | l,u | l,u,a | r,a |
| Palatal | Velar | Uvular | Pharyngeal |

And of course each of these can serve as part of the representation of a secondary stricture or double articulation as well – again using the same limited set of combining operations as before.

We already have the formal relations available: a secondary stricture is naturally interpreted as governed by a primary, i.e. subjoined to it: the basic category is dominant (a palatalized X is an X, not a palatal). So, for any X:

(11.37)
$$
\begin{array}{ccc}
X & X & X \\
| & | & | \\
l,i & l,u & r
\end{array}
$$

And so on. And palato-alveolars can be characterized as palatalized alveolars, i.e. |l ⇉ l,i|, thus getting them in as well, if not as a simple positional class.

A double articulation, on the other hand, like a labial-velar [kp] or a labial-palatal [ɥ], has two strictures of equal rank: hence in this framework co-dependent. Combining the articulatory and categorial representations for these two, we get:

(11.38)
$$
\begin{bmatrix} l,u \leftrightarrows u| \\ |C| \end{bmatrix} \quad \begin{bmatrix} |l,i \leftrightarrows u| \\ |V \rightrightarrows V,C| \end{bmatrix}
$$
$$
[\widehat{kp}] \qquad\qquad [ɥ]
$$

(Not unreasonably, we can take consonantal approximants as 'liquids').

Two major articulatory components remain to be specified: |λ| 'laterality' and |n| 'nasality' (their interpretations are straight-forward, equivalent to [+lat], [+nas]). Thus an alveolar lateral and nasal would be:

288

(11.39) $\begin{bmatrix} 1,\lambda \\ V \Rrightarrow V,C \end{bmatrix}$  $\begin{bmatrix} 1,n \\ V \Rrightarrow C \end{bmatrix}$

[l]  [n]

Nasals – unlike any other segments – are assigned a unique double specification: |n| in the articulatory gesture and |V⇒C| in the categorial. This may appear redundant, but there is a double justification: (a) phonetically nasals are unique by virtue of their nasality (of course); (b) phonologically they are unique in that even though they may group with other sonorants (hence the |V|), they do not seem to enter into the lenition scale, and often show 'stronger' or more obstruent-like properties than liquids. In addition, of course, they must be kept distinct from nasalized liquids, e.g. [ĩ]. Thus compare a nasalized [ĩ], a palatal nasal, and [ĩ]:

(11.40) $\begin{bmatrix} i,n \\ V \end{bmatrix}$  $\begin{bmatrix} 1,i,n \\ V \Rrightarrow C \end{bmatrix}$  $\begin{bmatrix} 1,n \\ V \Rrightarrow V,C \end{bmatrix}$

[ĩ]  [ɲ]  [ĩ]

Note that |λ| and |n| never appear alone, but always in combination.

## 11.6 **The initiatory gesture**

The preliminary discussion of gestures in §6.5 suggested a simple dichotomy of laryngeal and supralaryngeal, so that the mere location of an item in the larynx assigned it to a gesture. But argumentation in dependency theory supports the claim that this is oversimple: phonation proper (glottal activity) plays a rather different role from initiation (glottal attitude + airstream). That is, intralaryngeal and sublaryngeal configurations may have a part to play in both categorial and initiatory gestures. As the use of the |V| component suggests, 'voice', while physically laryngeal, is in its association with periodicity of output a categorial property, whereas glottal stricture and airstream have a different status. For instance: vocal-fold vibration is independent of glottalic initiation (voiced implosives vs. voiceless ejectives, both glottalic) and of airstream direction (voiceless ejectives and clicks, voiced pulmonic stops and implosives).

So we might suggest that the set of segmental properties as a whole is distributed among the gestures in this way (after Ewen 1980: §5.2.3):

289

(11.41)

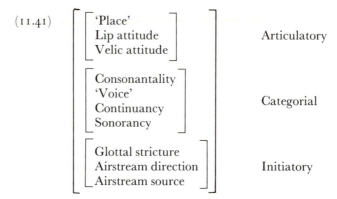

(| 'Place' | Lip attitude | Velic attitude |) Articulatory

(| Consonantality | 'Voice' | Continuancy | Sonorancy |) Categorial

(| Glottal stricture | Airstream direction | Airstream source |) Initiatory

('Place' is a cover-term for backness and height of vowels, and for place in the traditional sense for consonants: see §6.3.)

The first initiatory primitive is |O| 'glottal opening'. This defines only a static configuration, and says nothing about vocal-fold activity. All segments except [ʔ], glottalized consonants, ejectives, and (unaspirated) clicks will have |O| somewhere in their initiatory gesture. But how is the initiatory gesture related to the others, in particular the categorial? The schema (11.41) might suggest the kind of relation shown between categorial and articulatory gestures in (11.38–40); but overall phonetic properties and phonological behaviour suggest a different approach. Following Ewen (1980), we will assume that the initiatory gesture enters into its own dependency relations with the categorial, so that |O| if present may be governing, co-dependent, or dependent. We can suggest a basic set of relations of this type (for some justifying argument see §11.7):

(11.42)

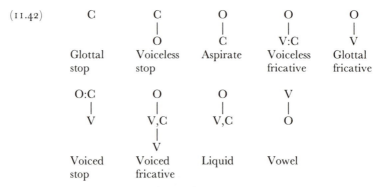

| C | C | O | O | O |
|---|---|---|---|---|
| \| | \| | \| | \| | \| |
| O | C | V:C | V |
| Glottal stop | Voiceless stop | Aspirate | Voiceless fricative | Glottal fricative |

| O:C | O | O | V |
|---|---|---|---|
| \| | \| | \| | \| |
| V | V,C | V,C | O |
| | \| | | |
| | V | | |
| Voiced stop | Voiced fricative | Liquid | Vowel |

For specifying airstreams, two additional initiatory primitives have been suggested: |G| 'glottalicness' and |K| 'velaric suction'. There

290

is no specification as such for directionality; the different segment types are characterized in terms of the relation of categorial to initiatory gesture as follows:

(a) For pulmonic egressives, there is no specific relation between initiatory and categorial (see (11.42)).

(b) For glottalic egressives, |G| governs the categorial |C|.

(c) For glottalic ingressives, there are actually two airstreams: the glottis moves downwards, but some voiced air moves up as well. Hence there is an |O| component (for glottal opening), as well as a |G|, but this time in a dependent position.

(d) For simple velaric ingressives, |K| appears in combination with the categorial gesture; for complex ones, such as aspirated, voiced or nasalized clicks, it appears as dependent.

In outline, then, we have the following basic types:

$$
\begin{array}{ccccccc}
(11.43) & \text{G} & \text{C} & \text{C,K} & \text{C} \rightrightarrows \text{V} & \text{V} \rightrightarrows \text{C} & \text{O} \\
 & | & | & & | & | & | \\
 & \text{C} & \text{O,G} & \text{Click} & \text{O,K} & \text{O,K} & \text{C,K} \\
 & \text{Ejective} & \text{Implosive} & \text{Click} & \text{Voiced} & \text{Nasalized} & \text{Aspirated} \\
 & & & & \text{click} & \text{click} & \text{click}
\end{array}
$$

There are elements of arbitrariness in this characterization, and it is too soon to know whether these specifications will have as much heuristic value as some of the others. In the next section we will see how the suggestions in (11.42), which seem quite soundly based, can help to give a unified picture of lenition.

## 11.7 Lenition revisited

The positing of |O|, and hence the characterization of aspirates and [h], suggests that we ought to take a look at lenition again. We will find that it becomes rather more complex, but at the same time more coherent with respect to the hierarchy. Let us look first at the parameter 'opening' via aspiration, with velars as illustrative types:

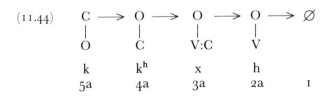

$$
\begin{array}{ccccccccc}
(11.44) & \text{C} & \longrightarrow & \text{O} & \longrightarrow & \text{O} & \longrightarrow & \text{O} & \longrightarrow & \emptyset \\
 & | & & | & & | & & | & & \\
 & \text{O} & & \text{C} & & \text{V:C} & & \text{V} & & \\
 & \text{k} & & \text{k}^{\text{h}} & & \text{x} & & \text{h} & & \\
 & 5\text{a} & & 4\text{a} & & 3\text{a} & & 2\text{a} & & \text{I}
\end{array}
$$

(The numbers relate to those in (8.13).) The first stage involves the shifting of |O| from dependent to governor, in which position it continues for the entire sequence. The rest involves weakening of the |C| component, first by co-dependent |V|, then by deletion. The shift |O⇉V:C|→|O⇉V| is equivalent to deoralization or sub-matrix deletion (§8.3.1); we assume that |O⇉V| with no |C| is equivalent to lack of an articulatory gesture. That is, every articulated (i.e. 'oral' in the sense of §5.3.2.1) segment has a |C| component; |V| is articulated only if it governs |O|. The picture of lenition that emerges is perhaps a bit surprising, but quite sensible in the end: |O| is the first component to be added, and it dominates to the end, whereas the rest of the sequence involves |V|-increase and |C|-decrease. Within lenition by opening, then, there are three distinct sub-processes, each of which decreases 'strength'.

If we take the sonorization route, we see a similar picture; only here the |V|-increase involves the additional stage |V⇉O|, i.e. vowel alone as prelude to zero. Because all the segments on this scale are voiced, we end up with governing |V|, i.e. a segment that still has its articulatory gesture. This sequence (again illustrated with velars) would be:

(11.45)

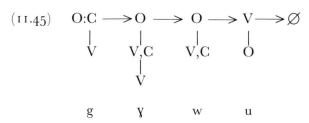

Put together, the whole lenition hierarchy (except for affrication, which is an 'alternate' route to aspiration) comes out as:

(11.46)

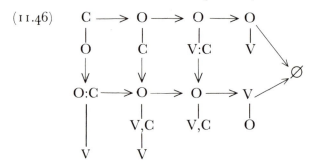

This is just a brief introduction to the basic formalisms and concepts of dependency phonology; for more extensive examples of its applications to real-language data, see the notes.

## NOTES AND REFERENCES

11.1 Dependency as a general concept has been most fully treated within the context of syntactic analysis, especially case-grammar: for details see **Anderson (1971), **Anderson (1977: §2.2). For the formal foundations of dependency theory, Hays (1964), Robinson (1970). The basis for the formalism used in this chapter is laid out in **Anderson & Jones (1974a), and Anderson & Jones (1977: ch. III). For a general sketch of the theory of dependency phonology, Anderson & Ewen (1980b). The most detailed exposition of the theory in general is unfortunately not published: **Ewen (1980).

11.2 On vowel representation, Ewen (1980: ch. 4), Anderson & Jones (1977: ch. III).

11.3 For a detailed account of *i*-umlaut and some other vocalic processes, Anderson & Jones (1977: ch. III).

11.4 On the categorial gesture, Ewen (1980: ch. 6), Anderson & Ewen (1980b: §4.1).

11.5 On the articulatory gesture, Ewen (1980: ch. 8), Anderson & Ewen (1980b: §4.2).

11.6 On the initiatory gesture, Ewen (1980: ch. 9), Anderson & Ewen (1980b: 4.3).

11.7 For a detailed study of lenition in dependency terms, Ó Dochartaigh (1980). Some other applications to specific problems are Jones (1979) on OE vocalic phonology, Jones (1980) on metathesis, Ewen (1977) on Scots vowel length, and Anderson (1980) on the history of English.

# 12

# Non-static phonology: connected speech and variation

## 12.1 **Preliminaries**

Except for the brief discussion of sandhi (§4.7), we have been exclusively concerned with organization at the word or morpheme level. In keeping with phonological tradition we have had little to say about phonological structure as it is deployed in the normal contexts of language use, or with the properties of connected speech. Nor have we considered variability; except for 'free variation' (§§2.4, 2.7) we have restricted ourselves to either/or structural properties, naturally described in terms of inventory statements or categorically applicable rules (even if with the odd invariant exception: §2.10).

In addition, when we talked of 'the structure of' any language, we assumed implicitly that a speaker is a speaker of one language-variety, and that this variety has a once-and-for-all statable structure and organization (phonological and morphophonemic) for all discourse situations – the 'system' that we take as our descriptive base, the subject for typology, etc. This is a rather gross simplification; but as long as we recognize it, and deal with the neglected complexities somewhere, a fairly benign one. This chapter is a mild corrective, designed to show, however briefly, the 'other face' of phonology, as well as to introduce some concepts that will prove useful in dealing with phonological change (ch. 13). The message is that the range of phenomena coming under the heading of phonology is greater than – and partly different in kind from – what's covered by phonemics, allophonics, and morphophonemics in the usual sense.

But the simplified version of structure we've been using does have a special analytical priority; the complicated and often messy things we consider here require it as a basis, and are largely incomprehensible without it. Variation and instability, the 'dynamic' aspects of

294

phonology, are uninterpretable save against an invariant, stable background. This is true of connected speech at various tempi, various levels of formality, and socially conditioned variation, all of which interact. And this complex set of interactions, as we'll see, is the basis for linguistic change – as well as the performance norm for non-changing speech communities.

## 12.2 **Connected and casual speech**

It's clear from our discussion of sandhi that there can be a difference between **citation forms** (CFs) of lexical items – the shapes they take in isolation, or in stressed positions in very careful speech – and their forms in (certain) syntactic contexts. It is also clear that modifications in connected speech can often have effects with higher-order systematic relevance: e.g. we can get what looks like allomorphic variation in particular larger-than-the-word contexts that arise through the 'accidents' of the way words get put together in syntactic constructions (e.g. 'linking-*r*' in English).

But beyond this, we must consider not only processes that are simply a function of contiguity in the speech chain, but also ones tied to tempo, and register and style as well. And we will see that language systems as wholes may have – within the same speaker – quite different properties at different tempi and in different styles. Or, to turn this around, that it often looks as if one ('monolingual') speaker may possess two or more 'different languages'.

As a first example, consider this string:

(12.1)     dːɪfx̩t̩tɹɪɪzə̃ãmːä̃ʔʃɤ̃ɹəβærɪʔt°

What language is this? How many words are in this utterance? It's obviously a language with long consonants ( [dː nː] ), nasalized vowels ( [ã̃ɪ] ), a bilabial fricative [β], a velar [x], and syllabic fricatives like [ʃ]. In fact, the language is my own variety of English, spoken in a rapid and casual style. It is a casual speech (CS) version of what, as a sequence of CFs, would be:

(12.2)     ðə dɪfɪkʌɫ̩ʔtɹɪ ʔɪz ðæʔt ãɪm nä̃ʔt ʃɤ̃ɹ ʔəbæʊʔt ʔɪʔt

That is, 'the difficulty is that I'm not sure about it'. At the level of (12.2) – where we usually 'do phonology' – it's not the case that English is a language with nasalized vowels, syllabic fricatives, long consonants, [β x]. Yet it's quite possible to get from one representation to the other by fairly simple rules: and (12.2) is a necessary basis for the processing by a hearer of (12.1).

The problem with (12.1), from the standpoint of what in the normal sense is 'the structure of English', is relating some of the segments and sequences that actually appear to expected ones. Perhaps this will become clearer if we put the two transcriptions together:

(12.3)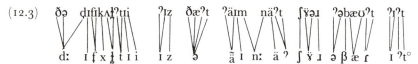

The mappings between CF and CS are often highly complex, e.g. the initial [dː] represents the sequence [ðə], plus the [d] of *difficulty* (two words into one segment as it were); [ə] for *that* is a more radical collapse, if without fusion. There are also very elaborate mappings such as that between the [m] in *I'm* and its CS representation: it seems to split off into two pieces, one of which is [˜] on the diphthong, and the other the first component of [nː].

So one thing we see here – apparently – is not simply coalescence and/or reduction of word length, but what could be interpreted as deletion or suppression of boundaries: conditions that hold within the word in CF cross word boundaries in CS, and boundaries occur 'inside' segments. (The assimilation of /m#n/ to [nː] = [nn] is not, by the way, a case of a word-level constraint being extended over boundaries in CS: while /NC/ clusters are homorganic within the word, this does not hold for /NN/: *enmity*, etc.) See §12.3 for more on boundary-suppression.

Why should this sort of thing be possible in CS? One way of looking at it is in terms of the knowledge and expectations of the participants in a conversation. Native speakers of a language 'know in advance' what messages consist of: WORDS, 'not odd acoustic bits and pieces' (Brown 1977: 4). Therefore the listener applies, in a CS situation, all his knowledge of linguistic structure: syntax and morphology, semantics and lexis – as well as pragmatic cues – and finally of course phonology. And he approaches the task of interpretation, under normal conditions, with the expectation that messages make sense, and he does his best to ensure that they do.

In other words, it is perfectly possible for the listener to 'hear' things that aren't there, or things quite different from what's actually being said – as long as he knows the variety of the language being spoken, or can guess at its structure and rules, and can compute the possible 'sources' of a given segment or sequence. And in doing so he 'hears' the underlying source, not what's said: ask a native speaker to repeat a reduced message like (12.1), and the chances are he'll repeat (and think he heard) something like (12.2).

That is, if he knows the rules by which CFs are 'converted' into their reduced, altered, coalesced CS counterparts, he can restore the missing bits – whether segments or boundaries – and convert the 'exotic' segment types into their 'ideal' representations. So the speaker listens not to what is – strictly – being said, but to what his knowledge of the basic structures of the language tells him ought to be being said. A state of affairs beautifully described by Sapir (1921: 56n): 'In watching my Nootka interpreter write his language, I often had the curious feeling that he was transcribing an ideal flow of phonetic elements which he heard, inadequately from a purely objective standpoint, as the intention of the actual rumble of speech.'

It is interesting that some of the segments speakers produce in CS are illegal in CF: so much so that they often have immense difficulty in pronouncing them in cold blood, as it were – e.g. when learning a foreign language and producing ITS CFs. For instance, as far as I know all varieties of English have [x] for /k/ in some CS contexts, and [ṼC] for [VNC]; yet any language teacher knows how hard it is to get English speakers to produce German /x/ or French nasalized vowels: the typical results are [k] and [VN] respectively – their 'sources' in the speaker's own CS. The aberrant items 'belong' in some very intimate way to CS, with its much lower level of conscious awareness.

CS modifications appear to derive essentially from characteristics of the speaker that come to the fore in CS ('physical sources') and properties of CS interactions ('social sources'). The former are rooted in anatomy and physiology, and the latter in the particular expectations about comprehensibility that are typical of CS, rather than more formal situations.

What appears to happen is that the faster and more casual speech becomes, the less it is 'focal' to the speaker's concerns, the less attention he pays to it. Therefore the inertial properties of the speech apparatus tend to take over: as it were a 'gravitational' effect, where decrease of attention leads to decrease of effort. To put it crudely, things tend

297

to get done the easiest way, movements flow along a path of least effort. As attention decreases, so does control; and both distinctiveness and distinctness decrease. Articulatory 'fine tuning' is less strictly maintained, so there is a general loosening of control over individual gestures, and an increase in coarticulation. (But all still, as we will see, under the constraints of language-specific rules.)

On this basis, the primary CS characteristics are: (a) increasing frequency of asssimilation, i.e. loss of distinction between neighbouring segments, often as a result of (b) suppression of boundaries, leading to the reorganization of word-size chunks of phonic material into syntactic groups with multiple membership, treated as single phono-logical words; (c) lenition, especially by opening of stricture; (d) vowel reduction (primarily shortening and centralization), with vowel-loss leading to syllabification of consonants; (e) shortening of long segments; (f) reduction of clusters.

These physical alterations are often enhanced by properties of the speech situation. If you expect your interlocutors to be able to follow a reduced and relatively indistinct message, there is less need to concentrate on the identities of individual segments, morphemes, words; there is an option for producing a rather blurry message from which the speaker will have to extract the relevant material. Thus the closer to you (in terms of relationship, membership of the same micro-dialect, social group, shared background knowledge and assumptions) the other speaker(s) turn out to be, the more skill in 'resynthesis' you can expect, and the less obliged you are to maintain clarity. The 'ideal' phonemic system and tactic rules of CFs become a kind of background against which the extremely messy products of CS can be interpreted.

### 12.3 Systemic effects, tempo hierarchies, and rule interactions

The typical CS modifications can lead, either alone or in combinations, to what appear to be radical restructurings of the basic phonological system. We will look at a few types here, mainly exemplified from my own variety of English.

(i) **Phonotactic restructuring.** Languages generally have fairly rigid constraints on phoneme sequences, in particular positions. Let us look for instance at word-initial clustering in English. One im-portant CF restriction is that initial obstruent clusters are canonically of the form stop + fricative (rarely fricative + fricative as in *sphere*); stop + stop, stop + fricative (unless that's how you interpret affricates) are generally ruled out except in loans from languages that have such sequences (*Dvořák*, *tsetse* – often legalized to /dəvɔːʒæk/, /sɛtsi/, etc.).

But many of these restrictions are suspended in CS, and exceedingly exotic clusters appear. As an example, I get [ts] in [tsɪimz] 'it seems', [θf] in [θfɹʌnʔt] 'the front', [ks] in [kstɹɪimʇɹi] 'extremely', [px] in [pxɔəz] 'because' (as well as [pk] in the same form). In CS, phonotactics may become almost 'accidental' or contingent: if you delete a vowel, as in *because*, you're stuck pretty much with whatever the vowel-loss has brought together. Though we might note that there are other constraints operating: if two obstruents are brought together, the cluster must be made homorganic for voice – normally in this dialect by regressive devoicing (i.e. *[bkɔəz] is impossible, and [bgɔəz], though properly homorganic, is simply unlikely).

(ii) **Phonemic restructuring.** This is usually the result of development of new segment types, not normally realizations of phonemes in CFs; examples have already been given of [β x f̩] in English. The effect of this kind of innovation may be relatively low-level, i.e. simply a matter of expanding the phonetic repertoire. But it can also have a more systematic effect: the emergence of new phonemic oppositions. For instance, the development of a new phone type may be simply a consequence of a general process of lenition. If you're going to lenite [k] and [b] you have little choice but [x] and [β]. And if lenition is virtually automatic, if it takes place so far below the level of conscious awareness that if – say – you 'think [b]' and produce [β], it still counts for you and your hearer as a potential token of /b/. The fact that (at CF level) English 'has no [β]' is irrelevant; its 'facthood' is relegated to background knowledge, and all that counts is voice and bilabiality.

But this can lead, at CS level, to the destruction of the old set of stop/fricative oppositions, and can produce a new fricative/fricative contrast [β]:[v], which acts like a 'normal' phonemic contrast. We then get minimal pairs like [kʰʌβɹd] 'cupboard' vs. [kʰʌvɹd] 'covered'. So while a language like Ewe has a /β/:/v/ contrast at CF level ([εβὲ] 'Ewe' vs. [ὲvὲ] 'two'), English has it only in CS. English is thus – at two different levels – typologically 'two different languages'. But, significantly, the new contrast will probably never be categorical: SOME tokens of CF /b/ will normally, given a long enough stretch of discourse even in the most casual styles, surface as [b]. But it would make little difference if they didn't: the forms would still be distinct (see further §12.4).

Another kind of restructuring occurs when, because of some interaction between processes, a phonetically illegal sequence not only appears, but becomes contrastive with a legal one. Here is a very complicated case in point. My dialect has, in common with most others, a CS rule of stop-deletion in final position before a word beginning with a consonant. Thus [hæːnd], [tʰæʊəɫ] 'hand', 'towel', but [hæːntʰæʊəɫ] 'hand-towel'. There is also a homorganic nasal-assimilation rule, which can operate across word boundaries, as in (12.1) [ãɪ̃ːä̃ʔt] 'I'm not'. If final stop-deletion occurs, and the resulting sequence contains a nasal and a non-homorganic stop, the nasal will assimilate: [hæːmpʰɪ̃ʔkt] 'hand-picked', where the [m] in *hand* (now homophonous with *ham*) presupposes 'prior' deletion of [d], giving [np] → [mp]. This much is simple enough. We can suggest a derivation:

| (12.4) | Input | hænd pɪkt |
| --- | --- | --- |
| | Length | hæːnd pɪkt |
| | Stop-del | hæːn pɪkt |
| | Assim | hæːm pɪkt |

Now the lengthening rule for /æ/ (see §§2.10, 8.5) applies before /m n/ but not /ŋ/: thus the above forms vs. [hæŋ] 'hang'. This is relevant to deletion and assimilation, as follows. In CF, there is – obviously – no possible contrast between [æŋ] and [æːŋ], since the latter is illegal. But the interaction of stop-deletion and nasal assimilation in CS in fact produces just such a minimal contrast, e.g. in [hæŋglaɪdəɹ] 'hang-glider' vs [hæːŋgɹɪnɛɪd] 'hand-grenade'. The process is simple:

| (12.5) | Input | hæŋ | glaɪdəɹ | hænd | gɹɪnɛɪd |
| --- | --- | --- | --- | --- | --- |
| | Length | — | — | hæːnd | — |
| | Stop-del | — | — | hæːn | — |
| | Assim | — | — | hæːŋ | |

Thus a 'false' contrast [æŋ] vs. [æːŋ] occurs in CS, where a minimal pair [hæŋ] 'hang' : [hæːŋ] 'hand' is born out of an interaction between one CF rule (lengthening), and two CS rules. There is thus a potential 'phonemic contrast' in CS that can't exist in CFs: structurally, the two are 'different dialects'.

Yet the contrast is easily referrable to the CFs, since if we know that a sequence can't occur AS SUCH in a CF, a CS occurrence must be something other than what it seems. And since we also know that stop-deletion is restricted to alveolars and velars in this dialect, [æːŋ] must derive from /ænC/; and since /t d/ are the most likely obstruents to delete anyhow, the speaker can recover /hænd/ simply by back-tracking the derivation. (Or we can model his comprehension by attributing something of the sort to his processing.)

(iii) **Morphosyntactic restructuring** via CS rules. An even more radical structural alteration occurs in my CS, apparently involving syntax as well. One would be surprised to find a dialect of English of which the following was true: 'the distinction between indefinite and definite nouns is produced by lengthening the initial consonant for definiteness'. This is pretty exotic – not even, one would think, Indo-European. Yet pairs of contrasting utterances like those in (12.6) are quite normal and easily distinguishable by native speakers:

(12.6)    (1a) Put [mɪɫk] on the table         [ = milk]
          (1b) Put [mːɪɫk] on the table        [ = the milk]
          (2a) I saw her by [ɫæmpɫäɪʔt]       [ = lamplight]
          (2b) I saw her by [ɫːæmpɫäɪʔt]      [ = the lamplight]

And so on for most other consonants.

But these are the most casual forms. There is in fact a hierarchy of modes of casualness/tempi which makes this apparent length/definiteness system into something quite different. If we take a series of increasingly rapid tempi (here labelled mnemonically, following a fairly conventional practice, with musical terms), we get:

| (12.7) | *Lento* | *Allegretto* | *Allegro* | *Presto* | |
|---|---|---|---|---|---|
| | ðə mɪɫk | ð̃mɪɫk | ʔmɪɫk | mːɪɫk | 'the milk' |
| | ðə nəʊz | ð̃nəʊz | ʔnəʊz | nːəʊz | 'the nose' |
| | ðə dɔəg | ð̃dɔəg | ʔdɔəg | dːɔəg | 'the dog' |

What look like minimal pairs in presto arise via a SEQUENCE of intrinsically ordered processes: the contrast [C]:[Cː] as a marker of definiteness is an artifact, not 'original' or 'structural'. We have in (12.7) a set of apparent implicational relations between tempi: each slower tempo serves as input to the next faster, and the faster ones only 'make sense' in the light of the slower ones – provided we know the rules.

The implicational or 'inferential' relation between tempi can be even more clearly illustrated by a complex of rules involving nasalization, syllabification of nasals, place assimilation, and the /p t k/ → [ʔ] rule. Some typical forms:

(12.8)
| | *Lento* | *Allegretto* | *Allegro* | *Presto* | |
|---|---|---|---|---|---|
| | bəmʔpɪmɔəf | bʌmʔpm̩ɔəf | bʌ̃ʔpm̩ɔəf | bʌ̃ʔm̩ɔəf | 'bump him off' |
| | sɛnʔtɪns | sɛnʔtn̩s | sɛ̃ʔtn̩s | sɛ̃ʔn̩s | 'sentence' — |
| | bæŋʔkɪŋ | bæŋʔkŋ̩ | bæ̃ʔkŋ̩ | bæ̃ʔŋ̩ | 'banking' |

In order to interpret this, we note one crucial fact: syllabic nasals occur in reasonably slow styles only if they follow a homorganic obstruent. Thus allegretto [sɛnʔtn̩s], but [bärəm] 'bottom', never *[bärm̩], etc. This overall constraint determines the interpretation of the faster forms, as follows: if a nasal is syllabic, it must derive from a homorganic /CN/ sequence. Such sequences may arise from vowel-deletion. But then nasalization, nasal-deletion, and reduction of glottalized stops may occur, leaving us with a minimally informative structure [ṼʔN̩].

But backtracking, even the presto forms are unambiguous. The voiceless stop can be recovered from [ʔ] via the nasal: a sequence [ʔn̩] can – by the criteria above – have no source but [ʔtn̩], so that lento [t] can be resynthesized out of [ʔn̩]. The nasal that followed the vowel can also be resynthesized, because of the CF homorganicity constraint: if you have [Ṽʔt], the only nasal that could have been there is [n]. Hence the lento forms emerge – if you know the rules.

But there is a slight complication which shows that you need to know lexis as well as rules. It is possible for /n/ to assimilate to a following stop, giving things like [wʌnʔkŋ̩] 'one can'; this can reduce to [wʌ̃ʔŋ̩]; and by the argument above, this would presuppose a lento *[wʌŋ ...]. Indeed it does; but here lexis comes in (is there a word /wʌŋ/?), as does the speech situation, since interpreting decontextualized sentences is an artificial task. Assuming the existence of a Mr Wung, then [wʌ̃ʔŋ̩] *do it* is interpretable as *Wung can do it* or *One can do it*; and presumably the problem is unlikely to arise.

The intrinsic relations between the rules in this complex can be seen more clearly in a rough formalization:

(12.9)     1 Vowel-deletion

$$\begin{bmatrix} V \\ -\text{stress} \end{bmatrix} \rightarrow \emptyset / [+\text{obs}]\_\_\_N$$

2 Nasal syllabification

$$\begin{bmatrix} N \\ \alpha[\text{artic}] \end{bmatrix} \rightarrow [+\text{syll}] / \begin{bmatrix} +\text{obs} \\ \alpha[\text{artic}] \end{bmatrix} \underline{\quad} \left\{ \begin{matrix} \# \\ C \end{matrix} \right\}$$

3 Nasalization

$$V \rightarrow [+\text{nas}] / \underline{\quad} N \left\{ \begin{matrix} \# \\ C \end{matrix} \right\}$$

4 Nasal-deletion

$$N \rightarrow \emptyset / \begin{bmatrix} V \\ +\text{nas} \end{bmatrix} \underline{\quad}$$

5 Glottal stop

$$\begin{bmatrix} +\text{obs} \\ -\text{voice} \end{bmatrix} \rightarrow \emptyset / ? \underline{\quad} \begin{bmatrix} N \\ +\text{syll} \end{bmatrix}$$

The nasal assimilation shows up another kind of restructuring, with interesting effects: what might be called **boundary-demotion**. In my speech the cluster [nk] is permissible across word boundaries in slower speech, but not within the word: *in-, un-* before velars virtually always end in [ŋ]. So one quite reasonable way of interpreting the [ŋk] in *one can* is in terms of restructuring of the boundaries, i.e. #*one*#*can*# → #*one* + *can*#. That is, # is 'demoted' to +, so that *one can* is a 'single word', like #*in* + *come*#.

For an even clearer example, consider the case of Scots vowel harmony. Many varieties have a VH rule applying mainly to the suffixes *-ie, -y*, which have a relatively close vowel if the preceding stressed vowel is close or half-close, and a relatively open one if the preceding stressed vowel is half-open or open. So:

(12.10)

| | | | | |
|---|---|---|---|---|
| (a) | pÿs | *puss* | pÿse | *pussy* |
| | ɬik | *leek* | ɬike | *(cock-a-)leekie* |
| (b) | ɬʌk | *luck* | ɬʌkɛ | *lucky* |
| | kë? | *kit* | kë?ɛ | *kitty* |

But in very casual speech, we get sequences like [ëʃːɛ] *is she*, where the citation forms are [ëʒ], [ʃiː]. Since the domain of VH is the disyllabic word, this looks like another boundary-demotion: #*is*#*she*# → #*is* + *she*#, where the whole complex is treated as a single word with [ɛ] as the suffix.

### 12.4 **Variation and variables: the social dimension**

In §12.1 we introduced the notion 'variation'; it's time now to give it some more substance. The various CS phenomena dealt with in §§12.2f are 'optional' – but I didn't make much of this. The particular kind of optionality involved is however not simply a matter of random application or non-application of a rule: the polarity optional/obligatory is not very helpful. What we have here is a matter of PROBABILITIES. A tempo hierarchy like (12.7) is not a listing of forms absolutely characteristic of particular tempi, but should be interpreted this way: given a particular tempo, at least a certain percentage of tokens meeting the SD of a tempo-specific rule will actually show its application. With increasing speed, the number of forms showing a CS modification will increase. So [mːɪłk] is a 'presto form'; but a stretch of presto utterance may perfectly well contain forms of the [ʔmɪłk] or even [ðə mɪłk] types – though proportionately fewer than an allegretto utterance, etc. The material there was not subject to quantitative analysis; but if we look at some that has been studied that way, we can get a much better idea of how typical variation works.

We'll begin, not with style or tempo variation, but with another kind: non-categorical rule application under social controls. That is, a rule sensitive to extralinguistic factors (class, age, sex, religion), and, within these parameters, to statistical controls which are correlated with them in a complex and rather mysterious way.

Let's look again at the Scots /t/ → [ʔ] rule (§6.5), which functions in many communities as a typical **linguistic variable**: a category whose incidence is tied to social factors, and serves as an index or marker of group identity. Recall the linguistic environment:

$$(12.11) \qquad t \rightarrow ʔ/\acute{V} \left( \begin{bmatrix} C \\ -obs \end{bmatrix} \right) \underline{\qquad} \begin{Bmatrix} V \\ \# \end{Bmatrix}$$

In a recent study of Glasgow Scots (Macaulay & Trevelyan 1973) the application of (12.11) was investigated as follows: a group of informants of different class, age, sex and religion were recorded, and out of a stretch of running speech for each one, 80 tokens of 'potential [t]' in the (12.11) environments were selected (i.e. items like *that*, *butter*, *football*). Then the percentage of [ʔ] for /t/ was calculated for each speaker, and correlated with social parameters; thus for any class, sex, age, or class/age, class/sex complex, etc., the individual scores could be conflated to get a group average.

The analysis was based on a four-class division: I (professional and managerial), IIa (intermediate and junior non-manual, manual supervisory), IIb (skilled manual, self-employed non-professional), and III (semi-skilled and unskilled). Given this class stratification and a calculation of the percentage of [?] for each group, the results are:

(12.12)　　Class　　I　　　IIa　　　IIb　　　III
　　　　　　%　　　48.4　　72.9　　84.3　　91.7

These results can be seen graphically in (12.13).

(12.13)

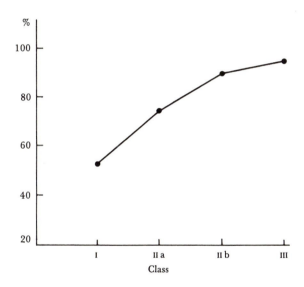

We will look at age, sex, and religion shortly.

But the pattern in (12.13) is actually a bit misleading. If we consider, not total [?], but percentage by linguistic environment, it turns out that class behaviour is not the same for all contexts. Given prepausal, intervocalic, and preconsonantal positions (e.g. *foot*, *butter*, *football*), we get the results shown in (12.14).

(12.14)

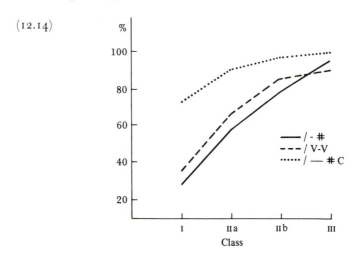

The class marking function of [ʔ] is obviously much greater in other environments than pre-C (not surprising, if you consider how much more striking [fʉʔ] for *foot* is than [fʉʔbɔɫ] for *football*). So [ʔ] itself is not a potent discriminator: the differences between classes I and III are much smaller here than for other positions. Removing this environment, then, we get the following figures (here broken down further for sex: ♂male, ♀female):

(12.15)

| Class | I | IIa | IIb | III |
|---|---|---|---|---|
| All | 30.9 | 60.2 | 79.7 | 90.4 |
| ♂ | 30.9 | 74.7 | 80.0 | 93.6 |
| ♀ | 30.9 | 45.6 | 79.4 | 87.1 |

It's clear that for social class IIa (most strikingly), and for III, sex is another determinant; as is rather commonly the case in Western industrial societies at least, there is a strong tendency for women in lower social classes to approximate more closely to the usage of higher classes than for men.

If we break down the figures by age, we find something else:

(12.16)

| | Class | I | IIa | IIb | III |
|---|---|---|---|---|---|
| ♂ | Adult | 11.3 | 41.6 | 89.1 | 92.3 |
| | 15 yr | 25.0 | 92.6 | 81.7 | 95.6 |
| | 10 yr | 56.2 | 89.9 | 69.4 | 92.8 |
| ♀ | Adult | 9.3 | 12.5 | 66.4 | 88.0 |
| | 15 yr | 24.8 | 45.7 | 77.8 | 94.1 |
| | 10 yr | 58.7 | 78.7 | 94.1 | 79.2 |

There's not much here in the way of uniform patterning; the overall trends for men and women are clear, but within the groups the age-structures are not consistent. This overall lack of consistency suggests that there's no community-wide change in progress; but it does show that for each group and subgroup there is an appropriate percentage of [ʔ]-use that in some way seems to be 'known' to the speaker – or at least, to avoid this kind of psychologistic claim, is coded into his behaviour. The difference between the patterning by sex alone and by sex + age comes out in the two graphs, (12.17) and (12.18).

(12.17)

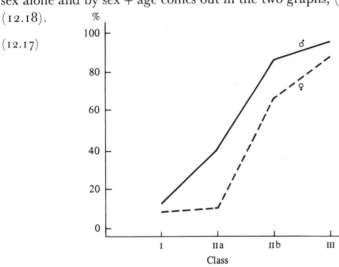

[ʔ] by sex and social class

(12.18)

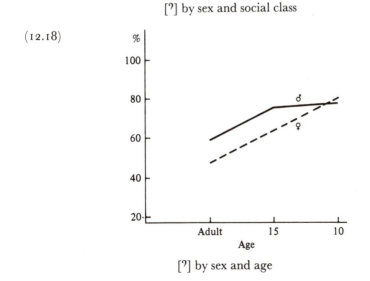

[ʔ] by sex and age

307

The age-grading suggests an apparent ongoing frequency rise among women, and a levelling-off among men; but it would require a good deal of long-term observation before we could tell if this represents a trend in [ʔ]-use, or simply an intergenerational development that remains constant from generation to generation of speakers.

Finally, to illustrate the further potential complexity of the control of a variable, consider religion: not on the face of it a likely factor, but given the political and demographic history of the West of Scotland, a reasonable one to look at:

| (12.19) | Class | I | IIa | IIb | III |
|---------|-------|---|-----|-----|-----|
| | Catholic | 33 | 77 | 52 | 88 |
| | Non-Catholic | 32 | 46 | 82 | 91 |

Again, a typical community-wide pattern (if different in detail and direction from other patterns within the social structure of the [ʔ]-variable): minimal differentiation at the top and bottom of the class hierarchy, and striking differences in the middle. A similar pattern shows up in the age-structure of religious differences as well, but I think we've seen enough to illustrate what a variable looks like.

Now the sociolinguistic aspects of this situation are not our basic concern; they are introduced merely because they are part of the description of how rule (12.11) functions. From the point of view of phonology (not 'sociophonology') we've uncovered yet another type of alternation, this time keyed to extralinguistic factors, and with a structure that can really only be stated in terms of a community, not a speaker.

But it's also worth noting the particular kind of dependency uncovered here: unlike a categorical rule, (12.11) does not predict – even for a speaker whose class, age, etc. are known – whether any SINGLE token, or even any relatively short sequence, will show [ʔ] if the SD of the rule is met. Rather it predicts that given a sufficiently large number of tokens, the AVERAGE number of [ʔ] will approximate closely to the appropriate group figure. Each speaker will of course have a slightly different absolute score over a sample of utterances, but it will be within fairly characteristic limits of tolerance for his group.

So this rule is a rather odd sort of animal: what is generally called a **variable rule**. Its environments, when it's properly stated, code both extralinguistic parameters and a set of probability-weightings, for both social and linguistic contexts.

The Macaulay & Trevelyan study does not deal with [ʔ] for the other voiceless stops, nor with stylistic variation; I have no quantitative evidence on these matters. But on the basis of observation of Scottish speech, I would think that a quantitative study would show two further aspects: (a) that while /t/ → [ʔ] is the most striking instance, /k/ and /p/, in the same environments also go to [ʔ]; likelihood of application increases in the order /p/ < /k/ < /t/; (b) there will be a strong stylistic correlation, such that for any environment, the more casual the style (for any class), the greater the likelihood of application.

This kind of interaction between class and style is a common property of rules of this type: consider graph (12.21) of the variable (ng) in Norwich (/n/ vs. /ŋ/ in unstressed *-ing*: high scores = high proportion of /n/).

(12.20)

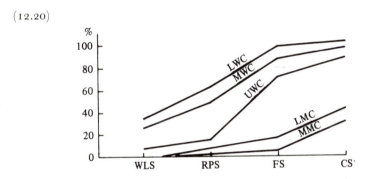

(L, M, U = Lower, Middle, Upper; WC, MC = Working class, Middle class; WLS = Word list style, RPS = Reading passage style, FS = Formal speech, CS = Casual speech. These constitute a descending scale of formality.)

The rule involved might be stated – linguistically – as:

(12.21)
$$\eta \rightarrow n / \begin{bmatrix} V \\ -\text{stress} \end{bmatrix} \underline{\quad} \#$$

But this tells us very little. Note how the variability works: there is a sharp overall differentiation between WC and MC, but it seems to be most striking at a particular point in the STYLE continuum. And the highest /n/-scores for MMC speakers in CS are just about the same as those for MWC speakers in RPS. Class and style are related scales, in that a move down the formality hierarchy, within one social class, looks – in terms of frequency – rather like a move down the class hierarchy, ignoring style.

What are we to make of variable rules and the community-wide structure of a variable? Questions of 'psychological reality' and the like (§§9.4f) become difficult here, since it seems inconceivable that a variable rule in any real sense 'belongs to' any particular speaker – though it certainly guides his behaviour. Do we want to attribute the capacity for such statistical monitoring to the speaker? To say that he 'knows' the appropriate percentages of particular forms for his class, his age, for a given style, etc., and that he can adjust his performance to make it conform? Or do we rather want to suggest that a variable rule is a description of a mysterious and (at present) uninterpretable set of controls on the linguistic output of a community as a whole, not attributable to any individual?

These issues have not been very well discussed in the literature, and I leave them for now as ones that deserve to be puzzled over. The basic problem is the kind of knowledge that has to be attributed to a speaker if ALL of this is to be in his individual control. (Note that this is quite different from the problem of how a child might acquire 'abstract segments': with variables, the facts are relatively superficial and available to investigators; with 'underlying forms', the 'facts' themselves are artifacts of a particular type of analysis, and cannot be 'observed' except by someone who believes in them to begin with.)

## 12.5 Individual variation: the lexical dimension

The (ʔ) and (ng) variables discussed in the last section are two-valued: there is no exponent between [n] and [ŋ], and nothing to speak of between [ʔ] and [t] (degree of glottalization, release, etc. are probably non-significant). And, as we said, every speaker appears to produce some tokens of each value.

But there are some variables that have a much wider spread of values, and can show extremely complex patternings for individual speakers. Here we find not only variation in phonetic exponents, but LEXICAL variation as well: the environments that show particular weightings for the implementation of a variable-value are often at least partly lexeme-specific. Take for instance the frequently discussed New York City variable (æh): this involves raising of /æ/ in various 'long' environments (see the data in §2.10). The closest values are of the type [ɪə], the openest around [æː]. The greatest degree of raising seems to be before N(C) and voiceless fricatives, with voiced stops following a close second. (Hence the New York dialogue: A: What's your little boy's name? B: Ian. C: Ann? What a funny name for a boy. Speaker A is a native with [ɪən] for both, speaker B from another social class or an outsider.)

But if one looks at profiles of individual speakers, one finds (a) a considerable scatter of values for this nucleus, and (b) that certain lexical items appear to 'lead' in degree of raising. Consider the profiles for three New York speakers in (12.23–12.25) (after Labov *et al.* 1972, vol. II, figs. 3–3a, 3–4a, 3–5); the figures represent plots of the frequencies (in $H_z$, or cycles per second) of $F_1$ against $F_2$ for the vowels, with the lexical items in places corresponding to their nuclei (see §6.6 for the interpretation of charts like this: for our purposes they may be said to represent the 'vowel space'; the vertical axis = height and the horizontal = backness, with front at the left and high at the top).

(12.22)

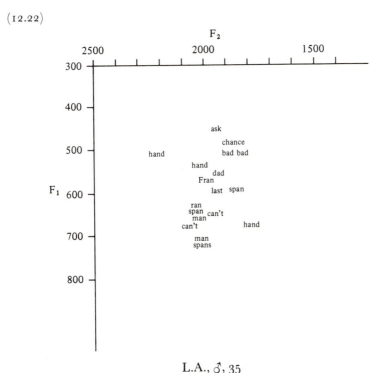

L.A., ♂, 35

(12.23)

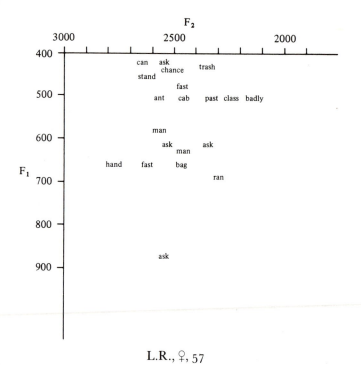

L.R., ♀, 57

(12.24)

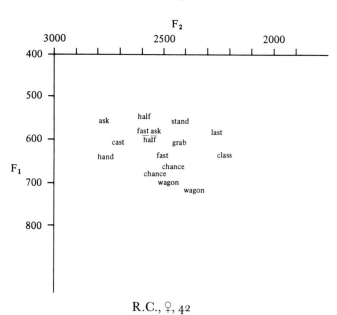

R.C., ♀, 42

Each speaker shows particular lexical items scattered over the vowel space: thus for L.A., *hand* has realizations that are quite front and close, as well as fairly central ones (the first mora roughly [ɪ] ~ [æ] – these charts tell us nothing clear about the second mora). But *hand* 'leads' for frontness over all other items, and no other -NC word reaches the same position; though *ask* is closer, if more central. If we look at L.R., we find again that *hand* is the frontest, but both *stand* and *ant* are closer, while *man* is intermediate, and *ran* is backer (this may be a phonetic effect, due to the preceding pharyngealized /r/). And R.C. shows, like the others, a very close *ask* (here almost as front as *hand*), but a much backer *stand*. In all cases *hand* seems to be the frontest of the -N(C) words, and *stand, can't, chance* are considerably backer. And so on; with more material, we would find more of the same kind of patterning.

Leaving aside the complex sociolinguistic factors involved here, the thing to note is the domain of the raising: while it's true, for instance, that the rule applies before -N(C), it's not equally true in degree (nor probably in frequency, though that information isn't available here) for all words. So we find that the word is a possible environment for variation as well, and in a historical change (which this data partly represents) a rule may be 'added' to a language not only with social and stylistic constraints, but with lexical ones as well. Some rules apply variably, that is, with respect to individual lexical items.

We have an immensely complex picture here, with numerous kinds of interlocking conditioning. A rule itself appears to be indexed for the statistics of its applicability with respect to extralinguistic factors (class, sex, style, etc.); and each lexical item it could potentially apply to is indexed with respect to the range of applications, primarily in terms of degree, but in most cases probably frequency as well. This kind of variability has profound implications for models of phonological change, as we'll see in ch. 13; we might say that without it, there would be no linguistic change at all.

## NOTES AND REFERENCES

12.2 There is not a great deal on casual speech as such available in easily accessible form; and still less is theoretically oriented. Much of the best material, which might serve as a basis for more theoretical treatments, is scattered in the form of incidental observations in works dealing with other subjects, or in particular language descriptions. For a good introduction to the general area, *Heffner (1950: ch. VII), which gives numerous examples. For particular languages, there is a wealth of information on English (RP), in Gimson (1962: ch. 10). Perhaps the most sophisticated and detailed treatment of the whole area is the account of English casual speech in *Brown (1977): probably the best work available on the phonetics/phonology of connected speech in general.

For theoretical work (with a good deal of data), there is the pioneering study by Zwicky (1972); see also Dressler (1973, 1975), and the detailed study of tempo/style hierarchies in Viennese German in **Dressler *et al.* (1972). For a recent treatment of this area in general, **Linell (1979: §§6.3.2, 10.3.4, 10.6.1, 10.7, 10.9–12). On the special area of 'phonostylistics' (the interrelationship of phonology and style), the classic work is that of Rubach (1977a, 1977b), which deals with Polish and English, as well as theoretical issues. For other studies, Hooper (1978) (with special reference to 'sonority' hierarchies and syllable structure); Cearley (1974) and Lee & Howard (1974) (rule ordering in casual speech).

12.3 The material in this section mainly represents the beginning of a research programme of my own, and I know of no literature precisely on this topic; though much of the materal cited above inspired this approach.

12.4 The literature on sociolinguistic variation is enormous: for bibliography see the references in Labov (1972, Labov *et al.* (1972), Hudson (1980), Chambers & Trudgill (1980), Romaine (1982). The work cited in this section is in a tradition pioneered by William Labov (1966), and carried on by many others (e.g. Trudgill 1974; the source of the Norwich example). For relatively accessible introductions to the study of variation, *Hudson (1980: ch. 5), *Chambers & Trudgill (1980: chs. 4–6, 9). For variable rules, **Labov (1972), Chambers & Trudgill (§§9.3–4). For a difficult but important critical study of the whole tradition of 'variationist' sociolinguistics, **Romaine (1982).

12.5 On the lexical dimension in variation, Chambers & Trudgill (§10.3) and references there; we will return to this issue in §§13.4.2ff.

# 13

# Phonological change

## 13.1 What changes? Phonetic change and phonologization

Throughout this book I have alluded to changes of various types, in different contexts: for purposes of theoretical argument (ME open syllable lengthening, §6.2, the GVS, §7.2), to illustrate process types (ch. 8), or in discussing the source of problematic MP alternations (Hungarian, ch. 9). I have called all these 'phonological changes', without being more specific, or trying to distinguish significantly different kinds of change. This chapter attempts to remedy this.

Just what do we mean by 'change'? The simple answer is: any appearance of a new phenomenon in the phonetic/phonological structure of a language, e.g. a new allophone, a new contrast, loss of an allophone or contrast, a new MP alternation or loss of an old one. But as this catalogue suggests, not all changes have the same status, or the same consequences for overall linguistic structure, or even involve the same mechanisms.

Let's start with a gross example. Consider the (impossible?) change from system I to II:

$$(13.1) \qquad \begin{array}{llll} i & u & y & \mathrm{ɯ} \\ e & o & \quad\rightarrow\quad \emptyset & \mathrm{ɣ} \\ & \mathrm{ɑ} & & \mathrm{ɒ} \\ \quad\quad\; \mathrm{I} & & \mathrm{II} \end{array}$$

From a phonemic point of view, nothing at all has happened; the systems have the same number of contrasts, the same spatial distributions, and the same type of oppositional structure: non-low vowels of opposite backness have opposite rounding, and the low vowel has the opposite rounding to the non-low members of its series, and the same rounding as the non-low members of the opposing series. If we

315

consider 'significant' change to be only structural or phonemic, then (13.1) is not a case of historical change.

But of course it is, and fairly major at that. This crude illustration suggests that we need to distinguish carefully between phonetic and phonemic change, but NOT to the extent of devaluing the former. One in fact is impossible without the other, and as we will see, just about everything rests in the end on phonetic change.

We will explore the possibilities raised by phonetic/phonological interaction in the course of language history by looking at a series of events in the early history of English. Before the advent of *i*-umlaut (§§8.2.1, 10.2.3), the ancestor of attested Old English had a phonemic system of this type:

(13.2)

| i꞉ | i | | u | u꞉ | | p | t | k |
|----|---|---|---|----|---|---|---|---|
| e꞉ | e | | o | o꞉ | | b | d | g |
| æ̌꞉ | æ | | ɑ | ɑ꞉ | | f | θ | x |
| | ɑi | ɑu | iu | | | | s | |
| | | | | | | m | n | |
| | | | | | | r l j | w | |

(Most of the consonants also occurred long as well.)

The following forms represent the categories we will be concerned with:

(13.3)    /kunjæ/ 'kin'          /guldjɑn/ 'gild'
          /kinni/ 'chin'         /geldjɑn/ 'yield'

At this period (call it stage 1), the only allophonic rule of note affecting these forms is GEMINATION: lengthening of consonants after a short vowel and before /j/:

(13.4)
$$\varnothing \rightarrow \begin{bmatrix} C \\ \alpha[\text{artic}] \end{bmatrix} / V \begin{bmatrix} C \\ \alpha[\text{artic}] \end{bmatrix} \underline{\quad} + j$$

So:

(13.5)                         Stage 1
          /kunjæ/ → [kunnjæ]     /guldjɑn/ → [guldjɑn]
          /kinni/ → [kinni]      /geldɑn/ → [geldɑn]

We have 'underlying' /nn/ vs. 'derived' [nn] from /Vnj/.

The first major change in the series leading to the modern pronunciation is a PALATALIZATION, of the type:

(13.6)    $\begin{bmatrix} k \\ g \end{bmatrix} \rightarrow \begin{bmatrix} c \\ ɟ \end{bmatrix} / \underline{\quad\quad} \begin{bmatrix} V \\ -\text{back} \end{bmatrix}$

The results are:

(13.7)

Stage II

/kunjæ/ → [kunnjæ]      /guldjɑn/ → [guldjɑn]
/kinni/ → [cinni]       /geldɑn/ → [ɟeldɑn]

In addition to the two kinds of geminates, we now have the alternations [k] ~ [c], [g] ~ [ɟ].

This is followed by I-UMLAUT, which fronts back vowels before a following palatal approximant (/i/ or /j/), giving us:

(13.8)

Stage III

/kunjæ/ → [kynnjæ]      /guldjɑn/ → [gyldjɑn]
/kinni/ → [cinni]       /geldɑn/ → [ɟeldɑn]

The phonemic structure is still intact; and now we have added the alternation [u] ~ [y] (for these forms; there are of course others as well, like [uː] ~ [yː], [o(ː)] ~ [ø(ː)], etc.). To clarify the sequence, here is a historical derivation representing the PHONETIC OUTPUTS of the stages so far:

(13.9)

|                  | /kunjæ/ | /kinni/ | /guldjɑn/ | /geldɑn/ |
|------------------|---------|---------|-----------|----------|
| Stage I          | kunnjæ  | kinni   | guldjɑn   | geldɑn   |
| Stage II (Pal)   | kunnjæ  | cinni   | guldjɑn   | ɟeldɑn   |
| Stage III (Uml)  | kynnjæ  | cinni   | gyldjɑn   | ɟeldɑn   |

Note that even at III, with the phonetic diversity produced by gemination, palatalization, and umlaut, there is still no systemic change; there are no new contrasts, and the parameters of distinctiveness are the same as before. All new phonetic material is predictable from context.

But now a series of changes occurs with dramatically different effects. These include (a) deletion of /j/ in post-root syllables; (b) deletion of /j/ and final vowels after heavy root syllables (e.g. VCC); and (c) other modifications, such as lowering of final /i/ to /e/. We'll be concerned here with (a–b).

The phonetic effects of this rule-complex, which I will call AFFIX MODIFICATION, (AM) for short, can be seen if we add another stage to derivation (13.9):

(13.10)     Stage ɪv (AM)     kynn     cinn     gyldɑn     ɟeldɑn

But these phonetic changes have produced three PHONEMIC effects:

(i) The distinction between derived and underlying [nn] (or any other geminates) vanishes, because gemination is no longer predictable from a following /j/. All geminates are now phonemic.

(ii) The allophonic alternation [u] ~ [y] becomes a phonemic contrast, since the trigger for [y] is no longer present.

(iii) Since we can no longer distinguish underlying and derived front vowels (by (ii)), the velar/palatal distinction becomes contrastive: there is no surface environment for predicting which front vowels will cause palatalization and which won't. (That is, at stage ɪɪɪ we could have a synchronic grammar with the rules Pal/Uml applying in that order; at stage ɪv, on any reasonably concrete analysis, that option is gone.)

Since the data has been selected to give forms as similar to each other as possible, one could object: after all, [k] and [c] could still be allophones of /k/, with [k] appearing before front vowels only if they're rounded. But we can dispose of this with some other forms, e.g. [kennɑn] 'to know' from stage ɪ /kɑnjɑn/ vs. [ceːn] 'torch' from stage ɪ/keːn/.

The primary systemic event here is **phonologization**: the development of contrastive status by former allophones, through loss of the conditioning environments. We now have phonemic /y c ɟ/. And the same for other vowel-sets, e.g. /yː/ in [dryːʝe] 'dry', stage ɪ /druːgi/, /ø/ in [døxter] 'daughters', stage ɪ /doxtri/, /øː/ in [føːt] 'feet', stage ɪ /foːti/.

### 13.2 **Split and merger**

The phonologization of front rounded vowels and palatal stops is **phonemic split**, which can be visualized this way:

(13.11)

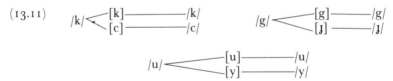

So the simple loss of certain elements in final syllables has produced a **restructuring**: instead of (13.2) we now have the more complex systems:

(13.12)

| iː | i | yː | y | u | uː | p | t | c | k |
|----|---|----|---|---|----|---|---|---|---|
| eː | e | øː | ø | o | oː | b | d | ɟ | g |
| æː | æ |    |   | ɑ | ɑː | f | θ |   | x |
|    |   |    |   |   |    |   | s |   |   |
|    | ɑu |   | ɑi | iu |  |  | m | n |   |
|    |   |    |   |   |    |   | r | l | j | w |

But there are further systemic effects. Since not all of the umlaut vowels are qualitatively different from their sources, the loss of environment can also produce the opposite result from split, (partial) **merger**. For example /æ/ umlauts to [e], which happens to be the value of /e/; and when the environments are lost, this [e] is indistinguishable from phonemic /e/. What starts as overlap (see §2.7) becomes a 'transfer' of allophones to a different phoneme. Thus /kænjɑn/ → [kennɑn], and the [e] here is the same as that in /ɟeldɑn/, etc. Similarly, the umlaut of /ɑː/ is [æː], producing another merger. So:

(13.13)     /æ/⟍―[æ]――/æ/

/e/――⟍[e]――/e/

But there is still more to this historical sequence. The next change affects the palatals produced at stage II, PALATAL SOFTENING. This is of the form:

(13.14)  $\begin{bmatrix} c \\ ɟ \end{bmatrix} \rightarrow \begin{bmatrix} tʃ \\ j \end{bmatrix}$

This is context-free, which is crucial. Note that in addition to [tʃ], which does not exist before, the other output is [j]; and there is already a /j/ in the system. The result here is a COMPLETE merger, not partial as in (13.13). So /ɟ/ vanishes from the system, and all of its allophones merge with those of /j/:

(13.15)       Merger          Old system          New system

/ɟ/⟍                    p  t  c  k          p  t  tʃ  k

⟍/j/          b  d  ɟ  g          b  d      g

/j/⟋                    · · ·                · · ·

r  l  j  w          r  l  j  w

This is a 'system-destroying' merger, unlike that of the [e]-allophones of /æ/ with /e/, which affects only the **lexical incidence** of a segment, not the shape of the system itself.

13.3 **Morphophonemic rules, morphologization, and analogy**

In §§13.1–2 we looked at two possible effects of purely phonetic change: phonologization through split following loss of conditioning environment, and loss of contrast through merger, either partial or complete. But both the processes and their effects were purely phonetic: there was no reference or relevance to higher-order categories.

Still remaining with Old English, we can move on to the next 'higher' stage in the effects of phonetic change: change in the status of alternations, from e.g. phonetic to morphophonemic. Let's return to *i*-umlaut: in the early stages, before the umlaut vowels were phonologized, it served a number of different roles:

(i) Non-alternating (lexical)

Numerous forms simply had final /i/ or /j/ in them, which umlauted back or low front vowels: /druːi/ 'magician' → [dryːi], /koːni/ 'keen' → [køːni], /kunjæ/ → [kynnjæ], etc. Here there are no paradigmatic alternations involved; after umlaut, a lexeme of this type simply had a different allophone of its stem vowel.

(ii) Alternating (morphological)

(a) Inflexional. Many OE paradigms had /i/ or /j/ in suffixes for certain members and not others. For example, nouns of the type /foːt/ 'foot' had /i/-suffixes in dative sg and nom/acc pl, but not elsewhere; and some verbs had /i/ suffixes in 2 and 3 person present indicative sg, but not in 1 sg or infinitive:

(13.16)

| Nom sg | foːt | Pres 1 sg | fɑre 'I go' |
|--------|------|-----------|-------------|
| Gen | foːtes | 2 sg | færis |
| Dat | føːti | 3 sg | færiθ |
| Acc | foːt | Inf | fɑrɑn |

(b) Derivational. Many productive derivational processes involved umlauting suffixes, e.g. the verb-forming /-jɑn/, which converted an adjective or noun to a verb, or the past sg of a strong verb to a causative (among other things):

(13.17)

| Simplex | Derived |
|---------|---------|
| trum 'firm' | trymmjɑn 'make firm' |
| bloːd 'blood' | bløːdjɑn 'bleed' |
| drɑːf 'he drove' | dræːfjɑn 'to herd' |

And so on. At this pre-OE stage, the umlaut alternations, while phonetically conditioned, have a potential morphological function: the suffixes are doing the primary 'work' of coding the morphological distinctions, but because of the morphological structure of certain forms, umlaut has an 'incidental' secondary coding function. There's no systemic distinction between lexical umlaut ([kynnjæ]) and morphological ([trymmjɑn]).

But what happens when the umlaut vowels are phonologized? There's a shift in the status of those forms where a morphological environment was responsible for umlaut; for with phonologization, the new phonemic alternations are **morphologized**: i.e. they are now MP alternations, and umlaut is an MP rule proper. Thus:

(13.18)  /trum/ ~ /trymmɑn/
         /bloːd/ ~ /bløːdɑn/
         /fɑre/ ~ /færeθ/
         /draːf/ ~ /dræːfɑn/

(Attested OE *trum/trymman, blōd/blēdan, fare/fær(e)þ, drāf/drǣfan.*)

Umlaut is now coded into the exponents of particular morphological categories or processes, and is as much a morphological indicator as the affixes themselves: thus 'umlaut + /eθ/' marks 3 sg, the vowel alternations mark 'simplex' vs. 'derived', and so on.

But observe: the shifts from allophonic to phonemic status, and from allophonic rule to MP rule, are all brought about by phonetic processes. The shift to MP is virtually an accident: purely the result of certain phonological configurations happening to occur in places that were also morphologically relevant (wherever else they might occur).

But this now opens up the possibility of a new use for umlaut. Once an alternation is no longer under phonetic control, the constraints on its use can be relaxed. If umlaut can signal (say) 'plural', then there's an option for its extension to forms that (historically) have no right to show it. Now in English this didn't happen; umlaut in fact retreated, and was displaced by the *-s* plural (otherwise the plurals of *book, nut* would be *\*beech, \*nit*: cf. German *Buch/Bücher, Nuβ/Nüβe*). But in German there was considerable extension, as in *Baum/Bäume* 'tree' (OHG *boum/bouma*), *Wort/Wörter* 'word' (OHG *wort/wort*), etc. And in Yiddish, which derives ultimately from various German dialects, umlaut has remained productive in this new sense into the 20th century: not only in early non-Germanic words like *toxes/texeser* 'arse', *kol/keler* 'voice' (from Hebrew), but late English borrowings like *švits-šop/-šeper* 'sweat-shop'.

This sort of redeployment of a rule, usually called **analogical extension**, is a clear sign of its death as a phonological rule, and its movement into the morphology. The death of a phonological rule, and its conversion to an MP rule, can have the contrary effect as well: the extension of umlaut to environments where it was not historically justified represents the encroachment of a 'minority' rule on an ever-increasing set of paradigms, but minority rules (as in English) can just as well retreat. In English the -*s* plural took over all but a handful of nouns; in Dutch, all the umlaut plurals disappeared, and were taken over by -*s* or -*n* plurals, both of which were commoner early types. This kind of reorganization is usually called **analogical levelling**.

## 13.4 The mechanism of sound change

### 13.4.1 *'Regularity' and reconstructability*

What exactly happens when 'a phonetic/phonological change occurs', or a language 'innovates'? Throughout this book so far I've treated changes as simple one-off 'events' in history: a rule $X \to Y$ is 'added to' a language, and a new segment results. This is a natural assumption; we characteristically see only the end results of a historical change (i.e. we only get the meal, and are not usually let into the kitchen: but see §§13.4.2–3 for a brief glimpse inside). And indeed with hindsight this is a more or less correct view – though it needs a more sophisticated treatment, as we'll see.

The reason we tend to think of the meal only and not the kitchen is the characteristic picture produced by historical change. For instance, consider the distribution of initial /p/ and /f/ in certain obviously related words in Indo-European dialects:

(13.19)   (a) *father*: Swedish *far*, Latin *patēr*, Greek *patēr*, Sanskrit *pitár*.
   (b) *farrow*: German *Ferkel* 'boar', L *porcus*, 'pig', Lithuanian *paršas* 'castrated pig'.
   (c) *foot*: Swed *fot*, L *pēd*-, Gr gen sg *podós*, Skr *pād*-, Lith *pādas*.
   (d) *-fold*: G *-flat*, l *du-plu-s* 'doubled', Gr *ha-pló-s* 'single'.
   (e) *five*: G *fünf*, Gr *pénte*, Skr *pañča*, Lith *penki*, Welsh *pump*.

(All orthographic forms or transliterations: all that counts is that *p* = /p/ and *f* = /f/.)

Regular correspondences like this are clearly due (a) to common origins for these forms in the parent language, and (b) to the fact that the changes that produced the forms in the daughter dialects were regular. In other words, we would reconstruct an ancestral */p-/ in all these items, and suggest that one of the definitions of the Germanic subfamily of Indo-European (English, German, Swedish ...) was 'a change of */p/ to /f/'. This backward projection of cross-language distributions into prehistory is called **comparative reconstruction**; and a great deal of our present, relatively secure knowledge of language history is based on this technique, applied to innumerable sets of attested forms like (13.19), in many language families. And its primary justification is the assumption that given regular correspondences, and presuming regular change (see below for more precise definition) we should be able to reverse the effects of change – providing of course that not all the languages change in parallel.

So on the basis of the Germanic /f/ and /p/ in the other dialects, we assume an innovation in the IE dialect ancestral to Germanic, of the form /p/ → /f/. And since we get similar stop/fricative correspondences at other places of articulation (*three*: L *trēs*, *heart*: L *cord-*), we actually have something like this:

(13.20)
$$\begin{bmatrix} +\text{obs} \\ -\text{cont} \\ -\text{voice} \end{bmatrix} \rightarrow [+\text{cont}]$$

(This is of course the spirantization subcase of Grimm's Law: §7.3.) And we even find that 'exceptions' to this are regular: e.g. the unspirantized stops in *star* ( = L *stella*), *spew* ( = L *spuō*) can be predicted from the preceding obstruent (a case of 'protection': see §8.3.2).

This regularity means further that we can distinguish native from borrowed forms: in English pairs like *father*:*paternal*, *heart*:*cardiac*, *three*:*triad*, the second member – since it does not show spirantization – must come from another IE language (here Latin, Greek, Latin respectively). And, in addition, we can use these clearcut correspondences to establish relations between less obvious forms: English *fly* and Lithuanian *plaũkti* 'swim', *feather* and the second element in L *acci-piter* 'hawk', Greek *ptéruks* 'wing', Sanskrit *pátati* 'he flies'. The phonological regularities allow us to recognize the validity of the less transparent semantic connections.

Such a procedure makes sense only under a strong regularity assumption: if phonological change were random the regularities could not arise. Thus /p t k/ → /f θ x/ in all Proto-Germanic morphemes containing them in the appropriate places. Sound change is envisioned as a relatively instantaneous and fundamentally exceptionless process. This view is often called the **Neogrammarian Hypothesis**, after a 19th-century school of German linguists who first formulated it as a working principle. The aim of the Neogrammarians was to make historical linguistics a 'science', which in the 19th-century context meant (crudely) a theoretical discipline with 'laws' like those of classical physics. (Indeed, the characteristic term for what we've been calling 'rules' or 'innovations' was *Lautgesetze* 'sound-laws'.) The basic principle was set out by Osthoff & Brugman (1878) as follows: 'every sound change, inasmuch as it occurs mechanically, takes place according to laws that admit no exception ... all words in which the sound subjected to the change appears in the same relationship are affected by the change'.

The methodological necessity of such a position is clear: as Osthoff & Brugman continue:

> Only he who adheres strictly to the principle of sound laws, this mainstay of our whole science, has firm ground under his feet ... There are, on the one hand, those who needlessly ... admit of exceptions to the sound laws governing a dialect, who except either individual words or classes ... from a sound change which has demonstrably affected all other forms of the same type, or who postulate a sporadic sound change which has taken place only in isolated forms ... and finally, there are those who will say that the same sound, in the very same environment, has changed in some words in one way, in other words another.

These three classes of 'irregularists', they say, end up as victims of 'subjectivism and arbitrariness'. And, on the face of it, they seem to be right: if sound change is not mechanical and exceptionless, unaffected by morphosyntax or lexis, how would we either (a) get the characteristic regular correspondences we do get, or (b) have any hope of reconstructing unattested language states?

13.4.2 *Lexical diffusion and the origin of regularity*

The Neogrammarian claim seems, paradoxically, to be both true and false. Globally it is true, or as close as makes no difference; locally it is probably always false. The next two sections are an attempt to justify this odd assertion, and make some sense of it.

Consider the reflexes of ME /a/ in certain environments in three dialects of English: E. Yorkshire standard, RP, and New York City standard:

| (13.21) | ME | -at# | -as# | -asC | -ad# | -an# |
|---|---|---|---|---|---|---|
| | Yorks | a | a | a | a | a |
| | RP | æ | ɑː | ɑː | æ | æ |
| | NYC | æ | æː | æː | æː | æː |
| | | *cat* | *pass* | *fast* | *bad* | *pan* |

This looks like a classic case of regular correspondence; on the basis of (13.21) we can reconstruct a reasonable scenario for the development of *cat, pass, bad*:

| (13.22) | | Yorks | | | NYC | | | RP | | |
|---|---|---|---|---|---|---|---|---|---|---|
| | ME input | kat | pas | bad | kat | pas | bad | kat | pas | bad |
| | (1) Raising | — | — | — | kæt | pæs | bæd | kæt | pæs | bæd |
| | (2) Lengthening | — | — | — | — | pæːs | bæːd | — | pæːs | — |
| | (3) Retraction | — | — | — | — | — | — | — | pɑːs | — |
| | Output | kat | pas | bad | kæt | pæːs | bæːd | kæt | pɑːs | — |

This accounts for the data; but in fact NYC and RP have a common ancestor, 17th-century Southern British English, and split from each other at a point (late 17th-early 18th century) subsequent to lengthening before /s/ and prior to lengthening before /d/ (as is obvious). This will be relevant shortly. So the true historical development would show common history up to the first lengthening, and separate histories during which RP undergoes retraction and NYC another lengthening:

(13.23)

| | | Common ancestor | | |
|---|---|---|---|---|
| | ME input | kat | pas | bad |
| | (1) Raising | kæt | pæs | bæd |
| | (2) Lengthening I | — | pæːs | — |

RP ——————————— NYC

| | Input | kæt | pæːs | bæd | | | Input | kæt | pæːs | bæd |
|---|---|---|---|---|---|---|---|---|---|---|
| | (3) Retraction | — | pɑːs | — | (3) Lengthening II | | — | — | bæːd |
| | Output | kæt | pɑːs | bæd | | | Output | kæt | pæːs | bæːd |

(Actually, Lengthening I occurs before /f θ s ns/, and Lengthening II before voiced stops, voiced fricatives, and nasals: see below.)

The eventual result is the vowel-length distribution in NYC described in §§2.10, 8.5. But as we noted, the allophonic lengthening rule has a number of exceptions, some systematic, others apparently unsystematic. And all are of one particular kind: short [æ] where we would expect long [æː]. To recapitulate, some major examples are: [æ] in *can* (aux), *have*, *has* vs. [æː] in *can* (n), *halve*, *jazz*; [æ] in *adze*, *cadge* vs. [æː] in *adds*, *badge*. The short vowels in auxiliary or potentially auxiliary verbs seem to reflect a morphosyntactic constraint on the allophonic rule; so, too, perhaps does short *and* (long *hand*). But *adze*, *cadge* seem unmotivated: they are just lexical idiosyncrasies.

In §2.10 I used these exceptions as examples of the problem of 'failure' of allophonic rules; but now that we see the origin of the length alternations in a historical perspective, things are more serious. If the plausible Neogrammarian account of change is valid, this is precisely the sort of correspondence we should not get: sound change is insensitive to morphosyntax and lexical identity.

Now note in addition that lengthening before /s/, etc. seems to be exceptionless: there are no phonetic *[æs], *[æf], and the like. So it looks as if one rule, Lengthening I, is 'Neogrammarian', while Lengthening II is not. Formally, the two rules would be of the same type, i.e.:

(13.24)

Lengthening I

$$\begin{bmatrix} V \\ +\text{front} \\ +\text{low} \end{bmatrix} \rightarrow [+\text{long}] / \underline{\quad} \begin{bmatrix} +\text{obs} \\ +\text{cont} \\ -\text{voice} \end{bmatrix} \begin{matrix} \# \\ C \end{matrix}$$

Lengthening II

$$\begin{bmatrix} V \\ +\text{front} \\ +\text{low} \end{bmatrix} \rightarrow [+\text{long}] / \underline{\quad} \left\{ \begin{matrix} \begin{bmatrix} +\text{obs} \\ +\text{voice} \end{bmatrix} \\ C \\ \begin{bmatrix} -\text{obs} \\ +\text{nas} \\ -\text{back} \end{bmatrix} \end{matrix} \right\}$$

So what's different is not the rules, but, apparently, something about how they applied.

Note now that the exceptionless rule is the older one, and the one with exceptions is the younger (by how much is uncertain, but I think at least a century or so). Now we can suggest a solution: the problem with the Neogrammarian model is that it is non-historical: it neglects TIME. That is, our 'punctual' model of the implementation of a change is wrong. Changes, apparently, need time to BECOME exceptionless; they don't start out that way.

What are we suggesting? A model in which a change is not to be looked at as an EVENT, but as a PERIOD in the history of a language. It looks as if change may be (a) gradual, (b) selective with respect to the lexicon, and (c) sensitive to morphosyntax.

Unfortunately, we have very little useful data on the progress of these lengthenings over time; but from information we have about other changes, in English and many other languages, it looks as if change typically proceeds by what is called **lexical diffusion**. Perhaps the best analogy to this is the course of an epidemic of infectious disease. A population consists of some members who are susceptible to infection, and some who are not; an epidemic begins with one or a few cases, and the rate of infection characteristically increases for a certain time, and more of the susceptible population are infected more quickly. Then the rate of infection begins to tail off, until the epidemic 'runs its course', and dies away – often leaving a good number of potentially eligible victims unaffected. The course of an epidemic, then, is typically representable as an S-curve of the sort shown in (13.25).

(13.25)

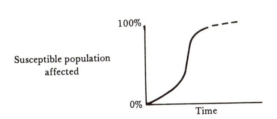

Just as an epidemic diffuses through a susceptible population in an S-curve of numbers against time, so a sound change diffuses through a lexicon – as far as we can tell from the cases that have been studied in detail. Here the items in the lexicon meeting the SD of the change are the susceptible population, and the change goes through this group, 'looking for' suitable items to 'infect'.

Given a curve like (13.25) as the normal course of a change, then, both the typical Neogrammarian regularity and the kind of irregularity shown by NYC /æ/ under Lengthening II fall out quite naturally. It's all a matter of where you happen to intersect the curve.

Thus we intersect the Grimm's Law curve after completion, but Lengthening II (apparently) somewhere before. This raises the possibility of a new phenomenon entirely: that a change will die before its incidence hits 100%. Lengthening I has gone all the way; Lengthening II has been caught somewhere near the top of its curve, perhaps in the end of the levelling-out phase. But we can't tell whether it will ever go to completion; a future generation of historians will have to decide that.

But things are more complicated still, as usual. To keep to our biological metaphor, changes are born, mature, and die; and sometimes they die before expected maturity. The metaphor is in fact apt, as the S-curve is the typical shape of growth processes in biological systems. We have an initial **lag phase**, when the process in question is getting organized, followed by a steeply rising curve (**log phase**, for mathematical reasons that don't concern us here), and a flattening-out as the process slows down, approaching the maximum growth supportable by the environment, i.e. an **equilibrium**.

In Lengthening II, we have intersected a growth curve either approaching equilibrium, or at an equilibrium point just short of 100% implementation. But there's another possibility we haven't considered, which is that a change may never get out of the lag phase, but, to coin a term, may **abort**. That is, if we find a change that has only affected a few items, it might be that we've caught the lag phase of a normal curve; but if there has been no progress towards log phase for, say, several centuries, then we may assume an aborted curve. The change has got started, but never proceeded, and left the bulk of its population of potential victims unaffected.

A case in point is the nuclei of standard Southern English *food* (/uː/), *good* (/ʊ/), *blood* (/ʌ/), all of which etymologically have ME /oː/. By the Great Vowel Shift (§7.2), the expected reflex of ME /oː/ is /uː/; so we should, if change is Neogrammarian, have \*/guːd/, \*/bluːd/. The two 'deviant' nuclei arise as follows. In the 17th century, there was a change whereby all short /u/ became /ʌ/; later on, any short /u/ that happened to arise (by, say, shortening of /uː/) were unaffected, as the /u/ → /ʌ/ change had reached the end of its curve. Such /u/ became /ʊ/ by a later stage.

Thus *blood* represents the result of an early shortening of /uː/ from ME /oː/ (Shortening I), and *good* a later shortening of /uː/ (Shortening II). Diagrammatically:

(13.26)

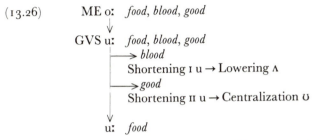

ME oː   *food, blood, good*

GVS uː   *food, blood, good*
⊢⟶ *blood*
    Shortening ɪ u → Lowering ʌ
⊢⟶ *good*
    Shortening ɪɪ u → Centralization ʊ

uː   *food*

Let's call /uː/ forms 'normal', /ʌ/ forms 'Short ɪ', and /ʊ/ forms 'Short ɪɪ'. If we look at a large population of susceptible items, we find a curious distribution:

(13.27)   *'Normal'*: broom, boon, boot, booth, brood, broom, cool, coop, doom, food, goose, gloom, groom, groove, hoop, lose, loose, loom, loon, mood, moon, moor, moot, noon, noose, ooze, pool, poop, proof, roof, root, shoot, smooth, snood, soon, soothe, spoon, stool, tool, tooth
    *'Short ɪ'*: blood, flood, glove
    *'Short ɪɪ'*: book, brook, cook, crook(ed), foot, good, hook, hoof, hood, look, poor, rook, shook, soot, took, wood

So 'normal' items represent a full curve, i.e. the uninterrupted development of the /oː/ → /uː/ change; but the other two categories show curves aborted in lag phase; only this small group of items seems to have been hit by the shortenings. (In some dialects, e.g. in the north of England, even fewer forms are Short ɪɪ: of the list here only *foot, good, hood, wood*, seem consistently short, the others having /uː/.)

We can see now that the LEXICON is in a sense the key, the primary domain for phonological change (even if the innovations, in the end, are statable in phonological terms). Sound change is characteristically **lexically gradual**, and diffuses over time. Neogrammarian 'regularity' is not a mechanism of change proper, but a result. The Neogrammarian Hypothesis might better be called the 'Neogrammarian Effect': Sound change TENDS TO BECOME REGULAR, given enough time, and if curves go to completion.

13.4.3   *Phonetic gradualness: variation and change*
    So phonological change is lexically gradual, and the classical regular correspondences arise only when we intersect completed diffusion curves. But even the more complex S-curve model, with its time-dimension, is an oversimplification: there's still another

'irregularity' to consider. Recall the data on New York [æː]-raising in §12.5. We saw there that a given speaker may have a number of different realizations of the nucleus resulting from that process, and that not only are different words affected to different degrees, but even tokens of the same lexical item may occur with different nuclei in utterances of the same speaker.

Let's put this in a historical perspective. We know from external evidence that the 'oldest' type of nucleus here is [æː] – i.e. the output of Lengthening I or II, depending on environment. And the 'youngest' or most innovatory type is the very close [ɪə]. The direction of the shift has been upward, with diphthongization supervening at about the point (in 'articulatory space' and time) when the value [ɛ] for the first mora is reached. Extrapolating from the formant charts (12.22–4), and assigning rough transcriptions to particular positions, we can find something like this for selected words:

(13.28)  (i)  L.A. *hand*: [ǣː] ~ [ɛ̈ə] ~ [ɪə]
         (ii) L.R. *ask*: [ɛə] ~ [ɛ̈ə] ~ [ɪ̈ə]

That is: each speaker has (from this data) at least three possible nuclei for each word; and the nuclei cover a range from quite near the oldest type of form to the most innovating. And the same pattern is clear for other lexical items as well.

This seems to be characteristic of change in progress: the most innovatory forms coexist with considerably older types, at least at certain points. And the change proper is completed largely by alterations in the frequency of particular types (as well as the introduction of new ones, following the overall 'direction' of the change). As time goes on the newer forms constitute an increasing proportion of speaker output, and the older ones gradually disappear.

We can model this in a simple way, taking arbitrary (but not improbable) figures for the frequency of forms at varying stages along the phonetic growth-curve of a change for a given lexical item. Imagine the change [æː] → [ɪə] going to completion by this kind of innovation-and-variation process: the precursor to the lag phase is a 100% frequency for [æː], and the end of the tail-off is 100% for [ɪə]. So we might have:

(13.29)   Input:       [æː] (100)
          Lag-onset:   [æː] (90) ~ [ɛə] (10)
          Stage 1:     [æː] (30) ~ [ɛə] (50) ~ [eə] (20)

Stage 2:      [ɛə] (30) ~ [eə] (50) ~ [ɪə] (20)
Stage 3:      [eə] (20) ~ [ɪə] (80)
Completion:   [ɪə] (100)

(This is of course only a schematic idea of the KIND of thing that happens, not a set of accurate 'real' figures, or a typical number of stages. Indeed, we really don't have figures for the entire course of a curve like this, because the idea that such processes are observable is not much more than two decades old, and no one change has been studied in real time from beginning to end. But the partial results we have so far suggest this type of process.)

We have now added two new dimensions to our picture of change: alongside lexical gradualness we have (variable) **phonetic gradualness** (see §13.4.4 for another aspect of this). Given a correspondence of input A and output B, the arrow in the expression 'A → B' is actually a shorthand representation of increase of B-frequency and decrease of A-frequency (plus relations of the same kind between increasingly innovative 'intermediate' forms).

Now presumably a pattern like (13.29) would hold for each affected lexical item; though groups of items may of course enter the curve simultaneously or nearly so. Thus the whole curve for a change like [æː] → [ɪə] would really be the sum of a set of overlapping curves, with each item at a different 'place' on its curve, and each place being some kind of average over a set of variants. But all the curves – perhaps at varying rates – would be heading in the same direction.

So the overall smooth S-curve for a change is an abstraction from (a) individual lexical curves, and (b) variable and phonetically gradual phonetic implementation along these curves. But the final historical effect is a levelling-out, so that the single-curve abstraction in fact BECOMES TRUE of the change as a whole. Thus we distinguish, in the broader historical perspective, between the change-as-a-whole and the piecemeal mechanism of its implementation.

This is a very important conceptual distinction, which many scholars (in particular the 'generative' school) still fail to make. Change is never 'catastrophic'; it only looks that way if we intersect a curve at two points sufficiently far apart, and neglect (or, as is more often the case, do not have available) the details of transition. But since contemporary studies of change in progress seem to reveal the variation-and-diffusion pattern with great consistency, we must always assume it to have been the case in the past as well.

331

But note that this kind of interpretation is neither a 'refutation' of the Neogrammarian Hypothesis (strictly), nor an indication that it's wrong to talk about a language 'innovating by adding a rule $A \rightarrow B$'. It's all a matter of perspective, and what we happen to be interested in. So from the viewpoint of the history of English it is perfectly correct to say that the GVS involved 'a rule raising /oː/ to /uː/', even though this must have proceeded variably, and in small steps, and was interrupted by sporadic changes. And from the Indo-European or Germanic viewpoint the Grimm's Law spirantization included '/p/ → /f/' – even though this surely involved at least one intermediate stage ( [pf] or [pʰ], see lenition hierarchy (8.13) ). The only place in fact where the Neogrammarian model is clearly wrong is in disallowing sporadic change; and this is largely the result of their not having had the information available for looking at change in the double perspective of input–output relations AND progress through time. Once we allow for progress-curves of a certain shape, and the possibility of abortion in lag phase, we can fit sporadic change as well into a unified – if very complex – model. It is no different in principle from 'regular' change, since all regular change is sporadic in lag phase; it's all a matter of completion.

### 13.4.4 *Phonetic gradualness and 'missing links'*

When we say that phonetic change is 'gradual' we don't – or shouldn't – necessarily mean that it's 'infinitely' gradual, as some writers have supposed. Indeed, the classic argument against the notion of gradualness (misinformed, but influential) is that it implies 'infinitesimal' change, and allows no principled limits on the size of the intermediate steps between input and output (King 1969). This purports to make gradualness an incoherent concept, but fails to, as we'll see, since the problem is a false one.

We can approach this through individual variation, which as we've seen is the prime mechanism of change anyway. Consider one simple type of change, lenition (§8.3). We already know that Germanic voiceless fricatives and /h/ arise from original voiceless stops, via the Grimm's Law spirantization (§13.4.1): how many stages (if any) ought we to assume between, say, an input [p] and output [f], or [k] and [h]? Or, to take a more extreme case, between an input [p] and output zero, as in the development of IE initial */p/ in Old Irish (L *pater*:OIr *athir*, L *porcus*:OIr *orc*, L *piscis* 'fish':OIr *īasc*). Is there any evidence for the type and/or degree of gradualness we ought to posit?

One possibility is to project, from the range of lenition, variants in the output of a speaker of some language, and check this against other evidence. The argument to follow is intricate and partly speculative, but it gives an idea of how a number of different types of evidence might converge on this problem. The primary justification for this strategy is simple: a speaker can serve as a potential model for a historical process, since community-wide change over time presupposes a summation of individual changes, and a study of the individual might give us an idea of **speaker capability**. In particular, how large or small are the units or **'quanta'** of variation, and hence of change? That is, if a speaker controls the possibility of 'going from' one segment to another lower down the hierarchy (8.13) this movement may be taken as a possible quantum or basic unit: a move of that size is a 'possible sound change'.

I will use my own speech as a first example. Looking at careful pronunciations, we find that voiceless stops occur in two non-coarticulated forms: unaspirated [p t k] and aspirated [pʰ tʰ kʰ]. The range [k]–[kʰ], then, might be a candidate for a quantum. Looking further, into CS variants, we find that initial [kʰ] can appear as [kx] or [x]: CF [kʰʌm] 'come', CS [kxʌm] ~ [xʌm]. This corresponds to a sub-sequence of the hierarchy:

(13.30)

So we needn't, perhaps, invoke any steps smaller than these. But can we get directly from say [k] to [x] without an intervening aspirate or affricate? In weak intervocalic position (V̇___V), the evidence is that we can: the variants [bækɪŋ], [bæxɪŋ] 'backing' appear, but not as far as I can tell *[bækxɪŋ]. So it looks as if direct intervocalic spirantization of a voiceless stop is legal, but there are some doubts about initial position (for this language anyhow).

So we do have some (weak) support for the legality of a direct Stop → Fricative move (though in a historical-developmental context, with variation of course). But what about the development of initial /h/ in Germanic, from IE */k/ (*heart*: L *cord-*)? Can we go directly from [k] to [h]? The evidence I know of from English and other IE languages, as well as non-IE ones (see below) suggests that this is too big a jump: we need an intervening oral fricative as a prelude to a de-oralized one (§§6.5, 8.3.1). For example, the only cases I have of substitution of [h] for something else involve /θ/ ([hǽŋks] 'thanks', etc.); and there are other well-documented cases of /h/ from voiceless fricatives, e.g. in Greek (*hépta* 'seven', cf. L *septem* which represents an older type), and in contemporary Spanish where /s/ ~ /h/ is common. This kind of material suggests that [k] → [x] → [h] is possible, but not [k] → [h] (we will return to this shortly).

And a look at the Germanic evidence suggests that this argument is reasonably sound. Original */k/ shows up as /h/ initially in most cases (*heart*, G *Herz*), and in some cases (non-initially) as /x/ (G *Nacht* 'night', cf. L *noct-*). And even in English some dialects retain /x/ here, e.g. varieties of Scots with /nɛxt/, /nixt/.

And what about deletion? We've established that it might be reasonable to posit a stage (say) */xert/ in the development of *heart*, *Herz*; and the English loss in *night* clearly goes via [x], and probably, by analogy, [h]: so somewhere between */nixt/ and late ME /niːt/ (the predecessor of modern /nait/), we might want to suggest *[niht]. And we know that [h] can delete, since we have evidence from forms under low stress in virtually all varieties of English (e.g. [ɪm] 'him'), and the general or sporadic loss in many others. All of this suggests that we might be able to formulate 'size-principles' for consonant change, particularly lenition. A few representative principles or constraints might be:

(13.31)  (i)  No obstruent except [h] may delete.
         (ii) Stop → Fricative is allowed, but (probably) non-preferred; Stop → Affricate/Aspirate → Fricative is better, perhaps more so initially than medially.
         (iii) Stop → [h] is disallowed, but Fricative → [h] is legal and in fact expectable.

These principles are projected from synchronic data, with a little historical backup; and this gives us a kind of 'anchor' for the more speculative thinking we have to do when direct historical testimony is lacking.

But (13.31) needs some revision. For instance, many dialects of English with '[ʔ] for /t/' (§§6.5, 12.4) seem to contravene (13.31(i)). These are, as far as I know, always really cases of [ʔt] → [ʔ], i.e.

[t]-deletion. And there are frequent losses of stops in clusters, e.g. in speakers with [hændz] ∼ [hænz] 'hands', but no *[hænðz], *[hænhz]. So we must probably adopt a less restrictive version of (13.31(i)), like:

(13.32)     (i′)  No oral obstruent may delete directly, except: (a) if it is part of a multiple articulation, or (b) part of a homorganic cluster.

> *Rider*: This condition may be further weakened if there is a language-internal or universal prohibition on what MIGHT result from implementation of the preferred principle.

The language-internal rider would operate for English in blocking *[nðz], *[nhz], which never appear under any circumstances. And there may be a universal constraint against sequences of the [nhz] type, which demand two glottal-state changes and two orality changes in one coda.

This sounds like fudging (and indeed it partly is). But in the current state of our knowledge it looks as if we haven't much choice. The point is that there are probably general principles governing the size of possible moves in sound change (here using lenition as a simple example); and that, since nothing ever happens in isolation, these will interact with language-specific phonotactics, and general constraints stemming from preferred and non-preferred gesture-sequences, determined by 'preferences' of the human articulatory machinery and its users.

This very preliminary argument is not a hard-and-fast theory, but an indication of how to go about making one, and a guess about what it would look like. We can at least see that infinite graduality does not have to be seriously considered as a mechanism of change; and that there are reasonable arguments for deriving a theory of the size of possible sound changes from an examination of the size of possible distances between synchronic variants.

This could have profound implications for the accounts we give of language history. Let's take a simple example: if principle (13.31(i)) or its variant (13.32(i′)) are essentially correct, and if (13.31(iii)) is well-founded, we must look afresh at certain historical correspondences, and reinterpret them. Consider these two correspondence-sets:

(13.33)     (a) Indo-European
                    L porcus  :        OIr orc
                       pater  :            athir
                       piscis  :            īasc
            (b) Dravidian
                    Tamil pōku  :  Kannaḍa hōgu      'go'
                         pāl  :            hālu      'milk'
                         pal  :            hallu     'tooth'

In the IE cases, we have a /p/ : φ correspondence; in Dravidian we have /p/ : /h/. Are these genuine correspondences, or ought the picture to be more complex? For IE, we have evidence from other dialects suggesting that there was at least one intermediate stage, namely /f/, between /p/ and zero. That is, in Germanic (*farrow, father, fish*). This suggests that we ought to reconstruct at least [p] → [f] → [h] → φ for Old Irish as well: i.e. it has gone 'one step further' than Germanic, but without leaving evidence of the intermediate stage (perhaps as a function of the time the language was written down with respect to its development). And in fact there are some scattered items in Celtic that seem to confirm the end of this: Irish *én* 'bird' (cf. L *penna*) and Old Cornish *hethen* 'bird'; and perhaps OIr *hil* 'many' (cf. OE *fela*, Gr *polús*). These might be relics of aborted lexical diffusion; but they tend to support the general principle, and argue that given the synchronic variation evidence, plus more certain historical material, we ought to assume the intermediate stage [h].

Going further afield, consider the following reflexes of Proto-Uralic */-k-/:

(13.34)   Finnish     Yurak     Yenisei Samoyed     Vogul
          -k-         -h-       -h-                 ∅

If we had only Finnish *joki* 'river', and Vogul (*jõõ* (*õõ* = [ɤː]), we'd posit direct [k] → φ; but fortunately we have in the dialects a kind of overall picture of the change, preserving various stages, and supplying our [h]. And the Germanic material cited earlier suggests that we ought to have [x] as well; this is missing, but we can supply it now with some confidence.

We can now turn this class of interlocking arguments on to the Dravidian /p/:/h/ correspondence. Here we have only these two segments, and no dialects with initial fricatives. But the evidence we've been looking at from other languages suggests that the Oral stop → Oral fricative → [h] sequence is so much the commonest type that in the absence of strong counter-evidence we ought to assume it: thus an intervening [f] or [ɸ] in Dravidian.

So we project from actual surviving data to a history, using principles derived largely from variation in currently observable languages, and bolstered by those histories we know in more detail. The picture we then get is like this:

(13.35)

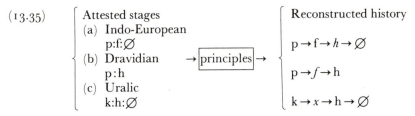

| Attested stages | Reconstructed history |
|---|---|
| (a) Indo-European p:f:∅ | p → f → *h* → ∅ |
| (b) Dravidian → principles → p:h | p → *f* → h |
| (c) Uralic k:h:∅ | k → *x* → h → ∅ |

Our principles have provided us with hitherto unsuspected **missing links** (as I like to call them): we have used synchronic observation to create history. And note that by using the lenition hierarchy as a template against which to look at history, we can say that given correspondences [p]:[h]:ɸ, this represents a SEQUENCE of developmental types: even though of course there is no ancestor–descendant relation among the three dialects in question (Germanic isn't 'older than' Celtic, etc.). In fact, what we are saying is this:

(13.36)

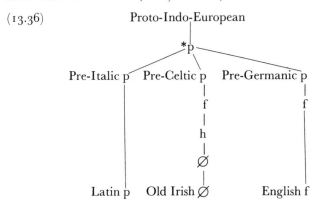

A correspondence [p]: ∅ then implies that the ∅-dialect went through the stages [f], [h] if it started from [p]. And similar arguments can be constructed for all types of change, though some (like vowel change) are more difficult.

But a word of warning: the fact that some types of change are gradual (and this applies to most) doesn't mean that all are. In particular, at least two types (true metathesis §8.4.3 and epenthesis §8.4.1) are in general clearly not. You can apparently get from zero to something immediately, but not from something to zero, except within very strict limits. And some articulatory changes as well, like the /x/ → /f/ change in English (*rough, laugh* from OE *rūh, hlæhhan*), or velar → labial in Rumanian (*opt* 'eight', *lemn* 'wood', Latin *octo, lignum*), are also clearly non-gradual.

## NOTES AND REFERENCES

13.1 For a thorough (if dated) introduction to the study of phonological change, *Bloomfield (1933: chs. 20–1); see also *Hockett (1958: chs. 41–54). On the relations between phonetic change and phonologization, see the classic study of *i*-umlaut by *Twaddell (1939), and Hill (1936); also Hockett (1958: chs. 52–4).

The account of Old English here and in §§13.2–3 is rather conservative and 'concrete'; for a more radical and 'abstract' account, within the GP framework, Lass & Anderson (1975).

13.2 The classic treatment of split and merger is **Hoenigswald (1960). For other accounts Hockett (1958: ch. 53), Bynon (1977: chs. 1–2). In general my treatment here (as might be gathered from the views on abstractness in ch. 9) is rather traditional and 'surfacist'; for discussion of phonological change in the TG tradition see the pioneering (though now dated) treatment in *King (1969), and the exposition in *Bynon (1977: ch. 3). The first three chapters of Bynon give a good historical overview of changing interpretations of sound change and its relation to linguistic structure.

13.3 On analogy, *Bloomfield (1933: ch. 23), Hockett (1958: chs. 50–1), **Anttila (1972: ch. 5), Bynon (1977: ch. 1, 5–5.2).

13.4.1 On regularity and reconstruction, Bloomfield (1933: ch. 18), Hockett (1958: chs. 57–60), **Anttila (1972: chs. 10–13), Bynon (1977: ch. 1, §§1.3–7.2).

13.4.2–3. The best introduction to the theory of lexical diffusion is a very important paper by **Chen (1972). See also Chen & Hsieh (1971), and Chen & Wang (1975), and their references. The material on ME /a/ and its developments is based largely on Lass (1976a: ch. 3).

13.4.4 On 'missing links', see **Lass (1978), which sets out (in a slightly over-enthusiastic way) the principles behind this section.

# APPENDIX
# PHONETIC AND OTHER
# SYMBOLS

The phonetic symbols used in this book are those of the IPA; the only major departure is the use of [ä] for a low central vowel, instead of IPA [ɐ]. In the charts below I have placed in parentheses alternate symbols which you are likely to find in writings in non-IPA traditions; below each chart is a list of diacritic markings which should help you to interpret unfamiliar symbols in the book.

Vowels

In the chart below, R = rounded, UR = unrounded.

| | Front | | Centralized | | Central | | Centralized | | Back | |
|---|---|---|---|---|---|---|---|---|---|---|
| | UR | R | UR | R | UR | R | UR | R | UR | R |
| Close | i | y (ü) | | | ɨ | ʉ | | | ɯ | u |
| Half-close | e | ø (ö) | ɪ (ɩ) | ʏ | ɘ | ɵ | ÿ | ʊ(ѻ) | ɤ | o |
| Half-open | ɛ | œ (ɜ) | | | ɜ | | | | ʌ | ɔ |
| Raised | | | | | | | | | | |
| open | æ | | | | | | | | | |
| Open | a | | | | ä | | | | ɑ | ɒ |

(Blanks in the chart do not represent non-existent segment types, but rare ones, or ones not mentioned in this book.)

Diacritics: [V:] = long; [V·] = half-long; [Ṽ] = nasalized; [V̟] = advanced; [V̠] = retracted; [V̞] = lowered; [V̇] = centralized; [V̥] = voiceless; [V̯] = non-syllabic.

Notes

(a) In some traditions, e.g. much U.S. writing, [æ] covers both [æ] and [a], and [a] is often used for [ɑ]. This has to be figured out from context.

(b) Generalized symbol for central non-close, non-open V: [ə].

(c) Diphthongs are always written as vowel-sequences, e.g. [ai]; some writers tend to use [j w] for non-syllabic close vowels, e.g. [aj] = [ai].

# Appendix

## Consonants

| | Bilabial | Labiodental | Dental | Alveolar | Alveo-Palatal |
|---|---|---|---|---|---|
| Stop | p  b | | ʈ  ɖ | t  d | t  ɖ |
| Fricative | Φ  β | f  v | θ  ð | s  z | ɕ  ʑ |
| Nasal | m | ɱ | ṇ | n | |
| Lateral | | | ƛ | l | |
| Trill | | | | r | |
| Tap | | | | ɾ | |
| Approximant | | ʋ | | ɹ | |

| | Palato-alveolar | Retroflex | Palatal | Velar | Uvular | Pharyngeal |
|---|---|---|---|---|---|---|
| Stop | | ʈ  ɖ | c  ɟ | k  g | q  G | |
| Fricative | ʃ  ʒ | ʂ  ʐ | ç  j | x  ɣ | χ  ʁ | ħ  ʕ |
| Nasal | | ɳ | ɲ | ŋ | N | |
| Lateral | | ɭ | ʎ | | | |
| Trill | | | | R | | |
| Tap | | ɽ | | | | |
| Approximant | | ɻ | j | ɰ | | |

Diacritics:   [C̃] = nasalized;   [C̥] = voiceless;   [C̟] = advanced; [C̠] = retracted;   [C͡C] = double articulation;   [C̡] = palatalized (also [Cʲ]); [Cʰ] = aspirated; [Cʷ] = labialized; [Cᵒ] = unreleased.

## Notes

(a) In paired symbols above, the first is voiceless, the second voiced.

(b) Affricates are usually represented as stop + fricative sequences, though [č ǰ] for palato-alveolar/palatal affricates are common, as are [c ʒ] for [ts dz] (mainly in Slavonic linguistics).

(c) Ejectives (glottalic egressives) are indicated as [p' t' k'], etc.; implosives (glottalic ingressives) as [ɓ ɗ ɠ], etc.; breathy voiced (murmured) segments as [b̤ d̤ g̈], etc.

(d) Special symbols for double articulations: [ɥ] = labial/palatal approximant; [w] = labial-velar approximant.

(e) Voiceless glottal fricative [h]; voiced glottal fricative [ɦ]; glottal stop [ʔ].

(f) Lateral fricatives: [ɬ] voiceless, [ɮ] voiced.

(g) Clicks: [ʇ] dental, [c] post-alveolar, [ʖ] lateral.

## Non-phonetic symbols

| | |
|---|---|
| → | is realized as; becomes; is rewritten as |
| ≡ | is equivalent to |
| ≠ / ≢ | is not equal/equivalent to |

| | |
|---|---|
| [  ] | phonetic representation; in generative phonology, any non-underlying representation |
| /  / | phonemic/phonological representation |
| > | precedes; is hierarchically preferred to |
| {  } | morphemic representation; disjunction of elements; set of elements (depending on context) |
| ~ | varies with; negation (e.g. X ~ Y 'X varies with Y', ~ X 'not X') |
| < | is less than |

# REFERENCES

The following abbreviations for journals, publishers, etc. have been used throughout:

BSOAS        *Bulletin of the School of Oriental and African Studies*
CLS          *Papers from the Regional Meetings, Chicago Linguistic Society*
FL           *Foundations of Language*
JL           *Journal of Linguistics*
Lg           *Language*
LI           *Linguistic Inquiry*
TCLP         *Travaux du Cercle Linguistique de Prague*
TPS          *Transactions of the Philological Society*
UCLA WPP     *UCLA Working Papers in Phonetics*
WLG          *Wiener Linguistische Gazette*

Abercrombie, D. (1967). *Elements of general phonetics*. Chicago: Aldine.

Albrow, K. H. (1966). Mutation in spoken North Welsh. In Bazell *et al.* (1966).

(1975). Prosodic theory, Hungarian and English. *Grazer Linguistische Studien* 2.5–20.

Allen, W. S. (1951). Some prosodic aspects of retroflexion and aspiration in Sanskrit. *BSOAS* 13.939–46. Repr. Palmer (1970).

(1962). *Sandhi*. The Hague: Mouton.

(1973). *Accent and rhythm*. Cambridge: CUP.

Anderson, J. M. (1969). Syllabic or non-syllabic phonology. *JL* 5.136–43.

(1971). *The grammar of case*. Cambridge: CUP.

(1975). Principles of syllabification. *York Papers in Linguistics* 5.7–20.

(1977). *On case grammar*. London: Croom Helm.

(1980). On the internal structure of phonological segments: evidence from English and its history. *Folia Linguistica Historica* 1.165–91.

Anderson, J. M. & Ewen, C. (1980a). *Studies in dependency phonology*. Ludwigsburg Studies in Language and Linguistics, 4.

(1980b). Introduction: a sketch of dependency phonology. In Anderson & Ewen (1980a).

Anderson, J. M. & Jones, C. (1974a). Three theses concerning phonological representations. *JL* 10.1–26.

(1974b). *Historical linguistics*, 1. Amsterdam: North-Holland.

(1977). *Phonological structure and the history of English*. Amsterdam: North-Holland.

Anderson, S. R. (1974). *The organization of phonology*. New York: Academic Press.

(1976). Nasal consonants and the internal structure of segments. *Lg* 52.326–44.

(1982). The analysis of French shwa. *Lg* 58.534–73.

Anttila, R. (1972). *An introduction to historical and comparative linguistics*. New York: Macmillan.

Árnason, K. (1980). *Quantity in historical phonology: Icelandic and related cases*. Cambridge: CUP.

# References

Asher, R. E. (1966). The verb in spoken Tamil. In Bazell *et al.* (1966).

Bach, E. & Harms, R. T. (1968). *Universals in linguistic theory*. New York: Holt, Rinehart & Winston.

Basbøll, H. (1977). The structure of the syllable and a proposed hierarchy of distinctive features. In Dressler & Pfeiffer (1977).

(1981). On the function of boundaries in phonological rules. In Goyvaerts (1981).

Bazell, C. E., Catford, J. C., Halliday, M. A. K. & Robins, R. H. (1966). *In memory of J. R. Firth*. London: Longmans.

Bell, A. & Hooper, J. B. (1978). *Syllables and segments*. Amsterdam: North-Holland.

Bendor-Samuel, J. T. (1960). Some problems of segmentation in the phonological analysis of Terena. *Word* 16.348–55. Repr. Palmer (1970).

Bloch, B. (1941). Phonemic overlapping. *American Speech* 16.278–84. Repr. Joos (1957), Makkai (1972a).

(1948). A set of postulates for phonemic analysis. *Lg* 24.3–46.

Bloomfield, L. (1933). *Language*. New York: Holt.

(1939). Menomini morphophonemics. *TCLP* 8.105–15. Repr. Makkai (1972a).

Botha, R. P. (1971). *Methodological aspects of transformational-generative phonology*. The Hague: Mouton.

Bright, W. (1966). Dravidian metaphony. *Lg* 66.311–22.

Brosnahan, L. F. & Malmberg, B. (1970). *Phonetics*. Cambridge: CUP.

Brown, G. (1970). Syllables and redundancy rules in generative phonology. *JL* 6.1–18.

(1972). *Phonological rules and dialect variation*. Cambridge: CUP.

(1977). *Listening to spoken English*. London: Longmans.

Bruck, A., Fox, R. A. & La Galy, M. W. (1974). *Papers from the parasession on natural phonology, April 18, 1974*. Chicago: CLS.

Bynon, T. (1977). *Historical linguistics*. Cambridge: CUP.

Carnochan, J. (1951). A study of quantity in Hausa. *BSOAS* 13.1032–44. Repr. Palmer (1970).

(1960). Vowel harmony in Igbo. *African Language Studies* 1.155–63. Repr. Palmer (1970).

Catford, J. C. (1977a). *Fundamental problems in phonetics*. Edinburgh: University of Edinburgh Press.

(1977b). Mountain of tongues: the languages of the Caucasus. *Annual Review of Anthropology* 6.283–314.

Cearley, A. (1974). The only phonological rule ordering principle. In Bruck *et al.* (1974).

Chalmers, A. F. (1978). *What is this thing called science?* Milton Keynes: Open University Press.

Chambers, J. K. & Trudgill, P. (1980). *Dialectology*. Cambridge: CUP.

Chao, Y-R. (1934). The non-uniqueness of phonemic solutions of phonetic systems. *Bulletin of the Institute of History and Philology, Academia Sinica*, IV, 4.363–97. Repr. Joos (1957).

Chen, M. (1972). The time dimension: contribution toward a theory of sound change. *FL* 8.457–98.

(1974). Natural phonology from a diachronic viewpoint. In Bruck *et al.* (1974).

Chen, M. & Hsieh, H. I. (1971). The time variable in phonological change. *JL* 7.1–14.

Chen, M. & Wang, W. S-Y. (1975). Sound change: actuation and implementation. *Lg* 51.255–81.

Chomsky, N. (1957). *Syntactic structures*. The Hague: Mouton.

(1965). *Aspects of the theory of syntax*. Cambridge, Mass.: MIT Press.

(1972). *Language and mind*. New York: Holt, Rinehart & Winston.

Chomsky, N. & Halle, M. (1966). Some controversial questions in phonological theory. *JL* 1.97–138.

(1968). *The sound pattern of English*. New York: Harper.

Clayton, M. L. (1981). Word boundaries and sandhi rules in natural generative phonology. *Lg* 57.571–90.

Clements, G. V. (1977). The autosegmental treatment of vowel harmony. In Dressler & Pfeiffer (1977).

Coates, R. A. (1977). The status of rules in historical phonology. Unpublished PhD thesis, University of Cambridge.

Cohen, D. (1974). *Explaining linguistic phenomena*. Washington, D.C.: Hemisphere.

Cohen, D. & Wirth, J. (1975). *Testing linguistic hypotheses*. Washington, D.C.: Hemisphere.

Comrie, B. (1981a). *Linguistic universals and language typology*. Oxford: Blackwell.

(1981b). *The languages of the U.S.S.R.* Cambridge: CUP.

Crothers, J. (1978). Typology and universals of vowel systems. In Greenberg *et al.* (1978).

Crystal, D. (1982). *Linguistic controversies*. London: Arnold.

Davidsen-Nielsen, N. (1978). *Neutralization and archiphoneme. Two phonological concepts and their history*. Copenhagen: Akademisk Forlag.

Davidsen-Nielsen, N. & Ørum, H. (1978). The feature 'gravity' in Old English and Danish phonology. *Acta Linguistica Hafniensia* 16.202–13.

de Chene, B. & Anderson, S. (1979). Compensatory lengthening. *Lg* 55.505–35.

de Groot, A. W. (1939). Neutralization d'oppositions. *Neophilologus* 25.127–46.

Dekeyser, X. (1978). Some considerations on voicing with special reference to spirants in English and Dutch: a diachronic-contrastive approach. In Fisiak (1978).

Derwing, B. (1973). *Transformational grammar as a theory of language acquisition*. Cambridge: CUP.

Dingwall, W. O. (1971). *A survey of linguistic science*. College Park: University of Maryland, Linguistics Program.

Dinnsen, D. (1977). *Current approaches to phonological theory*. Bloomington: Indiana University Press.

Dixon, R. M. W. (1977). *A grammar of Yidiɲ*. Cambridge: CUP.

Donegan, P. J. & Stampe, D. (1977). The study of natural phonology. In Dinnsen (1977).

Drachman, G. (1977). On the notion 'phonological hierarchy'. In Dressler & Pfeiffer (1977).

Dressler, W. U. (1973). On rule ordering in casual speech styles. *WLG* 4.3–6.

(1975). Methodisches zu Allegro-Regeln. In Dressler & Mareš (1975).

(1977). *Grundfragen der Morphonologie*. Österreichische Akademie der Wissenschaften, Sitzungsberichte, 315.

(1981). External evidence for an abstract analysis of the German velar nasal. In Goyvaerts (1981).

Dressler, W. U., Gasching, P., Chromec, E., Wintersberger, W., Leodolter, R., Stark, H., Groll, G., Reinhart, J. & Pohl, H. D. (1972). Phonologische Schnellsprechregeln in der Wiener Umgangssprache. *WLG* 1.1–29.

Dressler, W. U. & Mareš, F. V. (1975). *Phonologica 1972*. München: Fink.

Dressler, W. U. & Pfeiffer, O. E. (1977). *Phonologica 1976*. Innsbruck: Innsbrucker Beiträge zur Sprachwissenschaft.

Dressler, W. U., Pfeiffer, O. E., Rennison, J. & Dogil, G. (1981). *Phonologica 1980*. Innsbruck: Innsbrucker Beiträge zur Sprachwissenschaft.

Einarsson, S. (1945). *Icelandic. Grammar, texts, glossary*. Baltimore: Johns Hopkins Press.

Eliasson, S. (1981). Analytic vs. synthetic aspects of phonological structure. In Goyvaerts (1981).

Ewen, C. J. (1977). Aitken's Law and the phonatory gesture in dependency phonology. *Lingua* 41.307–29.

(1980). Aspects of phonological structure, with particular reference to English and Dutch. Unpublished PhD thesis, University of Edinburgh.

Fallows, D. (1981). Experimental evidence for English syllabification and syllable structure. *JL* 17.309–18.

Firth, J. R. (1935a). Phonological features of some Indian languages. *Proceedings of the Second International Conference of Phonetic Sciences*. Repr. Firth (1957).

(1935b). The use and distribution of certain English sounds. *English Studies* 17. Repr. Firth (1957).

(1948). Sounds and prosodies. *TPS* 127–52. Repr. Firth (1957), Palmer (1970), Makkai (1972a).

(1957). *Papers in linguistics 1934–1951*. Oxford: OUP.

Fischer-Jørgensen, E. (1975). *Trends in phonological theory*. Copenhagen: Akademisk Forlag.

Fisiak, J. (1978). *Recent developments in historical phonology*. The Hague: Mouton.

Fodor, J. & Katz, J. J. (1964). *The structure of language: readings in the philosophy of language*. Englewood Cliffs: Prentice-Hall.

Foley, J. (1977). *Foundations of theoretical phonology*. Cambridge: CUP.

Fromkin, V. (1965). On system-structure phonology. *Lg* 41.601–9. Repr. Makkai (1972a).

(1971). The non-anomalous nature of anomalous utterances. *Lg* 47.27–52.

Fudge, E. C. (1969). Syllables. *JL* 5.253–86.

Fujimura, O. (1974). *Three dimensions of linguistic theory*. Tokyo: TEC.

Gamkrelidze, T. V. (1978). On the correlation of stops and fricatives in a phonological system. In Greenberg *et al.* (1978).

Gimson, A. C. (1962). *An introduction to the pronunciation of English*. Leeds: Arnold.

Gleason, H. A. Jr (1961). *An introduction to descriptive linguistics*. New York: Holt, Rinehart & Winston.

Gordon, E. V. (1957). *An introduction to Old Norse*, 2nd edn Oxford: Clarendon Press.

Goyvaerts, D. (1980). *Aspects of post-SPE phonology*. Ghent: E. Story-Scientia.

(1981). *Phonology in the 1980s*. Ghent: E. Story-Scientia.

Goyvaerts, D. & Pullum, G. K. (1975). *Essays on the Sound Pattern of English*. Ghent: E. Story-Scientia.

Greenberg, J. (1963). *Universals of Language*. Cambridge, Mass.: MIT Press.

(1966a). Language universals. In Sebeok (1966).

(1966b). Some generalizations concerning glottalic consonants, especially implosives. *Stanford Working Papers on Language Universals* 2.

Greenberg, J., Ferguson, C. A. & Moravcsik, E. (1978). *Universals of human language*. Volume 2, *Phonology*. Stanford: Stanford University Press.

Gussmann, E. (1978). *Explorations in abstract phonology*. Lublin: UCMS, Instytut Filologii Angielskiej.

Hale, K. (1973). Deep-surface canonical disparities in relation to analysis and change. An Australian example. In Sebeok (1973).

Halle, M. (1959). *The sound pattern of Russian*. The Hague: Mouton.

(1962). Phonology in generative grammar. *Word* 18.54–72. Repr. Fodor & Katz (1964), Makkai (1972a).

(1964). On the bases of phonology. In Fodor & Katz (1964). Repr. Makkai (1972a).

(1970). Is Kabardian a vowelless language? *FL* 6.95–103.

Harms, R. T. (1968). *Introduction to phonological theory*. Englewood Cliffs: Prentice-Hall.

(1973). How abstract is Nupe? *Lg* 49.439–46.

Harris, J. (1969). *Spanish phonology*. Cambridge, Mass.: MIT Press.

Harris, Z. S. (1960). *Structural linguistics*. Chicago: University of Chicago Press.

Hays, D. G. (1964). Dependency theory: a formalism and some observations. *Lg* 40.511–25.

Heffner, R-M. S. (1950). *General phonetics*. Madison: University of Wisconsin press.

Henderson, E. J. A. (1951). The phonology of loanwords in some South-East Asian languages. *TPS* 131–58. Repr. Palmer (1970).

(1966). Towards a prosodic statement of Vietnamese syllable structure. In Bazell *et al.* (1966).

Hill, A. A. (1936). Phonetic and phonemic change. *Lg* 12.15–22. Repr. Joos (1957).

Hill, T. (1966). The technique of prosodic analysis. In Bazell *et al.* (1966).

Hockett, C. F. (1942). A system of descriptive phonology. *Lg* 18.3–31. Repr. Joos (1957), Makkai (1972a).

(1954). Two models of grammatical description. *Word* 10.210–34. Repr. Joos (1957).

(1955). *A manual of phonology.* Baltimore: Waverley Press.

(1958). *A course in modern linguistics.* New York: Macmillan.

Hoenigswald, H. (1960). *Language change and linguistic reconstruction.* Chicago: University of Chicago Press.

Hooper, J. B. (1972). The syllable in phonological theory. *Lg* 48.525–40.

(1976). *An introduction to natural generative phonology.* New York: Academic Press.

(1978). Constraints on schwa-deletion in American English. In Fisiak (1978).

Householder, F. W. (1965). On some recent claims in phonological theory. *JL* 1.13–34. Repr. Makkai (1972a).

(1966). Phonological theory: a brief comment. *JL* 2.99–100.

(1971). *Linguistic speculations.* Cambridge: CUP.

(1977). How different are they? In Dinnsen (1977).

Hudson, R. (1980). *Sociolinguistics.* Cambridge: CUP.

Hurford, J. R. (1977). The significance of linguistic generalizations. *Lg* 53.574–620.

Hyman, L. M. (1970). How concrete is phonology? *Lg* 46.58–76.

(1973a). The feature [grave] in phonological theory. *Journal of Phonetics* 1.329–37.

(1973b). Nupe three years later. *Lg* 49.447–52.

(1975). *Phonology: theory and analysis.* New York: Holt, Rinehart & Winston.

Isačenko, A. (1963). Der phonologische Status des velaren Nasals im Deutschen. *Zeitschrift für Phonetik* 16.77–84.

Itkonen, E. (1978). *Grammatical theory and metascience.* Amsterdam: Benjamins.

Jakobson, R. (1929). Remarques sur l'évolution phonologique du russe. *TCLP* 2.

Jakobson, R., Fant, G. & Halle, M. (1951). *Preliminaries to speech analysis.* Cambridge, Mass.: MIT Press.

Jakobson, R. & Halle, M. (1956). *Fundamentals of language.* The Hague: Mouton.

Jones, C. (1979). Rounding and fronting in Old English phonology. *Lingua* 46.157–68.

(1980). Some characteristics of sonorant–obstruent metathesis within a dependency framework. In Anderson & Ewen (1980a).

Jones, D. (1950). *The phoneme: its nature and use.* Cambridge: Heffer.

Jones, S. (1929). Radiography and pronunciation. *British Journal of Radiology,* N.S.3.149–50.

Joos, M. (1957). *Readings in linguistics 1.* Chicago: University of Chicago Press.

Kaye, J. (1981). Recoverability, abstractness, and phonotactic constraints. In Goyvaerts (1981).

Keller, R. E. (1961). *German dialects: phonology and morphology.* Manchester: Manchester University Press.

King. R. D. (1969). *Historical linguistics and generative grammar.* Englewood Cliffs: Prentice-Hall.

Kiparsky, P. (1968a). How abstract is phonology? Indiana University Linguistics Club. Repr. Fujimura (1974).

(1968b). Linguistic universals and linguistic change. In Bach & Harms (1968).

(1971). Historical linguistics. In Dingwall (1971).

(1979). Metrical structure assignment is cyclic. *LI* 10.421–42.

Kisseberth, C. (1970). On the functional unity of phonological rules. *LI* 1.291–306.

Koerner, R. F. K. (1975). *The transformational-generative paradigm and modern linguistic theory.* Amsterdam: Benjamins.

Koestler, A. (1978). *Janus, a summing up.* London: Hutchinson.

Kohler, K. (1966). Is the syllable a phonological universal? *JL* 2.207–8.

(1974). Contrastive sentence phonology. *Journal of the IPA* 4.87–91.

Koutsoudas, A. (1972). The strict fallacy. *Lg* 48.88–96.

(1975). *The application and ordering of grammatical rules*. The Hague: Mouton.

Koutsoudas, A., Sanders, G. & Noll, C. (1974). On the application of phonological rules. *Lg* 50.1–28.

Kuipers, A. (1960), *Phoneme and morpheme in Kabardian*. The Hague: Mouton.

Labov, W. (1966). *The social stratification of English in New York City*. Washington, D.C.: Center for Applied Linguistics.

(1972). The internal evolution of linguistic rules. In Stockwell & Macaulay (1972).

Labov, W., Yeager, M. & Steiner, R. (1972). *A quantitative study of sound change in progress*. 2 vols. Philadelphia: U.S. Regional Survey.

Ladefoged, P. (1971). *Preliminaries to linguistic phonetics*. Chicago: University of Chicago Press.

(1975). *A course in phonetics*. Chicago: University of Chicago Press.

Ladefoged, P., De Clerk, J., Lindau, M. & Papçun, G. (1972). An auditory-motor theory of speech production. *UCLA WPP* 22.48–75.

Langacker, R. W. (1972). *Fundamentals of linguistic analysis*. New York: Holt, Rinehart & Winston.

Lass, R. (1974). Linguistic orthogenesis? Scots vowel quantity and the English length conspiracy. In Anderson & Jones (1974b).

(1975). How intrinsic is content? Markedness, sound change, and 'family universals'. In Goyvaerts & Pullum (1975).

(1976a). *English phonology and phonological theory: synchronic and diachronic studies*. Cambridge: Cambridge University Press.

(1976b). On generative taxonomy, and whether formalisms 'explain'. *Studia Linguistica* 30.139–54.

(1978). Mapping constraints in phonological reconstruction: on climbing down trees without falling out of them. In Fisiak (1978).

(1980). *On explaining language change*. Cambridge: CUP.

(1981). Undigested history and synchronic 'structure'. In Goyvaerts (1981).

(1983). Quantity, resolution and syllable geometry. *Stellenbosch Papers in Linguistics* 10.

Lass, R. & Anderson, J. M. (1975). *Old English phonology*. Cambridge: CUP.

Laver, J. (1980). *The phonetic description of voice quality*. Cambridge: CUP.

Lee, G. & Howard, I. (1974). Another mouthful of divinity fudge. In Bruck *et al.* (1974).

Lehmann, W. P. (1967). *A reader in nineteenth-century historical Indo-European Linguistics*. Bloomington: Indiana University Press.

Lindau, M. (1975). Features for vowels. *UCLA WPP* 30.

Lindau, M., Jakobson, L. & Ladefoged, P. (1972). A cross-linguistic study of the feature 'Advanced Tongue Root'. Paper presented to the 82nd meeting of the Acoustical Society of America (1971). Abstract in *Journal of the Acoustical Society of America* 51.5.

Linell, P. (1979). *Psychological reality in phonology: a theoretical study*. Cambridge: CUP.

Lisker, L. & Abramson, A. S. (1971). Distinctive features and language control. *Lg* 47.767–85.

Love, N. (1981). *Generative phonology: a case study from French*. Amsterdam: Benjamins.

Lyons, J. (1962). Phonemic and non-phonemic phonology: some typological reflections. *International Journal of American Linguistics* 28.127–34. Repr. Makkai (1972a).

McCarthy, J. J. (1979). On stress and syllabification. *LI* 10.443–65.

Macaulay, R. K. S. & Trevelyan, G. D. (1973). *Language and employment in Glasgow*. Report to the Social Science Research Council. Revised version: Macaulay, R. K. S. (1977). *Language, social class and education: a Glasgow study*. Edinburgh: Edinburgh University Press.

McCawley, J. D. (1967). Le rôle d'un système de traits phonologiques dans une théorie du langage. *Langages* 8.112–23. English version in Makkai (1972a).

McIntosh, A. (1956). The analysis of written Middle English. *TPS* 26–55.

Maddieson, I. (1980a). A survey of liquids. *UCLA WPP* 50.93–112.

(1980b). Vocoid approximants in the world's languages. *UCLA WPP* 50.113–19.

Makkai, V. B. (1972a). *Phonological theory. Evolution and current practice*. New York: Holt, Rinehart & Winston.

(1972b). Vowel harmony in Hungarian reexamined in the light of recent developments in phonological theory. In Makkai (1972a).

Malmberg, B. (1963). *Phonetics*. New York: Dover.

Martinet, A. (1936). Neutralization et archiphonème. *TCLP* 6.46–57.

(1955). *Economie des changements phonétiques*. Bern: Franke.

Matthews, P. H. (1972). *Inflectional morphology*. Cambridge: CUP.

(1974). *Morphology*. Cambridge: CUP.

(1979). *Generative grammar and linguistic competence*. London: Allen & Unwin.

(1981). *Syntax*. Cambridge: CUP.

Moulton, W. G. (1947). Juncture in modern standard German. *Lg* 23.212–26. Repr. Joos (1957).

Nartey, J. N. A. (1979). A study in phonemic universals – especially concerning fricatives and stops. *UCLA WPP* 46.

O'Connor, J. D. (1973). *Phonetics*. Harmondsworth: Penguin.

Ó Dochartaigh, C. (1980). Aspects of Celtic lenition. In Anderson & Ewen (1980a).

Ohala, J. (1974). Phonetic explanation in phonology. In Bruck *et al.* (1974).

Ohala, M. (1974). The abstractness controversy: experimental input from Hindi. *Lg* 50.225–35.

Osthoff, H. & Brugman, K. (1878). *Morphologische Untersuchungen auf dem Gebiete der Indogermanischen Sprachen*. Leipzig: Hirzel. Relevant portions translated in Lehmann (1967).

Palmer, F. R. (1965). The 'broken plurals' of Tigrinya. *BSOAS* 17.548–66. Repr. Palmer (1970).

(1956). 'Openness' in Tigre: a problem of prosodic statement. *BSOAS* 18.561–77.

(1970). *Prosodic analysis*. Oxford: OUP.

Pike, K. L. (1943). *Phonetics*. Ann Arbor: University of Michigan Press.

(1947). *Phonemics*. Ann Arbor: University of Michigan Press.

Popper, K. R. (1972). *Conjectures and refutations*. London: Routledge & Kegan Paul.

(1973). *Objective knowledge*. Oxford: OUP.

Postal, P. M. (1968). *Aspects of phonological theory*. New York: Harper.

Prokosch, F. (1938). *A comparative Germanic grammar*. Baltimore: Waverley Press.

Pulgram, E. (1970). *Syllable, word, nexus, cursus*. The Hague: Mouton.

Pullum, G. K. (1978). *Rule interaction and the organization of a grammar*. New York: Garland.

Ringen, J. (1975). Linguistic facts: a study of the empirical scientific status of transformational generative grammar. In Cohen & Wirth (1975).

Rischel, J. (1974). *Topics in West Greenlandic phonology*. Copenhagen: Akademisk Forlag.

Roach, P. (1982). On the distinction between 'stress-timed' and 'syllable-timed' languages. In Crystal (1982).

Robins, R. H. (1957). Aspects of prosodic analysis. *Proceedings of the University of Durham Philosophical Society 1, Series B*, I.1–12. Repr. Palmer (1970), Makkai (1972a).

Robinson, J. (1970). Dependency structures and transformational rules. *Lg*. 46.259–85.

Romaine, S. (1982). *Sociohistorical linguistics*. Cambridge: CUP.

Rubach, J. (1977a). *Changes of consonants in English and Polish. A generative account*. Wrocław: PAN.

(1977b). Contrastive phonostylistics. *Papers and Studies in Contrastive Linguistics* 6.63–72.

(1980). *Cyclic phonology and palatalization in Polish and English*. Warsaw: WUW.

(1982). *Analysis of phonological structures*. Warsaw: PWN.

Sampson, G. (1974). Is there a universal phonetic alphabet? *Lg* 50.236–59.

(1975). One fact needs one explanation. *Lingua* 36.231–9.

(1980). *Schools of linguistics. Competition and evolution*. London: Hutchinson.

Sapir, E. (1921). Language. New York: Harcourt, Brace.

Saussure, F. de (1916). *Cours de linguistique générale*. Paris: Payot. English version, *A course in general linguistics*, tr. W. Baskin (1959). London: Owen.

# References

Schane, S. A. (1968). On the non-uniqueness of phonological representations. *Lg* 44.709–816.
  (1971). The phoneme revisited. *Lg* 47.503–21.
  (1972). Natural rules in phonology. In Stockwell & Macaulay (1972).
  (1974). How abstract is abstract? In Bruck *et al.* (1974).
Sebeok, T. (1966). *Current trends in linguistics III. Theoretical foundations.* The Hague: Mouton.
  (1973). *Current trends in linguistics XI. Diachronic, areal and typological linguistics.* The Hague: Mouton.
Sedlak, P. (1969). Typological considerations of vowel quality systems. *Stanford Working Papers on Language Universals* 1.
Shuy, R. & Bailey, C-J. (1974). *Towards tomorrow's linguistics.* Washington, D.C.: Georgetown University Press.
Sigurd, B. (1965). *Phonotactic structures in Swedish.* Lund: Uniskol.
  (1975). Linearization in phonology. In Dressler & Mareš (1975).
Skousen, R. (1975). *Substantive evidence in phonology.* The Hague: Mouton.
Smith, N. V. & Wilson, D. (1979). *Modern linguistics: the results of Chomsky's revolution.* Harmondsworth: Penguin.
Sommerstein, A. (1977). *Modern phonology.* London: Arnold.
Stampe, D. (1969). The acquisition of phonetic representation. *CLS* 5.443–54.
  (1973). A dissertation on natural phonology. Unpublished PhD thesis, University of Chicago.
Stanley, R. (1967). Redundancy rules in phonology. *Lg* 43.393–435.
Steinberg, D. & Krohn, R. (1975). The psychological validity of Chomsky and Halle's vowel shift rule. In Koerner (1975).
Stetson, R. M. (1928). *Motor phonetics, a study of speech movements in action. Archives Néerlandaises de Phonétique Expérimentale* 3.
Stockwell, R. P. & Macaulay, R. K. S. (1972). *Linguistic change and generative theory.* Bloomington: Indiana University Press.
Swadesh, M. (1934). The phonemic principle. *Lg* 10.117–29. Repr. Joos (1957), Makkai (1972a).
Thrane, T. *et al.* (1980). Typology and genetics in language. *Travaux du Cercle Linguistique de Copenhague* xx.
Trubetzkoy, N. S. (1936). Die Aufhebung der phonologischen Gegensätze. *TCLP* 6.29 45. Repr. Vachek (1964a).
  (1939). *Grundzüge der Phonologie. TCLP* 7. English version, trans. C. Baltaxe (1969). *Principles of phonology.* Berkeley: University of California Press.
Trudgill, P. (1974). *The social differentiation of English in Norwich.* Cambridge: CUP.
Twaddell, W. F. (1935). On defining the phoneme. *Language Monographs* 16. Repr. Joos (1957).
  (1939). A note on Old High German umlaut. *Monatshefte für Deutschen Unterricht* 30.177–81. Repr. Joos (1957).
Vachek, J. (1964a). *A Prague school reader in linguistics.* Bloomington: Indiana University Press.
  (1964b). On some basic principles of 'classical' phonology. *Zeitschrift für Phonetik, Sprachwissenschaft und Kommunikationsforschung* 17.409–31. Repr. Makkai (1972a).
  (1966). *The linguistic school of Prague.* Bloomington: Indiana University Press.
Vago, R. (1973). Abstract vowel harmony systems in Uralic and Altaic languages. *Lg* 49.597–605.
Vennemann, T. (1970). The German velar nasal. *Phonetica* 22.65–82.
  (1974a). Phonological concreteness in Natural Generative Grammar. In Shuy & Bailey (1974).
  (1974b). Words and syllables in Natural Generative Grammar. In Bruck *et al.* (1974).
Waddington, C. H. (1977). *Tools for thought.* London: Cape.

Wang, W. S-Y. (1968). Vowel features, paired variables, and the English vowel shift. *Lg* 44.695–708.

Waterson, N. (1956). Some aspects of the phonology of the nominal forms of the Turkish word. *BSOAS* 18.378–91. Repr. Palmer (1970).

Wood, S. (1974). The articulatory description of vowels. *Lingvistika Månadsmeddelanden, Juni–Juli 1974.* Lund: Institutionen för Lingvistik, Lunds Universitet.

(1975a). Tense and lax vowels – degree of constriction or pharyngeal volume? *Working Papers* 11.109–34. Lund: Phonetics Laboratory, Lund University.

(1975b). The weakness of the tongue-arching model of vowel articulation. *Working Papers* 11.55–107. Lund: Phonetics Laboratory, Lund University.

(1979). A radiographic analysis of constriction locations for vowels. *Journal of Phonetics* 7.25–43.

Wunderlich, D. (1979). *Foundations of linguistics.* Cambridge: CUP.

Zwicky, A. (1970). The free-ride principle and two rules of complete assimilation in English. *CLS* 6.579–88.

(1972). Note on a phonological hierarchy in English. In Stockwell & Macaulay (1972).

(1973). Taking a false step. *Working Papers in Linguistics* (Ohio State University) 14.100–12.

(1974). Homing in: on arguing for remote representations. *JL* 10.55–70.

(1975a). The strategy of generative phonology. In Dressler & Mareš (1975).

(1975b). Settling on an underlying form: the English inflectional endings. In Cohen & Wirth (1975).

351

# GENERAL INDEX

**Boldface** entries indicate definitions or illustrative discussions of technical terms.

Abaza 160
abbreviatory notations 190ff; angled
    brackets 193f; braces 14, 23, 192
Abipon 151
Abkhaz 150f, 153, 155, 160
absolute neutralization **208ff**; arguments
    against 211ff
abstract analysis **68**; 203–35
abstract segments **208ff**
adjunction **275**
Adyghe 160, 161; vowels 139
Adzera: vowels 143, fricatives 151
affricates: dependency analysis 284; English
    26f; feature analysis 89f, 108, 111f;
    systemic status 147f
Afrikaans 49
Ainu: nasals 156; obstruents 147, 152;
    vowels 143
Akan 119
Akha: vowels 146
Albanian 132; vowels 145
Aleut: vowels 142; nasals 157
allomorphs **13**; bound vs. free **60f**;
    conditioning **14**
allophone **18**; 11–38
allophonic rules *see* rules
Altaic 269
alternants **59**
alternation **4**; *see also* morphophonemic
    alternation
Amahuaca: stops 148; vowels 143
Amharic: sibilants 153
Amnesha: vowels 136
analogical extension **322**
analogical leveling **322**
anaptyxis **184ff**
angled brackets *see* abbreviatory notations
Ao: stops 148
aperture/sonority **139**
aphaeresis **187**

Apinayé: nasals 156
apocope **187ff**
Arabic: Moroccan 142; pharyngeals 76, 84
Araucanian: nasals 156, 287
*arbitraire du signe* **2**
archiphoneme **41**; 39–54; representatives of
    49ff
Armenian: /h/ 179; stops 149
'as-if' argument **25ff**
aspiration 91, 148f; as lenition 178, 182,
    291ff; dependency analysis 290ff
assimilation **99**, **171ff**; acoustic 175ff;
    bimodal **175ff**; contact vs. distant **171**;
    fusional **173**; glottal state 175; gravity 99;
    lip attitude 174; NC 199ff; non-process
    interpretation 238ff; place 173f;
    progressive (perseverative) vs. regressive
    (anticipatory) **171**; stricture 174; velic 174f
Ateso 119
autosegmental phonology 269
Avar 155; obstruents 150, 152ff
Azerbaijani: vowels 146; vowel harmony 269

background knowledge **7**
ballistic movement **108**
Bantu 200
basis of comparison **43**
Beembe: vowels 144
Bengali: stops 149
biuniqueness **24**, 27ff
boundaries (termini) **33f**; demotion **303f**
braces *see* abbreviatory notations
breathy voice 43, 90, 149, 155
bridging function **59**
Bulgarian: nasals 157
Burera: consonants 147; lack of fricatives
    151
Burmese: obstruents 149, 153; vowels 145

canonical form **23**

353

carrier **188**
casual speech 294–314; characteristics of
    297f; as evidence for reconstruction 333
categorical properties **20**
Caucasian 155; vowel systems 140, 160f
Cayapa: vowels 141
Celtic 177
chains, push and drag **126**ff
Cham: vowels 146
Chamoro: stops 149
Chipewyan: affricates 91; liquids 158; nasals
    156; vowels 144
Chuave: stops 149
Chuckchi 269; obstruents 148; vowels 144
Chuvash: vowels 144
citation form **30**, **295**ff
classical phonemics **16**ff
clicks: areal restriction 155; dependency
    analysis 291; feature analysis 93; Zulu 150
Coast Salishan 156
cognitive bias 92, 103
coincidence **274**
combination **274**
commutation **19**
comparative reconstruction **322**ff
compensatory lengthening **259**f
complementarity **99**f, 122, 166
complementary distribution *see* distribution
componentiality **272**
conditioning (of allomorphs):
    grammatical/lexical/phonological **14**
conflation **192**
consonant systems 21f, **146**ff
consonant/vowel relations **108**ff
conspiracy **187**ff
constituency **12**, 271f; of syllables 252ff
constraints: on abstractness 222ff; on
    reconstruction 332ff
context-free change **133**
contrast: minimal **19**f; in phoneme definition
    14ff; suspension of 26ff, 39–54, 55–74,
    203–35
co-vowel **138**
creaky voice 90, 159
Cree: vowels 140
Crow 159
Czech: syllabic consonants 84

Danish: stop neutralization 50; vowels 86
de-articulation **179**
deep vs. surface **62**, 203–35
deletion 186ff; in lenition 177ff; of obstruents
    333ff
de-oralization **179**
dependency **272**; mutual vs. strict **274**;
    271–93

descriptive order **60**
diacritic use of features **214**
Dieguño 156; nasals 287
diphthongization: as dissimilation 174
diphthongs 91f, 112f; dependency analysis
    275; falling vs. rising 275; systemic status
    136ff; *see also* long vowels, mora, quantity
direction of derivation **162**ff
disjunction **97**, 193
distinctness **78**
distribution: complementary **18**ff; defective
    **19**, 51ff; macro- vs. micro- **15**; parallel **19**
double articulation **2**
Dravidian 155, 180, 200; /h/ 336f
Dutch 3, 46, 49, 108, 133; umlaut 321f
Duwamish 156

Early Modern English 174, 286
ease of articulation **199**f
ejectives **20**, 149; dependency analysis 291;
    feature analysis 93
English: /æ/-lengthening 34ff, 134f, 192f;
    history 325ff; /æ/-raising 311ff; affricates
    25ff, 90; article deletion 301; aspiration
    16f, 265; casual speech 295ff, 333;
    diphthongs 109, 123; effects of /r/ 111;
    epenthesis 184ff; glottal stop 27ff, 302f;
    liquids 158; MP alternations 58, 138; nasal
    assimilation 300, 302f; nasalization 24,
    302f; nasals 157; NC spellings 34;
    obstruents 149; prosodic analysis 242f;
    /r/-sandhi 71f; /sC/ clusters 52f; semivowels
    159; stop-deletion 300; syllabification
    263ff; syllable structure 254; /t/-weakening
    179; /t/ : /d/ neutralization 30f; taps/flaps
    122f;
    varieties: Hiberno-English 22;
        Liverpool 183; New York City *see*
        *within this entry* /æ/-lengthening
        /æ/-raising, article deletion, casual
        speech, liquids, nasalization; RP 122,
        124, vowels 144; Southern U.S. 137,
        174, 181, 184, 200, 286; Tyneside
        110; Yorkshire 92
environment bar **23**
epenthesis **184**ff
Eskimo: Alaskan, vowels 143; Greenlandic,
    nasals 156; stops 148
Estonian: overlength 109
etymological relations **226**
evaluation measure **196**
exponent **15**
external evidence 214ff
extrinsic ordering *see* rules

false segmentation **34**

false step **65**
family universals **155**
features **42**, 75–124; agreement vs.
 disagreement *see* variables; acoustic vs.
 articulatory 76, 97ff; binary **77**f; cavity
 **84**ff; classificatory vs. phonetic function
 **79**; cover **76**f; distinctive **75**ff; Jakobsonian
 75ff; length of stricture **89**; lip attitude **88**;
 major class **83**ff; manner **89**; non-binary
 104ff; primary stricture **84**f; secondary
 aperture **89**; sequential values 111ff; source
 **90**f; tongue-body **85**f; use in description 93
features, specific: anterior 84; aspirated 91;
 back 85; consonantal 83; constricted 90;
 continuant 89f; coronal 84f; delayed
 release 89f; distributed 89; egressive 93;
 fricative 108f; front 86f; glottalic 93;
 glottalic pressure 93; glottalic suction 93;
 grave 99f; high 85; high (non-binary)
 106f; inrounded 88; lateral 89; long 92;
 low 85; murmur 90; nasal 89; obstruent 83;
 oral 84; premature release 91; rate 108f;
 round 88; stop 108f; strident 90f; syllabic
 83; tense 91f; velaric 93; velaric suction
 93; vibration 108f; voice 90
filters **187**f, 255
Finnish: lenition 181ff, 336;
 morphophonemics 228f; vowels 145
foot **248**f
form and substance **2**
formants **101**, 120f, 175f
fortition **177**ff
Fox: vowels 136f
free ride **66**, 205
French 3, 4, 133, 181; liquids 158;
 nasalization 174, 232; neutralization of
 vowels 50; obstruents 152; semivowels 159;
 vowels 146
front rounded vowels: distribution 143f

Garo: vowels 143
geminates **92**, 175, 181f
generality **81**, 204ff, 203–35; 231
generative phonology 203–35
Georgian: liquids 158; vowels 143
German 2, 53, 91, 108, 120, 136, 157, 158,
 179; final devoicing ( = neutralization of
 voice) 40f, 55ff, 95f, 164ff, 170, 226f, 229;
 juncture 36f; nasal assimilation 200;
 obstruents 23, 39f, 149, 152; palatalization
 36ff, 96; redundancies 94f; rule of
 permitted finals 61; segment inventory 94;
 velar nasal 205ff, 214ff; vowels 145;
  varieties: Alsatian vowels 146f; Austrian
  176; Swiss 108, vowels 146; Viennese
  217ff

Germanic 179; lenition 180, 333ff
gesture 113ff, 285ff; articulatory **282**, 285ff;
 categorial **282**ff; initiatory **282**, 289ff;
 laryngeal **115**ff; oral **115**ff
glottal segments: as undifferentiated
 obstruents 113ff; as defective 117, 179f;
 *see also* /h/, lenition
glottal stop: for /p t k/ in English 27ff,
 302f; Scots 114ff, 123, 304ff
Gothic 190
governor **272**
gradualness: lexical *see* lexical diffusion;
 phonetic 329ff
grapheme/allograph **15**
Great Vowel Shift **126**ff, 137, 174
Greek 132, 179, 182
Grimm's Law 130, 182, 322ff

/h/: sources of 179, 333ff; *see also* glottal
 segments, lenition
Hawaiian: liquids 158; obstruents 147, 151;
 passive 222; semivowels 159; vowels 144
head **272**
heterorganic **199**
heuristics **33**
High German Sound Shift 108
Hindi: aspiration 4; breathy voice 90
historical recapitulation 213f
holons **257**
Holtzmann's Law 181
homogeneity assumption **102**ff
homophony 29
homorganic segments **48**
Hopi: nasals 157
Hungarian 98, 179; neutral vowels **208**;
 vowel harmony 172f, 208ff, 244ff; vowels
 145

Iai: nasals 157; vowels 146
Icelandic: long vs. short vowels and
 diphthongs 112f; obstruents 148, 152;
 /u/-fronting 133; voice assimilation 175
Ilocano: vowels 140
implosives 149; dependency analysis 291;
 feature analysis 93
independent motivation **67**
indexical information **17**
index of oddity **155**
Indo-European 155; lenition 335ff
initiator power **248**
instrumentalism **166**
interludes **267**f
intrinsic ordering *see* rules
invariance of meaning **13**
Irish 22
isochronism **249**

Italian 181; liquids 158; vowels 145
Itonama: vowels 144
*i*-umlaut *see* umlaut

Javanese: vowels 145
juncture phonemes **36f**

Kabardian: vowels 16of
Kannaḍa: lenition 180; liquids 158;
    metaphony 172; nasals 46ff, 116ff, 157,
    238ff; obstruents 43, 150; semivowels 159;
    syllables 228
Kharia: vowels 144
Klamath 151
Koiani: fricatives 151
Kpelle: vowels 145
Kui 179
K'üri: vowels 139
Kuvi 179

labials, lack of 151
lag/log phase **328**
language acquisition 212f, 220
Latin: accentuation 194f; assimilation 175,
    200; consonant-stem nouns,
    morphophonemics 64ff; /h/ 179
length **254**
lenition **177ff**; dependency analysis 283ff,
    291ff; Dravidian 336f; Germanic 180,
    333ff; Indo-European 335ff; Kannaḍa
    180; Old English 98; Old Spanish 180;
    Romance 181f; Spanish 174; Uralic 98,
    181ff, 336ff
lexical diffusion **327ff**
lexical incidence **319**
lexicon **12**, 205, 226f; in historical change
    324ff
linearity **24**, 30f
linearization **185**
linking **197**
liquid **22**
Lithuanian: vowels 144
long consonants 91f, 108ff
long-domain phenomena **244ff**
long vowels 91f, 108f, 112; bimoric analysis
    174, 253ff; systemic status 135ff

Malayalam: liquids 158; nasals 287
Maltese: vowels 136
Manda 179
Mandarin: vowels 143
Maori 19, 23; morphophonemics 220ff;
    obstruents 147, 151
Maranungku 163
Marathi: nasals 164
Margi: semivowels 159; vowels 141, 142
markedness **45**, 132ff, 196ff

markers **243**
marking conventions 196ff
Maxakali: nasal sandhi 175
Mazahua: vowels 146
Mazateco: vowels 143
mediated relation, mediator **204**f
mentalism, mental representations *see*
    psychological reality
merger **319**
metaconditions **25**
metaphony **171**f; *see also* umlaut, vowel
    harmony
metarules **118**, 129
metathesis **188ff**
Middle English: /a/ 325ff; epenthesis 286;
    long vowels 128; /o:/ 328f; open-syllable
    lengthening 105f; syllable structure 268
Middle Korean: and gravity 98f
minimal pair **20**
mirror-image environments **195**
missing links **322ff**
Mixtec: nasals 156
Mohawk 19
monophthongization: as assimilation 174;
    Late West Saxon 286
Montenegran: vowels 139
mora **253**f
morph **13**
morpheme **11**
morphologization **320ff**
morphophoneme **57**f
morphophonemic alternations **57**, 55–74,
    203–35
morphophonemic level 57ff
multiple articulations 87f; dependency
    analysis 288
multiple strategy **199**f
murmur *see* breathy voice

Naga: vowels 145
nasality: sequential in segments 113
nasals, lack of 156
Nasioi 159
natural vs. unnatural **196**
natural classes **80**; labials/velars 97ff;
    dentals/palatals/velars 285ff
natural context-sensitivity **200**
Natural Generative Phonology 223ff
naturalness 195ff
Navaho; semivowels 159; vowels 143
negative condition **187**
Nengone: vowels 145
Neogrammarian Hypothesis **324ff**
neutralization **40**f, 39–54; English 30f;
    German 40f, 55ff; Kannadµa 46ff; multiple
    46ff; positions of vs. positions of relevance **41**;

neutralization *cont.*
　types 49ff; vs. defective distribution 51ff
neutral position **84**f
neutral vowels *see* Hungarian
non-systemic entities **17**
non-uniqueness/indeterminacy **27**
no ordering condition **223**f
Norwegian: high vowels 86
nuclei **137**
null strategy **200**
Nunggubuyu 287; obstruents 148, 151

observation language **7**
obstruents **22**, 83
Occam's Razor **38**
Old English: affix modification 317f;
　breaking 174, 193f; gemination 316;
　metathesis 188, 190; late West Saxon
　monophthongization 286; palatalization
　316f; palatal softening 319; short vowel
　neutralization 51, 165f; stop weakening 98;
　syllable quantity 250ff; umlaut 280ff, 317f
Old High German 180, 181
Old Icelandic: syllable structure 257ff
Old Irish: lenition 322ff
Old Norse: assimilation 175; fortition 181
Old Spanish: lenition 180
Old Swedish: 259
onomatopoeia **9**
ontology **103**
opening **178**ff, *see also* lenition
open juncture **36**ff
openness *see* sonority
open syllable **23**
oppositions: bilateral **43**; constant vs.
　neutralizable **40**f; equipollent **46**; gradual
　**45**f; isolated **44**f; multilateral **43**f; privative
　**45**; proportional **44**; structure of **41**ff
ordering *see* rules
Ostyak 98, 139, 179; nasals 146; vowels 146
overlapping: phonemic **27**ff; syllables *see*
　interludes
overlong segments 108f

palatalization: English 16ff, 169f; German
　36ff, 96; Old English 316f
Papago: morphophonemics 189f; nasals 156;
　obstruents 149, 152; vowels 144
paradigmatic dimension **242**, 271
paraphrase class **204**
parasite vowels **184**
Pashto: nasals 156
pattern congruity **27**
peak **252**; monomoric vs. bimoric **254**ff;
　simple vs. complex **137**f
Pengo 179

Persian: vowels 144
phonematic units **240**
phoneme **18**, 11–38; contrast and phonemic
　status 18ff; distinctive vs. identifying
　function 52f; inventories **21**, 125–68;
　primacy of **24**; unspecified 160ff
phonetic motivation **196**, 198ff
phonetic plans **228**
phonetic similarity **19**
phonological space **129**
phonologization **198**, **318**f
phonotactics **21**, 298f
place (prosodic) **243**
Polish 3, 23, 49, 200; semivowels 159; stress
　260f
Polynesian 222
polysystemic vs. momosystemic **163**ff
power of theories 211f
Prague School 39–54
precedence **272**ff
predictability: in morpheme definition **13**; in
　phoneme definition 17ff
prenasalization 112f
pretheoretical terms **6**
primitives **25**, 75–101, 102–24, 236ff;
　dependency 275ff
privilege of occurrence **15**
procedural/operational definition **20**
processes, phonological **59**, 169–202; *see also*
　rules
process morphophonemics **59**ff, 73, 203–35
productive alternations **58**, 223ff
proper analysis **95**
proper vs. improper bracketing **267**f
prosodic analysis/phonology **240**ff
prosodies **239**ff; types 242ff
protection **181**ff
prothesis **184**ff
Proto-Dravidian 180
Proto-Germanic 180
Proto-West Germanic 259f
Proto-Uralic 98
psychological reality 9f, 103f, 191, 212f, 214ff

quantity **254**ff
Quileute 156

realism 166
realization **11**, 12ff
recoverability 231f
reduction 76, 236f, 285f
redundancy **17**, 79
reduplication **189**
regularity vs. irregularity: in sound change
　322ff; in structure 68, 205

restructuring: historical 318ff;
  synchronic: morphosyntactic **301f**;
    phonemic **299**f; phonotactic **298**f
rhotic vs. non-rhotic *see* English, /r/-sandhi
Romance 200; lenition 181f
Rotokas: nasals 156; obstruents 149, 151
rule features **209**
rules: allophonic **20**, failure of 34ff;
  articulatory reduction **230**; formalisms 23,
  95ff, 169–202; morphological spell-out
  **223**; morphophonemic **58**, 223;
  morphophonological proper **230**ff;
  mutation **60**; optional vs. obligatory **28**;
  ordering: **14**, 60, 67f, 207f, disjunctive
  **194**f, extrinsic vs. intrinsic 208, 223ff;
  universal 234; perceptual redundancy **229**;
  phonotactic **229**; P-rules **223**; rescue **65**;
  reordering **216**f; sandhi **223**; syllable **223**;
  telescoping **216**; vacuous application **95**;
  variable **308**f; **via** 223f
Rumanian 338
Russian 3, 23, 49

Samoan 159
sandhi 69ff, **70**; English 71f, 173, 175;
  internal vs. external 74; Sanskrit 70f, 173
  175, 279f; Swedish 72, 187f
Sanskrit *see* sandhi
schema 122, 192ff; expansion of **192**;
  subrule **192**
schwa **110**
Scots 108, 129; epenthesis 186; /ĕ/ → [ʌ]
  rule 195; glottal stop 114ff, 123, 304ff;
  semivowels 159; /u/-fronting 133f; vowel
  harmony 303f; vowel length 32f, 37f
secondary strictures 87f; dependency analysis
  288
segmental coding **59**
segmentalization **185**
segments, internal structure 111ff
Sentani: obstruents 149, 151
separation of levels **25**, 36ff
shifts: chain 127ff; constraints/conditions on
  **130**; cyclical 129ff
simplicity 25ff, **81**, 211f
Sindhi: obstruents 149
Snoqualmie 156
sonorant **22**, 83
sonority: in lenition 178f; in syllables **264**
sonorization 178ff, 283f; *see also* lenition
Spanish: liquids 158; morphophonemics
  224ff; spirantization 174, 180
speaker capability 333
speech errors 219f
speech pathology 219
speech tempo 298ff, 301f

spirantization **171**
split **318**f
static vs. dynamic 169, 241f, 294f
storage vs. computation 205ff
strength 177ff; hierarchy 178ff, 182; *see also*
  lenition
strengthening *see* fortition
structural change **95**
structural description **95**
subjunction **275**
submatrix **115**
substantive evidence 214ff
sulcalization **124**
Sundanese: nasalization 174f; vowels 145
suppletion 63, 205, 226f
Svarabhakti **184**
Swahili 3
Swedish: assimilation 200; diphthongs 92,
  107; sandhi 72, 187f; syllable quantity
  255ff; syncope 187, 231; vowels 44, 88,
  91
syllables: as domains for stress 240ff;
  boundaries 262ff; bracketing 266ff; coda
  **252**; constituency 252ff; dependency
  analysis 273f; hypercharacterized/overlong
  **256**; long/heavy **254**; margins **264**; motor
  theory **248**; onset **252**; overlap **266**; peak
  **252**; phonetic vs. phonological **250**;
  quantity **250**ff; rhyme **252**; short/light **254**;
  tactic vs. more tiers 256f
symmetry 25ff
synchronic **35**
syncope **187**
syntagmatic dimension **63**, 271
system vs. structure 271
systematic phonemic/phonetic levels **223**
systemic entities **17**

Tamil 174, 180; metaphony 172; obstruents
  161ff
Taoripi: nasals 156
taps/flaps: English 30f; feature analysis 108f
taxonomic linguistics **12**
taxonomy **4**
testability 33
thematic vowels **64**
Tillamook: stops 151
timing, syllable vs. stress **248**f
Tlingit: stops 151
trading-relations **207**
True Generalization Condition 223f
Turkish: vowel harmony 269; vowels 145
typology 125, 125–68

Ubykh 160; stops 147

umlaut **172**; Germanic *i*- 172, 197f;
  morphologization 320ff; Old English 280ff,
  317f, 321f; Old High German 321;
  phonologization 320ff
underlying form **59**; artificial **61**
underlying vs. derived **68**
Unique Underlier Condition **63**, 203–35
universals 125, 125–68; absolute vs.
  implicational vs. statistical **131**
unobservables **9**
unplaced features **239**
Uralic 179, 269; lenition 98, 181ff, 336ff

variables 106; dependent **238**; for feature
  agreement 116ff; disagreement 123; Greek
  letter 116f; sociolinguistic **304**ff
variation: free **21**; in linguistic change 311ff;
  quanta of **333**f; sociolinguistic 304ff
Vogul 181f, 336
vowel harmony **172**, 269; Hungarian 172f,
  208ff, 244ff; *see also* Azerbaijani, Turkish
vowel space 121f
vowel systems 139ff; linear **139**, 160f;
  quadrangular **139**; triangular **139**

vowels: auditory/articulatory asymmetry
  118ff; dependency analysis 275ff; height
  85ff, 106f, 118ff; multi-parametric
  characterization **121**f; peripheral vs.
  interior **140**f

Wapishana: nasals 156; vowels 143
weak vs. strong clusters 267f
weakening *see* lenition
Welsh 3; initial mutations **177**f, 243
Western Desert 163, 286; obstruents 148,
  151
Wichita: vowels 143

Yenisei Samoyed 336
Yiddish: phoneme system 21, 138; liquids
  158; nasals 156; umlaut 321f; vowels 143
Yidiɲ: stops 148
Yugakhir: stops 149
Yurak 179, 336

Zulu: stops, clicks 150

# INDEX OF NAMES

Abercrombie, D. xviii
Aitken, A. J. 38
Albrow, K. H. 269
Allen, W. S. 74, 201, 269, 270
Anderson, J. M. 270, 293
Anderson, J. M. and Ewen, C. 293
Anderson, J. M. and Jones, C. 267, 270, 293
Anderson, S. R. 113, 123, 201, 233, 270
Anttila, R. 338
Árnason, K. 270
Asher, R. E. 269
Basbøll, H. 270
Bell, A. and Hooper, J. B. 270
Bendor-Samuel, J. T. 269
Bloch, B. 38
Bloomfield, L. 59, 60, 61, 62, 73, 74, 227, 338
Botha, R. P. 233
Bright, W. 201
Brosnahan, L. F. and Malmberg, B. xviii
Brown, G. 100, 314
Bruck, A. *et al.* 235
Bynon, T. 338
Carnochan, J. 269
Catford, J. C. 101, 123, 124, 168, 248, 250
Cearley, A. 314
Chalmers, A. F. 10, 166
Chambers, J. K. and Trudgill, P. 314
Chao, Y-R. 38
Chen, M. 201, 338
Chen, M. and Hsieh, H. I. 338
Chen, M. and Wang, W. S-Y. 338
Chomsky, N. 10, 103, 191, 196, 202, 204, 212
Chomsky, N. and Halle, M. 77, 82, 103, 104, 167, 233
Clayton, M. L. 235

Clements, G. V. 269
Coates, R. A. 73
Cohen, D. 9
Cohen, D. and Wirth, J. 234
Comrie, B. 167, 234, 269
Crothers, J. 137, 139, 140, 141, 143, 167, 168
Davidsen-Nielsen, N. 50, 53
Davidsen-Nielsen, N. and Ørum, H. 101
de Chene, B. and Anderson, S. 270
de Groot, A. W. 52
Dekeyser, X. 201
Derwing, B. 10, 234
Dinnsen, D. 235
Dixon, R. M. W. 167, 168
Donegan, P. J. and Stampe, D. 202
Drachman, G. 201
Dressler, W. U. 73, 202, 216, 217, 218, 219, 220, 314
Dressler, W. U. *et al.* 314
Einarsson, S. 201
Eliasson, S. 234, 235
Ewen, C. J. 270, 277, 278, 289, 290, 293
Fallows, D. 270
Ferguson, C. 167
Firth, J. R. 164, 165, 168, 239, 268, 269
Fischer-Jørgenson, E. 38, 53, 73, 100, 233
Foley, J. 183, 201
Fromkin, V. 219, 269
Fudge, E. C. 270
Gamkrelidze, T. V. 167
Gimson, A. C. 314
Gleason, W. A. Jr 38
Gordon, E. V. 201
Goyvaerts, D. 234, 235
Goyvaerts, D. and Pullum, G. K. 235
Greenberg, J. 167
Greenberg, J. *et al.* 167

Gussmann, E. 235
Hale, K. 221, 222
Halle, M. 100, 168, 233
Harms, R. T. 100, 123, 202, 234
Harris, J. 224
Harris, Z. S. 38, 58, 73
Hays, D. G. 293
Heffner, R-M. S. xviii, 314
Henderson, E. J. A. 168, 269
Hill, A. A. 268, 338
Hockett, C. F. 38, 73, 136, 137, 139,
    140, 142, 147, 156, 167, 168, 338
Hoenigswald, H. 338
Hooper, J. B. 224, 229, 230, 235, 262, 263,
    264, 265, 266, 270, 314
Householder, F. W. 9, 60, 202, 233
Hudson, R. 314
Hurford, J. R. 202
Hyman, L. M. 38, 74, 101, 201, 202, 233,
    234
Isačenko, A. 233
Itkonen, E. 10
Jakobson, R. 53, 75, 91, 103
Jakobson, R. and Halle, M. 100
Jakobson, R. *et al.* 75, 100, 103
Jesperson, O. 264
Jones, C. 270, 293
Jones, D. 38
Jones, S. 124
Joos, M. 38
Kaye, J. 234
Keller, R. E. 168, 201
King, R. D. 332, 338
Kiparsky, P. 100, 191, 234, 235, 270
Kisseberth, C. 202
Kniezsa, V. 168
Koestler, A. 237, 268
Kohler, K. 270
Koutsoudas, A. 234
Koutsoudas, A. *et al.* 234
Kuipers, A. 168
Labov, W. 314
Labov, W. *et al.* 167, 311, 314
Ladefoged, P. xviii, 101, 108, 111, 122, 124,
    168
Ladefoged, P. *et al.* 120, 124
Langacker, R. W. 202
Lass, R. 9, 10, 38, 84, 100, 101, 122,
    123, 132, 167, 179, 201, 202, 270, 338
Lass, R. and Anderson, J. M. 38, 51, 100,
    101, 123, 201, 338
Laver, J. xviii, 101
Lee, G. and Howard, I. 314
Lindau, M. 119, 124
Linell, P. 10, 228, 230, 231, 232, 235, 314
Lisker, L. and Abramson, A. S. 101

Love, N. 235
Lyons, J. 269
McCarthy, J. J. 270
Macaulay, R. K. and Trevelyan, G. D.
    304, 309
McCawley, J. D. 76, 100
McIntosh, A. 9
Maddieson, I. 157, 158, 159, 168
Makkai, V. B. 38, 201, 233, 234
Malmberg, B. xviii
Martinet, A. 54, 167
Matthews, P. H. 10, 38, 73, 74
Moulton, W. G. 36, 37
Nartey, J. N. A. 151, 153, 154, 156, 168
O'Connor, J. D. xviii
Ó Dochartaigh, C. 293
Ohala, J. 201, 202, 234
Ohala, M. 234
Osthoff, H. and Brugman, K. 324
Palmer, F. R. 268, 269
Pike, K. L. 23
Popper, K. R. 8, 10
Postal, P. M. 167, 233
Prokosch, F. 167
Pulgram, E. 270
Pullum, G. K. 234
Ringen, J. 10
Rischel, J. 168
Roach, P. 270
Robins, R. H. 202, 240, 241, 245
Robinson, J. 293
Romaine, S. 314
Rubach, J. 233, 235, 314
Sampson, G. 100, 214, 268
Sapir, E. 297
Saporta, S. 167
Saussure, F. de 2, 264
Schane, S. A. 38, 202, 233, 234
Sedlak, P. 137, 167
Sigurd, B. 201, 202, 270
Skousen, R. 215
Smith, N. V. and Wilson, D. 10
Sommerstein, A. 38, 233, 234, 268
Stampe, D. 202
Stanley, R. 100
Steinberg, D. and Krohn, R. 234
Stetson, R. M. 248, 270
Swadesh, M. 38
Thrane, T. *et al.* 167, 202
Trubetzkoy, N. S. 40, 41, 42, 44, 46, 52, 53,
    54, 139, 140, 161, 167
Trudgill, P. 314
Twaddell, W. F. 38, 338
Vachek, J. 53, 233
Vago, R. 209, 212, 213, 234, 241
Vennemann, T. 223f, 233, 234, 235

Waddington, C. H. 268
Wang, W. S-Y. 100
Waterson, N. 269

Wood, S. 101, 123, 124
Zwicky, A. 74, 183, 235, 314